Founders of Modern Political
and Social Thought

CICERO

FOUNDERS OF MODERN POLITICAL AND SOCIAL THOUGHT

SERIES EDITOR
Mark Philp
University of Warwick

The *Founders* series presents critical examinations of the work of major political philosophers and social theorists, assessing both their initial contribution and their continuing relevance to politics and society. Each volume provides a clear, accessible, historically informed account of a thinker's work, focusing on a reassessment of the central ideas and arguments. The series encourages scholars and students to link their study of classic texts to current debates in political philosophy and social theory.

Published in the series:

JOHN FINNIS: *Aquinas*
GIANFRANCO POGGI: *Durkheim*
MAURIZIO VIROLI: *Machiavelli*
CHERYL WELCH: *De Tocqueville*
RICHARD KRAUT: *Aristotle*
MALCOLM SCHOFIELD: *Plato*
JOSHUA COHEN: *Rousseau*
FREDERICK ROSEN: *Mill*
MALCOLM SCHOFIELD: *Cicero*

Cicero

Political Philosophy

Malcolm Schofield

OXFORD
UNIVERSITY PRESS

UNIVERSITY PRESS

Great Clarendon Street, Oxford, OX2 6DP,
United Kingdom

Oxford University Press is a department of the University of Oxford.
It furthers the University's objective of excellence in research, scholarship,
and education by publishing worldwide. Oxford is a registered trade mark of
Oxford University Press in the UK and in certain other countries

© Malcolm Schofield 2021

The moral rights of the author have been asserted

First Edition published in 2021

Impression: 5

All rights reserved. No part of this publication may be reproduced, stored in
a retrieval system, or transmitted, in any form or by any means, without the
prior permission in writing of Oxford University Press, or as expressly permitted
by law, by licence or under terms agreed with the appropriate reprographics
rights organization. Enquiries concerning reproduction outside the scope of the
above should be sent to the Rights Department, Oxford University Press, at the
address above

You must not circulate this work in any other form
and you must impose this same condition on any acquirer

Published in the United States of America by Oxford University Press
198 Madison Avenue, New York, NY 10016, United States of America

British Library Cataloguing in Publication Data
Data available

Library of Congress Control Number: 2020937542

ISBN 978–0–19–968491–5 (Hbk.)
    978–0–19–968492–2 (Pbk.)

DOI: 10.1093/oso/9780199684915.001.0001

Printed and bound in Great Britain by
CPI Group (UK) Ltd, Croydon, CR0 4YY

Links to third party websites are provided by Oxford in good faith and
for information only. Oxford disclaims any responsibility for the materials
contained in any third party website referenced in this work.

In memory of Miriam Griffin

Preface

This book explores the Cicero who wrote of his 'incredible and unparalleled love for the *res publica*' (*de Or.* 3.13). His work in political philosophy stands as the first surviving attempt to articulate a holistic rationale for republicanism and a sustained account of its different elements. These might be summarized in words of Mark Philp, general editor of the series in which this book appears:[1]

> I take republican thought to share three distinctive features: that political order and stability rests ultimately on sustaining the civic virtue of the citizens of the state; that the end of politics is the common good of the citizens; and that the achievement of civic virtue and the common good is a fragile achievement for which there are certain social, material, cultural, and, above all, institutional prerequisites.

In this study Cicero's pioneering contribution to that kind of republican thought is tracked through studies of some of his major themes, which include some that still have resonances today as in earlier periods of the history of the West. The book focuses mainly on the three major writings that he devoted to political philosophy: *On the commonwealth*, *On laws*, and *On duties*—the third of these formally speaking a general treatise on practical ethics, but in reality addressed to the young man expected and expecting to enter public life, and much of it concentrating on conduct in the public sphere.

Cicero himself played a significant part as a leading figure in the turbulent politics of the last two or three decades of the Roman Republic, not least through his oratory. The political and ethical stances he takes in his speeches are intimately related to his official theorizing. The same is true of his correspondence with friends and acquaintances when he discusses pressing political issues or questions of character or behaviour. Treatment of material in letters and speeches accordingly figures strongly in some chapters. There is quite a lot of history and historical context in their pages (my approach to Cicero's political philosophizing is, I think, broadly in line with the 'Cambridge' style associated particularly with the name of Quentin Skinner). I have attempted, often in the footnotes, to give some idea of the state of controversy about interpretation of the history, so far as it has presented itself to me in my own inevitably selective and unsystematic reading of the truly massive amount of publication devoted to it.

All three of the major theoretical works are accessible in good English translations. The book does not attempt comprehensive coverage of their contents, nor of all the very extensive scholarship relevant to them or to the particular themes selected for discussion. The dialogues *On the commonwealth* and *On laws*, in particular, are highly crafted and often subtle pieces of writing, as are Cicero's letters (*On duties* strikes me as on the whole more straightforward, although less so in Book 3 and in other passages where we know or may suspect that Cicero is not following more or less closely his Greek model Panaetius). I have attempted to communicate some sense of this in my discussions and in some of the translations from the original Latin (and occasionally Greek), which are my own unless otherwise indicated. The book does aim to give readers a feel for what one might call the Ciceronian state of play, and through references to the bibliography to supply some guidance on how that might be followed up. But it does not presuppose much prior familiarity with Cicero or Roman history, nor knowledge of Latin vocabulary. Translations of particular terms are provided when they make their initial appearance in the text, and as may be helpful at other junctures. Abbreviations in references to classical authors and their works in general follow those used in the fourth edition of *The Oxford Classical Dictionary* (Oxford: Oxford University Press, 2013).

The idea for this book was conceived when I responded to an invitation from the University of Oxford to give Carlyle Lectures on the history of political thought. Like the lectures, it is designed to be of interest both to those concerned with the history of Western political thought who would appreciate an assessment of Cicero's contribution to their discourse, and to students and scholars of Cicero in particular and the history, literature, and especially philosophy of the ancient Western world more generally. The material it presents is much developed from the lectures, but it retains their overall scope and trajectory, which are briefly sketched in section 5 of Chapter 1. I have been working and giving talks on Cicero for many years, and have benefited from many comments by colleagues and discussions with them. I am grateful to Margaret Atkins for helpful criticisms of my first draft of the Introduction, and to Mark Philp and an anonymous reader for the Press for some most thoughtful comments on my final draft. I am particularly indebted to Mark and to Peter Momtchiloff at OUP for their encouragement and patience with my slow progress. It has been my good fortune to work since then with Jayashree Thirumaran, assisted by Phil Dines as copy editor and other colleagues, who has taken my manuscript from submission through to publication with exemplary efficiency and friendly courtesy. The lectures themselves were delivered in Hilary Term, 2012. My thanks go to the Carlyle committee for the honour of their invitation, and particularly to their chairman, George Garnett, for his helpfulness throughout and for the generosity of his hospitality. It is a pleasure once again to thank the Warden and Fellows of All Souls College for accommodating me most comfortably, for the warmth of the welcome at their table, and for some stimulating discussions. Many Oxford friends and colleagues showered me with their own invitations.

The book is dedicated to the memory of one such. It is from her that I have learned most about its subject and about the ways in which that might profitably be tackled. In the prologue to her own posthumously published collected papers, she wrote of her determination from the outset to straddle ancient history, literature, and philosophy in her research.[2] I hope I have been able in my own fashion to follow her example.

MS
Cambridge, February 2020

Notes

1. Philp 1996: 387–8.
2. Griffin 2018: vii.

Acknowledgements

Material used or adapted from previous publications of mine appeared originally as follows:

Chapter 2: 'Cicero's definition of *res publica*', in J. G. F. Powell (ed.), *Cicero the Philosopher*. Oxford: Clarendon Press, 63–83. Published in 1995.

'Liberty, equality, and authority: a political discourse in the later Roman Republic', in D. Hammer (ed.), *A Companion to Greek Democracy and the Roman Republic*. Chichester: Wiley-Blackwell, 113–27. Published in 2015.

Chapter 4: 'Cosmopolitanism, imperialism, and justice in Cicero's *Republic* and *Laws*', *History of Political Thought.Net* 2: 5–34. Published in 2013.

Chapter 5: 'Republican virtues', in R. Balot (ed.), *The Blackwell Companion to Greek and Roman Political Thought*. Oxford: Wiley-Blackwell, 199–213. Published in 2009.

'The fourth virtue', in W. Nicgorski (ed.), *Cicero's Practical Philosophy*. Notre Dame, Indiana: University of Notre Dame Press, 43–57. Published in 2012.

Chapter 7: 'Debate or guidance? Cicero on philosophy', in F. Leigh (ed.), *Themes in Plato, Aristotle, and Hellenistic Philosophy: Keeling Lectures 2010–18*. London: *BICS* Supplement 141. Published in 2020.

I am grateful for permission to reuse passages from these articles.

Contents

1. Introduction: Contexts — 1
   1. Cicero in the Western tradition — 1
   2. A brief life — 4
   3. Rehabilitation — 7
   4. Writing political philosophy — 14
   5. Prospect — 19
2. Liberty, Equality, and Popular Sovereignty — 27
   1. *Libertas* in Roman political discourse — 27
   2. Senate and people — 32
   3. Liberty and equality — 36
   4. Equality and liberty in *On the commonwealth* — 40
   5. Popular sovereignty — 46
3. Government — 61
   1. *On the commonwealth* — 61
   2. The consensus of justice — 64
   3. Kingship, aristocracy, popular rule: their drawbacks — 69
   4. Consilium and political stability — 75
   5. History and theory — 78
   6. Crisis and leadership — 83
   7. *On laws* — 90
   8. Conclusion — 93
4. Cosmopolitanism, Imperialism, and the Idea of Law — 105
   1. Cosmopolitanism — 105
   2. Cicero's conception of law — 112
   3. The law code — 116
   4. Laws 'for all good and stable nations' — 122
   5. Justice and imperialism — 125
   6. Conclusion — 135

5. Republican Virtues 147
   1. Civic virtue 147
   2. Roman virtues 152
   3. Justice 159
   4. *Magnitudo animi* 166
   5. *Verecundia* 170
   6. The republican citizen 175
6. Republican Decision-making 185
   1. Citizen decision 185
   2. Principles, rules, and the casuistry of exceptions 193
   3. Civil war 197
   4. Tyranny 203
   5. Friendship 208
   6. Tyrannicide 214
7. Epilogue: Philosophical Debate and Normative Theory 229
   1. Introduction 229
   2. Silencing debate 232
   3. Full-throttled debate 238
   4. Final thoughts 240

Bibliography 245
Index of Passages 263
General Index 275

1
Introduction: Contexts

1. Cicero in the Western tradition

In approaching Cicero's political philosophy, it may paradoxically be helpful to begin with someone who took a distinctly jaundiced view of what Cicero stood for—but at the same time thereby testifies to his massive historical importance. The thinker in question is Thomas Hobbes, who in the twelfth chapter of *de Cive* mounts a forthright attack on the 'seditious doctrine' that 'Tyrannicide is Lawfull'. In fact, he says, that puts the position he has in his sights too weakly: 'Nay, at this day it is by many Divines, as of old it was by all the Philosophers, Plato, Aristotle, Cicero, Seneca, Plutarch, and the rest of the maintainers of the Greek, and Roman Anarchies, held not only lawful, but even worthy of the greatest praise.' Whether Hobbes could have cited chapter and verse for his claim so far as it relates to Plato or Aristotle may be doubted: the torments tyrants suffer in the just punishment to which they are subjected in the afterlife are what we may most vividly recall from Plato, for example.[1] Plutarch does seem to take it for granted that tyrannicide is something admirable, without articulating any principled stance on the issue (so, for example, *Phil.* 2–3). As for Seneca, however, there is the passage in which he criticizes Marcus Brutus's assassination of Julius Caesar as 'contrary to Stoic teaching, because he feared the name of king'—when 'the best form of government is under a just king' (*Ben.* 2.20).

But for Cicero Hobbes is spot on. In the *de Officiis* (*On duties*), a work which from the twelfth century AD onwards had entered 'the bloodstream of Western culture',[2] to be read in Hobbes' time and for many decades prior and subsequently by every well-educated person, Cicero argues that assassinating a tyrant is an honourable act, not contrary to nature, and indeed a positive duty. The health of the body as a whole sometimes requires the amputation of limbs that have started to deaden and are harming the other parts. In the same way, the savagery and monstrous bestiality of the tyrant has to be removed from the body (so to speak) that we are all part of as humans (*Off.* 3.32). That argument would not have impressed Hobbes. He was dismissive of the tyrannicide's claim to the moral discernment needed for the judgement that some particular ruler—as it might be Caesar—was exercising his rule tyrannically. He thought it also gave the green light to the 'dissolution of any Government', good or bad, 'by the hand of every murtherous villain'—and constituted a recipe for 'Anarchy'. Anarchy was indeed the immediate consequence of Caesar's murder on the Ides of March, an act that Cicero had applauded and sought to justify as liberation from tyranny (contemporary political and geopolitical resonances perhaps ripple through the mind).

A time when Cicero (or indeed Seneca or Plutarch) could have been mentioned as political philosopher in the same breath as Plato and Aristotle seems remote (and not merely mentioned, given that it is *his* stance on tyrannicide that is in truth being recalled by Hobbes, rather than anything one could find in their writings). All the same, Cicero has gradually been edging his way back into political philosophy's current frame of reference. Re-examination of the republican tradition in Western political thought, initiated above all by the work of Quentin Skinner, has done much to prompt this development. At the heart of that revaluation has been demonstration of the dominant influence of 'those writers whose greatest admiration had been reserved for the doomed Roman republic: Livy, Sallust, and above all Cicero'. These were the authors invoked in Renaissance Italy 'as a means of defending the traditional liberties of the city-republics'.[3] In the efflorescence of English republican theorizing of the mid-seventeenth century, ancient Rome, as represented in their writings, remains an important point of reference. It was in the eighteenth-century enlightenment that Cicero's 'authority and prestige' reached its peak.[4] As for the America of the Founding Fathers: 'The nostalgic image of the Roman Republic'—mediated through writers such as Cicero, Sallust, and Tacitus—'became a symbol of all their dissatisfaction with the present and their hopes for the future'.[5] The twenty-three-year-old John Adams would declaim Cicero's speeches against Catiline alone in his rooms at night.[6] According to the *Secret History* of the French Revolution penned by Danton's journalist ally Camille Desmoulins, 'the first active, activating republican of the Revolution',[7] it was reading Cicero at school that inspired the French to love of liberty and hatred of despotism.[8]

In contemporary political philosophy, a version of the Roman ideal of political freedom (or as Skinner calls it, with reference to the recourse to the ancients in the early modern period, the 'neo-Roman') has been given perhaps unexpected new life. The most notable and influential treatment is probably that developed by Philip Pettit, especially in his 1997 book *Republicanism: A Theory of Freedom and Government*. His core thesis is the claim that reflection on the Roman and neo-Roman tradition enables us to identify a concept of freedom as 'non-domination', which fits on neither side of Isaiah Berlin's dichotomy between negative and positive liberty. Adoption of non-domination as the political ideal would, Pettit argues, give us a *via media* between liberalism and communitarianism. In particular, it would give us the possibility of a more radical and active notion of what government should provide and how civil society should work than the negative liberty of protection from coercion and interference that liberalism makes fundamental, and a less contentious way of approaching the idea of the common good than adoption of communitarianism, insofar as that is 'tied up with particular, sectarian conceptions of how people should live'.[9] Pettit insists that non-domination is not just a particular application of the concept of negative liberty.[10] More important than not being coerced is *not being in a state of dependence on the uncontrollable and arbitrary will of another, even if that other is not at the moment actually exercising that will to effect coercion.* A benevolent despot may never in fact coerce you or threaten to do so, but (as Skinner puts it) your dependence ultimately on his power and will 'is in itself a source and a form of constraint', which when you recognize that 'will serve in itself to constrain you from exercising a number of your civil rights'.[11] This, in Pettit's formulation, is 'an older, republican way of thinking about freedom', which 'had its origins in classical Rome, being associated in particular with the name of Cicero'.[12]

The Cicero presented so far has been something of a canonized figure: a 'name', as Pettit puts it, to be invoked in later centuries when authority is needed whether for situating and recommending a philosophical position, or alternatively (as with Hobbes) when such authority is being subverted. In the main body of this book I am going to undertake the enterprise—very much in the spirit of Skinner's own project—of trying to get closer to a historical Cicero, above all through and in his own writings (now available in good editions with English translations in the Cambridge series *Texts in the History of Political Thought* that Skinner co-edits),[13] read against the context of the turbulent era in which he lived. At the same time, I propose to explore those elements in his political thought that remain of abiding interest for moral and political philosophy, especially but not only in a republican register. In the remaining sections of this introductory chapter, I first offer a brief life of Cicero (section 2). Then I attempt some explanation of the current resurgence of interest in his philosophical writings in general (section 3). There follows a discussion of the qualifications Cicero suggests are needed for writing political philosophy (section 4). Finally, there will be a short account of the agenda for the rest of the book (section 5).

2. A brief life

Rome and the tortuous and intermittently brutal and bloody course of its politics in the final decades of the collapsing Republic are by the standards of most other periods of ancient Greek and Roman history particularly well documented, and never more intensively studied and debated than in present-day scholarship. Cicero, 'vain, insecure and ferociously clever',[14] was himself a central player, though increasingly less central than he wished to be, in the constantly shifting political landscape: a landscape that can be charted from his own often changing or opportunistic standpoint through the great volume of surviving forensic and political speeches, letters, theoretical writings of different kinds, even poetry, that he himself composed. We know more about Cicero (106–43 BC)—sometimes from day to day and week to week—than about anyone else in classical antiquity.[15]

Not surprisingly, therefore, in modern times it has been Cicero's life in politics rather than his thought that has attracted most of the attention. His family were well-to-do and highly educated provincial landed gentry, from Arpinum in the hill country of Italy sixty miles south-east of Rome. It was comparatively rare for anyone from that kind of background to break into the intensely competitive world of politics at Rome, dominated as it was by a well-established aristocratic elite, and then to make it as Cicero did to the very top, when he was elected one of the two consuls for 63 BC at the earliest possible age of 43 (*de Leg. Agr.* 2.3–4). It was his power as an orator that had made him a force to be reckoned with. Soon after a politically courageous exercise in successful advocacy in his first major performance in the courts (in 80 BC), he began to climb the political ladder, steadily building and exploiting his reputation as an advocate. In 66 BC, the year in which he held the important office of praetor, he undertook his first significant venture in political oratory, supporting the appointment of the powerful military leader Pompey to a further command in the East (to deal with Mithridates, King of Bithynia, a territory bordering the southern coast of the Black Sea). Then three years later came the consulship, and with it supreme executive responsibility.

This was Cicero's finest hour, which in the future he would constantly recall as the critical moment when he saved from disaster the *res publica*—the Roman state conceived as a commonwealth, or political enterprise in which the interests of all major sectors of society were at stake. The threat he identified was an incipient popular uprising led by a disaffected member of the nobility: the so-called Catilinarian conspiracy. Catiline himself was killed in the military operation the consuls launched against him. But following a vote in the senate supporting such action, Cicero had some of his leading associates summarily executed. Putting Roman citizens to death without trial or opportunity of appeal, however expedient it might have been judged, was an act that would inevitably provoke controversy. In fact, it violated the very law giving protection against such action to which Cicero himself had appealed in denouncing the provincial governor Verres seven years before: *Verr.* 2.5.163).[16] He was soon accused of tyrannical behaviour, and his enemies eventually had him forced into exile (in 58 BC).

Thanks partly to Pompey's good offices, he was able to return to Rome the following year and to resume public activity. But the warlords Pompey, Caesar, and Crassus now exercised increasing control of political life, mostly in concert with each other, and in the early summer of 56 BC, after they had renewed their pact, it was indicated to Cicero that he needed from now on to be careful over what line he took in his political pronouncements. This was in a way testimony to the weight his voice still carried; and Cicero did not entirely withdraw from the public scene. But his wings had been clipped. And it was now—from 56 to 51 (when he took up in the summer the governorship of the province of Cilicia, in modern south-west Turkey)—that he first turned in his adult years to serious theoretical writing. To these years belong *On the orator*, *On the commonwealth* (discussed in Chapter 3 below, but also in sections of Chapters 2 and 4), and probably *On laws* (apparently never finally completed or put into circulation; the main focus of discussion in Chapter 4, but figuring in Chapters 3 and 7 also). It was in these latter two works, both unfortunately now fragmentary, where—together with the later *On duties*—Cicero made his primary contributions to political philosophy.

As he was returning from his year in Cilicia in the autumn of 50 BC, war between Caesar and Pompey was looming. The conflict got seriously under way in the summer of 49, when after much vacillation (worked out often in philosophical terms in his letters of the period: see Chapter 6), Cicero ended up himself joining the bulk of the conservative senatorial faction with Pompey's army in Greece. Following Pompey's defeat in August 48, he returned to Italy, and received a pardon from Caesar in July 47. In the following year, Caesar won the last major battle of the civil war, at Thapsus in north Africa on modern Tunisia's Mediterranean coast, and the intransigent Stoic Marcus Cato, general of the defeated republican forces, committed suicide, thereby achieving undying fame. Caesar now ruled Rome, in the exceptional but historic office of 'dictator'.[17] Cicero recognized that there was virtually no further role he could perform in public life, and turned once again to writing. Between 46 and the end of 44 he composed an impressive volume of further theoretical writing, initially on oratory, but then a sequence mostly of philosophical works. Most of these were written in the dialogue form pioneered by Plato and other associates of Socrates. In effect, they would constitute something within striking distance of an encyclopedia of the whole of philosophy for the edification of Roman readers.

March 44 however saw the assassination of Caesar by Brutus, Cassius, and their associates (Cicero had not himself been enlisted in the conspiracy, and in fact seems to have been midway through composition of his *On divination* at the time: *Div.* 2.6–7). In the late summer of that year Cicero resumed public activity in earnest, and early in September made the first of his attacks on Mark Antony, Caesar's political heir, in the famous sequence of speeches known as the *Philippics*, which were to continue until April 43. But he continued his philosophical writing, and in the latter months of 44 completed *On duties* (*de Officiis*), his guide to the virtues to be expected of the man in public life (see Chapters 5 and 6).[18] With the following year (43) came renewed military hostilities, and in November a rapprochement between the new ascendant warlords: Antony, Marcus Aemilius Lepidus, and Caesar's adopted son Octavian, eventually to become the emperor Augustus. A list of opponents to be eliminated was drawn up, and on 9 December the hitmen called on Cicero.

Cicero therefore met a miserable end, conscious not only of the frustrations and failures of his own life in politics, ever since the triumphant year of 63, but even worse of the demise of everything he had championed, including the very possibility of a participatory republican politics and of the oratory of which he had been the master. In the prefaces to the philosophical dialogues of 45, in particular, he makes it plain that their composition is the occupation of an enforced leisure he would prefer not to have to be filling. He saw his true role as involvement in the public sphere, promoting the good of the *res publica* by political activity. The choice between the philosophical and the political life is in fact flagged as a key issue in both *On the commonwealth* and *On duties*, with the decision going unequivocally in favour of political engagement. Nonetheless Cicero also represents his philosophical writings as service to the *res publica* in another mode. They will equip Romans with the basis of a philosophical education, focused above all on ethics: how to live. They will do so by speaking to Romans in their own Latin language, which—as he intends to demonstrate—possesses resources for the purpose quite the equal of those available to Greek, if not indeed richer.

3. Rehabilitation

'Through these hasty compositions', wrote D R Shackleton Bailey, distinguished editor and aficionado of Cicero's letters, 'Greek thought, especially of the two and a half centuries after Aristotle, filtered down to mould the minds of Christian Fathers and eighteenth-century philosophers—a stupendous triumph of popularization, which has had its day.'[19] That statement—in a biography of Cicero published in 1971—was a particularly eloquent expression of a view of his philosophical writings that has had wide currency. Ever since Plato and Aristotle in the nineteenth century regained effective recognition in the consciousness of educated people as the philosophical giants of classical antiquity, his philosophical stock has undeniably lost value. He has often been perceived as merely derivative, not even attempting anything more than faithful reproduction of his sources, and for all his unquestionable fluency second-rate.

But perceptions in recent decades have been changing. Three reasons for this development are worth highlighting: reflecting respectively philosophical, literary, and historical assessments of the philosophical works. One key factor has been a revival of philosophical interest in Hellenistic philosophy. The power and subtlety of the theories and arguments advanced in the three centuries after Aristotle (who died in 322 BC) by Stoics and Epicureans and the sceptics of the Hellenistic Academy, the debates in which they engaged with each other, the way they conceived of their entire philosophical projects, and their impact on the Western philosophical tradition, are all now better understood and rather more appreciated.[20] So if most of Cicero's philosophical writing presents his readers with the philosophizing of the Hellenistic schools, this focus has made him more, not less, attractive. The clarity and precision of his treatments of this material may sometimes disappoint. By and large, however, time spent with them yields significant rewards. Few scholars who work seriously on Cicero today are unaware of this transformation of the standing of his philosophical writings in the eyes of those who engage with 'Cicero the philosopher', to use the title of a respected and influential collection of essays published twenty-five years ago now.[21]

He himself was neither Epicurean nor—as is sometimes supposed—Stoic, although (as he tells us in an autobiographical section of his dialogue *Brutus*) from his early twenties he worked with the Greek Stoic Diodotus, who was to live in his house for the best part of forty years (*Brut.* 309). His initial study of philosophy was pursued with Philo of Larissa, the head of Plato's Academy in Athens, who had however fled to Rome in 88 BC. He subsequently resumed serious philosophical study for a period of six months with another Academic, Antiochus of Ascalon, during a long visit to Athens and Asia Minor in 79–77 BC (*Brut.* 306, 315). Cicero venerated Plato, and felt himself most at home with the Platonic dialogue, both as a literary vehicle for philosophy and for its articulation, perpetuated in the Academy, of philosophy as debate, not attempting the conclusive demonstrations that the treatise writing of the other schools often aimed to supply. The spirit of Plato permeates his own first major writings on rhetoric and philosophy of 56–51 BC.[22] In the writings of 45–44 BC he is explicit in identifying his own position as that of the Academic sceptic, which requires that one argument should be pitted against another—and if one of the two seems in the end closer to the truth than the other, that is the most humans are legitimately entitled to conclude, and in any case a matter for the judgement of the reader. I have argued elsewhere that Cicero's dialogues of this period are genuinely more balanced and open-ended—and in these respects more dialogic—than Plato's, with whom he is sometimes unfavourably compared.[23]

The higher standing of his philosophical writings is not simply a function of enhanced appreciation of Hellenistic philosophy. Literary scholars who approach texts as cultural artefacts have become fascinated with the way Cicero projects his own voice and stance in his philosophical writings, and with what he brings to the material he presents, as a cultivated member of the Roman elite, alert to the delicacy of the negotiation between Greek language and culture and Roman, and frequently insistent that the long-established values and institutions of the Republic are in disrepair and perhaps under threat of oblivion as he writes.[24]

The Romanization of Greek philosophy was a project whose difficulties and opportunities Cicero frequently discussed in the prefaces he wrote to his dialogues, at times rather defensively, but often *con brio*: 'I thought it mattered a lot for the glory and honour of the citizen body (*civitas*)', he says in the preface to *On the nature of the gods*, 'to give ideas of such importance and so greatly respected a place in Latin literature' (*ND* 1.7).[25] Among other devices he employed for the purpose was his choice of speakers for his dialogues and of the locations in which he set them: not the teenagers or Sophists Plato's Socrates encounters in gymnasia or in the town houses of moneyed Athenians, but distinguished Roman politicians, represented as well versed in philosophy, occupying their leisure in the gardens of grand country villas. The implication is that philosophy is in fact already well ensconced in Roman elite culture, and not in the least incompatible with the serious traditional public business of statesmanship.[26] But in his dialogue settings and speaker selection Cicero also had another and darker agenda.

Most of the speakers in the philosophical dialogues of 45–44 BC, not just Cato (advocate of Stoicism in Books 3 and 4 of *On ends*), would lose their lives fighting in the republican cause soon after the fictive occasions on which Cicero had them conversing on philosophical themes. Through such a pointed choice of cast he never lets readers forget what he sees as the disastrous loss of that cause. But for the most part the message remains a subtext. The most obvious exception is the first theoretical composition of the later sequence, the *Brutus* of 46 BC, a history of Roman oratory whose preface and concluding pages (*Brut.* 1–10, 329–33) openly bewail the 'night' which has engulfed the Republic. Nearly ten years earlier, in *On the orator*, the untimely demise in 91 BC of Crassus, the leading speaker,[27] had evoked in Cicero's writing what Ingo Gildenhard has characterized as a similar 'mood of pessimism and gloom' and 'sense of impending catastrophe' (*de Or.* 3.1–12).[28]

No less important for the re-evaluation of Cicero's contribution to the literature of philosophy has been change and diversification in the writing of Roman history, as of history more generally. If fifty years ago you had asked a Roman historian how the Roman Republic was governed, 'oligarchy' would have been the short answer, and indeed—however elaborated—the core of a long answer too. In the minds of English-speaking readers that view had been given brilliant and influential crystallization in Ronald Syme's *The Roman Revolution* of 1939.[29] Peter Brunt, writing in 1988, began a chapter of his book on the fall of the Roman Republic with a sketch of Syme's view of the political discourse of the late Republic:[30]

> In the political struggles of the late Republic frequent appeals were made on all sides to *libertas*. For Syme they were essentially fraudulent. 'Liberty and the laws are high-sounding words. They will often be rendered, on a cool estimate, as privilege and vested interests.' The name of liberty was usually invoked in defence of the existing order by the minority of rich and powerful oligarchs. 'The ruinous privilege of freedom' was extinguished in the Principate for the higher good of 'security of life and property'.

Brunt expressed the view—which has since in one form or another become something approaching a new orthodoxy—that this analysis was improbably reductionist:[31]

> Though Syme was right in holding that on the lips of the nobility it often veiled their selfish attachment to power and its perquisites, he was wrong in my judgement in suggesting at least by insinuation that it was no more than a catchword, proclaimed in conscious cynicism, and that some, perhaps most, of them did not sincerely believe that the liberty or power they possessed under the Republican constitution was essential to the public good. In the same way the common people were surely attached to the different personal and political rights which their spokesmen subsumed under the name of liberty by sentiment and tradition, as well as by consciousness of the concrete advantages which these rights secured to them.

Or to put the argument somewhat differently, Syme had crucially left two things out of the picture. One was indeed the people, whether that increasingly small percentage of Roman citizens which was constituted by the non-elite male population of the city itself, or the whole body of citizens, now including the increasingly large numbers of recently enfranchised Italians and of army veterans settled in the Italian hinterland.[32] Just how much power the Roman populace exercised at assemblies where they would vote along with the propertied classes (whose votes were more heavily weighted) on legislation and in electing magistrates, or in the mass meetings where politicians would attempt to gain support on issues that assemblies were to decide, or as the audience thronging trials before magistrates or standing courts, has been intensely debated for more than a quarter of century.[33] Rent-a-crowd had its ancient equivalents. Nonetheless there is no denying that Roman aristocrats had to expend a great deal of time and energy in persuading popular gatherings. And it is clear that in the constantly shifting political landscape of the late Republic it became increasingly difficult for the senate to remain cohesive and to guarantee consistent control of them.[34] More specifically, despite significant senatorial resistance, the popular assemblies were able between 140 and 50 BC to vote into being laws constraining the senate's discretionary power (for example, to assign command of major wars), defending popular rights and powers, and establishing material benefits for the *plebs*, the ordinary citizens of Rome.[35]

The other, and closely connected, drawback to Syme's assessment was his treatment of ideology. Ideology might better be seen not as primarily cynical window dressing, but as 'itself an instrument of power, perhaps the most effective (and certainly the cheapest) one there is'.[36] Nicola Mackie—author of those words—continued:

> The effectiveness of ideology—what distinguishes it from 'propaganda'—lies in its capacity to appear as more than an instrument of naked class- or self-interest; its capacity, that is, to base itself on 'objective' moral standards, and so fire the enthusiasm of those in whose interest it is, and also convince (or at any rate disconcert) those in whose interest it is not. Only this conception of ideology can explain the role played by it in Roman politics in the late Republic.

As with the role of the people, there has been plenty of debate over quite how ideology informed political stances, and whether there were any fundamental ideological differences between politicians who clashed on important matters of policy.[37] But once ideology is recognized as a key factor in the shaping of political agency, and so as indispensable for historical explanation, Roman political philosophy has an immediate claim on the historian's attention.

'Modern accounts of the Roman Republic', wrote the historians Mary Beard and Michael Crawford back in 1985,[38] 'tend to place its cultural and religious history at the margins'. However:

History is not merely about events and actions, but also about how they were perceived and discussed. The development, for example, of moral and political philosophy in the late Republic, bringing with it new ways for the Roman governing class to understand and justify their own conduct, is just as important as the political events themselves.

Understanding of the configurations and dynamics of the entire culture of a past society has since then come to seem central business for historians, where once it was accounts of constitutional structures and their development, economic survey and analysis, and particularly political narrative that were their main if not exclusive preoccupation. If we focus on Rome in the final decades of the Republic, it was clearly not just the parameters of power and of social and economic reality within which politics was conducted that were shifting. Much else in the contexts within which Romans lived their lives was changing too: what Beard and Crawford describe as a 'cultural explosion', involving 'progressively broader bands of the Roman and Italian elite'.[39]

In her 1997 book *La Raison de Rome* Claudia Moatti[40] argued that the diffusion of writing and the proliferation of forms of written technical or specialized discourse—including grammar, rhetoric, historiography, geography, ethnography, antiquarian learning, law, philosophy, theology—represented much of it a critical reinvention of tradition and a remedy for loss of collective memory, as well as testimony to expanding horizons, both imperial and more metaphorical. She recalls some words addressed by Cicero to his contemporary, the prolific antiquarian Varro, in the preface to his *Academic books* of 45 BC (*Acad.* 1.9):[41]

We were wandering and straying like visitors in our own city when your books led us, so to speak, right home, and enabled us at last to appreciate who and where we were. It is you who have revealed to us how old our native city is, how its successive periods are to be demarcated, the laws governing our rites and priesthoods, how we were brought up at home and trained for war, the topography of our regions and local districts, the names, classifications, duties, and origins of everything in the spheres of both the divine and the human.

Rediscovery and recovery of Roman identity, in a city now full of public buildings monumentalized with Greek colonnades and columns in the Greek architectural orders, are what Cicero celebrates here in Varro's vast enterprise.[42] But more characteristically, and perhaps most memorably in the preface to Book 5 of *On the commonwealth* (*Rep.* 5.1–2), Cicero elsewhere bewails the well-nigh irretrievable loss of what the Romans conceived as their traditional way of life. The *mos maiorum*, 'the ways of our forefathers', an austere and public-spirited code of values focused on *virtus* (understood principally as the courage required of a citizen in the constant warfare of Rome's early centuries), and transmitted within the family from father to son, had been allowed to start crumbling away. In truth, as Moatti suggests, Varro was turning living tradition (so far as it still lived) into text—indeed into a database.[43] Once internalized ancestral knowledge becomes objectified ancient history. In the hands of Varro, and Cicero too, authority begins to leach away from custom to reason.

The general pattern of change Moatti describes indubitably began to affect the way Romans lived their lives in quite palpable ways. Teachers of rhetoric and Greek philosophy, for example, like the Greek Sophists of an earlier age, were in the late Republic already providing a form of higher education for which tradition had felt no need—and which was to become widespread through much of the Roman world under the empire. Julius Caesar's reform of the hitherto arbitrary and chaotic calendar is another notable case of a change—with quite general impact on the structure of living—which illustrates the general pattern. Before his intervention, making the civic calendar follow the solar year, the religious authorities could without much warning insert extra days or months, ostensibly to achieve better correlation with the lunar cycle. The result (as the historian Suetonius put it) was that 'harvest festivals did not come in summer nor those of the vintage in the autumn' (Suet. *Iul.* 40.1). Here is Wallace-Hadrill on the subject:[44]

Calendar reform, while on the surface a technical matter of sorting out a confused traditional practice, entailed a far deeper shift of social authority and control of knowledge: from a republican society in which a 'nobility' maintained its preeminence by a superior knowledge of Roman discourse—in this case, through the right of the pontifical college to 'know' the year—to a court society in which knowledge, far from being concentrated in a single power group, was diffused among experts, whose authority was endorsed by the ruler.

This assessment relates, of course, to the beginnings of the post-Republic era. Yet as Moatti says, the development in question could not have occurred had not Caesar been the beneficiary of the intellectual achievements of the late Republic, and its appetite for new kinds of knowledge and for the uses to which that knowledge might be put.[45]

Caesar and Cicero make an interesting comparison and contrast. Caesar was a blue-blooded member of the old aristocracy, who thought however—or certainly behaved as though he thought—that the old order of things had had its day. Cicero, on the other hand, had broken into the charmed circle of the ruling republican elite from outside (and was passionately committed to its survival as such). But he was not just a 'new man' in that sense. His whole literary career may be read as a work of self-invention. Catherine Steel writes:[46]

> He first entered public life as an orator; his reputation, and success, were intimately bound up with his capacity to speak persuasively. To supplement those achievements with a permanent written record of what was said was to enter a different arena and one which many of Cicero's distinguished predecessors had not; this was a move which involved new audiences, new opportunities for criticism and the creation, conscious or not, of a record of who and what Cicero had been over the course of many years. And Cicero supplemented oratory with poetry and with rhetorical and philosophical treatises: in both cases he developed a new kind of writing, and new capacities for being a public figure in written form.

It was flattery, of course, but Caesar had a point when he said in praise of Cicero—or so the elder Pliny tells us (*NH* 7.117)—that advancing the frontiers of the Roman mind rather than its empire was the more significant achievement. Caesar's verdict gains in persuasiveness when we set Cicero's philosophical work in a more general context of cultural change and innovation—in which as it happens Caesar too was heavily invested, as witness not only his reform of the calendar, but the geographical and ethnographic excursuses in his *Gallic War*, and his planned 'codification' of the law.[47]

4. Writing political philosophy

The best qualification for writing political philosophy—Cicero thinks—is political experience at the highest level. This is the thesis he advances in its strongest form in *On divination*, in a passage (*Div.* 2.10–12; cf. *de Or.* 1.210–13) where he is using a Socratic form of argument, derived from the Academic sceptic Carneades (214–129 BC), to impugn the credentials of divination as a proper discipline with its own proprietary field of knowledge. Suppose, he asks, we are enquiring into what is good or bad, or into what our duties are:

these are questions for philosophy, to be tackled by philosophers, not practitioners of divination. Suppose, on the other hand, we want to know 'what is the best form of government for the commonwealth, what laws or what customs are beneficial or the opposite'. Are we to summon soothsayers from Etruria, or do we let leading citizens of distinction, experienced in politics, determine the question? That line of thought might seem to separate the provinces of moral philosophy and political theory, and again of reflection and experience, rather sharply (discussion of that issue is pursued in Chapter 7). In the preface to *On the commonwealth* Cicero had taken a more catholic approach. There are philosophers, he says, who have not held public office themselves, but because they have done a lot of research and writing about the commonwealth have performed a particular public function (*Rep.* 1.12): we think—as indeed Cicero must be doing—above all of Plato.

As for himself, Cicero strikes a relatively modest note in this same context, no doubt by way of *captatio benevolentiae*. His credentials for authorship of a work on the topic are his combination of experience of office, where he has achieved 'something memorable', and 'a certain capacity for explaining political principles not only by virtue of being practised at it, but through an appetite for learning and teaching' (*Rep.* 1.13). In other words, we may expect an account of 'the best form of citizen body' (*civitas*: *Rep.* 1.33, 2.65, cf. *Leg.*1.20) or 'commonwealth' (*res publica*: *Rep.* 2.41, *Leg.* 1.15, 20) informed by his own political experience, and by his facility in exposition, enhanced by his study of philosophy. Those resources are precisely what *On the commonwealth* (composed in the years 54–51 BC) goes on to dramatize, in proxy form through fictive dialogue between Roman statesmen of an earlier era. Dialogue, not treatise, is in Cicero's view—inherited from Plato—the way to do and write philosophy.[48] Plato was for Cicero the prince among philosophers. He himself identified with Plato in all his richness and abundance as a writer and thinker, but also as a model for the politically engaged intellectual.[49] *On the commonwealth* is a dialogue in a Platonic mode. The conversation it stages is imagined as occurring in 129 BC, a few years after the turmoil of the tribunate and death of the reforming politician Tiberius Gracchus. The principal speakers in a large cast are Scipio Africanus and Gaius Laelius, who are portrayed not only as paragons of political wisdom, but as deeply cultivated men steeped in philosophy, and well able to articulate their arguments.[50]

Thus Laelius proposes that it is as a leading figure in the commonwealth that Scipio is particularly suitable for tackling the subject, but also because he has studied politics with Panaetius and Polybius, two Greeks who are especially expert in this field (*Rep.* 1.34)—an indication that we can expect the theories developed in the dialogue to owe a good deal to their work (as we can indeed confirm in the case of Polybius, though nothing of Panaetius survives).[51] But Cicero is careful to have Scipio himself stress his own Roman upbringing: he is a *togatus*, a Roman citizen, who thanks to his father's care was early on inflamed with a desire for learning (here Scipio's words are made to echo those Cicero had applied to himself previously), but has been 'educated much more by experience and home learning than by books' (*Rep.* 1.36). *On the commonwealth* will in due course argue that the excellence of the Roman constitution is the outcome of a long and complex experiential process: the empirically tried and tested product of historical development of a whole nation, not the utopian invention of a solitary Greek theorist (*Rep.* 2.21–2; Cicero's devotion to Plato had its robustly critical elements).

Last but not least, the other participants expect eloquence of Scipio (*Rep.* 1.37), although it is Laelius's set piece in Book 3 that is greeted as a paradigm of oratory (*Rep.* 3.42). This reflects the verdict of the later *Brutus* (*Brut.* 83–5) that while both were orators of the first rank—Scipio noted for the weight, *gravitas*, with which he spoke, Laelius for mellifluousness, *lenitas* (*de Or.* 3.28)—Laelius was the more celebrated, although Cicero goes on to give his own opinion that many of Scipio's surviving speeches were the equal of what was apparently regarded as one of Laelius's finest. Cicero believed that both philosophy and statesmanship needed eloquence if they were to be at their best. 'I have always judged philosophy in its perfect form', he says at the beginning of the *Tusculan Disputations* of 45 BC (*Tusc* 1.7) 'to be philosophy which on the most important questions can speak expansively (*copie*) and with embellishments (*ornate*)'—in other words, in the grandest of the rhetorical styles discussed in his theoretical treatments of oratory. Similar notes are not infrequently struck in others of his philosophical prefaces and elsewhere. And although sometimes his philosophical prose is in practice more appropriately 'even (*aequabile*) and restrained (*temperatum*)', as he claims in the preface to *On duties* (*Off.* 1.3), there are indeed many important sustained passages in the philosophical writings where expansiveness and embellishment are precisely what is attempted and achieved.

It is significant that when in both the 50s and in the mid-40s Cicero to a greater or lesser extent turned away from public activity to literary composition, on each occasion the first subject to which he devoted attention was oratory—or rather, the orator.[52] *On the orator* (55 BC) was the first of all his dialogues, its composition immediately preceding that of *On the commonwealth*. It was no technical handbook (indeed 'an anti-textbook'), but in a quite different mode 'his most elaborate and far-reaching work of rhetorical theory'. John Dugan, author of that assessment, comments:[53]

> The over-arching ideological goal of this work is to celebrate the power of oratory to maintain the safety and stability of Rome. Cicero's ideal orator stands in opposition to the military dynast, and is thus a revival of the role he created for himself after his suppression of the Catlinarian conspiracy in 63 when he claimed that his oratory was as vital to Rome's salvation as Pompey's military conquests. *De oratore* offered a nostalgic idealization of the orator at a time when speech seemed powerless to influence Roman politics.

The urbane conversations of *On the orator* are themselves conceived as conducted in a villa in the Italian countryside at a time of political crisis at Rome (91 BC).[54] The participants discuss the crisis late into the evening of the day before their two days of philosophical debate (*de Or.* 1.26).

Cicero does not allow us to forget that political context. In the preface to Book 3 he calls to mind the death of the principal speaker, Lucius Licinius Crassus, not long after his imagined colloquium. He presents a dramatic account of confrontation in the senate back in Rome itself between Crassus and the consul Philippus, who was attempting to block legislation promoting (among other things) agrarian reform and the extension of citizen rights to the Italians, as well as restoring a senatorial presence on juries on criminal courts. Crassus, he tells us, made the most powerful speech of his life, and a thronged assembly passed the resolution he moved. But within a week he was dead from pleurisy. That prompts from Cicero a jeremiad on the savagery of Roman politics over the next few years, which was to compass the violent deaths of the other main participants in the dialogue. Perhaps, he suggests, it was providential that Crassus did not have to witness any of that (*de Or.* 3.1–12).

It is hard to avoid reading this preface as implicit reflection on the fragility of civilized political order, something highlighted on the very first page of the work (*de Or.* 1.2–3), and of the vulnerability of oratory and statesmanship to violence—indeed Cicero goes on to make the reflection explicit, with specific reference to his own current situation (*de Or.* 3.13). Something very similar is true of the preface to the *Brutus*, the first of Cicero's writings in the largely philosophical 46–44 BC sequence.[55] There articulation of the same contrast—through use of the metaphor of *arma*, 'weapons', 'arms'—is made the chief focus of the introduction it supplies to the history of oratory at Rome that occupies the main body of the work. News of the death of the greatest orator of the previous generation, Hortensius, had reached him as he was returning from his governorship of Cilicia as civil war was brewing. It prompted melancholy reflection on the difference between the Rome of that day and the Rome of the present, when civil war and its consequences have taken a terrible toll. He exclaims (*Brut.* 7):

> I am anguished that the public life of the commonwealth has no need of the weapons of counsel, of insight, of authority, which I had learned to handle, and to which I had accustomed myself—weapons that were the right ones both for a man preeminent in public affairs and for a well-ordered polity with soundly based and effective codes of conduct. In fact, if there ever was a moment in our public affairs when from the hands of citizens acting in anger the authority and eloquence of a good citizen could have wrested arms, it was emphatically then that any chance of peace was shut off, whether through the miscalculations people made or because of their fear.

Oratory in the service of statesmanship—the activity that gives him his own identity—has been denied the opportunity to promote peace and harmony that it deserves and Rome needs.

What Cicero in the *Brutus* mourns in the death of Hortensius is the loss of the voice of a good *citizen* speaking with wisdom and authority in the forum of the Roman people (*Brut.* 2–6). He knows very well that great statesmen are not always eloquent (*de Or.* 1.6–8), and that powerful and effective oratory can wreck the commonwealth as well as advance its interests: the jurist Scaevola is made to put just that argument early on in *On the orator* (*de Or.* 1.35–8). Nevertheless, it is hard to doubt that Cicero would have endorsed the claim that he has had Crassus already articulate (*de Or.* 1.34): 'In the control (*moderatio*) and wisdom of the perfect orator are especially to be found not only his own high standing (*dignitas*), but the safety of countless private citizens and of the commonwealth more generally.' And when in the preface to the *Brutus* he talks of the 'weapons' (*arma*) of counsel, insight, and authority—attributes which as we shall see in Chapter 3 are identified as the principal requirements of statesmanship in *On the commonwealth*, indeed frequently throughout his writings—he has in mind above all the eloquence that orators such as Hortensius and he himself command.[56]

Cicero's voice is in fact heard most obviously in the introductory commentary with which he prefaces each of his theoretical works (and indeed usually their individual books), and in some of the concluding comments he makes at the end of them. There are exceptions. In *On laws* he makes himself the leading speaker for the entirety of the conversation. His disagreements with his brother Quintus, in Book 3 in particular, come across as authentic. *On duties* has the form not of a dialogue but of something like an extended letter to his son. Particularly in his works of political philosophy the concern to address in different ways the condition of the Roman commonwealth is inescapable. Moreover, the scholarship of recent decades has shown in detail just how much continuity there is between (for example) theological ideas expounded in his philosophical dialogues and appeal to divine providential order in his oratory;[57] or again, as Chapter 6 will argue, between the ethical and political frames of reference within which he debated (in letters written to his intimate friend Atticus) what course of action he ought to pursue as Pompey and Caesar squared up for civil war, and the theoretical approach to the duties of the man in public life that he argues for five years later in *On duties*.[58] Shackleton Bailey had complained:[59] 'His ideas and experience were never in easy communication' (i.e. with each other). Claims like that now look increasingly hard to sustain.

5. Prospect

What becomes inescapable is a deliberately existential dimension to Cicero's project of writing philosophy. The philosophy is preoccupied with ideals: the perfect orator, the best form of government and the best citizen, and so on. But particularly in the intensely and obsessively autobiographical prefaces to the philosophical writings, Cicero is constantly alerting his readers to the unstable and dangerous times they and he are living through, and to the threats they pose to a stable political and social order and to any scope for the wisdom and eloquence of statesmanship that might nurture it. For the reader of *On the commonwealth*, *On laws*, and *On duties*, this means that their author is in effect inviting engagement with the theories these treatises propose and work through by use of a double lens: one for concentrating on those theories themselves, the other for registering the commentary on Rome's current problems that may thereby be intended, even if not explicitly articulated. Such an exercise may then prompt further questions about the overall purpose of the works themselves: how far Cicero had any hope that his ideals could be realized or approximated, how they look in the light of discussion of related issues in the letters or the speeches (that question gets some examination in many of the chapters that follow, but especially Chapter 6), and whether his thought measured up to the formidable challenges for understanding and political action that were facing the Romans of the late Republic.

Such a project for enquiry might prove rather disappointing if the questions Cicero explores were not intrinsically interesting, and if the way he handles them were uninviting or the intellectual equipment he brings to bear on them underpowered. So, at any rate, readers interested in ancient Greek and Roman philosophy and political theory might be inclined to think. Fortunately, Cicero's mind is fascinating to watch at work: poised as it is between rhetoric and dialectic, assertion and debate, with the demands and pieties of allegiance in counterpoint with chronic scepticism and indecision. Nor is he short of theoretical ambition and sophistication.

The ideas we shall be examining find resonances, sometimes more so than is true of Greek political philosophy, in subsequent Western political thought. And the book will accordingly be organized by topic, not as a comprehensive exposition of the successive writings on political philosophy in the Ciceronian corpus, although some account of each of them will be given as we go along. In fact, reflecting the existential character of Cicero's thinking about the foundations of politics, Chapter 2 will look at the idea of political liberty that he takes largely as read in the philosophical works, but which bulks large in his speeches of all periods, and in the discourse of late Republican politics more generally as we find it reflected in other writers, notably the historians Sallust and Livy.

Cicero in the preface to Book 3 of *On the orator* refers to his own 'incredible and unparalleled love for the *res publica*' as what has involved him in calamity (*de Or.* 3.13). And in one way or another the *res publica* will be the natural focus of each of the discussions that occupy the four subsequent chapters. Chapter 3 deals with Cicero's theory of government in *On the commonwealth,* and above all with the authority and counsel needed to sustain it, including the need in critical situations for the 'best citizen'—by dint of his insight and political virtue—to seize the helm of the commonwealth. Chapter 4 looks at the theory of justice and law, particularly as applied to Rome's constitutional arrangements and its conduct of empire, that is presented in *On laws* and *On duties* as well as *On the commonwealth*, and at the tensions with the cosmopolitan outlook that he also espouses. In Chapter 5 the topic of the distinctively civic and republican virtues—something in which the long tradition of republicanism in Western political thought remained deeply interested—is taken up, as we meet them as well as the cardinal virtues in various among Cicero's writings. Chapter 6 examines the complex casuistry of republican decision-making, as we find it both in Cicero's internal agonizing in letters to his friend Atticus about which way to jump in the looming civil war between Caesar and Pompey, and in the theoretical treatment of conflicting priorities in *On duties*, where his discussions extended to the ethics of tyrannicide (particularly in relation to friendship: also debated in his correspondence). Finally, in an Epilogue we step back and consider with Cicero the problem facing a thinker who wants philosophy to lay firm foundations for the *res publica*, as he tells us in *On laws*, and who values political activity as the highest calling for a citizen (as both *On the commonwealth* and *On duties* insist), and yet sees philosophy as a business of ongoing, inevitably open, and never quite conclusive debate.

Cicero's works on political philosophy will emerge as a massive, if flawed, achievement, which resonated through Western minds often powerfully for many centuries. So far as we know, no previous, nor indeed subsequent, Roman writer attempted anything comparable to the full-scale theory of government and constitutional order, or the related account of political leadership and of the duties and challenges of citizenship, together with an exploration of the moral and intellectual attributes they require, such as Cicero presented in these writings. To develop that agenda, he drew adroitly both on a rich and complex Greek literary and philosophical heritage and on native Roman tradition, history, and way of life. Its intellectual coin was not just ideas but ideals. Yet this is idealism tempered by consciousness that ideals, if they are to be taken as having serious claims to command assent or aspiration, need to allow for an appropriate way of responding to contingent realities. Consciousness is in truth a rather tame term to apply to the reflections, often agonized, of a major political figure, caught up in the death throes of the republican system of government (as he often bewailed) of one of the great powers in global history, who was trying to find intellectual and moral resources adequate to cope with threats to all that he himself held dear, and with the dilemmas practical and theoretical that these threw up. There are obvious deficiencies in his treatments of political leadership, of imperialism and the imperial state, and of tyrannicide (to take prominent examples among those discussed in the chapters that follow), and again in the theoretical resources—despite their other considerable strengths—with which he attempted to tackle these issues. Here he was largely reflecting failures of the Roman republican system itself, and the limitations, in these areas at any rate, of the conceptual universe it inhabited.

Notes

1. There was certainly an ancient tradition, known to Plutarch, associating Plato's Academy with encouragement of tyrannicide (see for example his life of Philopoemen: *Phil.* 1.3–4; for other evidence of the tradition, see Sedley 1997: 53). But Plutarch is at pains to distance Plato himself from anything of the sort (*Dio* 22.1); and he signals his disapproval of Julius Caesar's assassination (*Comp. Dion. et Brut.* 2.1–2). One would-be tyrannicide does earn his plaudit: the fourth-century Theban general Pelopidas is admired as a freedom fighter who died in battle against a tyrant he tried to kill (*Pel.* 34.5).
2. Dyck 1996: 43.
3. Skinner 1990: 300.
4. Wood 1988: 1–13 offers a brief survey.
5. Wood 1969: 53. But quite how widespread or efficacious a symbol it was has proved a debatable issue. Even Adams and Jefferson, Cicero's most prominent admirers, could on occasion express themselves much more sceptically on the subject of ancient Roman virtue: see Reinhold 1979, Rahe 1994. Certainly the Founders were 'ambivalent' (Rahe 1994: 77).
6. Bailyn 1967: 26. On Adams' devotion to Cicero, see Reinhold 1994.
7. Parker 1937: 37. Despite the title of his book—*The Cult of Antiquity*—Parker could find only a few other revolutionary figures, albeit including the prominent Girondins Jacques Pierre Brissot, and Madame Roland, as well as Robespierre himself, who made much of the ancient Rome or of the Ciceronian defence of the Republic that were familiar to them from their classical education. But see also n.8 below.
8. Sellers 2010: 822. The more recent discussion of Dubin 2016 provides evidence of the importance of the Roman Republic, and particularly of Cicero's triumph over the Catilinarian conspiracy, in the French revolutionary imaginary.

9. Pettit 1997: 120.
10. This claim is the subject of an interesting debate in which Skinner and Pettit engaged with Matthew Kramer and Ian Carter in Laborde and Maynor 2008: 31–130.
11. Skinner 1998: 84.
12. Pettit 1997: 5, 19. Pettit has restated his version of republicanism many times, for example in Pettit 2012. The classical credentials of the construction of neo-Roman republicanism associated with his and Skinner's work have not gone unquestioned. A learned and trenchant article, at points however tendentious, by Clifford Ando is an interesting example (see especially Ando 2010: 183–95, with useful bibliography at 183 n.2; see also Chapter 2, p. 31). But criticisms often reflect contemporary concerns: 'Democrats', says John McCormick (McCormick 2011: 141), 'should worry when philosophers employ the language of "republicanism"'.
13. See Griffin and Atkins 1991, Zetzel 2017a; but see too Walsh 2000, Fott 2014.
14. Thonemann 2018: 14.
15. An attractively written biographical account which gives due prominence to Cicero's intellectual interests is Rawson 1975.
16. See Brunt 1988d: 332–4; Drummond 1995. Cicero for his part had argued that there is no way an enemy of the *res publica* can be a citizen (*Cat.* 4.10).
17. See Chapter 3, section 6 p. 89 n.72 for a brief account of the office.
18. *On duties* was for many centuries one of the most studied of all ancient Latin texts, hugely influential as a guide for conduct: see Dyck 1996: 39–49, Walsh 2000: xxxiv–xlvii.
19. Shackleton Bailey 1971: x–xi.
20. Two useful introductions to Hellenistic philosophy are Long 1986 and Sharples 1997. A major collection of texts with translation and commentary is Long and Sedley 1987; see also Inwood and Gerson 1997. A comprehensive philosophical presentation and analysis is supplied in Algra, Barnes, Mansfeld, and Schofield 1999.
21. Powell 1995. See also Griffin and Barnes 1989, Barnes and Griffin 1997.
22. Schofield 2017a.
23. Schofield 2008.
24. See for example Gildenhard 2007.
25. See for example Baraz 2012, who suggests that what she diagnoses as unacknowledged contradictions in Cicero's defence of the enterprise threaten its coherence as a 'balancing act' between its Greek and Roman identities.
26. See for example Steel 2005. The implication contained a considerable element of exaggeration, as Cicero himself found himself admitting on one occasion

when he decided to change the cast of the dialogues that eventually became his *Academic books*. Its arguments 'were more technical than anybody could ever suppose they [viz. the original speakers] dreamed of' (*Att.* 13.19.3–5). On the other hand, it is clear from his correspondence that some of Cicero's own friends, significant political figures included among them, were indeed philosophically informed, often professed philosophical stances of their own, and could enjoy playing with philosophical vocabulary and ideas: see Griffin 1995 [= Griffin 2018: 461–74] and 1997 [= Griffin 2018: 495–509].

27. An earlier Crassus than the wealthy warlord co-opted into a power pact by Pompey and Caesar (as mentioned in section 2, pp. 5–6).
28. Gildenhard 2013: 259. For more on this facet of *Brutus* and *On the orator*, see section 4 pp. 17–19. *On the commonwealth* contains a prediction (*Rep.* 6.11–12) that the great Scipio would as dictator save the Republic from the turbulence associated with the activities of the populist Gracchi, if he can escape the impious hands of his relatives (he died in 129 BC in mysterious circumstances, soon after the supposed date of the gathering portrayed in the dialogue: a piece of staging parallel with that mounted in *On the orator*). Cicero's original readers themselves were left to draw the analogy with the perils confronting the Republic at the time of the dialogue's composition and initial circulation.
29. Syme 1939. Syme's chapter on 'political catchwords' (149–61) remains a riveting read.
30. Brunt 1988d: 282.
31. Brunt 1988d: 282–3.
32. Brunt 1988c: 240–80 argued that mostly rejected demands for agrarian reform, particularly from veterans, were a principal leitmotiv in Roman politics throughout most of the last century of the Republic, and that it was willingness of landless veterans to take up arms again which was the instrument by which it was eventually destroyed.
33. Some recent contributions to the argument are Millar 1998, Mouritsen 2001, Morstein-Marx 2004, Tan 2008, Morstein-Marx 2013, Mouritsen 2017. A useful brief summary of some main issues is Yakobson 2006.
34. See especially Morstein-Marx 2004.
35. Morstein-Marx 2013.
36. Mackie 1992: 66.
37. For contrasting recent perspectives see for example Wiseman 2009, for whom a Cicero (as voice of the entrenched aristocratic elite) and a Caesar (within a populist tradition he is seen as inheriting) do subscribe to opposed value systems (he speaks of 'two rival ideological camps'), and Mouritsen 2017, for whom the cohesiveness of the ideology which all political agents shared helps explain why

there was never any fundamental challenge in the last century of the Republic to its basic constitutional structure. Elements of both interpretations are endorsed by Mackie 1992, who shows however that ideological divisions were radical enough to pose a potentially destructive threat to the stability of that structure, a fear that Cicero frequently expressed.

38. Beard and Crawford 1985: 12. As Andrew Wallace-Hadrill has observed, Syme's 'Roman revolution', with its stress on the rise of Italian elites within the post-republican political settlement, was already 'explicitly a social revolution', but 'also implicitly a cultural one' (Wallace-Hadrill 1997: 4).
39. Beard and Crawford 1985: 20.
40. Moatti 1997 (English translation: Moatti 2015). By one of those coincidences that frequently occur in scholarship, a similar argument, albeit inevitably covering less ground, was published simultaneously by Andrew Wallace-Hadrill, in an article prefiguring some of the themes of a later monograph: see Wallace-Hadrill 1997, 2008. Rawson 1985 had already assembled much pertinent evidence. For a briefer survey: Griffin 1994 [= Griffin 2018: 432–60.
41. Moatti 2015: 104.
42. As is pointed out in Wallace-Hadrill 1997: 14, according to Augustine this seems to be how Varro himself conceived his project (CD 6.2.48). See also Feeney 2007.
43. Moatti 2015: 149.
44. Wallace-Hadrill 2008: 248.
45. Moatti 2015: 142; cf. 2–3.
46. Steel 2005: 12; for a full-scale development of this kind of assessment, with specific focus on the rhetorical treatises, see Dugan 2005.
47. See Moatti 2015: 60–7, 126–8.
48. Schofield 2008.
49. Schofield 2017a.
50. Their intellectual interests need not be doubted. But while Laelius may have been 'masterly' in 'matters of political calculation', hence perhaps his nickname 'Sapiens' ('the wise') (Astin 1967: 81), Scipio's political career was much of it marked by populist methods, placing 'his own advancement above both usage and the law', helping 'to create a political atmosphere in which such methods could be tolerated and, because of their evident success, imitated' (Astin 1967: 242–3). Astin (ibid.) concluded that 'he is not without responsibility' for the 'epoch-making eruption into violence and bloodshed' of 133 BC, notably the assassination of Tiberius Gracchus.
51. Scholars once believed in the historical existence of a Scipionic intellectual circle at Rome, with the four figures just mentioned at its core. The inadequacy

of the evidence for this construction was powerfully demonstrated in Strasburger 1966, which however noted that there was credible independent evidence of Scipio's friendship with Posidonius, and also with Panaetius (Laelius, too, and Scipio's nephew Tubero, one of those also imagined in *On the commonwealth* as present at the gathering, are said to have studied with him). Strasburger thought that Scipio's interest in philosophy would not have extended beyond practical ethics and philosophy of life, but it seems arbitrary to exclude the possibility that, as Laelius is made to affirm, he did discuss the principles of politics with these Stoics (and the *Cyropaedia* of Plato's contemporary Xenophon, his favourite reading, is a treatment of the best way to exercise power, at least as Cicero construes the work: *QFr.* 1.1.23). In more recent scholarship, Scipio's enthusiasm for Greek *paideia* more generally is stressed by Sommer 2013; the attempt to ascribe to Panaetius a school of philosophy operating in Scipio's house by Barlow 2018: 115–16 is based on an absurd misreading of Cic. *Mur.* 66. On Panaetius see further Chapter 5, section 3 p. 159 and nn.42 and 43.

52. From the time of his earliest studies Cicero had developed a strong interest in Greek rhetorical theory, of which he had expert command; and perhaps not coincidentally it was getting help from Greek teachers in improving his speaking technique that he claims to have been the principal motive for his travels of 79–77 BC to Athens and points east (*Brut.* 313–16). As a very young man (he suggests actually as a teenager) he had written and circulated a still surviving two-volume treatment of the subject entitled *On invention* (*de Or.* 1.5), presumably his very first published literary composition.

53. Dugan 2013: 31. Mankin 2011: 1–50 supplies an excellent detailed account of *On the orator*. See also Fantham 2004.

54. See section 3 p. 9.

55. For an assessment of the political import of *Brutus*, see Steel 2002–3.

56. Cicero is sometimes thought to have overemphasized the significance of oratory in Roman republican politics. But the influential work of Morstein-Marx 2004 does something to redress the balance in his favour; and van der Blom 2016 argues convincingly for the importance of public performance and self-presentation (albeit not confined to oratory, and in oratory not to Ciceronian norms of eloquence) in the building of a successful political career.

57. See especially Gildenhard 2011.

58. See especially Brunt 1986.

59. Shackleton Bailey 1971: x.

2
Liberty, Equality, and Popular Sovereignty

1. Libertas in Roman political discourse

Propaganda is perhaps the place to begin, with a coin in the British Museum collection, minted in the latter years of the Roman Republic. It is given a conjectural date of 54 BC by Michael Crawford, in *Roman Republican Coinage*.[1] The obverse—heads—represents *LIBERTAS* (Liberty) as a goddess. The reverse—tails—shows us *BRUTUS*, as a magistrate walking between his official retinue of lectors and preceded by an attendant. The coin evidently recalls one of the defining moments in early Roman history, as Romans conceived it, and in the Romans' sense of their national past. The Brutus in question has to be Lucius Junius Brutus, one of the leaders of the coup that overthrew Tarquin the Proud, last of the Roman kings, and father of the man responsible for the rape of Lucretia as Roman tradition had it. Brutus then became one of the first two consuls under the newly inaugurated Republic. The coin commemorates him as Rome's great liberator and as symbol of its constitutional integrity as a republic. The inference—from this and a similar coin representing his ancestors—is that the moneyer who had the coins struck was Marcus Junius Brutus, who ten years later was to be a leading participant in the assassination of Julius Caesar.

The coin issue must have been designed to make a political point: perhaps to warn against the despotic ambitions of Pompey in particular, against whom Brutus had particular cause for animus; perhaps—from someone who had not yet held public office—to announce his own political pedigree as he prepared to run for election (he was to become praetor in 53 BC); perhaps both. His pedigree could not have been more impressive. When in the autumn of 44 BC political pressure on Caesar's murderers mounted,

Cicero in the second *Philippic* against Mark Antony (never in fact delivered as a speech) responded to the charge that he himself had incited them to the act with a barrage of pointed rhetorical questions, including this one (*Phil.* 2.26): 'Was it my authority (*auctoritas*) that stimulated the Brutuses [i.e. Marcus and his distant cousin Decimus] to liberate our county, when everyday they would see the image of Lucius Brutus, and one of them Ahala too [i.e. on display—doubtless—in their ancestral homes].'[2]

Liberation from tyranny was what the Roman Republic was all about. Everybody agreed about that. But consensus ended there. For who were the tyrants, and who the liberators? Only a few years earlier than Brutus's coin issue, for example, sentiment turned against Cicero. After suppressing the Catilinarian conspiracy in 63 BC, he had been acclaimed by a popular assembly as father of the country (App. *B.Civ.* 2.7; cf. Cic. *Pis.* 6). In 58 BC, however, he was driven into exile. As the historian Dio reports in his matter of fact manner (Dio Cass. 38.17.6): 'His property was confiscated, his house was razed to the ground as though he were a public enemy, and they dedicated its site for a temple of Liberty.' By the next year, the mood had swung again, and Cicero was back in Rome, suing—in the end successfully—for the restoration of his property. In one of the speeches he made in this connection, he berates Publius Clodius, the populist politician close to Julius Caesar who as tribune had promoted the vote to have him exiled. After itemizing Clodius's infractions of civic liberties in making the confiscation (*Dom.* 110): 'So is it an image of liberty that you have installed in that house, the house which was itself a proof of the exceeding cruelty of your own absolute power (*dominatus*) and of the exceeding wretchedness of the servitude (*servitus*) of the Roman people?'[3] To Clodius, it was Cicero who had behaved like a tyrant, when as consul he had had Catiline's leading associates executed without trial: hence the triumphalist consecration of the site of his house to Liberty. To Cicero, that got things exactly the wrong way around: Clodius's actions showed *him* to be the enemy of the people, intent on *depriving* them of their liberty by his attack on their saviour in the critical days of 63 BC. His 'temple of Liberty' was in reality a temple to nothing but Licence (*Leg.* 2.42).

That is just a glimpse of the way the idea of political liberty saturated Roman self-identity: in their conception of the *res publica* (i.e. the Roman commonwealth and the public interest), their sense of their own history, their political arguments, their propaganda, and their religion. Above all, for

Romans liberty was an ideal and (it was hoped) a reality to fight for. For us Roman liberty has had its resonances in our cultural inheritance. We all remember the point in Shakespeare's *Julius Caesar* when after Caesar mutters: '*Et tu, Brute*. Then fall, Caesar', and so dies, the first cry that goes up (from the lips of the conspirator Cinna) is: 'Liberty! Freedom! Tyranny is dead!' (*Julius Caesar* II.1). And we noted in the previous chapter how, in the last twenty-five years, historians have come to see the ideal of what the Romans spoke of as a free people, *populus liber* (or sometimes *civitas libera*, 'free polity' or 'free citizen body'),[4] as a governing preoccupation in a whole tradition of republican thought: in late medieval Italy, particularly as represented in Machiavelli's *Discorsi* on Livy; in writers of the English commonwealth period; and in the American Founders.

The keynote of the neo-Roman discourse[5] is the insistence that if a state is to flourish and to provide its citizens with what Milton described as 'the civil rights and advancements of every person', it must be free from domination by any other political power and from servitude to the arbitrary will of a tyrant. It represents the notion of freedom famously mocked by Hobbes in *Leviathan*. There he says of the inscription of the word LIBERTAS on the city turrets of the self-governing republic of Lucca, that its citizens have no more liberty than they would if they lived in Constantinople, under the rule of an absolute monarch. The neo-Roman assumption, by contrast, is that 'any understanding of what it means for an individual citizen to possess or lose their liberty must be embedded within an account of what it means for a civil association to be free.'[6] That is the way people thought in the Roman Republic, too, to judge from the literary evidence, and in particular from Cicero's voluminous surviving writings—the letters, the forensic and political speeches, the philosophical treatises—and the historians Sallust and Livy, who were so important for the neo-Roman writers discussed by Quentin Skinner and others.

Thus Cicero's younger contemporary Sallust explains that the rule of the Roman kings was directed at 'preserving liberty and growing the *res publica*', before it turned into arrogance and domination (Sall. *Cat.* 6.7). He represents the tribune Gaius Memmius as warning assemblies of the people to defend themselves against the nobles and not to 'abandon the *res publica* or their own liberty' (*Jug.* 33.30).[7] Cicero celebrates the great contribution of all sectors of Roman society in putting down the Catiline insurrection, through being spurred to defend the safety of their country by concern for private fortunes, for the common *res publica*—and for liberty, sweetest of all possessions (Cic. *Cat.* 4.16). The prime focus of much political discourse about *libertas* was in fact the *res publica* and the rights of the Roman people as a people, not (as in Pettit's contemporary version of republicanism) the freedom of 'an individual person or persons', even if many of those rights did guarantee the protection and powers of the individual citizen.[8]

The bottom line was independence from foreign rule. At the very beginning of their history it was in this sense that the early kings were said to have preserved liberty, and that the Romans defended with their arms 'liberty, country, parents' (Sall. *Cat.* 6.5). But not being subject to tyranny or (in the time of the Republic) kingship was no less fundamental. Livy tells us that when the Romans were urged by a neighbouring power to restore the Tarquins, they replied (2.15.3): 'The Roman people exists not under kingship, but in liberty', a sentiment that in effect captures the theme of the second book of his history as a whole. Tacitus famously begins the *Annals* with the sentence (*Ann.* 1.1.1): 'The city of Rome was originally in the possession of kings; liberty and the consulate were instituted by Lucius Brutus.' We have already seen Cicero charging Clodius with imposing servitude on the Roman people by his attempt (as Cicero alleged) at absolute control; and in attacking Mark Antony after Caesar's assassination, he concludes the sixth Philippic with the words (*Phil.* 6.19, addressed to a popular assembly): 'Other nations can endure slavery: the birthright of the Roman people is liberty.'

The emperor Augustus was to deploy the same rhetorical contrast, in the opening sentence of the work that he had inscribed all over the Empire as *The Achievements of the Divine Augustus* (*Mon. Anc.* 1.1): 'I emancipated the commonwealth, oppressed as it was by the control (*dominatio*) of a faction, into liberty.' Here a republican trope is deliberately echoed,[9] most immediately in the form Julius Caesar had given it when he defended his return under arms from Gaul to Italy, thus triggering civil war. Caesar explained that he did so 'to emancipate into liberty himself and the Roman people, oppressed as it was by the faction of a few' (*BCiv.* 1.22.5).[10] The use in these contexts of the vocabulary of absolute power, slavery, and emancipation is striking. It was meant not only to evoke Rome's long history as a republic ever since the overthrow of the Tarquins, but to appeal to something at the core of a Roman citizen's sense of himself. As Peter Brunt observes, 'the contrast between master and slave was omnipresent and vivid in Roman daily life.' He goes on:[11]

This must have made a man more intensely conscious of whatever freedom he possessed. His own rights were more precious by contrast with the rightlessness of the slaves around him. No doubt this gave a special emotive force to 'freedom' and 'slavery', when they were employed as political slogans.

The historian Clifford Ando aptly comments that in its political usages, the word *libertas* was drastically 'undertheorized'. Cicero (in his theoretical writings no less than in his oratory), Sallust, Livy, and the rest are generally content to trade off 'the binarism of slave and free' without further elaboration.[12] But as a basic individual status understood in those terms, freedom at Rome in effect came in varying degrees. For example, the son of a citizen father could be 'his own master in relation to . . . functions concerning the life of the community', carrying all the responsibilities of a citizen himself. However he remained 'inescapably under the power of his father [as head of the family] in many aspects of his private life', including ownership of property.[13] In the public sphere it was citizenship, as the quotations below will indicate, that was the guarantee of the liberty a Roman enjoyed, as realized in the exercise of political and legal rights.[14] Roman political *libertas*, for all its insufficiency of explicit definition, was accordingly very much a positive value, antithetical to subjection or servitude, but not conceived solely or often primarily in terms of their absence.

In many political contexts, talk of liberty in effect meant political self-determination as represented in popular sovereignty (those are our terms, not the Romans'), and in the constitutional guarantees and the legal rights which went with that—thanks to a long if often obscure sequence of political gains achieved over several centuries. Livy begins Book 2 of his history of Rome, and his account of what he describes as the newly gained freedom of the Roman people in the first years of the Republic, by announcing that he will show how the control (*imperia*) exercised by laws was made more powerful than that of men (2.1.1). Cicero standardly couples *ius* and *iura* (right, rights) with *libertas*. Addressing a popular assembly at the very outset of his term as consul in 63 BC, he talks of how 'this *civitas* (polity, citizen body) far excels others in its right of liberty (*iure libertatis*)', in that appointment to any position of power, civic (*imperium*) or military (*potestas*), is in the hands of the people in its assemblies. Creation of the board of decemvirs (panel of ten) proposed by Publius Servilius Rullus, he argues, would effectively bring back kings, and the end of 'your right, power (*potestas*), and liberty' (*Leg. agr.* 2.29).[15] To quote Brunt once more:[16]

The legal rights that Romans most explicitly and commonly subsumed under the title of freedom are of two types: immunity from arbitrary coercion and punishment by magistrates, and some degree of political power.

Having—and being able to renounce—the citizenship entitling us to such rights[17] represented the 'firmest of foundations' (*fundamenta firmissima*) for our liberty, Cicero told a jury in 56 BC: the basis too of 'our empire (*imperium*)', and why through their extension to other Italian communities the name of the Roman people has become so known and respected (*Balb.* 31).

2. Senate and people

Sallust passes a grim verdict on partisanship in the last decades of the Roman Republic (*Cat.* 38.3):

All who troubled the commonwealth pretended concern for the public good, with slogans that sounded honourable, some maintaining that they were defending the rights of the people (*populi iura*), others that they were intent on maximizing the authority (*auctoritas*) of the senate. But they were contending each for his own control of events (*potentia*).

Nicola Mackie had some interesting words on Sallust's perspective:[18]

Retired politicians live on the sidelines of politics, and rake over events whose outcome has often been less than desirable. Disaster born out of good intentions hardly seems to make sense. One can perhaps more easily come to terms with what has happened, and establish control over the past, by assuming that all participants got what they deserved. But politics thrives on the ambiguous rightness of each side in the dispute, not on the admitted wrongness of both.

Sallust's contrast here of the rights of the people with the authority of the senate is what we must now consider.

The people was the sovereign body, and its decisions in legislation and elections were needed to legitimize the outcomes of the processes in question. These and other powers, such as the Roman version of *habeas corpus* (*provocatio*), or again the powers of the tribunes to act on behalf of the *plebs* (the ordinary mass of citizens), were exercises of that sovereignty—of its liberty.[19] What the senate mostly exercised, by contrast, was *auctoritas*, authority. That authority can be described as authoritative influence deriving formally from its constitutional role, which was to act as the chief forum for deliberating public policy and for advising the consuls and other senior magistrates on the decisions they needed to take in order to implement it—since executive decisions were for elected politicians ('magistrates'), not the senate itself.[20] This was undoubtedly a rather extraordinary form of 'influence'.

The senate was for long the one relatively cohesive and stable political entity at Rome, its membership consisting in all who had previously held senior elected office. It was permeable by 'new men' such as Cicero, but descendants of the same wealthy landowning 'patrician' families appeared generation after generation. Its influence when at its height represented enormous power, even if formally speaking that remained 'advice', or 'leadership' (*hêgemonia*), as Livy's Greek contemporary Dionysius of Halicarnassus conceptualized it in his *Roman Antiquities* (e.g. *Ant. Rom.* 6.71.3, 6.74.3, 6.85.1, 7.50.4; cf. Plu. *Rom.* 13.4). That advice was formally expressed in *senatus consulta*, which were conceived as resolutions magistrates would ignore at their peril, with a particularly grave resolution 'of last resort' (what Julius Caesar once called the *senatus consultum ultimum* (*BCiv.* 1.5.3)) purportedly authorizing emergency action (overriding the laws) to protect the commonwealth from unusual danger.[21]

Senate and people together—*senatus populusque Romanus*—came to be regarded as what gave Republican Rome its constitutional identity, as the emperor Augustus signalled when he claimed to have restored the commonwealth from his own power to the *arbitrium* (decision-making) of the senate and the Roman people (*Mon. Anc.* 34.2)—and as was of course given symbolic expression in the acronym SPQR, on countless coins and inscriptions as well as on military standards.[22] In fact, senatorial authority and the liberty of the people were in constitutional terms complementary. And despite his gloom about the late Republic, Sallust himself is probably implying that there was a time when they actually did function as such (cf. *Iug.* 41.2). As late as 44–3 BC, the pairing of senatorial authority and the liberty of the people remains an almost ritualistic Ciceronian trope. In the *Philippics* (the speeches he wrote in autumn and winter 44–3 BC, mostly against Mark Antony) he wants to talk of the twinned fundamental political values that anyone who cares for the *res publica* will commit himself to upholding and championing (*Phil.* 4.5, 10.23, 13.33, 47).

The dynamics of popular liberty and senatorial authority did run in opposite directions, however: broadly, and too roughly speaking, democratic and oligarchic respectively. Livy writes the entire history of the early Republic as an unceasing sequence of struggles between these countervailing forces—something which Machiavelli in his *Discorsi* was to judge the recipe for the Republic's durability and success. For all that, it has been observed that none of those who in the late Republic maintain that 'they were defending the rights of the people' (as Sallust put it), 'appears ever to have represented conflict between Senate and People as fundamentally an institutional one',[23] even if, from the opposite standpoint, Cicero in a philosophical dialogue can represent his brother Quintus as calling for the abolition of the key popular institution of the tribunate (*Leg.* 3.19–22).[24] The issue was thought to turn on 'men, not ideology'[25]—or as Sallust put the point elsewhere (*Jug.* 41.5), on the 'unrestrained desire' of the nobility for *dignitas* (respect proportionate to their status and achievements and *auctoritas*),[26] and of the people (*populus*) for more liberty.[27]

What does Sallust mean by 'people' here? The sovereign citizen body itself? Or the *plebs*: the mass of ordinary citizens as distinct from the political elite, and as such just one of two segments of the whole citizen body? When members of the political elite addressed a popular gathering (*contio*)—which could be summoned only by a consul or tribune or other senior elected officer of state—with speeches often relating to legislative proposals shortly to be put formally to a voting assembly (*comitia*), they invariably addressed those present as *Quirites*. That was the archaic Latin word for 'citizens', preserved in the formal designation of the Roman state as *res publica populi Romani Quiritium*, 'the commonwealth of the citizens of the Roman people' (Varro, *Ling.* 6.86.1). In other words, whatever the make-up and size of the crowd before them, they treated it as 'the actual embodiment of the *populus Romanus*'[28]—as the sovereign body itself. In truth, any such crowd could consist only of a small subset even of those citizens domiciled in or visiting Rome, let alone those who lived elsewhere in Italy.[29] Nonetheless, this was 'the venue where political leaders sought to influence . . . that portion of the citizenry who actually exercised the sovereign right of the *populus Romanus* to decide by vote most of the fundamental matters of the Commonwealth'—above all legislation and elections.[30]

At the same time a *contio* was, and was sometimes acknowledged to be, a gathering of the *plebs*.[31] In Cicero's speech to the people against Rullus's agrarian law, the assumption that audience and speaker share exactly the same concerns, values, and aims—above all commitment to the *res publica* and the liberty of the Roman people—is sustained throughout. He charges Rullus at one point both with breach of 'faith with the Roman *plebs, Quirites*' (as their tribune), and failure 'to play fair with you and your liberty' (as the citizen body of the Roman people) (*Leg. agr.* 2.20). When Sallust portrays a populist leader addressing the citizen body at a *contio*, he too may be made to couple 'betrayal of the authority of the senate, betrayal of the power vested in you (*imperium*)' in a single clause (*Iug.* 31.26), just as Cicero might have done in addressing the *populus* as sovereign body. But the speaker in this instance—the tribune Gaius Memmius, in 111 BC—had begun his address with an attack on the 'power of the faction' that is threatening the *res publica* (31.1). That is then equated with the 'arrogance of the few' (31.2), who are differentiated from the 'Roman *plebs*' and people of 'your order' (31.7). The tribune Gaius Licinius Macer is represented as beginning his speech to a *contio* in 73 BC in traditional style with the salutation '*Quirites*' (repeated at various junctures: *Hist.* 3.48.1, 8, 15, 16, 24). But he too lambasts the 'domination (*dominatio*) of the few' (*Hist.* 3.48.6; cf. 28),[32] and he is explicit that it is the *plebs* who are their victim (*Hist.* 3.48.28).

Cicero, at the time of the civil war a leading representative of the anti-populist senatorial 'faction' in Caesar's eyes, would for his part see claims by a Catiline or a Clodius to be defending the liberty of the Roman people as masking an attempt to enlist the support of the common people—the *plebs*, the *multitudo*—in what was in reality a bid for tyranny. When he refers to *populares* he generally means 'popularist' in describing a political actor in these terms: i.e. someone who may talk of the interests of *populus*, the sovereign citizen body, but is really aiming to please the masses—as in his classic distinction between those in public life who wish to be and to be considered *populares*, on the one hand, and *optimates*, 'the best sort', on the other (*Sest.* 96). This was the sense in which, when addressing elite audiences, he counted Gaius Gracchus as the *popularis* or popularist par excellence (*Dom.* 24; cf. *Sest.* 103, where however the Gracchi stand in contrast with the present crop of so-called *populares*, who are—he claims—rejected by the *populus* itself: *Sest.* 104-19). In addressing a *contio* he could even represent himself as truly *popularis* (*Leg. agr.* 2.6–7); unsurprisingly refer in more admiring terms to the favourable treatment of the *plebs* by the Gracchi (*Leg. agr.* 2.10, 81); and report how he had professed himself willing to support legislation beneficial to the Roman *plebs* (*Leg. agr.* 2.12).[33]

3. Liberty and equality

In 2001 Henrik Mouritsen wrote:[34]

> *Libertas* was the common ideal invoked by all Romans who aspired to power, no matter what their political views and methods might otherwise have been .... All political acts and arguments must be justified within the ideological framework of the liberty of the *res publica* and the *populus Romanus*. And precisely because it was such a fundamental tenet of the identity of the Roman state, all political agents could draw moral capital from it and exploit it for their own purposes.

In 1988 Peter Brunt had expressed the following view:[35]

> Liberty was often on the lips of politicians. It meant different things to different people. For the ordinary citizen it comprised not only his safeguards for personal protection under the law but also his capacity as a voter, which the ballot enabled him to use with more independence; for the senator his right to speak freely on matters of state, and to have an effective voice in decisions; to both alike it was thus equivalent to a share in political power. The citizen could use his vote to secure material advantages, and the power of senators brought them lucrative perquisites. It is, however, unlikely that men consciously prized liberty as no more than an instrument for these purposes.

These two statements are evidently not incompatible. The differing vantage points of citizen and senator articulated by Brunt are best interpreted as two particularly salient ways in which agents occupying different points within the political system were able to draw from the single ideological framework described by Mouritsen the moral capital that they perceived as available within it—and indeed as what should be guaranteed for them by something fundamental: the *libertas* of the *res publica* itself.

It is true enough that 'Cicero ... was passionately attached to liberty, the liberty of the senators': their freedom to 'take decisions without fear or pressure.'[36] That is what he was clear that he and senators generally thought they had lost when in 56 BC the 'few' (Pompey and the other two warlords) took control of Roman politics, and the objective that experienced statesmen embraced of exhibiting '*dignitas* in stating our opinions, *libertas* in public affairs (*res publica*)' was 'totally eliminated' (*Fam.* 1.8.3). What would freedom from tyranny add up to, if those charged with principal responsibility for wise government could not speak their minds without fear or favour? When, in the next chapter, we examine the theory of government set out a few years later in *On the commonwealth* and *On laws*, it will also become evident how restricted he thought the political rights exercised by the *populus* or the *plebs* ought to be, despite what he describes (also in 56, but before Pompey's power pact) as the wisdom of those who established the constitution of the Republic in wanting the senate 'to protect and increase the liberty and interests of the *plebs*' (*Sest.* 137).

But there is no reason to doubt that the ideological framework of the liberty of the *res publica* and the *populus Romanus* remains the overall context in which he wrote and thought. That framework was capacious enough to accommodate the development of fiercely opposed conceptions of how the various interests and values that the liberty of the Roman people was supposed by all parties to secure should be weighted—and about what was a true exercise of liberty and what merely 'licence', to use the term for abuse of freedom and power, whether on the part of the *plebs* and their advocates or on that of the nobility or the holders of *imperium*, that Cicero, Sallust, and particularly Livy all liked to deploy.[37] Thus in Book 3 of *On the commonwealth*, Lucius Furius Philus, one of the company who make up the dialogue's cast, is made to say (*Rep.* 3.23): 'If the people has the greatest power, and everything is governed by its decision, that is called liberty, but is really *licentia* (licence).'

So much for the present on liberty itself. What of any connection with equality? Liberty clearly took centre stage from time to time in political controversy in the last years of the Republic. Evidence by contrast that equality was much talked about in such contexts is hard to find—although Brunt observes (albeit on a related point) 'how little the sources preserve of the sentiments to which *populares* appealed'.[38] Wirszubski's still largely authoritative study *Libertas* (1950), in itemizing 'major points at issue' (with regard to liberty) during this period, offers no instances, other than Cicero's view that politicians from outside the charmed circle of the nobility should be treated with equivalent esteem (and by implication given similar opportunity for advancement).[39] But that matter does not seem to have been mostly or explicitly argued in terms either of liberty or of equality. Concerns with equality do not figure at all in the account of 'the political struggle in the first century BC' over liberty offered in Valentina Arena's more recent *Libertas and the Practice of Politics in the Late Roman Republic* (2012).[40]

We could not, of course, infer that equality was regarded as of little political significance. Cicero for his part is certainly committed to the principle of equality before the law. But it is most directly connected in his writings with legal justice and the rights of citizenship. In *On duties* he takes it to be one of the key characteristics of the good citizen that he should live with the citizens in fair and equal right (*aequo et pari iure*) in his private capacity (*Off.* 1.124), although he does earlier indicate a connection with liberty when he states that among free peoples and 'in equality of right' (*iuris aequabilitate*) one should cultivate 'an affable temper and what some call "elevation of mind"' (*Off.* 1.88). Similarly, a prime duty laid upon those in government is to 'make every effort to enable each person to keep that which is his through the fairness (*aequitate*) of justice and the courts', protecting both poor and rich alike from the threats to which they are differently but typically beset (*Off.* 2.85).

The same kind of thinking can be found in Cicero's forensic oratory. *On behalf of Caecina* (69 BC) is a speech full of appeals to equity in interpretation of law (*aequitas*).[41] At one point in it, when rounding off a denunciation of any attempt to undermine law governing the relations between citizens (*ius civile*), he concludes (*Caec.* 70):

In truth, if it is done away with, there is no way of sorting out what belongs to you or to someone else, and there is nothing that can count as equal ground shared by everyone (*aequabile inter omnes*) nor can there be one thing relating them all.

In defending Gnaeus Plancius (54 BC), like Atticus a 'knight' (*eques*) or member of the business class, he explodes at any possibility of a suggestion that a member of that class could not speak as freely as he wished (while allowing that Plancius's father had misjudged what was appropriate) (*Planc.* 33):[42]

Where is our famous tradition (*mos*), where that equality (*aequitas*) of right, where that ancient liberty, which though overwhelmed by the evils of civil strife, should by this time have been raising its head, at last revived and taking an erect stance?

So here, at any rate, equality is associated with liberty.

In all of these statements, Cicero clearly assumes that the principles he invokes are unchallengeable and will not be challenged. His tactic is rather to remind his readers or hearers, more or (in *On duties*) less forcefully, that they need the impartial implementation they all too often fail to get. The appeal to 'ancient liberty' is particularly significant. Romans in the first century BC thought that it was in the political struggles of the early Republic that basic civic freedoms had been won. According to Livy, a key episode was the suspension of the constitution in the middle of the fifth century BC following a long period of class antagonism. The tribunes had asked for measures to be proposed by a panel of legislators, drawn from both the *plebs* and the patricians, which would be advantageous to both sides and would represent the equalizing of liberty (*aequandae libertatis*) (3.31.7). Their request succeeded (except that the panel appointed was exclusively patrician). A board of ten (known to historians as the Decemvirs) to draw up fresh legal provisions was appointed.

In due course the Decemvirs, in reporting on their proposals, claimed that they had indeed equalized rights (*iura*) for all, high and low (3.34.3, cf. Tac. *Ann.* 3.27; something once achieved under the kings, according to Cicero: *Off.* 2.41). The so-called Twelve Tables (originally Ten, on Livy's account) seem to have represented publication in written form of what had been for the most part customary law.[43] Evidently what they meant was that it was now incontrovertibly established that all citizens had the same rights where private law (as it would later be categorized) was concerned. And that does indeed seem to have been the case. Whether it was quite all that the tribunes had in mind (as Livy represents them) is another matter.

There followed, he tells us, some months of turbulence, brought that to a temporary end by the election once again of two consuls (Lucius Valerius Potitus and Marcus Horatius Barbatus) in 449 BC. Livy's narrative of the turbulence and his account of the legislation Valerius and Horatius are said to have promoted indicate what for the *plebs* remained unfinished in the business of equalizing liberty.[44] The one thing that agitated the plebeians was how they could recover the power of the tribunes, their champions under the constitution and the 'bulwark for liberty' (3.37.5)—but a function suspended like other elective offices for the duration of the Decemvirate. Valerius and Horatius duly emerged as 'leaders of the masses' (3.49.3).

Three key laws of the Republic, designed to safeguard 'the liberty of the *plebs*' (3.55.2), are said to have been the outcome. One made resolutions of the *plebs* in one of the formal assemblies (the *comitia tributa*) binding on the Roman people. A second restored the citizen's right of appeal to the people if impeached (*provocatio*), 'a unique bastion of liberty'. A third gave the office of tribune (and some other functions intimately concerned with the rights of the *plebs*) the protection of religious sanction (3.55.3–7). Thus was 'the power (*potestas*) of the tribunes and the liberty of the *plebs* firmly established' (3.56.1). 'Equal liberty', as the *plebs* and their protagonists saw it, ought to mean not just that any individual citizen should have the same rights in the private sphere as any other, but crucially that they as a body should have legally protected political rights, which would give them collectively powers balancing those of the patricians (as vested in the consulate and the senate). Cicero put the general gist more colourfully in the last of his tracts against Verres in 70 BC (*Verr.* 2.5.163):[45]

> Sweet name of liberty! Exemplary rights of our citizenship (*civitas*)! Law of the Porcian clan, laws of the Sempronian family! Powers of the tribunes, yearned for with heavy hearts, and eventually restored to the Roman *plebs*!

Most present-day historians of Rome are sceptical that Livy had any real historical warrant for articulating what was at stake in the struggle that he recounts in the political vocabulary which he introduces in telling his story. 'We do not of course know', says Brunt of those Livy represents as demanding 'equal liberty', 'how they actually argued their case; annalistic representations necessarily mirror the ideas of their own age.'[46] What sources Livy drew upon in this context, particularly in highlighting equal liberty as a focus of argument, must be a matter for speculation. Some historians think agnosticism is the only prudent option.[47] Others have favoured as the principal suspects the historian Licinius Macer (died 66 BC),[48] otherwise known as a populist politician to whom Sallust in his *Histories* gives a stirring speech delivered in 73 BC (*Hist.* 3.38), and Valerius Antias, whose history is usually dated to 80–60 BC, but by some to the 40s BC.[49] Perhaps we should stick to repeating that Romans in that century saw the period of the Struggle of the Orders as the time when equality under the law and civic rights for all were first achieved.

4. Equality and liberty in *On the commonwealth*

When Cicero represents Scipio, principal speaker in most of *On the commonwealth*, as developing early in Book 1 the cases that could be made for kingship, aristocracy, and democracy as forms of government, he made equality and liberty central to the argument for popular rule. If Livy's account of the political settlement that emerged from the Struggle of the Orders is anything like right, then a division of powers and responsibilities as between consul and senate, on the one hand, and the *plebs*, on the other, was achieved in the fourth century. But such an outcome fell far short of democracy, and indeed—it might be thought—of real liberty or real equality. Precisely such a criticism is articulated when Scipio puts (without himself endorsing) the argument for what its advocates would recognize as true popular rule.

The key stretch of reasoning begins with a passage that probably reflects much populist rhetoric of the late Republic, as notably in the beginning of the speech to the *plebs* of 73 BC which Sallust attributes to Licinius Macer—where however there is no talk of 'equal' liberty (*Hist.* 3.48.1–6). Scipio says (*Rep.* 1.47):[50]

How can liberty be equal (I won't speak about kingship, in which slavery is not even hidden or ambiguous) in those polities in which everyone is free in name only? They vote, they entrust commands and offices, they are canvassed and asked for their support, but they give what must be given even if they are unwilling, and they are asked to give to others what they do not have themselves. They have no share in executive power (*imperium*), in public deliberation, or in the panels of select judges, all of which are apportioned on the basis of pedigree or wealth.

That sounds, as it must have been intended to sound, like a summary from one point of view of the Roman Republic's constitution.

But at this point Cicero has Scipio make a further move, which is perhaps unlikely to have been advanced by any Roman *popularis* politician. Scipio draws a contrast between Rome and a 'free people' (i.e. truly free, as this argument would have it—that is, a people enjoying popular rule: cf. *Rep.* 1.46) such as Rhodes or Athens—though unfortunately the detail of the contrast is lost.[51] *Populares* had not been arguing for democracy as such or in so many words, nor is appeal to any Greek parallel known to have figured in their rhetorical repertoire. The debate Cicero is staging at this point in *On the commonwealth*, on the other hand—about the comparative merits of kingship, aristocracy, and popular rule—is in origin a thoroughly Greek debate, which we meet first in the pages of Herodotus (albeit represented in the form of a discussion between leading figures in the Persian nobility: 3.80–2). It was given classic expression in Book 3 of Aristotle's *Politics*, often seen as the main source Cicero must be supposed to be exploiting here, whether directly, or indirectly, through Peripatetic reworkings.[52] The association of equality with liberty that Scipio already assumes at the start of the extract quoted is likewise familiar from Greek sources, most pertinently Plato and

Aristotle, even if it could already be heard on the lips of Romans in Cicero's time.[53]

If no more than a severely truncated line of reasoning to do with Athens and Rhodes had survived of the rest of the argument for popular rule, our frustration would have been intense. But the gap before the text picks up again is small. When it resumes, the register of Scipio's advocacy of popular rule again sounds thoroughly Roman while apparently drawing also on Greek political thought (*Rep.* 1.48):

> But if peoples hang on to their right (*ius*), nothing, they say, surpasses that in distinction, liberty, happiness: since they are masters of laws and courts, of war and peace, of international agreements, of the life or death of any one individual, of their finances. This only, they think, is properly called *res publica*, that is, the property or business (*res*) of the people; and so it is normal for the property of the people to be claimed (*vindicari*) into liberty from the domination of kings and aristocrats (*optimates*) alike.

Here the specification of 'laws and courts, of war and peace, of international agreements' as what needs to be controlled by the people exactly mirrors what Aristotle sees as the primary scope of public deliberation (*Pol.* 4.14, 1298a3–5), which at Athens was indeed under popular control. At the same time, there are further resonances with the rhetoric of Licinius Macer. One might also think of the radical language used by the classic populist Gaius Gracchus, in a speech to the people of 123 BC (as reported by Aulus Gellius), when he is recommending them to act radically, in such a way as 'more easily to manage (*administrare*) your advantages and *res publica*'. 'Managing' public business (*res publica*) is in Roman discourse standardly taken to be the job of magistrates and senate, not of the people as such.[54] The identification of *res publica* as the property or business of the people is most immediately a reference to the definition of the concept given shortly before on his own account by Scipio himself (*Rep.* 1.39). We will be discussing that in the final section of this chapter.

The democratic argument for popular rule is then clinched in the following passage by appeal to egalitarian principle (*Rep.* 1.49):

> Since law (*lex*) is the bond of citizen association, and the justice (*ius*) of law is equal (*aequale*), then by what justice can an association of citizens be held together, when the status of citizens is not equal (*par*)? For even if making financial resources equal (*aequari*) is not appealing, even if everyone's mental capacities cannot be equal,

definitely the rights (*iura*) of those who are citizens in the same commonwealth ought among themselves to be equal. For what is a citizen body (*civitas*) other than an association in justice (*ius*)?⁵⁵

This is a pregnant piece of argumentation, which will require some midwifery if it is to deliver its significance.

Any Greek source material Cicero may have used here has been comprehensively Romanized, and by Cicero the non-democrat himself, particularly where the basic philosophical justification for democratic equality is concerned. First, we get the claim that law is the bond of citizen association. This initial premise is not in the least unRoman. Indeed, as James Zetzel points out in his commentary on *On the commonwealth*,⁵⁶ Cicero's formulation puts one in mind of a famous purple passage in a speech to the court of 66 BC (over ten years earlier), when he says of the laws (*Clu.* 146): 'This is the bond that secures the esteem (*dignitas*) we enjoy in this commonwealth, this is the foundation of liberty, this is the source of fairness in justice (*aequitas*). The intellect and mind and thinking and judgement of the citizen body (*civitas*) are located in the laws.'⁵⁷ The second premise—that the justice (*ius*) of law is equal—is if anything still more Roman, as we saw in section 3.

The consequence Cicero draws from his two premises, and then spells out further in terms of equal rights, is both entirely logical and again thoroughly Roman. If a citizen society is bonded by law enshrining equal justice, then it follows that its members—the citizens—must have an equal status if they are to receive justice: they must have equal rights. That is precisely what Cicero thinks himself—and indeed takes to be uncontroversial as applied to private individuals. They should live in fair and equal justice with other citizens (*Off.* 1.124). The Twelve Tables may have done little to ensure that the *plebs* as a class had political rights that achieved a balance with those reserved for patricians. As mentioned above, the main achievement was to give definitive written formulation to customary private law. That will presumably have counted as an equalization of laws inasmuch as it provided any citizen, rich or poor, plebeian or patrician, with the same access in principle to knowledge of an established corpus of laws that applied to all equally as citizens, and that did not discriminate in content between citizens. Hence the outrage when (at least as the Romans came to believe) the Decemvirs added their two further tables of '*un*equal' (unfair) laws (*iniquarum legum*) to an original ten, including the notorious rule prohibiting intermarriage between plebeians and patricians (e.g. Cic. *Rep.* 2.62–3).

This is Cicero at his original best: acute and fertile.[58] He makes the Greek democratic argument for equal rights achieve a general formulation of citizen equality, which at that level of generality would constitute not just a valid deduction, but one any contemporary Roman would be more than happy to embrace—as the very foundation of Roman civil order. But of course, to work as a rationale for democracy the argument has to be taken more specifically as appealing to a conception of what *political* justice consists in if it is to generate the conclusion that all citizens should have equal *political* rights. And that is something no longer uncontroversial, nor what was operative in the Roman Republic, where (for example) the power of the vote was weighted heavily in favour of the propertied classes.

Nor is it what Scipio is made to argue on his own account. In a first sketch of the weaknesses of each of kingship, aristocracy, and popular rule, he has already taken the line that if, as in a radical democracy, all political business is transacted by the people itself, there is palpable injustice.[59] We like him might think of Athens, where all forms of political participation—above all eligibility to vote and to be elected to any office—were open to all adult male citizens equally. That is an equality (*aequabilitas*), Scipio objects, that is *in*equitable (*iniqua*). It provides for no distinctions in rank (*dignitas*) (*Rep.* 1.43). Democratic equality—identified as that 'equality of right (*aequabilitas iuris*) which free peoples (i.e. democracies; cf. *Rep.* 3.46) embrace', and as such 'what people call equality'—fails to live up to its name (*Rep.* 1.53).[60]

But a requirement to embed some form of equality in any form of constitution that will be durable is not rejected by Cicero. Instead he takes the view that it needs to be finessed. Near the end of Book 1, he has Scipio summarize the mixed theory of government that he does himself advocate (*Rep.* 1.69):

I give my approval to there being something preeminent and regal in a *res publica*, to something being bestowed and assigned to the authority of its leading men, and to certain matters being kept for the judgment and will of the mass of the people. This structure possesses, firstly, a particularly important kind of equality (*aequabilitaem quandam magnam*): something which free persons cannot do without for very long.

What sort of equality is this? In a comparable passage of Book 2 (*Rep.* 2.57), Scipio speaks of an equal 'balance' (*compensatio*) of 'right (*ius*), duty, and responsibility', ensuring sufficient (*satis*) power for those in governing positions (*magistratibus*), sufficient authority in the deliberation of the leading men, and sufficient liberty for the people. In short, such a form of *res publica* needs to be 'equal (*aequabilis*) relative to all the orders of the citizen body' (*Rep.* 2.62; cf. 2.42).

When Scipio speaks of a different and 'particularly important kind of equality', he means to rescue the political application of the term from exclusive democratic or egalitarian control, and give it a superior connotation.[61] Quite how that superior notion is to be theorized, the reader is not given much guidance. An influential article by Elaine Fantham amplified a suggestion by the historian Claude Nicolet that Cicero intended here an allusion to the Greek theory of 'the truest and best equality', conceptualized as assigning 'more to the greater and less to the lesser' (Plato, *Laws* 6.757b–c; elsewhere called by Plato 'geometric equality': *Gorg.* 508a, cf. Aristotle, *EN* 5.3, 1131a10–b24).[62] But such an interpretation does not reflect any use of the language of proportionality on Cicero's own part: Fantham herself shows convincingly that the standard connotation he attaches to *aequabilis*, 'equal', is 'impartial, unvarying, consistent, evenly distributed'.[63] Nor is it supported by his decidedly neutral talk of 'something' or a 'sufficiency' relative to the contributions or rights distinctive of the different 'orders' or constituencies or sectors within a *res publica*.

The concept of an equal 'balance' that Scipio is made to introduce likewise tells against interpretation in terms of proportionality. The metaphor of the balance might better be seen as an echo of the historian Polybius's analysis of the Spartan 'mixed' constitution as devised to work by an 'equilibrium and balance' of opposing forces sustained by mutual fear (Polyb. *Hist.* 6.10.6–11; the analysis is then applied less schematically to Rome: *Hist.* 6.15–17). At the end of Book 2, however, Scipio envisages the kind of constitutional structure that he is advocating as working (in more Platonic fashion: *R.* 4.443c) like a harmony composed of dissimilar sounds (*Rep.* 2.69): 'What musicians call harmony with regard to song is concord in a polity or citizen body (*civitas*).'[64] He appears to be thinking of mutual recognition by the 'orders' of the equitableness of their differing contributions and entitlements as the mechanism that keeps the *res publica* in equal balance. Thus the leading men will consider it equitable that the freedom of the mass of people should be given effect in exercise of their will and judgement in elections and legislation, while the people in turn will accept as equitable that distinction in leaders is honoured in their being accorded authority.[65]

To conclude: Cicero is wanting to retain the ordinary connotations of 'equal', making it apply however not (as in democratic ideology) to the right of every citizen to hold elected office and the like, but to the proper exercise in each case of the different roles appropriately played by those different orders or constituencies.[66] That is what he judges an equitable form of equality. He is meaning to avoid at least the appearance of proposing that any of the roles, or the basis for them, is more important than any other. In *On laws*, he will speak of 'a calibration (*temperamentum*) whereby lesser folk thought that they were on an equality with the leading men' (*Leg.* 3.24).[67] That statement, franker than anything said in *On the commonwealth*, makes it clear that Cicero was aware that his formula for equitable balance could be regarded as a charade no better than a thinly veiled justification for aristocracy.

5. Popular sovereignty

The Roman citizen body was sovereign: every magistrate was made a magistrate by election in its assemblies, every law required its assent.[68] There is however no expression in Latin that actually means 'sovereignty' (or anything at all close to it). In particular contexts translators and dictionaries sometimes render a word such as *maiestas* as 'sovereignty', particularly in the expression *maiestas populi Romani*. But as Brunt says, 'it is a vague term' (its root sense[69] being 'superiority'); and regarding the capital charge of violating the people's *maiestas*, he speaks of 'a crime so ill-defined that the assembly could construe it by its own pleasure'.[70] Nonetheless belief in popular sovereignty is clearly evidenced in the way Cicero and Livy alike tell Rome's early history.

On Romulus's death, Cicero tells us in Book 2 of *On the commonwealth*, the people did not tolerate an attempt of the senate to rule without a king. They demanded one, 'adopting' (*adscivit*) on the senate's nomination the foreigner Numa Pompilius, and in their assembly 'making an order' (*iusserat*) that he be king (*Rep.* 2.23-5). Livy gives a more elaborate variant of this same account, which differentiates carefully (as Cicero—typically of *On the commonwealth*—does not) between the political pressure exerted by the *plebs* and the order made by the *populus* as citizen body in its assembly (1.17.7–11).⁷¹ After Numa's death Cicero has the people 'create' (*creavit*) Tullus Hostilius king (2.31; Livy says—this time without qualifications—'ordered' (*iussit*): 1.22.1). Similar claims are made about Ancus Marcius (2.33; cf. Livy 1.32.1) and Lucius Tarquinius (2.35; cf. Livy 1.35.6). Servius Tullius's reign is represented by Cicero as having started with nothing more than the 'consent and consensus' of the citizens; Livy makes it effectively a *coup d'état*, and mentions only the absence of a popular order and the consent of the senate (1.41.6). According to Cicero Servius moved quickly to obtain the people's 'command' (2.38; no hint of that in Livy).

These variations on what must be a common inherited tradition doubtless reflect different priorities in the agenda of the two writers, with Livy wanting to indicate that under kingship any manifestation of popular sovereignty at Rome was limited and fragile, whereas Cicero hopes we will accept that a *res publica*, and a genuine and enduring element of popular sovereignty and its acceptance, already existed when Rome was ruled by kings. For he has already in Book 1 given what Augustine calls his 'brief definition' of *res publica*—any *res publica*—as *res populi* (*Rep.* 1.39), which is both explicated as a claim about popular sovereignty (as we shall see in what follows) and yet interpreted as allowing for any one of the three basic forms of government—the rule of one or few or the *populus* itself—to be valid constitutional systems (as will be discussed in Chapter 3).

The Latin expression *res publica* has a notoriously elastic range of uses. It is 'public[-spirited] activity', 'public affairs/business', 'the public interest', 'the public sphere', 'the way the community runs its affairs', 'the community' itself (or in that sense 'the commonwealth', as the prime locus of public activity/the prime beneficiary of the public interest), 'the community constituted by the *civitas* or *populus*', and—particularly in rousing patriotic contexts—'the country'. There are as many things that it is not. It is not the Republic, as contrasted with the monarchy of the early kingship or the autocratic system of government under the Roman emperors—indeed *res publica* was the way the Roman state continued to be referred to right to the end of the Empire. It might alternatively be supposed that Cicero's title means 'On the political system'. After all, he clearly intends it as a translation of the title of Plato's dialogue *Politeia* (which we therefore call 'Republic', although 'political system' is what *politeia* means),⁷² as is made pretty explicit in *On laws* (*Leg.* 1.15, 2.14). But Cicero also indicates that the actual subject of his own work (as indeed of Plato's: *Tusc.* 2.27) is more fully and accurately articulated as 'the best condition of the *res publica*' (*Leg.* 1.15) or 'of the *civitas*' (*Rep.* 1.33), which is the expression that comes closest to 'best *politeia*'.

Nor is it helpful in theoretical contexts to construe *res publica* as meaning 'state' either, although that is often how the title of Cicero's dialogue is rendered both in English and other European languages. Talk of the state enters and becomes focal to political discourse in the early modern period. Quentin Skinner once argued that it involved the idea of an impersonal authority distinct and indeed alienated from the community of citizens and the powers vested in that community.[73] No such idea, he pointed out, developed in ancient Greece or Rome. Skinner's more recent survey and analysis of the use of the term 'state' in early modern England yields a more sceptical outcome:[74]

> To investigate the genealogy of the state is to discover that there has never been any agreed concept to which the word *state* has answered. The suggestion, still widely canvassed, that we can hope to arrive at a neutral analysis that might in principle command general assent is I think misconceived.

In the context of Cicero's definition, the options for how he might there be taking *res publica* narrow rapidly. What he offers in the identification with *res populi* is something close to an etymology. In the second century BC, the spelling was actually at least sometimes *res poplica* ('the popular *res*'); and there is an argument for thinking that in the third it had been *res populica*, 'the derivation from *populus* not yet obscured by changes in orthography'.[75] Peter Wiseman, who makes that argument, comments further: 'The phrase meant "the People's property" or "the People's business".' So far as I am aware, no other Roman writer explicitly parses the expression in this way: this is Ciceronian theory. On the other hand, Cicero presumably anticipated that there would be little resistance to his assumption that this captures something fundamental in what Romans in general understood by *res publica*. As Miriam Griffin pointed out, for a Roman reader *res populi* 'serves as a reminder that *res publica* is the legal correlative of *res privata*' (private property).[76] At the same time, something stressed by Claudia Moatti should not be forgotten: that *res* was how the subject of a legal action was referred to, 'the affair as well as the asset'. Accordingly, '*res publica* is the world of affairs about which the citizens have conflicts or debates, and about which they act in common'.[77]

I shall assume that 'the people's business', or 'the affairs and interests of the people', is the best way to take the phrase initially (the salience of the property metaphor—which is indeed in play in Cicero's text—will become apparent in due course). So understood, *res publica* is not far removed in sense from talk in Greek political philosophy of 'the common good/advantage' (as in Aristotle), and still closer to the expression 'the common affairs of the multitude' (*ta koina tou plêthous*: Polyb. 6.8.3) which occurs in Polybius's theory of constitutions and constitutional change, a discussion evidently well known to Cicero. When Dionysius of Halicarnassus, a historian of the Augustan age, came to render *res publica* into Greek, for example in narrating the Struggle of the Orders, 'the common [thing]' (*to koinon*) was his solution (e.g. *Ant. Rom.* 5.67.3, 67.5, 68.1, 68.3, 68.5; 6.38.3, 68.3). Hence the rendering 'commonwealth' I am using for the title of his dialogue, following most recently James Zetzel in his translation for the Cambridge Texts in the History of Political Thought series.[78]

Cicero wants his definition to do two related jobs. One is simply to register the claim that sovereignty in a *res publica* is vested in the people. The Romans may have had no word meaning 'sovereign' or 'sovereignty'. But they did have the genitive case. And in the collocation *res populi*, the genitive *populi* is a genitive of belonging or ownership. To state that the public interest and the conduct of public affairs are something owned by the people is effectively to assert that they have ultimate rights in them superior to those of any possible contender. Such an assertion may reasonably be construed as tantamount to a doctrine of popular sovereignty, or even as the first clear articulation of the idea of it in Greek or Roman thought. The other thing the formulation achieves is an implicit indication of how to determine whether what might be thought to be a *res publica* really is a *res publica*, and thereby a criterion for judging the legitimacy of different forms of government. Both the identification of *res publica* with *res populi*, and the definition of a *populus* with which he goes on to amplify it, play this criterial role. That supplementary clause runs as follows (*Rep.* 1.39):

A people (*populus*) is not any group of human beings assembled in just any way, but an assemblage of a *multitudo* (lots of them: a mass) which forms an association through the consensus of justice (*ius*)[79] and through sharing in advantage (*utilitas*).

A people is a particular sort of assemblage: a large number of human beings; and what makes it the body that it is is a oneness of mind shaped by justice—

presumably embodied in just institutions, above all fair laws—and mutual advantage.

It is in the latter part of Book 3 of *On the commonwealth* that Cicero puts the formulae he has articulated in Book 1 to work as criteria of legitimacy. Although scrappily preserved in the manuscript, enough continuous text survives for us to see how he carried the project through (cf. also August. *CD* 2.21). Here he is, for example, making Scipio talk about tyranny (*Rep.* 3.43):

> So that 'people's business'—that is, the *res publica*: who would speak of that, when the entire population was crushed by the cruelty of one individual, and there was no single bond of justice nor consensus and association of an assemblage—which is what a people is?

There are two charges levelled against tyranny in this sentence. First, the ruler in question (we do not know who it was Scipio has been discussing) ruled unjustly, without due regard to what was due to the people as rightful owners of the *res publica*. Second, the conditions requisite for being a people (as defined at *Rep.* 1.39) were not met—no bond of justice held them together, nor was there any real community of outlook or interest at all. In short, no such thing as a people was any longer in actual existence. And even if you were to speak of it as such, it was in no position to exercise any rights over what was or should have been its own. That last point is made explicit in the immediate sequel, where Scipio turns to the tyrannical rule of Dionysius of Syracuse, and concludes his discussion in these words (*Rep.* 3.43):

> Nothing belonged to the people, and the people itself belonged to a single individual. So where there is a tyrant, in that case we should not say that there is a flawed commonwealth (as I did yesterday), but—as logic now compels us to affirm—that there is no commonwealth at all.[80]

In short, under tyranny the people's affairs are conducted as though they were not its affairs, but those of the ruler. There is effectively nothing belonging to the people. The requirements needing to be met if there is to be a *res publica* or commonwealth are therefore not satisfied. But the conditions requisite for there being a people in the first place are not met either. Tyranny destroys the fabric of law and justice and of mutual advantage essential to its very existence as such.

The next stretch of Cicero's text, dealing with oligarchy, is perhaps the most interesting and important for his treatment of popular sovereignty. It reads as follows (*Rep.* 3.44):

SCIPIO: So you see that not even that collectivity which is wholly in the control of a faction can truly be called a *res publica*?
LAELIUS: Yes, I am unequivocally of that view.
SCIPIO: And you are absolutely correct in your judgment. For what *res* then belonged to the Athenians, when after the great Peloponnesian War the notorious Thirty governed the city without any semblance of justice? Did the ancient glory of the state, or the remarkable beauty of the town, or the theatre, gymnasia, porticoes, or the noble entrance arches or the citadel, or the marvellous works of Phidias, or the spectacular harbour of Piraeus make it a *res publica*?
LAELIUS: Hardly—for indeed there was no *res populi*.
SCIPIO: What about Rome? When the decemvirs were in power for that notorious third year, with no right of appeal to the people, since liberty itself had lost its legal standing (*vindiciae*)?
LAELIUS: There was no *res populi*—and in fact the people acted to recover its own *res*.

As this passage progresses, the connotation 'property' carried by the word *res* is ever more insistently suggested, until in Laelius's final response it becomes the dominant meaning.[81] The Latin expression *rem suam recuperare* is the standard expression in Roman law for recovery of one's own property.[82] The property analogy continues in the next section of argument, on mob rule. Although the manuscript text breaks off mid-sentence, Scipio evidently reasoned that if the people themselves behave like tyrants or the Thirty or the Decemvirs, then it will be imperative for them to be deprived of control of their *res*, just as the law gives control (*potestas*) over the property (*bona*) of the insane to their relatives (*Rep.* 3.45). As Miriam Griffin observes, *res publica* is now being treated as 'the legal correlative of *res privata*: instead of ownership of property by an individual, we are considering ownership of property by the *populus*.'[83]

Hence a clue to Cicero's thinking. The notion that the *populus* should own its own *res* is not itself the point. What Cicero has in view is an idea about rights that the metaphor enables him to express. If the people possesses its own *res*, then it follows that it has rights over its management and use. And the ability to exercise those rights is what popular sovereignty and—as Scipio says outright—political liberty and its legal basis consist in. Cicero was no democrat. He was far from believing that the power of the *populus* over its *res* should be unlimited, or that there should be no constraints on popular liberty. But he is clear that it should have some such power, and that consequently a degree of political liberty is essential to a true *res publica*.

A comparison with Aristotle's talk of concern for the common good or advantage as a test of a correct constitution might be made. Aristotle operated with a notion of the city as a collection of citizens whose interests the constitution or political system is there to safeguard. By focusing his discussion by contrast on the notion of *populus* and its rights, Cicero effectively creates an entirely new theory, cast in a legal vocabulary that has no parallel in Greek generally, nor in Greek political philosophy in particular. Its legal inspiration makes it a distinctively Roman contribution to political thought, and arguably the very invention of the idea of political legitimacy.[84]

Notes

1. Crawford 1974: 455–6.
2. Cicero refers to another of Marcus Brutus's ancestors (this time on his mother's side): Gaius Servilius Ahala, who in 439 BC had killed Spurius Maelius, a populist politician suspected by the political establishment of harbouring tyrannical ambitions. The coin representing Lucius Junius Brutus as champion of liberty has a sibling, with Lucius Brutus on the obverse and Ahala on the reverse. See again Crawford 1974: 455–6; also Wiseman 2009: 17–18, 190.
3. The more usual term for the absolute power that a slave-owner exercises over his slave is *dominatio*, often used in political contexts to connote no more than 'control', 'rule'. But in attacking Clodius and subsequently (after Julius Caesar's assassination) Mark Antony, Cicero employs the related expression *dominatus*, to mean the absolute power a tyrant exercises over his subjects: as here, where the Roman people is by that same token characterized as enslaved. In truth, it seems highly unlikely that Clodius had 'the slightest intention of overthrowing the government' either in 57 BC or later (Tatum 1999: 145).

4. A large battery of textual references is assembled in Hellegouarc'h 1972: 548 n.10. Talk of a 'free *res publica*', however, is rarely found: significantly, we meet it in authors of the late Republic perhaps only in a letter of the 'liberators' Brutus and Cassius to Mark Antony in August 44 BC, and in Cicero's thirteenth Philippic of March 43 (*Fam.* 11.3.4, *Phil.* 13.6: see Hodgson 2017: 196).
5. See Chapter 1, section 1 p. 3 for 'neo-Roman'.
6. Skinner 1998: 23.
7. See Hellegouarc'h 1972: 545 n.2; Brunt 1988d: 299.
8. Pettit 1997: 52.
9. Wirszubski 1950: 103–6.
10. But otherwise not much emphasis was given to *libertas* in propaganda by or on behalf of either Julius Caesar or Augustus: see Raaflaub 2003: 36–7, 58–67.
11. Brunt 1988d: 288; Arena 2012: 30–44 documents the politically symbolic cultural expressions of that consciousness.
12. Ando 2010: 210.
13. Arena 2012: 25. Needless to say, freeborn wives of Roman citizens were subject to more drastic disabilities (see Arena 2012: 25–6).
14. Arena 2012: 28.
15. For the resonances evoked by 'decemvirs', see section 3 pp. 38–9, pp. 43–4.
16. Brunt 1988d: 297.
17. For a fuller summary of Roman citizen rights under the Republic as Cicero and Livy conceived them, see Atkins 2018: 43–9, and more comprehensively Arena 2012: 45–72.
18. Mackie 1992: 73. As she points out, in his last literary composition, *On duties* of 44 BC, Cicero voiced a very similar reflection, with specific reference both to Athenian politics (evidently in the latter stages of the Peloponnesian War) and to Rome's civil wars (*Off.* 1.85): 'Some appear as "men of the people", others as supporters of "the best men", but few as champions of the whole community.'
19. 'The tribunate had been instituted in the early Republic to protect the commons against the senate, then dominated by patricians, of whom the nobility, including great plebeian families, were the successors in power' Brunt 1998b: 21). There were ten 'tribunes of the *plebs*', who could and often did exercise their prerogatives independently of each other.
20. But the senate had extensive actual powers (however conceptualized) over state finances and foreign affairs (Lintott 1999a: 18–22).
21. See Lintott 1999a: 89–93, on the purely customary standing of such resolutions, which seem to have referred in unspecific terms to action necessary to deal with threats to the *res publica*. A fuller treatment is Drummond 1995: Ch.4.

22. The formulaic expression *senatus populusque Romanus* is usage that first became current and increasingly frequent (in both literary and official documentary texts) in the final era of the Roman Republic. Augustus appropriated it, and coined the logo SPQR, as one among other devices designed to legitimate his regime as a restoration of the Republic. See Moatti 2017: 40–8.
23. Morstein-Marx 2004: 231. 'In Sallust's *Bellum Jugurthinum* the tribune Memmius, who waged a relentless campaign against leading nobles, presented himself as a defender of the *senatus auctoritas*', as Mouritsen 2017: 161 observes, diagnosing 'a set of rhetorical strategies defined by the constitutional structure of the Roman state'.
24. Cicero himself there takes the line that 'for this *civitas* such a power cannot be lacking' (*Leg.* 3.26).
25. Morstein-Marx 2004: 232.
26. This is what Caesar explicitly made his own overriding demand at the beginning of the civil war (*BCiv.* 1.7.7, 1.9.2). Cicero in an early work defined *dignitas* as '*auctoritas* deserving of devotion, honour, and respect' (*Inv.* 2.166).
27. On the politics of the late Republic interpreted as conflict between *libertas* and *dignitas*, see further Wirszubski 1950: 74–9, Brunt 1988d: 327–30, Mackie 1992: 52–9.
28. Morstein-Marx 2004: 15.
29. 'The implication is therefore that the large majority of the population never took part in the political process' (Mouritsen 2001: 128). Those of them who were present at a *contio* might well be a motley gathering. Cicero was in 59 BC complaining, no doubt *parti pris*, that '*contiones* were now dominated by disruptive Phrygians, Mysians, and similarly decadent "Greeks" (*Flac.* 17), not to mention Jews (*Flac.* 66–7)' (Morstein-Marx 2004: 16 n.67).
30. Morstein-Marx 2004: 12.
31. One might say that this simply mirrors what had actually happened with the Roman constitution. *Plebiscita*, resolutions of the *plebs*, a term which originally denoted the body of citizens who were not members of the original landowning families (the 'patricians'), initially required ratification by an assembly of the whole *populus* if they were to become law. But by the time of the late Republic their validity (thanks to the *lex Hortensia* of 287 BC) was unconditional. And in some contexts, *populus* is effectively equivalent to *plebs* (we shall see examples in Cicero's *On the commonwealth*). The double use of Greek *dêmos* is an obvious comparison; and as with *dêmos*, or with *plêthos* (the equivalent of *multitudo*) in Aristotle's *Politics*, it may sometimes be unclear which meaning of *populus* is being employed—perhaps to the writer himself.

32. He means principally the *nobiles* (*Hist.* 3.48.3), the 'inner circle of old aristocratic families', as sometimes Cicero does, too, when he talks in these terms (Mouritsen 2017: 123–6, 131–5, 145–7; cf. Wirszubski 1950: 37–9).
33. For further discussion of the politics of the *populares*, see Mackie 1992.
34. Mouritsen 2001: 11; cf. Mackie 1992: 52–9; Morstein-Marx 2004: 205–7, 220–2; Arena 2012: 14–72.
35. Brunt 1988b: 51.
36. Brunt 1988d: 327.
37. See Brunt 1988d: 320–1.
38. Brunt 1988d: 348.
39. Wirszubski 1950: 40–65 (especially: 52–5). Cicero does in a letter to a member of the nobility express the hope that his own achievements might have made him their equal (*Fam.* 3.7.5). *Aequa libertas* for senators collectively, in expressing their views in voting without having to fear the dominant nobility, is the one instance where (so far as I have found) the demand in so many words for 'equal liberty' is met in what might be contemporary writing. It occurs in one of the letters to Caesar ascribed to Sallust (Sall. *Ad Caes. Sen.* 2.11.2–4). The ascription is probably wrong, however. This text is now often thought to be a declamatory exercise from the early Empire, and is therefore dubious evidence for the late Republic.
40. Arena 2012: 169–243.
41. See Frier 1985: 120–4.
42. Here, unusually, *aequitas* might best be rendered 'equality', differently from the more standard 'fairness' or 'equity', corresponding to the adjective *aequus*, 'fair', 'equitable' (pp. 43–4). But the line is hard to draw, since treating all relevant persons equally, without partiality, is what the fairness of legal justice demands.
43. See Crawford 1996: II.555–721.
44. Cicero had already given it as his view that at this juncture in the Decemvirs' management of affairs a deficit in equality was the problem with the state of the constitution (*Rep.* 2.62).
45. Cicero refers first to legislation promulgated early in the second century BC and then (by the brothers Gracchi) towards its end, and secondly to the dictator Sulla's removal from the tribunes of most of their powers, and to their restoration in that same year of 70 BC.
46. Brunt 1988d: 337, referring by 'annalistic' here to the lost chronicles of Rome (surviving at best only in a few fragments and reports) that were often entitled *Annales*, 'yearbooks', composed by earlier historians writing during the last century of the Republic's existence. Livy, who also follows the year-by-year

annalistic scheme, is thought to depend on them for much of his material. See more recently Oakley 1997: 86–7. Needless to say, different historians take different and often divergent approaches to the 'Struggle of the Orders': see Raaflaub 2005a.
47. So e.g. Oakley 1997: 16–17, Cornell 2005: 62–6. Older writers tended to be more confident in identifying material deriving from particular annalist historians: e.g. Ogilvie 1965: 7–16 on Licinius and Valerius.
48. So e.g. Wiseman 1979: 45, Raaflaub 2005b: 2, 10.
49. So (with the later date) e.g. Wiseman 1979: 112–21; cf. Ungberg-Sternberg 2005: 88–90. But Rich 2005 argues powerfully for the usual date.
50. Translation adapted from Zetzel 2017a: 21.
51. The manuscript text of *On the commonwealth* breaks off at this point. Scipio has more to say about Rhodes at *Rep.* 3.48, before the text again peters out. The history of the manuscript is sketched very briefly in Chapter 3, section 1 pp. 61-2.
52. So, for example, Frede 1989: 84–94 (proposing Theophrastus as intermediary), Arena 2012: 83–5 (proposing Dicaearchus).
53. Plato *R.* 8.557a-558c, Aristotle *Pol.* 6.2, 1317a40-1318a10. See Raaflaub 1996, Schofield 2006: 107–12.
54. Aulus Gellius, *Noctes Atticae* 11.10.1; see for discussion Hodgson 2017: 25–32, 49–54.
55. Zetzel 2017a: 22 translates *ius* here, but not earlier in the passage, as 'law', for which Cicero used *lex* at its beginning. This reflects his view of its meaning in the definition of *res publica* at *Rep.* 1.39 (see section 5 below). But the final clause of the paragraph is evidently appealing to the key feature of law articulated in the opening sentence: equal justice. Otherwise it will not support the thesis that citizen rights must be equal. Other translators (the Loeb, Rudd, Fott) render *ius* correctly as 'justice'.
56. Zetzel 1995: 139.
57. Here, as throughout this book, *civitas* is rendered 'citizen body' (cf. Brunt 1988d: 299). Translators often treat *civitas* as 'the state', and in some contexts in Latin that would work. But the word derives etymologically from *civis*, 'citizen'. Since in the texts that most concern us Cicero is generally concerned with *civitas* as a participatory citizen commonwealth, as explicitly in this quoted passage, I have thought it best to adopt 'citizen body' as the default English equivalent—even in contexts where that specific connotation may not be salient. See Wood 1988: 126 for some excellent brief comments on Cicero's usage of the word in *On the commonwealth*.
58. Arena 2012: 122–4 proposes that Cicero is here drawing on ideas of Greek provenance that 'came to penetrate the Roman conception of politics and

inform its democratic discourse'. But as Arena herself concedes, 'little has been preserved of any intellectual tradition that is "non-optimate"' (Arena 2012: 168; see also section 3 p. 40 above). It is hard to think that anyone but Cicero himself was responsible for the construction of such a precise, concise, and elegant argument as this exercise in democratic reasoning, exploiting as it does the general conceptual repertoire he deploys in discussion of the *res publica* elsewhere in the dialogue, as well as Greek democratic ideology.

59. See Chapter 3, section 3 pp. 70, 74.
60. *Aequabilitas* seems to be Cicero's own coinage in *On the commonwealth* (from *aequabilis*, 'equal', introduced specifically to create a term for 'equality' that can be deployed in contrast to *aequitas* (as 'equity', 'fairness'), as in these passages. See for further discussion Fantham 1973: 285–7. The suggestion of Zetzel 1995: 152 that there is 'some confusion' in Cicero's switching between *aequabilitas* and *aequitas* at *Rep.* 1.53 seems to miss the force of its anti-democratic thrust.
61. But when he adds: 'which free persons cannot do without for very long', he presumably means 'in some valid form or other', such as the basic citizen rights specified above, pp. 32, 32–3, and 39–40.
62. Fantham 1973: 287–90; cf. Nicolet 1970: 64–5.
63. Fantham 1973: 286.
64. Cf. Mouritsen 2017: 13–14. Arena 2012: 112–13 suggests that Cicero draws on 'the Pythagoreans' notion of proportionality' here. Again, however, the language of proportionality is absent: Cicero is recalling Plato's treatment of the harmony of the soul in the *Republic* (R 4.443c–444a), and while ancient harmony theory was conceived in terms of a structure of musical sounds conforming in pitch to mathematical ratios, such structure is not the focus of either the Platonic or the Ciceronian context.
65. That would be one way of construing the *consensus* of justice binding them in partnership that is specified in the definition of a *res publica* (*Rep.* 1.39). See section 5 below, pp. 47–50.
66. If a Greek parallel were to be proposed, Isocrates' talk of a form of equality 'assigning to each what is appropriate' (not 'the same for all') (*Areopagiticus* 21) sounds the right sort of option. But I do not suggest that Cicero had any such previous text in mind.
67. See Chapter 3, section 6, p. 91.
68. The idea of popular sovereignty is not generally taken to entail responsibility for ongoing conduct of government, nor was it so understood at Rome (unlike Athens in this). The limits on the Roman assemblies' powers are briefly described in Wirszubski 1950: 17–20, and became a highly contentious issue in the late Republic: see for example Straumann 2016: 119–29. Popular

sovereignty is however often thought to imply that government must be conducted in accordance with the will of the people, and the phrase *voluntas populi*, 'the will of the people' (sometimes with the accent on their goodwill), is often on Cicero's lips in the oratory of his speeches against Verres, from *Verr.* 1.1.2 on, and subsequently right down to the *Philippics*, as at *Phil.* 1.36: see Paulson 2017: Chapter 4. In the philosophy of *On the commonwealth*, ensuring security of access to justice and ability to exercise rights is taken to be the fundamental implication (see below pp. 50–2).

69. Hellegouarc'h 1972: 314–20.
70. Brunt 1988d: 338–9; see further Harries 2007: 72–7, Williamson 2016: 335–7, and the magisterial study of Thomas 1991. Cicero once offered as a definition: 'To diminish *maiestas* is to detract in some way from the dignity or grandeur or power of the people, or of those to whom the people have given power' (*Inv.* 2.53).
71. The substance of the order is in his version weakened significantly. The people order merely that the senate should determine who should be king. Neither version is likely to have any genuine historical foundation. Presumably the tradition on which they play their variations reflected later preoccupations about the differing roles of senate and people in the constitution (cf. Ogilvie 1965: 87).
72. See Schofield 2006: 30–5.
73. Skinner 1989 (cf. Wood 1988: 125); 'extensively revised and much expanded' as Skinner 2002: 2.368–413.
74. Skinner 2009: 326.
75. Wiseman 2009: 1.
76. Griffin 2013: 98.
77. Moatti 2017: 36. She further comments that 'to have something in common does not mean there is a consensus on it.' But Cicero's definition entails—as *On the commonwealth* conceives the issues—that citizens do not form a true *populus* in possession of their *res* unless they are united in *consensus* and shared benefit.
78. Zetzel 2017a.
79. Zetzel 2017a: 18 renders *ius* here as 'law' (cf. n.55 above), as does Asmis 2004: 575–82; the Loeb has 'justice' and Fott 'right'. For a case in favour of 'justice', see Chapter 3, section 2, pp. 66–9 below and Schofield forthcoming 1, where it is argued that Cicero has in mind a consensus—shared by the major sectors of the population—that is *characteristic of* or *belongs to* access to justice or ability to exercise rights. It is both the outcome of such access or ability (and so perhaps represents one kind of use of the subjective or 'belonging' genitive) and a state

of mind focused on access to justice or ability to exercise rights (so perhaps counts also as a kind of objective genitive, with the force of 'in', 'in regard to').

80. For discussion of just how Scipio's assessment of the flaw in tyranny here differs from that implied in Book 1 (*Rep.* 1.44), see section VI of Schofield forthcoming 1.
81. Cf. Zetzel 2017a: 76 n.57, which points out that in Scipio's remarks on both Syracuse and Athens it is in fact the buildings of these cities that form their focus—'the physical possessions of the state'.
82. Griffin 2013: 98 [= Griffin 2018: 694].
83. Griffin 2013: 98 [= Griffin 2018: 694].
84. Mackie was not wrong to say of the Roman discourse of politics in the late Republic that, although they had no word equivalent to 'legitimacy', 'they talked about legitimacy all the same: that is, about who should govern the *res publica* and how', appealing to the key values discussed in this chapter. 'Concepts of legitimacy', she continued, 'were expressed not just verbally through these and other value-laden terms, but through the institutions and adjuncts of power' (Mackie 1992: 52). The claim being made here is more specifically that it is Cicero, in the passages quoted above from Book 3 of *On the commonwealth*, who comes closest to explicit articulation of an idea of legitimacy.

3
Government

1. *On the commonwealth*

Cicero took longer over the composition of *On the commonwealth* than on any other of his philosophical writings.[1] Work on it was already under way in May 54 BC: 'a pretty sticky, laborious job it is', he writes to his brother Quintus, who was probably its dedicatee (*QFr.* 2.13.1). Two months later he is complaining to his friend Atticus of the magnitude of the task, requiring a lot of leisure he just does not have (*Att.* 4.16.2–3). By October or November of the same year he has already composed two books of this treatment of 'the best system for a citizen body (*civitas*) and the best citizen (*civis*)', but is chopping and changing over the way the work is planned (*QFr.* 3.5.1–2). Something must then have slowed him down. Although he was no longer the political force he had once been, he was certainly in the thick of public affairs on a number of fronts, and looking back in 44 BC went so far in exaggeration as to say that he was 'at the helm guiding the commonwealth' (*Div.* 2.3). Coincidentally or otherwise, there is a dearth of surviving correspondence until May 51, which sees the completed dialogue apparently hot off the press. His protégé Marcus Caelius assures him (*Fam.* 8.1.14): 'Your work on politics is all the rage.' And we find Atticus reading it in July of that year (*Att.* 5.12.2), apparently 'devouring' it (*Att.* 7.3.2).

On the commonwealth now survives in a fragmentary condition. For centuries only its final section, the so-called 'dream of Scipio', was available as continuous text, thanks to the late antique writer Macrobius, along with fragments and summaries in Cicero himself elsewhere and in other Roman writers of the imperial period, notably Lactantius and Augustine. Then early in the nineteenth century a palimpsest was discovered in the Vatican Library, in which long stretches of Books 1 and 2, some pages of Book 3, and a few isolated passages from Books 4 and 5 could be made out. The palimpsest confirmed the evidence already available that in the first of the two central books (Book 3)—at the heart of the whole work—Cicero staged a debate about justice between associates of the great second century BC general and statesman Publius Scipio Africanus.[2]

The construction of *On the commonwealth* is elaborate, on a grand Platonic scale. There were six books, representing three conversations (each allocated two books) imagined as conducted on Scipio's estate just outside Rome over successive days of a public holiday (*Att.* 13.19.3, *Div.* 2.3, *Lael.* 14; cf. *Rep.* 1.14, 2.70, 6.8). The participants were Scipio himself, Laelius, and other leading political figures of the time, gathered in 129 BC at a critical moment for the Roman Republic, a few days before Scipio's sudden death (*Rep.* 1.14–18, *Lael.* 14). Books 1 and 2 dealt with 'the best system', Books 5 and 6 with 'the best citizen', while the central books (as in Plato's *Republic*) addressed more foundational topics: Book 3 justice as the foundation of political order, Book 4 the institutions, customs and practices needed to bring citizens up properly.[3] Thus the work in fact falls into two main parts: the first three books focused on the community, the second three on the citizen.

But such divisions of the material conceal the fact that the dialogue is in reality 'through composed', with each successive book taking up an issue left hanging at the end of its predecessor. Book 2 supplies the historical material on the 'mixed' constitution which Scipio adumbrates at the end of Book 1 (*Rep.* 1.70–1). Book 2 ends with a statement of the need to prove not only that the conduct of the *res publica* can be conducted without injustice, but that it requires *summa justitia* ('justice in the nth degree', *Rep.* 2.70). The fragmentary preservation of the text gives us no such concrete evidence for the remaining books. But it is easy enough to see how the outcome of Book 3—government indeed requires justice—will prompt the need for a treatment of the question of the institutions needed to instil virtue in citizens (Book 4); that will naturally lead on to an account of what the supremely good citizen is like (Book 5); and that in turn to how reliance on such a person, rather than standard constitutional mechanisms, is the answer when the *res publica* is in crisis (Book 6)—which is what Scipio's Rome, like Cicero's, now faces.

Cicero evidently conceived the work in the most ambitious terms, as a Roman riposte to the *Republic*. Plato is emulated in a strikingly independent and imaginative manner (perhaps most notably in the 'dream of Scipio' which ends the whole work, mirroring the myth of Er, the *Republic*'s final chapter, and placing the entire discussion in a cosmic and theological context). Yet at the same time he is subjected to criticism, for creating (in the words of Scipio's friend Gaius Laelius) a utopian ideal 'totally alien to human life and ways' (*Rep.* 2.21–2; cf. 2.3, 2.52).⁴ Its author was evidently very proud of *On the commonwealth*. In the catalogue of his philosophical writings composed in the spring of 44 BC Cicero gives it some prominence (*Div.* 2.3): and later that year he is recalling it with affection and satisfaction in the *Laelius* (*Lael.* 14, 25), a late dialogue on friendship which is presented as a sort of sequel to *On the commonwealth*.

Book 5 begins (*Rep.* 5.2) with a famous lament in the authorial preface (a standard literary ingredient in most of Cicero's philosophical writings): 'By our own vices, not by any accident, we hang on to the *res publica* in name only. In real substance we lost it long ago.'⁵ Not surprisingly, *On the commonwealth* has often enough been seen as an exercise primarily in nostalgia. As the framework of the Roman Republic was collapsing (the civil war of 49–48 BC and following that Caesar's dictatorship were only just round the corner), the best Cicero could apparently do—it might be said—was to wind the reel back and celebrate the Roman Republican constitution, represented as the living historical achievement of 'the best political system', as it was (or rather as he imagined it) nearly a century before, before the first radical challenge to its assumptions had been suppressed by the murder of the tribune Tiberius Gracchus. Add to that a perception that much of the thinking in *On the commonwealth* is not only uncritically conservative but derivative from Greek materials of one kind or another, together with the difficulties of reconstructing the argument of a damaged and (from Book 3 onwards) very fragmentary text, and a depressing conclusion beckons: what was meant to be Cicero's philosophical masterpiece has to be written off as a sad intellectual wreck.

When the state is failing, or its governmental system no longer commands much confidence, what is a political theorist to do? There is no obvious or remotely comfortable answer to the question, which is as pressing in the contemporary world, developed or developing, as it ever was for Cicero in his. His responses to the challenge do not fit an escapist diagnosis. *On the commonwealth* draws on a wide range of intellectual resources, mined from Plato, Aristotle, Stoicism, Polybius, Roman historians, and no doubt—directly or not—many other writers and thinkers, besides those whose names are dropped from time to time.⁶ It contains incisive thinking about the basis of political order and the key prerequisites of effective government, in the light of the fundamentals of justice and indeed of the cosmic scheme of things. It suggests the need to step back from current crises, while developing ideas about crisis management. At the same time, it evinces a deep distrust of blueprint solutions (taking humans as they are and not as they might be, as Rousseau might have put it), and a sense of the need to reckon with the forces which have shaped a society over time. It sees such enquiry as best conducted through debate.[7] Moreover, despite the lament and a sense of foreboding, the tone is often quite different. *On the commonwealth* begins and ends with argument for the supreme importance of opting for a public life devoted to the service of the commonwealth despite its perils and uncertainties (*Rep.* 1.1–12, 6.12–16, 28–9).[8] Nostalgia there is. But on offer is a lot more too.

What Cicero above all explores are three main ideas, which between them shape the entire development of the argument of the dialogue: the concept of a *res publica* itself; the *consilium* (deliberation) needed to govern it; and the leadership required to supply that *consilium* and to carry it through in action, whether in the ordinary functioning of the *res publica* or in moments of crisis when its integrity is threatened. Someone is called for who will be a 'director (*rector*) of the commonwealth and initiator of public *consilium*', as *On the orator* had articulated the job description (*de Orat.* 1.211). This chapter in discussing these themes tracks the dialogue's own movement between them. Section 2 presents further discussion of the initial definition of *res publica* (*Rep.* 1.39). Section 3 looks at Cicero's critique of kingship, aristocracy, and popular rule as systems for its government. Section 4 turns to the requirement for political stability and for *consilium* to secure it—with a 'mixed' system of government the recipe. Section 5 discusses Book 2's treatment of the historical evolution that resulted in that system's realization in Republican Rome. Section 6 explores Cicero's thoughts on what happens when—as in his own time—the system is in crisis, and his reflections on leadership. Section 7 offers some discussion of comparable constitutional material in the companion dialogue *On laws*. A brief conclusion follows in section 8.

2. The consensus of justice

The definition with which Cicero launched the entire argument of *On the commonwealth* was by any standards an impressive piece of theoretical work. It was to become a direct (or as often indirect) influence on a great deal of thinking about community and government throughout the middle ages and Renaissance, thanks to Augustine's citing and discussing it twice in the *City of God* (*CD* 2.21, 19.21).[9] Here it is in full (*Rep.* 1.39):

A commonwealth (*res publica*) is the business and interests of the people (*res populi*). A people (*populus*) is not any group of human beings assembled in just any way, but an assemblage of a *multitudo* (lots of them: a mass) which forms an association through the consensus of justice (*ius*) and through sharing in advantage (*utilitas*).

In its equation of *res publica* with *res populi*, the definition supplies the foundational idea of popular sovereignty. In its identification of *populus* with a mass of human beings who form 'an association through the *consensus* of justice and through sharing in advantage' (*Rep.* 1.39) it provides criteria for the legitimacy of a political system, in particular of different forms of rule.[10] But Cicero also has further mileage to extract from his formula. He uses it not merely to exclude tyranny or the rule of a junta or a mob as illegitimate forms of government (*Rep.* 3.43–8). He makes it the basis for the elaborate theory of good government that will occupy the rest of Book 1 and all of Book 2 of his dialogue. And its focus on justice will prompt the debate on the basic nature of justice—something which can claim objective validity, or alternatively a variable human construct of little value when set against the rational pursuit of self-interest—that occupied the bulk of the fragmentary Book 3.

In the prefatory remarks with which he has Scipio introduce the definition, Cicero is at pains to indicate that beginning this way is sound method, appropriate in investigation of any subject. If the name of the thing enquired into is agreed upon, its meaning needs to be explained at the outset: a principle for which Plato's *Phaedrus* was sometimes cited as authority (*Phdr.* 237b–c, as at *Fin.* 2.3–4). But the kind of explanation to be provided here will not be an elaborate philosophical account, discussing the origins of human society or piling up further definitions and alternative nomenclature: the sort of thing you might get from a professor. The subject is well known. Laelius and the rest of the assembled company are experienced and distinguished Roman statesmen, expecting Scipio to say something worth hearing about the topic, rather than dwelling on what exactly that topic is (*Rep.* 1.38). And in practice Cicero will often enough treat *civitas* (citizen body) as effectively the subject of the same enquiry as the one he will devote to *res publica* (*Rep.* 1.34) without attempting to discuss differences in their connotation.[11] For example, he speaks indifferently of the best condition of *res publica* and *civitas* (*Rep.* 1.33, *Leg.* 1.15), and again of the kingship species of both *res publica* and *civitas* (*Rep.* 2.41, 2.43, 2.51).

It is probably to be inferred that Cicero expects or hopes that the definition Scipio goes on to articulate will be fairly uncontroversial, even if refinements from different philosophical viewpoints could no doubt be proposed. In writing on rhetoric, he issues a pithy prescription for the definition of the name of something whose meaning is sought: 'brief, clear, reflecting what people think' (*Inv.* 2.53). Nonetheless something more ambitious is being attempted here than either that recipe or Scipio's disclaimers might lead one to suppose. First, the definition as an entire construct is apparently original with Cicero, whatever it may owe to Romans' political discourse or common assumptions, and to Aristotelian or Stoic philosophy. Second, as just noted, he extracts from it rather more specific and far-reaching theoretical consequences than reflection on the general idea of a *res publica* would appear necessarily to yield.

The ambition of Cicero's project will start to emerge as we focus on the notion of a people (*populus*) that he spells out in the definition, as 'an association (*sociatus*) formed through the consensus of justice and through sharing in advantage' (*Rep.* 1.39). 'Sharing in advantage' sounds relatively straightforward. In fact, in what survives of *On the commonwealth*, it receives no further examination, and is barely exploited at all in what we possess of the rest of the dialogue. The sort of thing Scipio has in mind is intimated in his description of the role of the 'calibrator' (*moderator*) of the *res publica* that he will posit (see section 5 below). He 'aims at a blessed life for the citizens, secure in wealth, rich in resources, abundant in renown, honourable in virtue' (*Rep.* 5.8).[12] It is the expression 'the consensus of justice (*consensus iuris*)', apparently experimental wording of Cicero's own, which turns out to be the element in the formula that is key for his discussion of government: if indeed 'justice' is the right way to render the Latin *ius*, which as Elizabeth Asmis has observed is 'especially difficult to translate'.[13]

Like previous commentators, Asmis notes the connotations of right (Recht) and law carried by the word: thus, for example, *ius connubii* was the legal 'right of marriage', i.e. the right to marry a Roman citizen. And like James Zetzel she opts here for 'law' as probably the least misleading English equivalent. That option, however, faces two immediate objections. One is that as soon as Scipio starts discussing forms of government, and their differing consequent arrangements for management of the *res populi*, he enters the reservation (to be examined shortly) that under kingship there is a deficit in access to *ius* (*Rep.* 1.43): clearly meaning 'justice', as Zetzel himself translates. The other is that in *On the commonwealth* Cicero uses *lex* when he wants to talk about law, whether in general or in more specific terms. Thus in Book 3 Philus makes the Spartan Lycurgus the 'discoverer of the best laws (*legum*) and the most equitable justice (*iuris*)' (*Rep.* 3.16); and Laelius talks of a universal moral law (*lex*: *Rep.* 3.33), but ends his speech by speaking of the need to respect right (*ius*) or rights (*iura*) (*Rep.* 3.41).

The translation difficulty is best tackled by recalling our discussion in Chapter 2 of the case for democratic equality that Cicero has Scipio develop a few pages later on in Book 1 (*Rep.* 1.49). The advocates of popular rule take as their basic premiss—presumably as inherent in the idea of a *populus* articulated in the definition—the assumption that a *civitas* (a citizen body) is nothing other (cf. *Rep.* 6.13) than an association or partnership in justice (*ius*). But the argument they construct on this basis separates out the law and the justice or right components in *ius*: 'Since law (*lex*) is the bond of citizen association,[14] and the justice or right (*ius*) of law is equal, then by what justice or right can an association of citizens be held together (*teneri*), when the status of citizens is not equal?' So it looks as though justice is indeed the fundamental concept Cicero has in mind when he talks in the definition of *ius*. But this is justice or right as guaranteed by law (compare again *ius connubii*), with the implication that law—provided it is without arbitrariness—is what makes justice work as justice, through ensuring equal treatment for those subject to it.

The democratic proposal that law is the bond (*vinculum*) of citizen association also promises to give us help in understanding something else about the definition: what Cicero means by the expression 'consensus of justice' (*consensus iuris*) in which the appearance of the word *ius* in embedded. That curious phrase occurs in classical Latin only here and in Book 3 (*Rep.* 3.45), where Laelius is referring back to Scipio's definition.[15] It is usually translated as 'agreement with respect to justice' or similar, as in the Loeb edition. But if that were the meaning we would not expect the genitive *iuris*. It seems more likely that Cicero is wanting to convey the idea of agreement or consensus or a common mind *created* by justice, or characteristic of a just order in society. Once that is in place, as guaranteed by law, a consensus reflecting it will obtain. Or as the advocates of popular rule put the point, law will bind the citizen association together.

Nor is it only they who talk in such terms. Scipio on his own account speaks of any of the three basic forms of government as being 'tolerable' provided that the bond which first bound people together in the association of the *res publica*—holds fast (*tenere* again). And he supports that position not by reference to consensus, but by identifying the relevant condition as fairness (*Rep.* 1.42). Later in Book 3 he will argue that under tyranny there could be no single 'bond of justice', nor consensus and association in an assemblage, which is what constitutes a people (*Rep.* 3.43). Here the clear assumption is again that the binding together of human beings effected by justice is the thing basic to the existence of a *res publica*. It is not explicit that this creates a consensus and the conditions for partnership. But the implication suggests itself. Certainly, in all three passages the emphasis is on the *existence* of justice as binding force, not agreement about it, as the prime prerequisite if there is to be a *populus* or *civitas* or *res publica*. It follows that it would be a mistake to take Scipio's formulation 'consensus of justice' as a version of a contractual theory of justice, such as that put forward by Glaucon in Book 2 of Plato's *Republic* (*R.* 2.358e–2.359b) and advocated by Philus in Book 3 (*Rep.* 3.23), nor as implying like Philus that justice is not natural, but a mere convention (only a 'creation of civil society (*civile*)', or as Rudd translates, a 'political phenomenon': *Rep.* 3.13; cf. *Leg.* 1.42).[16]

In sum, what emerges from the definition taken together with what we might call the *vinculum* passages is the following idea. Justice—the justice inherent in a legal order, if upheld by the governmental system—binds human beings together, and makes them into an association: a community. The relevant notion of justice is that of equity, as indicated not only by the passage on 'tolerable' forms of government, but (for example) in a passage from Cicero's later *On duties*, where he is talking about the origins of monarchy at Rome, and the installation of a king eminent in virtue who (*Off.* 2.41) 'by instituting equity (*aequitas*) held the highest in the land in equal justice (*pari iure*) with the lowest'. Or we may compare a passage further on in the same book of *On duties*, where the basic job of those who are to 'look after the *res publica*' is defined as bending their efforts to ensure that 'by the equity of justice (*ius*) and the courts (*iudicia*) each person may keep what is his own', with the poorer classes free from oppression and the wealthy not being deprived of their rights through envy (*Off.* 2.85). If we then ask *how* justice so understood functions as a bond, Cicero answers: by creating a consensus—presumably consensus that society is justly ordered.

So when he seeks to encapsulate in a single brief phrase his understanding of what that consensus is, he coins the novel expression the 'consensus of justice'—in an attempt to convey the notion of a universally shared state of mind, created *by* justice and the ability to exercise citizen rights, which is focused on the thought *that* there is such access to justice.[17]

3. Kingship, aristocracy, popular rule: their drawbacks

Kingship, aristocracy, popular rule: the debate on their respective merits went back at least as far as the fifth century BC Greek historian Herodotus, in a notable passage of his *Histories* (3.80–2), where a group of Persian nobles well placed to seize power are represented as arguing the pros and cons of the three systems.[18] What is most striking in Herodotus is the emphasis given not to the merits that their different champions identify, but to the gross defects diagnosed in each of them, there mostly designated as monarchy, oligarchy, and democracy, as they get considered in turn. First monarchy is represented as tyranny, by the advocate of 'equal distribution' (of power). Then the democracy he has proposed is characterized as mob rule by the spokesman for oligarchy. The cleverest speech is delivered last—itself a smart move—by the eventual victor in the power race, Darius. He attacks both oligarchy, as characteristically racked by internal divisions, and (once more) democracy, and among other points argues that when either system inevitably collapses, recourse has to be had to monarchy.

All these arguments, like others made in the Herodotean debate, regularly resurface in the subsequent Greek tradition, through Thucydides, Plato, and Aristotle, down to Scipio's friend Polybius, in the sixth book of his *Histories*. Polybius's theory—that changes from one constitution to another exhibit a recurrent cyclical form—clearly feeds into *On the commonwealth*'s intellectual framework, even if Cicero's Scipio makes it clear that he does not buy into it wholesale (*Rep.* 1.45, 65, 68, 2.45; cf. Polyb. 6.9.10–14). He will likewise follow Polybius in arguing that a mixed constitution, containing elements of all three, is superior to any individual one of them, although the terms in which he conceives the mixture as 'combined and moderately blended' are more Platonic than Polybian (*Rep.* 1.54, 69,[19] 2.69; cf. Polyb. 6.10, 18).[20] As for the three primary systems, Scipio rates them merely 'tolerable':[21] 'not perfect, nor in my opinion the best possible' (*Rep.* 1.42). Somewhat similarly to that Herodotean debate, a brief sketch of the principal drawbacks to each of the three primary systems even at their tolerable best (not, as in Herodotus, their worst) is first presented (*Rep.* 1.43–4), but then at greater length the case to be made in favour of each of them (*Rep.* 1.46–64).[22] Here, naturally enough, further criticisms are made of whatever systems are not being advocated.

It looks as though the drawbacks singled out for attention by Scipio in his initial sketch numbered just two (although he perhaps implies that he could have listed more: *Rep.* 1.44). Each of the primary systems is vitiated by what we might call a systemic deficit. And each is an inherently fragile form of government. A mixed constitution of the kind Scipio will go on to advocate will offer a remedy for both kinds of fault (*Rep.* 1.69). To start with he focuses first on the problem of deficit (*Rep.* 1.43). Although he does not make the point programmatically, the drawbacks of this kind that he identifies in the primary systems consist in shortfalls in the realization of the justice or fairness any *res publica* must secure for its citizens if there is to be a proper *populus* or political community at all, and in the way a system provides for *consilium* or deliberation about the management of the affairs of the *res publica*. Proper provision for *consilium* is identified, in the immediately preceding discussion (*Rep.* 1.42), as a key requirement for government. In fact, it will turn out that shortcomings in opportunity to participate in deliberation are on that very count unjust.

Scipio articulates his diagnosis of systemic deficits in the following terms (*Rep.* 1.43):

> In kingships, other people have too little share in justice and deliberation. In aristocracies, the mass of the population can scarcely have any share in liberty, when they are excluded from all communal deliberation and power. And when all public business is in the hands of the people, however just and moderate they may be, nonetheless equality itself is inequitable, since it involves no degrees of status (*dignitas*).

It will subsequently emerge that the problem with kingship, as well as aristocracy, could have been expressed more pithily as a deficit in liberty (*Rep.* 2.43: as Chapter 2 might already have led us to expect). Apart from the stylist's desire not simply to repeat himself, by deferring the charge of deprivation of liberty to what is said against aristocracy Cicero is evidently wanting to reflect with maximum impact its role in the populist anti-aristocratic rhetoric of contemporary Roman political discourse. The objection to democracy similarly reflects the insistence on the importance of *dignitas* by the Roman elite: a fragment of the real Scipio's own oratory is recorded making the ringing pronouncement that 'integrity gives birth to *dignitas*, *dignitas* honour, honour *imperium*, *imperium* liberty' (Malvocati, *ORF* 21.32). John Richardson provides an illuminating commentary:[23]

> Here personal virtue *(innocentia)*, once recognized *(dignitas)*, leads, by way of the magistracy voted to the individual by the people *(honor)*, to the acquisition of power in the state by the individual *(imperium)*; and thus to the culmination of the list with the freedom which guarantees not only the position of the state with regard to other states, but also the position of the individual within it.

Cicero's Scipio is not meaning to suggest that in none of the primary systems can there be any such thing as the 'bond of justice' or the consequent consensus supporting the social cohesion of a *populus*. If rule is exercised with equity (and preferably wisdom too) (*Rep.*1.42), there can still exist a valid form of *res publica*, despite the diagnosis of systemic defect. This emerges with particular clarity from a passage on kingship in Book 2 (*Rep.* 2.43):

> The kingship species of constitution is in itself not only not to be deplored, but conceivably to be ranked far ahead of the other simple forms (supposing I were to approve of any simple species of *res publica*)—but only so long as it retains the condition proper to it. Its proper condition requires that the safety and equality *(aequabilitas)*[24] and peace of the citizens be governed by one person's permanent power with justice and altogether wisely. But a people that is ruled by a king is quite lacking in many things, and above all liberty, which consists not in having a just master, but in having none.

Under a good king there will be considerable and effective respect on his part for the requirement that ordinary people should enjoy safety, peace, and equal rights in law—for the duty to ensure the maintenance of the *res populi* in the people's own interest. This might presumably be enough to secure a 'consensus of justice' and 'sharing in advantage' sufficient for the association that would constitute a *populus*. In other words, the basic conditions requiring to be met if there is to be a *res publica* could be satisfied.

The downside, as Scipio puts it in a comment on the Persian monarch Cyrus, taken as the paradigm of the just and wise king, is that the *res populi* was 'ruled by the decision of one person' (*Rep.* 1.43). The contrast between 'business of the people' and 'decision of one' indicates the problem first voiced in the complaint that 'other people have too little share in justice and deliberation'. The people do not have enough say in the government of what after all is theirs, even though it may be governed in their interest and governed supremely well. Still worse, any participation on their part in deliberation about its management is entirely at the king's discretion. The king is effectively their master, even if he is a 'just master'. There is therefore a deficit in liberty: 'servitude', as the advocates of popular rule are made to say subsequently (*Rep.* 1.47). So the 'bond of justice' may be in place, but citizens are left without a form of *ius* that might be thought inherent in the very idea of the *res populi* (cf. *Rep.* 1.48): a radical form of systemic deficit. It would doubtless have been regarded by many of Cicero's contemporaries as disqualifying monarchy as a possible form of *res publica*.

But it becomes apparent when he has Scipio turn to the defence of kingship as a system that he sees it as ideally embodying a crucially important principle of good government.[25] The point is first articulated (in Platonic and Aristotelian fashion)[26] as a principle of individual human psychology, couched interestingly enough explicitly in terms of *dominatio* (*Rep.* 1.60):

If there is a regal *imperium* (power to command obedience to orders)[27] in the minds of human beings, then there will be the domination of one thing: *consilium* (deliberation, judgement), of course, for that is the best part of the mind. And with deliberation dominating, there is no place for lust, none for anger, none for rashness.

The alternative envisaged is control of the mind by 'appetites—which are innumerable—or angry passions': the plurals suggest chaos. What is true of the mind is then argued to apply to the *res publica*: 'If that *res* is put in the hands of a plurality, you can see that there will be nothing to be in charge as *imperium*—unless *imperium* is one, there can be none.' Laelius wonders why so far as exercise of *imperium* is concerned, there need be any real difference between one person and a plurality, provided the plurality has justice (*Rep.* 1.61). Scipio's reply (*Rep.* 1.61–3) appeals to the wisdom of the human tendency to entrust its affairs to one expert rather than many, particularly in critical situations—severe illness or storms at sea, for example. The Platonic antecedents of his position become particularly noticeable at this point (cf. *R.* 1.332d–e, 6.489b–c, *Plt.* 296d–297b, 297e–298e). It looks as though Cicero is signalling that any satisfactory theory of government is going to have to take a Platonist conception of ruling seriously.

Such an interpretation would be consonant with the treatment of oratory in *On the orator*, composed shortly before *On the commonwealth*. Walter

Nicgorski points out that Cicero there has Lucius Licinius Crassus, the earlier dialogue's most important character, argue explicitly that 'it is not possible to understand the character and importance of the force and nature of a thing, unless it is put before one's eyes in a perfected condition' (*de Or.* 3.86). In the *Orator*, written nearly ten years later, he once more endorses this approach to characterizing what it takes to command the craft or powers of an orator. With explicit reference to Plato's theory of Forms, he repeats that to deal with any subject, the right procedure is to fix one's mind on the 'limit [i.e. perfect] form of that sort of thing (*ultimam sui generis formam speciemque*: *Or.* 10)'.[28] In the surviving text of *On the commonwealth*, Scipio does not articulate any similar methodological principle.[29] But the attraction monarchy at its best holds for Cicero, as for Plato, is its supreme embodiment of the union of power and *consilium*. Kingship will remain therefore important to think with, even if its potential for abuse mean that in practice the palm must go to a mixed system of government—in which nonetheless *consilium* will dominate.[30] It will end up transmuted into the non-regal figure that Scipio names—among other designations—the *rector* (director').[31]

Even the case advocating aristocracy as the best system concedes that if we could find a person to be ruler who was not prone to rapacity, but was able to present his own way of life as 'law' for the citizens, and who could single-handed accomplish everything satisfactorily, then there would be no need for more people to be involved in ruling. But in fact, 'the difficulty of making policy (*consilium*)' is what results in public affairs being transferred from a king to a plurality (*Rep.* 1.52). Whatever its abilities in *consilium*, however, aristocracy exhibits the same kind of systemic deficit as kingship. Under undiluted aristocracy the exclusion of the people 'from all communal deliberation (*consilium*) and power'—from all rights of political participation—means that they have 'scarcely any liberty'.[32] At Massilia (ancient Marseilles, where aristocratic rule is exercised with 'supreme justice') there is 'something that closely resembles slavery' (*Rep.* 1.43). Here, as in some of the passages to be discussed in the next two sections, the systematic ambiguity of 'the people' where talk of popular liberty is introduced, as sometimes (but by no means always) simultaneously the sovereign body and the *plebs* or common people, forces itself upon us.[33]

Particularly striking in the critique of kingship and aristocracy alike is Cicero's recurrent preoccupation with rights and opportunities to contribute to *consilium*. This reflects his basic conception of how a system of government should be understood. When first introducing his distinction between the three primary systems, he presents them as options for locating responsibility not simply for rule, but rule precisely by *consilium*: *consilium* is what 'must be assigned to one or to selected individuals or taken up by the citizenry in the mass and by everybody' (*Rep.* 1.41–2).

At first sight it looks as though the focus shifts elsewhere in the critique of democracy. Here certainly there is a rather different kind of deficit in *ius*. Scipio makes it clear enough that, provided the people itself rules without acts of unfairness or rapacity against the more affluent citizens (*Rep.* 1.42), indeed with justice and moderation, and (as in democratic Athens, when it did not descend into mob rule: *Rep.* 1.44) only by proper constitutional procedures (*Rep.* 1.43), then the conditions that must obtain for there to be a *res publica* will be satisfied.[34] It is not suggested that there is in that case any deficit in anyone's liberty or in recognition of civic rights. Nobody is denied the opportunity to contribute to communal deliberation. The problem is that although everyone may be treated equally, there is nonetheless something unfair or inequitable about that system: not in its particular applications, but in the very basis of the system itself.

At least in theory (unsustainable and unsustained in democratic practice: *Rep.* 1.53), popular rule fails to recognize differences in personal and family standing, the respect it is owed, and the authority it should enable someone who possesses it to command—in this context especially in offering *consilium* (so preoccupation with *consilium* remains close to the surface if no longer explicit). Cicero refers to failure to acknowledge 'degrees of status': *dignitas*. That word was constantly on his lips in his political oratory and his correspondence, always to insist on its importance, often to lament the threats he saw to its proper valuation, particularly where ability to give *consilium* in public debate was concerned (e.g. *Fam.*1.8.3; 4.14.1); and (as noted in Chapter 2)[35] it was the word Caesar used to articulate what he most valued and yet thought he had not been properly accorded (*BCiv.* 1.7.7, 1.9.2). That failure would have to count also as a deficit in justice, given the standard definition of the virtue of *iustitia*, accepted by Stoics and Aristotelians alike, as 'assigning to each his own', i.e. what is due to a particular person (see for example *Fin.* 5.67; cf. *Off.* 1.15).

This review of the defects vitiating the three primary systems of government, even at their best, pulls no punches. These flaws undermine two of the values—*libertas* and *dignitas*—to which the Romans were most deeply attached, from all we know about the late Republic. No wonder the diagnosis of just such flaws gets pride of place in Scipio's account. But he goes on to mention other destructive shortcomings inherent in the undiluted forms of rule (*Rep.* 1.44). The problem he is raising there (and indeed still discussing after a lacuna in the surviving text: *Rep.* 1.45) is one familiar from Polybius's treatment of the different kinds of political system in Book 6 of his *History* (Polyb. 6.4–9). It is all too easy for kingship—which after all is the domination of a single person—to lurch into tyranny; an aristocracy with just a few leaders into a junta like the Thirty at Athens; and the power of the people over all things (despite the claim subsequently to be made by its advocates for its exceptional stability: *Rep.* 1.49) into the irrational and irresponsible behaviour of the mob. In Book 2 Cicero will claim in an extensive discussion of the replacement of kingship by tyranny at Rome that, despite its intrinsic merits, kingship is of all these regimes the most unstable: through the defects of a single individual it can be sent headlong in the most destructive direction (*Rep.* 2.43). Or as he will comment later on (*Rep.* 2.50) in the same section (devoted to the reign of the last Roman king, Tarquin the Proud): 'The fortune of a people is a fragile thing when it rests on the will or the character of one person.'

4. Consilium and political stability

From each of these types of commonwealth, then, 'there is a path—a sheer and slippery one—to an evil condition that is its close neighbour' (*Rep.* 1.44). How in that case can the *res publica* show be kept on the right road? Dealing with that problem, and securing stability for the *res publica*, is the main business of the first two books of *On the commonwealth*. It was an issue the Greeks had tackled in their discussions of the 'best *politeia*': though Karl Popper associated it with Plato, it is for us most significantly dealt with by Aristotle in Books 4 to 6 of the *Politics*. In *On the commonwealth* it has already been placed on the agenda of the argument after the initial account of the *res publica* as *res populi* (*Rep.* 1.41).

In approaching the topic, Cicero first introduces that crucial idea of *consilium*, political deliberation, or the job or function of deliberation— policy. The claim is that a *populus* or *res publica* must be governed or directed (*regenda*) by deliberation of a certain sort—if it is to achieve a particular condition; namely, stability over time (*Rep.* 1.41). *Consilium*, its overriding importance for politics, how to secure it, how to legitimate it, get it right, and make it effective, what its forms need to be: these are the issues that are going to preoccupy Cicero. It is interesting that Philip Pettit starts the second main part of his *Republicanism*, devoted to theory of government, with a chapter on aims and policies characteristic of a republican stance, before then turning to constitutional forms. In the reflections offered in hindsight in the later edition, he suggests that this may have misrepresented the priorities of 'traditional republicanism', in which (as he construes it) commitment to republican process was more fundamental than concern with policy.[36] I suggest that Cicero would have thought he had got the order right first time round: the primary need in politics is for *consilium*, deliberation, policy, in the public interest. That is what has to be in charge. So constitutional theory will need to be worked out with the aim of ensuring direction by *consilium*.

The prime focus of *consilium* is to be the long-term stability of the *res publica*. Cicero indicates that such *consilium* must always relate in the first instance to 'that cause, the cause which brought the citizen body into being' (*Rep.* 1.41). 'That cause' must be a reference to 'the first cause of assembly' (i.e. of the formation of a *populus*), spelled out back at *Rep.* 1.39, as soon as the definition of *res publica* had been enunciated. Scipio had there observed:

> Now the primary cause of that assembling [the assembling of a *populus*] is not so much weakness as what might call a kind of natural herding together on the part of humans. For this species is not individualistic or solitary, but is so created that even when all things are there in abundance for them . . . [The text breaks off. It is likely that the sentence continued by saying something such as 'people could not cope living on their own'.]

The idea is the Stoic or Aristotelian one that community is natural to humans—contrary to what will be claimed in the sort of contract theory of justice that Philus is to present in Book 3 (*Rep.* 3.23)—as indeed is an impulse to develop the virtues (*Rep.* 1.41).[37]

So in thinking about long-term stability for the citizen body, *consilium* must make its priority the preservation of properly cohesive community. Scipio has at this point just specified that the *civitas* or citizen body must function as the *constitutio populi*, 'how the *populus* must be constituted' (*Rep.* 1.41).[38] So the condition on which any one of the three primary systems of government will be 'tolerable' requires the preservation of community as a body of citizens: by holding on to (*teneat*) 'that bond which first bound humans together in the association of the *res publica*' (*Rep.* 1.42). In other words, as Fott comments on the reference to 'the cause which brought the citizen body into being' (*Rep.* 1.41), the condition will be met provided that the citizens achieve a degree of unity through 'consensus of justice and sharing in advantage' (*Rep.* 1.39).[39] 'Concord in the citizen body', Scipio will say towards the end of Book 2 (*Rep.* 2.69), 'is the tightest and best bond of safety in every *res publica*—and that concord can no way exist without justice (*iustitia*).'

Nonetheless, as we noted at the beginning of this section, although each of the primary systems can achieve a measure of stability (Scipio says 240 years in the case of kingship at Rome: *Rep.* 2.52), all are vulnerable to breakdown on account of their inherent unfairnesses, as well as of the human weaknesses of those in power. Scipio's view is that the best chance of a more secure system will be provided if the sort of 'equal' structure advocated at the end of Book 1 is instituted.[40] As well as offering equality it has 'solidity' (*firmitas*). Given that nobody has a legitimate grievance over his assured standing within that structure, breakdown generally does not occur 'in this configuration of the *res publica*, combining different components and indeed calibrating their mixture, unless there are great vices in its leaders' (*Rep.* 1.69). The best statement of the system that Scipio envisages is given in a passage of Book 2 of the dialogue not many pages later than the remark about kingship referred to above. It goes as follows (*Rep.* 2.57):

> The unchanged condition of a commonwealth cannot be preserved unless there is an equal (*aequabilis*) balance in the *civitas* of rights, duties, and responsibilities (*iuris et officii et muneris*), so that there is sufficient power in the magistracies, and sufficient authority in the deliberation (*consilium*) of the leading citizens, and sufficient liberty in the people.

'Cannot be preserved' is too strong if understood without qualification, since the primary systems can be relatively stable: 'cannot reliably be preserved' is presumably what is meant.

The 'mixed' system of a balance of 'rights, duties, and responsibilities' (*Rep.* 2.57) is tantamount to a general sketch for something like a theory of separation of powers in any long sustainable *res publica*. The people are to act as the legislative and electoral body, the leading citizens the deliberative body; with the consuls and other magistrates as executive and judicial officers.[41] The idea of separation of powers, associated in the first instance with Montesquieu, is usually taken to be designed to replace mixed constitution theory.[42] But in Scipio's formulation that theory clearly envisages quite separate spheres of responsibility for the three elements he identifies in the *civitas*, even if at Rome boundaries between them were in practice blurred or breached. Key to the success of a *res publica* is recognition by all elements that deliberation must be what steers its course (cf. e.g. *Rep.* 2.56). Given such a recognition, each element—Scipio assumes—will normally be sufficiently content with the extent of its own distinctive rights and responsibilities, and with the performance of theirs by the other elements, as not to encroach on one another's provinces. Mutual consent, based on a perception that the system is fair (attaining *aequabilitas*), is the general order of the day: hence the talk of concord as 'the tightest and best bond of security in any *res publica*' (*Rep.* 2.69, where the Platonic musical analogy is salient).

5. History and theory

The theoretical specification of an 'equal' constitution given by Scipio in Book 2 of the dialogue (*Rep.* 2.57) occurs, however, in the course of a historical narrative of how Rome grew to be the sort of 'solid and robust *res publica*' that it did (*Rep.* 2.3; cf. 1.34). It is a narrative confessedly inspired by a work of Cato the Censor, a dominant political figure at Rome earlier in the second century BC, which we know to have been entitled *Origins* (Nep. *Cat.* 3.3). Scipio has been made to cite Cato for the thesis that 'there never was a genius so great that he could miss nothing', in explaining how it was that the Roman commonwealth was many generations in the making, and the product of many minds.[43] Cato is represented as having made much of the importance of the difference between the Roman and the characteristic Greek experience. Rome's constitution was in consequence of its gradual historical formation superior, in his view, to those many Greek polities whose political systems were—or were represented as being—the creation of a single lawgiver (as for example Lycurgus at Sparta), the model so important for Rousseau's construction of the legislator in Chapter 7 of Book 2 of *The Social Contract*.[44] Rome's founder Romulus, and its first king, is always a political leader, not a lawgiver who in the Lycurgan or Solonian manner steps aside from power after having established a template for a well-functioning polity, that it is then for others to accept and implement.

Scipio is represented as wanting thereby to show how the achievement of the best political system requires (as Cato is said to have put it) 'practical experience over a long period of history' (*Rep.* 2.2; cf. 2.21–2),[45] as well as employment of 'the same principles (*rationes*) that Plato recognised' (*Rep.* 2.52).[46] As a programmatic statement at the end of Book 1 had promised (*Rep.* 1.70), his account is at once a description of the Roman Republican constitution, as it had indeed evolved over more than 350 years up to his own time (demonstrating stability), and of the general 'type of *res publica* deserving most approval', a 'calibrated and thoroughly mixed composite of the three primary systems' (*Rep.* 1.45; cf. 54). The history told and the way the type is specified will require each in turn some commentary.

Much of what survives of Book 2 of *On the commonwealth* is taken up with an account of early Roman kingship. The story told has been aptly described as 'essentially a theoretical discussion within a historical framework', excluding 'all kinds of things that would have been included in a history' (that is, a history as a Livy would have written it), such as the Trojan legend, and sanitizing others, such as the rape of the Sabine women.[47] Or perhaps we might speak of theory nourished by history and history perceived in the light of theory. But for all the difficulties that might present, nonetheless to the problem of conceptualizing the way a constitutional structure that approximates an ideal might be created, the amalgam is arguably in principle a more intellectually appealing solution than is offered by the alternative hypothesis: of a single legislator's devising of the entire template. Certainly, one of the most intriguing elements in the arguments of *On the commonwealth* is the interdependence of theoretical and historical argument in its pages. It cannot be treated as a straightforward matter of an independent theory provided with confirmation drawn from empirically established history.

The picture painted of Romulus himself at the very beginning is instructive. There is nothing crude or primitive about Scipio's Romulus or the Rome he founded (Cicero makes him insistent on the point: *Rep.* 2.18–19). Various among his supposed achievements in what might nowadays be called state-building are discussed. Included among these is his discovery, so we are told, that there will be better government if a ruler is supported by the *consilium* of the best citizens and the *auctoritas* they bring with them (*Rep.* 2.15). This is no longer kingship unqualified: Romulus has his council of advisers. Yet perhaps surprisingly, he himself is presented as already a paradigm of *consilium* (*Rep.* 2.21):

Do you see how by the *consilium* of a single man not only was a new *populus* brought to birth, nor left wailing like a baby in its cradle, but already grown and adult?

The most important achievement in development of the political system as such, however, was in Scipio's eyes due to the later king Servius Tullius, credited with 'the greatest vision of all where the *res publica* is concerned' (*Rep.* 2.37). It was Servius who was responsible for the creation of the 'centuriate' assembly of the Roman people. This involved its division into nearly two hundred voting constituencies, so weighted that those to which wealthier citizens were assigned constituted nearly half of the total—to ensure that while no one was denied the *ius suffragii*, 'the right to vote', those with the greatest interest in the *civitas* and its prospering should count most in the voting (*Rep.* 2.39–40). Scipio can therefore conclude that under the monarchy there was both a senate and 'some popular right' (*Rep.* 2.43). Nonetheless kingship it was. And although it was to last more than a couple of centuries (presumably because it was already on the way to being a mixed constitution), the people had no real liberty—and it needed only one bad incumbent, exercising power tyrannically, for the system to be overthrown.

Laelius is at one point made to voice what has been interpreted as a note of scepticism about this thoroughly idealized teleological narrative.[48] Scipio is ascribing to reason, he says, some things that Romulus performed 'by chance or necessity' (*Rep.* 2.22). But the context militates against that kind of reading in any very strong version. Laelius is in fact complimenting Scipio for renouncing Plato's precedent in the *Republic* of creating himself the pure fiction of a stretch of virgin territory on which he could construct a political entity of his own choosing. Scipio has done better in preferring instead to ascribe to someone else his own rationale for an actual location that Romulus picked either by chance or from necessity.[49] No critical qualms are therefore expressed about idealization, even if there may be a touch of wryness in Laelius's comment. The message is that idealizing theory would do well (as Plato's did not) to take history seriously.[50]

The absence of pronounced sceptical qualms is confirmed by Laelius's immediate encouragement to Scipio simply to continue on the same narrative track, explicitly identified as designed to demonstrate development towards something resembling (*quasi*) the perfection of the *res publica*.⁵¹ Scipio responds by supplying further instances of 'royal virtue and wisdom' under subsequent kings (*Rep.* 2.24), notably Numa Pompilius's strengthening of religion and *clementia* (humanity of disposition), two things that 'most conspicuously contribute to the survival prospects of a *res publica*' (*Rep.* 2.27). After insisting that progress was always due primarily to native initiative, not absorption of foreign ideas, he speaks—in nuanced rebuttal of the tendency of Laelius's suggestion about Romulus—of the way 'the Roman people grew in strength not by chance, but through *consilium* and *disciplina*, discipline, although luck (*fortuna*) did not go against them' (*Rep.* 2.30). He goes on to insist on the historical reliability of his narrative by scotching, on chronological grounds, the tradition that Numa was a pupil of Pythagoras (*Rep.* 2.28–9).⁵²

The final chapter of Scipio's account evidently dealt with the first century of the Republic and the 'Struggle of the Orders'.⁵³ Good government comes to be threatened by two main disruptive forces, representing *vis* (coercive force) and *libertas* respectively: short-lived attempts at tyranny and oppression of various sorts, and (something for which Livy and particularly Machiavelli had much more sympathy) popular uprisings demanding and securing for the long-term rights that would curtail the powers of the magistrates and the senate. One way or another, however, 'calibration (*temperamentum*) was found' (*Leg.* 3.24), and the authority of 'the wisest and bravest' maintained, despite a greater degree of popular liberty (*Rep.* 2.59). Of the three major constituent elements in the citizen body, it is they who are always, in the Republican era, presented as the prime source of *consilium*. So for the system to remain stable, it needed to be their *auctoritas* that carried most weight in the way that rule was exercised. The last few pages of the narrative are lost, all but the end of the final sentence. It must be significant that its last three words (apparently about 'our ancestors') are ' . . . I judge that they preserved most wisely' (*Rep.* 2.63).

So much for the history. Now for the constitutional settlement it is claimed to have produced. Scipio's highly general formulation of his notion of a calibrated, stable system spoke of 'sufficient power in the magistracies, and sufficient authority in the deliberation (*consilium*) of the leading citizens, and sufficient liberty in the people' (*Rep.* 2.57). The reiterated 'sufficient' is particularly indicative. It implies that how exactly such matters are to be determined will be a task for judgement, in the light of circumstances as assessed from a vantage point of practical experience, custom, and the actual realities of class and power, not of theory alone. In other words, a proper theory of the best constitution cannot remain a matter of 'pure' theory, or of a precise formula valid for all time, but must grant a crucial role to experience and judgement.[54] Not for nothing was Scipio identified as the ideal person to discuss these matters, on account especially of 'his great talent and his unsurpassed wealth of experience in public affairs of the greatest moment' (*Rep.* 1.34–7; cf. 2.67). Here we may be reminded of Aristotle's characteristic approach to ethics and politics in the *Nicomachean Ethics* and Books 4 to 6 of the *Politics*.

The passage in Book 2 on *On the commonwealth* that prompts and introduces Scipio's specification of the calibrated system is particularly indicative. He is explaining how the original aristocratic form of the Republic broke down (*Rep.* 2.57):

Then there occurred something constrained to happen by the very nature of things. A little after the people had been liberated from kings, in fact about fifteen years later, they claimed more rights of their own (this was when Postumus Cominius and Spurius Cassius were consuls). Reason was perhaps lacking in this situation, but the very nature of politics often overcomes reason.[55]

Scipio then bids the assembled company to bear in mind the principles of calibration, presumably suggesting that the management of the existing aristocratic status quo was in breach of them. As he goes on to explain a bit later, the Romans' ancestors could perhaps however have found a rational plan for alleviating problems of debt (as Solon had done in Athens: *Rep.* 2.59), without having to cope with a rebellion that achieved some success. But either their leaders did not apply reason to the issues, or else their reasoning was faulty—in other words, it was not the *consilium* called for by the situation. Either way, the recalibration required was not perceived. The contingencies of politics in general, and more specifically the momentum of the natural cycle of constitutional changes, often have the effect of stifling reason or making it ineffective.

The aristocratic constitution that was in place when there occurred the upheaval whose origins Scipio describes here and in what follows is clearly conceived by him as a system that had achieved a degree of balance. He stresses not only the control of government by the leading citizens exercising supreme *auctoritas*, but also the freedom of the *populus* which acceded to that, as well as the great achievements in war of the consuls or dictators who exercised supreme *imperium* in that context. But there was not much of an active role for the people; and even their decisions in their assemblies were not valid unless approved by the patricians, a principle fiercely maintained in order to maximize the power of the nobility (*Rep.* 2.56). There were evidently the makings of instability here. The liberty to which the people was entitled was insufficiently implemented and protected.

Despite that, the consequent creation of two offices of plebeian tribune did not bring about any more radical change of system. Balance was evidently restored. The respect in which the senate was in general held remained intact. It was earned by their leaders' wisdom in *consilium* and bravery in war, their personal austerity, and the dedication with which they performed private acts of benefaction for individual citizens (*Rep.* 2.59).[56] There are a number of morals to be drawn, presumably not just about early Republican Rome, but applicable to politics more generally. One is that what may be sufficient liberty at one juncture may not be enough at a later time: the pressure of events, as well as the natural movement of the constitutional cycle away from aristocracy, may require recalibration. Another is that what enabled recalibration on the occasion that Scipio describes was not just a more effective guarantee of popular liberty, but equally the good judgement and the civic and personal virtue needed for the leaders of the community both to put the *res publica* back on track, and to retain the *auctoritas* on which their own position in the system depended.

6. Crisis and leadership

That feature of their position might be considered a fundamental conceptual difficulty for Scipio's balanced political system. While the magistrates and the people hold legally entrenched rights and powers, the leading citizens' *auctoritas* falls short of anything quite equivalent. The historian Henrik Mouritsen writes of the Roman constitution which Scipio takes to be the best embodiment of that system:[57]

A basic problem of Roman politics was that real power came to reside in the one body that formally held very little. The system therefore worked on the premise that the bodies that held the power did not exercise it. That applied to the *populus* in particular but also to the magistrates and tribunes, who were restrained by their brief tenure, collegiality, and peer pressure, and in the case of the lower magistracies their hopes of future preferment.

His verdict: 'Rome seems to have triumphed despite her constitution, because she had found a modus vivendi which neutralised the weaknesses inherent in her political make-up, above all its lack of a clear and workable division of powers'. To that Cicero would perhaps have said a 'yes and no'. When in the preface to Book 5 he bewails Rome's current condition,[58] the surviving extract begins with a quotation from Ennius, always regarded by him as its great national poet (*Rep.* 5.1):

> On ancient customs and the men of old
> Rome's commonwealth stands firm.

He then went on to comment that, but for that way of life, there would not have been such men, and without such men at the helm there would not have been that customary way of life, nor could it possibly have been so great and so extensive in its imperial reach. In other words, practice of the old Roman virtues of austerity and courage and proper religious observance produced men who sustained them, and were the foundation on which the *res publica* in all its power and glory was built. That style of thinking recurs elsewhere in Cicero's writings. A notable instance occurs early in the preface to the first of the *Tusculan Disputations* (composed in 45 BC), where he argues for the Romans' superiority in most things to the Greeks. It is indicative that he begins with the claims that they keep up their customs and established practices of life better, and that their ancestors calibrated the commonwealth with better practices and laws. He goes on to talk of their native courage and austere values (*Tusc.* 1.2).[59]

For Cicero, therefore, it appears that what contributes most to the durability of a *res publica* is a people's way of life, given shape by its established practices and laws, and the sorts of human being that it fosters, rather than its political system. The senate's lack of formal powers would not so much matter, so long as it functioned as a cohesive elite, and was staffed with men commanding respect and deference.[60] This is not far from Mouritsen's overall assessment of Roman Republicanism: 'The system worked because of strong social cohesion underpinned by a powerful ideological framework often summed up in the concept of *mos maiorum*, the traditions and norms passed down from the ancestors.'[61] Once historically that condition ceased to obtain, and elite cohesion in particular started to fracture, the respect upon which the mixed constitution relied similarly started to leech away.

The gulf between current reality and historical paradigm prompts the question whether Cicero thought his dialogue had anything to contribute to Rome's present state. He had once complained of the Stoic Cato that he delivered his political views as though he were speaking in Plato's ideal city, not among Romulus's dregs (*Att.* 2.1.8). Is Cicero himself not liable to a very similar objection? Catherine Steel observes that his speech *On behalf of Milo* (52 BC), at any rate in the version he prepared for posterity, makes 'enormous effort to conceal the failure of the institutions of government and to pretend that everything is as it always has been'.[62] Should the contemporaneous *On the commonwealth* be seen as further evidence of his shutting his eyes and hoping for the best, this time in his theoretical writing, too?

In fact, Cicero goes out of his way to indicate that, even at the time of the imagined conversations between Scipio, Laelius, and the rest towards the end of the second century BC, the Roman commonwealth was in a critical condition. In the very first exchange between the interlocutors, Aelius Tubero is made to refer to 'the present disturbance of the *res publica*' (*Rep.* 1.14). Laelius will before long revert to that theme in explaining why the discussion should in his view turn from astronomy to politics. Tiberius Gracchus's tribunate and subsequent death in 133 BC (just a few years before the dramatic date of the dialogue) have effectively divided both senate and people into two, and that in a dangerous international context. Restoring unity is of vital importance—which is why it is time for some political philosophy, to consider the 'best condition of a citizen body' (*Rep.* 1.31–3).[63] At the very end of the dialogue Scipio is told in a dream that the safety of the citizen body will depend on him alone: he will need to 'restore the *res publica* as dictator'—if he can escape assassination by close kin (*Rep.* 6.12: Cicero is implying that his death soon after was in fact murder).[64]

This framing of the conversations of *On the commonwealth* within the explicit context of political crisis looks much more like advertisement of an intention actually to address such issues within its fictive conventions than evasion of them would have led one to expect. It constitutes among other things an effective acknowledgement that even the 'equalized and calibrated' system of the mixed constitution, despite its vaunted durability, can be destabilized. Scipio is made to acknowledge this more or less explicitly, in an interesting passage near the end of Book 1, where he says that change to another system does not occur 'at all easily' in that kind of case (*Rep.* 1.65).

Dealing with political crisis had already received attention from Greek writers of political philosophy: it was presumably the subject of Theophrastus' lost work *Politics at critical moments* (D.L.5.44), assuming that this is the treatise of his which Cicero describes as dealing with 'political tendencies and critical moments that have to be controlled as the situation demands' (*Fin.* 5.11).[65] It turns out to be an explicit topic in *On the commonwealth* too, even if the detail of Cicero's handling of it is mostly lost. 'This', Scipio says at one point in his historical narrative (*Rep.* 2.45), 'is the essential thing for *civilis prudentia* (political judgement), the theme of my entire account: to see the paths and turns of commonwealths, so that when you know the direction in which things are going, you can hold them back or anticipate them.' Such 'paths and turns' in political systems of the primary kind ordinarily follow a regular pattern—a cycle (*Rep.* 1.45, 2.45)—although when we are given typical examples of revolutionary change from one to another, quite a bit of variation seems to be allowed for, with all tending to lead at some point 'to one form of tyranny or another' (*Rep.* 1.65–8).[66] Presumably the same would be true of the likely vicissitudes to which a mixed constitution might be liable.

If what is needed to cope with such critical moments is political judgement, what will supply it? Cicero's answer in *On the commonwealth* is clear: political leadership. Political leadership has not been a subject of major interest or theoretical attention in contemporary political philosophy, until the relatively recent turn to forms of realism. I cannot find any reference to it in Pettit's version of Roman or neo-Roman republicanism. But it was of course a major preoccupation of Machiavelli in *The Prince* and the *Discorsi*: something to which Mark Philp has drawn attention, in a book attempting to re-establish its importance as a concern that philosophers of politics need to address.[67] The man in the street certainly worries about political leadership. Nor does the current dominance across the globe of political strongmen at the helm make him sleep easier at night.

The importance Cicero attached to the topic, already foreshadowed in various passages of earlier books, is apparent from his decision to devote the whole of the final third of the dialogue to it, in the treatment of the 'best citizen' presented in the now very fragmentary Books 5 and 6. The *res publica* needs such citizens for its good government at all times, of course, not just in emergencies. Much of the history of Book 2 is designed to demonstrate that, just as the third book of Machiavelli's *Discorsi* promised (3.1.11):

In order to make it clear to all how much the action of particular men contributed to the greatness of Rome and produced in that city so many beneficial results, I shall proceed to narrate and to discuss their doings, and shall confine myself to this topic in this third and last book on this first Decad [i.e. the first ten books of Livy's history].

But the old Roman way of life is no longer cherished or even remembered, says Scipio; and that is due to a shortage of 'men': men with the traditional moral virtues—but also (this probably received more emphasis in Book 6, where response to crisis was discussed) the leader who commands *civilis prudentia*.

We get a person description for the role in a theoretical passage of Book 2, where Scipio contrasts the tyrant, exemplified by Tarquin, last of the Roman kings, with his antithesis (*Rep.* 2.51):[68]

Good, wise, skilled as (one might say) a guardian (*tutor*) and manager (*procurator*) of the interests of the commonwealth and the proper esteem due to its citizens (*dignitas civilis*). These should be titles of whoever is the director (*rector*) and takes the helm (*gubernator*) of the citizen body (*civitas*).

Cicero had had an earlier shot in *On the orator* at describing the person who 'brings his own experience and knowledge and concern to calibrating the *res publica*'. This, he says, is his definition (*de Orat.* 1.211):

The person who can hold and use those resources by which the interests of the commonwealth may be secured and developed, this person should be considered the director (*rector*) of the commonwealth and the initiator of public *consilium*.

Rector, 'director', seems to be the term Cicero most standardly employed in this connection in Books 5 and 6 of *On the commonwealth* (*Rep.* 5.5, 5.6, 6.1). Jean-Louis Ferrary is very likely right to suggest that this word, which as he says is very far from normal Roman political vocabulary, was adopted 'to underline the originality of his *optimus civis*' ('best citizen').[69] As he also points out, it is natural to connect it with an idea we met with way back at *Rep.* 1.41 (also *Rep.* 1.42, 47, 53, 2.15, 33). There, as will be recalled, Cicero made it a prime requirement that a *populus* or *res publica* be governed or directed by *consilium* (*regenda est*: note the use of the cognate verb from which the noun rector derives, also used in a pertinent passage of *On the orator*, where he talks of the need for someone who by *publicum consilium* will be a 'leader in directing the *civitas*': de Orat. 3.63).

Perhaps readers of *On the orator* had thought talk of a *rector* carried too many of those connotations that we associate with Il Duce or Der Führer. That might help to explain why in *On the commonwealth*, when Scipio reintroduces the notion of the *rector* at *Rep*. 2.51, he suggests that the words 'guardian' and 'manager' (estate manager is the sense in question) of the *res publica* in the public interest, and (significantly and characteristically) of 'the proper esteem due to its citizens', are terms we should use in conceptualizing and talking about this exceptional figure. These were to be the terms in which a decade later in *On duties* (*Off*. 1.85), Cicero would likewise propose that government of the *res publica* should be conceived (following Plato in the *Republic*, as he emphasized there):

As with the office of guardian, so management of the *res publica* should be conducted in the interests of those who are entrusted to one's care, not in the interests of those to whom management has been entrusted.

This is amplified in what in the Western tradition became the most celebrated of all Cicero's remarks about magistrates, i.e. officers of state (*Off*. 1.124):

It is the particular responsibility of a magistrate to appreciate that he assumes the role (*persona*) of the citizen body, and is obliged to uphold its *dignitas* and distinction, to preserve the laws, to dispense people's rights, and to be mindful of all that has been entrusted to his good faith.[70]

Who is Cicero's candidate for *rector*? In *On the orator* he gave a list of examples from the mid-second century BC: 'I would mention Publius Lentulus the leader of the senate, Tiberius Gracchus senior, Quintus Metellus, Publius Africanus [i.e. Scipio], Gaius Laelius, and innumerable others both from our own citizen body and from others' (de Orat. 1.211). *On the commonwealth* casts the net wider, at any rate by implication. In a monarchy, the person who fits the specification of the *rector* can be the king: as witness Romulus (*Rep*. 2.21). In a republic, he may be a regular magistrate (Cicero in 63 BC: *Rep*. 1.10); or someone who holds an extraordinary office (such as the position of dictator envisaged for Scipio: *Rep*. 6.12); or someone with no office at all (Lucius Junius Brutus, in expelling the Tarquins), who was 'the first in this citizen body to teach that in looking after the liberty of the citizens, no one is a private person' (*Rep.* 2.46). In both his oratory and his theoretical writings, Cicero frequently cites with admiration the assassination of the tribune Tiberius Gracchus (in 133 BC) by Scipio's cousin Publius Scipio Nasica, as the action of just such a private citizen, 'reclaiming the *res publica* into liberty' (*Brut.* 212; cf. *Cat.* 1.3, *Planc.* 88, *Tusc.* 4.51, *Off.* 1.76), and apparently had Laelius mention the deed as something deserving public honour in the conversation preceding Scipio's narration of his dream in Book 6 of *On the commonwealth* (Macrob. *In Somn.* 1.4.2–3).[71]

When the *res publica* is stable, *rectores* are needed (and obviously needed at any one time in numbers) among the ranks of the *principes*, the leading citizens who command *auctoritas*. But the need is most urgent in times of crisis. This is where exceptional action by a dictator or a single private citizen may be required.[72] Here therefore is the kind of person Cicero meant by speaking of the 'best citizen' as the second main subject of *On the commonwealth* (*QFr.* 3.5.1): someone who will in ordinary circumstances be one of the leading participants in the formation and (when an officer of the *res publica*) execution of public *consilium*, but will possess the ability in a crisis to seize the initiative—whether in an authorized official capacity or otherwise—in order to restore the system to proper functioning. This may require him to emulate the African or Indian who can gently control the huge elephant he rides (in his case, however, there are fierce emotions to be held in check by the power of his mind: *Rep.* 2.67).[73] Through the 'brilliance of the spectacle of his mind and his own life he is to present himself as a mirror to the citizens', in which they can see and be persuaded by what they themselves should aspire to (*Rep.* 2.69).[74]

That conception is offered as a proposal in political theory. But it is hardly credible, particularly given the literary means that *On the commonwealth* employs to emphasize political crisis as the context within which it theorizes, that Cicero does not suppose such a best citizen to be precisely what was needed at Rome as he composed the dialogue. Two years later that certainly seems to be the way he was thinking. In February 49 BC, as Pompey and Caesar squared up for the conflict of the civil war, he wrote to Atticus (*Att.* 8.11.1):

I spend all my time contemplating the importance of that man (*vir*) whom I portrayed conscientiously enough, in your opinion certainly, in my book. Do you have good recall of the calibrator (*moderator*) of the commonwealth to whom we would want to have recourse in everything? This is what Scipio says, I think in Book 5:[75]

As the goal for a helmsman is a successful passage, for a doctor saving his patient, for a general victory, so for this calibrator of the commonwealth it is a life of happiness for the citizens: securely defended, rich in the resources they command, high in reputation, honourably in their virtue. This is the task I want him to perfect, the greatest and best possible in human society.

And he goes on to comment bitterly on how far short of that standard Pompey falls: the thought of it has barely occurred to him. 'Here', as Andrew Lintott comments mildly, 'there is a suggestion of disappointment.'[76] Conceivably Cicero once had hopes that Pompey might be the man—following that third consulship just two years before which he had so much admired.[77]

7. On laws

No concrete positive evidence survives of *On laws'* date of composition. The consensus is that the surviving material from it reflects the Rome of 52–51 BC, with Clodius dead (*Leg.* 2.42), Pompey no longer consul but still living (*Leg.* 1.8, 2.6, 3.22 and 26), and no hint either of the civil war ahead or indeed of Cicero's imminent absence as governor of Cilicia (51–50 BC).[78] *On laws* was never put into circulation, and perhaps never completed, with Lactantius's *Institutes* (early fourth century AD) the first ancient work evidencing knowledge of the work as such or as a whole.[79] Most scholars now think that Cicero at any rate started writing it in 52–51, set it aside on leaving for Cilicia in the early summer of 51, and probably never returned to it.[80]

On laws advertises itself as a complement to *On the commonwealth*, mirroring what Cicero appears to have taken to be the relationship between Plato's *Republic* and *Laws* (*Leg.* 2.14).[81] This time Cicero takes on the role of main speaker himself, in conversation with his friend Atticus and his brother Quintus. Although the setting is clearly contemporary, when in Books 2 and 3 (after discussion of the foundations of law and justice in Book 1) he gets down to proposing a detailed legal code, he is explicit that its provisions are conceived as needing to be in harmony with the best form of *res publica* as proposed by Scipio in *On the commonwealth* (*Leg.* 2.23, recapitulating 1.20: 'all the laws must be fitted to that kind of *civitas*'). But it has been argued that Book 3 (devoted to magistracies, i.e. elected offices of state, and more broadly to the structure of governing institutions) in effect abandons Scipio's balanced constitution, and partly in response to the 'political chaos, violence and anarchy of the late 50s in Rome', now envisages an aristocracy requiring 'only the formal approval of the people'.[82]

As we shall see, however, although Cicero speaks in *On laws* from a vantage point rather more explicitly aristocratic than Scipio generally does, and his 'top-down view of republican politics'[83] becomes more emphatic than ever, in fact he makes no shift in position from *On the commonwealth*.[84] As for reaction to the immediate political situation, that makes itself differently apparent in the surviving sections of the commentary supplied by Cicero on the relevant chapters of his code (all of that on the first three and most of the fourth of its six sections are lost). Although what his main emphases were, or where they fell, we therefore cannot know, fortunately we do still possess a passage which strongly suggests something central to his entire project.

To register that there is no shift in basic theoretical position, we might note first that it is Atticus and particularly Quintus who are presented as expressing highly conservative anti-populist views, notably on tribunes and the secret ballot (*Leg.* 3.19–22, 26, 33–7). Despite his bitterly resented reverse at the hands of Clodius when tribune, Cicero himself is at pains to present his own stances as both more measured and more realistic about politics (*Leg.* 3.23–6, 33, 38–9). What he says in reply to Quintus makes it clear enough that he continues to see popular liberty as inalienable. The people retain the rights recognized under the balanced constitution, and have to be persuaded by one means or other to be guided by the 'authority of the leading men' in their exercise of them.

Accordingly, he supports Pompey's restoration of the powers of the tribunate in 70 BC, for paying attention 'not only to what was best, but also what was necessary' (*Leg.* 3.26).[85] He sees the institution as a safety valve: 'a calibration whereby lesser folk thought that they were on an equality with the leading men': *Leg.* 3.24. It enables the control of popular discontent, while at the same time he stresses its foundation in principle (*Leg.* 3.25):

Either the kings should not have been driven out, or the *plebs* had to be given liberty—real, not nominal, liberty. But they have been given it in such a way as to be induced by many excellent practices to acquiesce in the authority of the leading men (*auctoritati principum cederet*).

That verdict echoes the general drift of Scipio's approving account in Book 2 of *On the commonwealth* of the outcome of constitutional innovations in the earliest years of the Republic, including the establishment of the tribunate

(*Rep.* 2.55–9, the passage which includes his specification of the balanced constitution). Indeed, it replicates some of Scipio's actual wording: 'with the people's acquiescence, everything important was in the hands of the leading men exercising their authority (*auctoritate a principibus cedente populo*)' (*Rep.* 2.56).[86]

With the ballot, Cicero's position is presented as a middle way between a return to voting by voicing assent or dissent openly (which he owns he considers the optimal method: *Leg.* 3.33), and continuation of the secret written ballot at present in force.[87] On pragmatic grounds, he advocates retention of a written ballot free to the *plebs*, but open to inspection by their betters (*Leg.* 3.38–9). That way the *plebs* are given the form (*species*) of liberty—I think he means not a mere appearance of freedom, but a symbolic guarantee of true liberty (*quasi vindicem libertatis*, he has just said). Their betters, however, retain *auctoritas*. The upshot: elimination of any ground for dispute (so he claims hopefully). The bottom line was already put succinctly in Book 2: 'What holds the *res publica* together is that the *populus* is always in need of the *consilium* and *auctoritas* of their betters' (*Leg.* 2.30), again very much in harmony with the argument of Book 2 of *On the commonwealth*.[88]

In the material sandwiched between the treatments of these two issues comes a passage which seems to get much closer to the heart of Cicero's concerns over the contemporary Roman Republic. It runs as follows (*Leg.* 3.27–8):[89]

As to my law that *the senate is to be composed of those who have held office*, it is certainly a democratic measure to have no one reach the highest position unless he has been elected by the people (since the censors can no longer co-opt). But this fault is calibrated inasmuch as my law strengthens the senate's authority. The law goes on to stipulate: *Its decrees are to be given binding force*. For the fact is that, if the senate is in charge of public deliberation and policy (*consilium*), and everyone defends what it has decreed, and if the other orders are willing for public affairs (*res publica*) to be directed by the *consilium* of the leading order, then by calibration of rights—with power vested in the people, authority in the senate—that balanced and harmonious condition of the citizen body [i.e. as proposed by Scipio in *On the commonwealth*] can be sustained, especially if my next law is obeyed. Next comes: *The senatorial order is to be of unblemished behaviour—it is to be an example to the others*.

Cicero proposes the kind of balancing act that Sallust thought had eluded the Romans of the latter days of the Republic (*Cat.* 38.3).[90] Its overall effect would be to enhance the senate's authority by giving its decrees (presumably including resolutions 'of last resort') stronger legal standing, while defending the rights of the people. As he acknowledges, 'power' has to remain in the people's hands.[91]

But perhaps most significant is Atticus's reaction to Cicero's stipulation of 'unblemished behaviour' on the part of its members. Quintus thinks it would need the censor to interpret. Atticus goes further. It has the capacity to 'exhaust the whole company of judges, too'. To which Cicero protests that he was not thinking of the senate as it is at present, but of future contingencies (*Leg.* 3.29–30). In a moment or two he repeats: *It is to be an example to the others*, and comments: 'If we hold on to that, we hold on to everything.' What then follows is an extended sequence of argumentation for the thesis that 'just as the entire citizen body is apt to be infected by the desires and vices of its leaders, so it is improved and corrected by their restraint.' Significantly Cicero rounds off this excursus in these terms (*Leg.* 3.32):

The damage they do is not just because they themselves are corrupted, but also because they corrupt. They harm more by example than by their misdemeanours. My law, which applies to the whole order, can be narrowed further in scope. It takes just a few men—very few, in fact, enlarged by position and prestige—to corrupt or put right the morals of the citizen body.

This diagnosis was one he had voiced before, in a bitter passage of a letter of December 54 BC (*Fam.* 1.9.12–17),[92] and (he implies here) in *On the commonwealth*, apparently in one of the now lost parts of the dialogue (but see *Rep.* 1.69, on the effect of 'great vices' in the *principes*). He is making no secret of his view of the basic problem Rome needs to face. Moral rot is spreading from the entrenched aristocracy (*nobiles*, from whose ranks Catiline and Clodius had emerged), but above all from the likes of Julius Caesar (for whom only rarely does he express any esteem).[93]

8. Conclusion

On the commonwealth presents a powerful analysis of the foundations of political society, in its definition of *res publica* and the consequences it extracts from that.[94] But when it goes on to develop on that basis a theory of government, it is often found wanting for its failure to address, or even mention, some of the major problems of Cicero's own time: for example, the huge extension of Roman citizenship to embrace the whole of Italy, the transformation of *imperium* entailed by the prolonged military commands to which Caesar and Pompey were appointed, and the senate's failure to solve many of the other problems consequent on Rome's expanded imperial reach.[95] The 'best condition of the citizen body' proposed in the dialogue looks like a model that could work only in a smaller scale society, more cohesive, with a more settled traditional way of life. On the other hand, the ideal is not presented in the dialogue as an option that can be recovered immediately. The implicit message Cicero himself extracted from it in his letter to Atticus of February 49 was rather that the current political emergency called for the 'best citizen': a leader with real vision, or as he might have put it himself, one richly endowed in the capacity for the *consilium* to which *On the commonwealth* gives such priority.

In this it is not clear that Cicero was wrong. When Rome finally emerged from the turbulence of the late Republic and its aftermath of two decades of civil warring, it was Octavian—as the emperor Augustus—who ensured its recovery. And as Peter Brunt argued,[96] it was he who realized Cicero's ideal in practice: whether as articulated in the specification of aims for the 'calibrator of the commonwealth' in *On the commonwealth*, or as expressed in the list of what in *On behalf of Sestius* Cicero had made the 'foundations' of public peace (*Sest.* 98): 'religious observance, the auspices, the powers of the magistrates, the authority of the senate, the laws, our ancestral way of life, the courts, the judicial role of a magistrate, a regime of trust in public and economic life, provinces, allies, the prestige of empire, our military establishment, the treasury'. Brunt demonstrated that in virtually every one of these areas the emperor systematically rebuilt and reorganized to achieve the Augustan settlement. Liberty was the casualty. But whereas Cicero would doubtless have seen Augustus's rule as tyranny, it must be acknowledged that he does not himself list liberty among the prerequisites for public peace in *On behalf of Sestius* (he speaks of *otium* 'with *dignitas*'), nor among the goals of statesmanship in *On the commonwealth*.

Notes

1. For a good brief account of *On the commonwealth* and *On laws*, see the Introduction in Zetzel 2017a: vii–xxviii.
2. Discussed at length in Chapter 4 section 5, pp. 126–34.

3. The treatment of equality and popular sovereignty in Books 1 and 3 was discussed in Chapter 1. Various key themes of Books 1, 2, 3, 5, and 6 are discussed in this chapter, while issues particularly relating to cosmopolitanism and to justice and empire raised in Books 1, 3, and 6 receive attention in Chapter 4. For Book 4 see Zetzel 2001.
4. For fuller reflections on *On the commonwealth* as a Platonic work, and a more positive assessment of its conscious debt to Platonic rationalism than interpreters have often allowed, see Atkins 2013a: 47–79.
5. Words perhaps echoed in a remark attributed to Julius Caesar: 'The *res publica* is nothing: just a slogan (*appellatio*), without body and form' (Suet. *Jul.* 77). Already in December 61 BC Cicero was bemoaning to Atticus that the *res publica* was 'weak, wretched, and unstable' (*Att.* 1.17.8), and in the next letter (from January 60) in the surviving correspondence, that it could 'no longer survive (*stare*)' (*Att.* 1.18.2). A few years later, after the acquittal of his political opponent Gabinius, thanks he claimed principally to Pompey's lobbying in a climate of apprehension, he wrote to Quintus in October 54—during the early period of composition of *On the Commonwealth*—that '*res publica*, Senate, courts of justice' are nothing (*QFr.* 3.4.1; similar sentiments are voiced in a letter to Atticus of just that time: *Att.* 4.18.2). Such expressions of gloom became more frequent with the onset of the civil war (e.g. *Att.* 9.5.2, 9.7.1).
6. Laelius is made to refer to Scipio's very frequent discussions with the Stoic Panaetius in Polybius's presence (*Rep.* 1.34). There is good evidence that Scipio's historical original did number these two Greek thinkers among his friends (cf. Chapter 1 section 4, p. 16 and n.51). Laelius's formulation suggests that we are to think Panaetius' theorizing was more significant for the argument of *On the commonwealth*. What may or may not derive specifically from him has from time to time been conjectured, but in the total absence of concrete evidence agnosticism on the question is the only sensible option.
7. The importance of debate is given symbolic expression by Cicero's adoption of the dialogue form, and in particular by the pains he takes in Book 1's opening sequence (after the authorial preface) to present the participants as initially arguing fiercely with each other (*Rep.* 1.15–20). It was in the discussion of justice in Book 3 (only partially preserved), in the opposed speeches of Philus and Laelius, however, that complex sustained arguments for incompatible points of view were developed on a major scale (see further Chapter 4 section 5, pp. 126–34).
8. The pattern of expression of despair over the demise of the *res publica* alternating with insistence on the need for participation in public life, conceived largely in traditional republican terms, continues in *On duties* (44 BC), composed in the aftermath of Caesar'a assassination: see Griffin and Atkins 1991: xii–xv.

9. See Kempshall 2001.
10. See Chapter 2, section 5.
11. See Wood 1988: 125–6. At *Rep.* 1.41 Scipio equates *civitas* with *constitutio populi*. Quite what this means is not altogether clear, partly because Cicero seems to deploy the term *constitutio* in a variety of senses in *On the commonwealth* (as for example at *Rep.* 1.69, 2.37, 2.53). Ordinarily *civitas* is the political body itself. Perhaps Scipio's point here is that any proper *populus* (as defined at *Rep.* 1.39) must be constituted as a body composed of citizens (*cives*), i.e. persons possessed of citizen rights. In other words, on this interpretation *civitas* is not being given a novel meaning here. Rather, it retains its meaning as 'citizen body', and the proposal is that a people to be a people will be constituted as a body of citizens (cf. Chapter 2 section 4, p. 43). The sentence in which it occurs is focused throughout on the notion of *populus*: Cicero is intent on showing how first *civitas*, then *res publica*, relate to it.
12. Wood 1988: 128–9 refers to the definition of *utilitas*, 'advantage', in Cicero's early treatise on rhetoric, *On invention*. Here (*Inv.* 2.168–9) he accords pride of place to such elements in the *res publica* as relate to the 'body' of the *civitas*, listing agricultural land, harbours, money, a fleet, sailors, soldiers, allies as the means by which its safety and freedom are preserved' as basics, before going on to the greater abundancy of grand and beautiful buildings, exceptional wealth, and an extended international network of alliances. Cicero concludes that *utilitas* accordingly appears to be a matter of two things: security and power.
13. Asmis 2004: 578. She comments aptly (ibid. 579): 'The whole expression is compressed, apparently out of a desire for grammatical parallelism with *utilitatis communione*.'
14. Some recent scholarship (Asmis 2004: 580–2, 597–8; Harries 2006: 24–5) has made something of the resonances of the adjective *sociatus* in the definition of *populus* (elsewhere the noun *societas*, 'association': e.g. *Rep.* 3.43), as suggesting the Roman institution of a business partnership, undertaken for mutual benefit and relying on legally binding consent by the partners of one form or another. Given the claim (evidently not presented as contentious) made here about law, and given the 'business' connotation of *res*, one might indeed see some analogy with a business partnership sustained by *bona fide* contract, 'linking the strength of civil society to the moral component in private commercial dealings' (Zetzel 2013: 440). Both have a legal basis assuring those associating that they will be treated justly and share benefit.
15. It does not otherwise occur in surviving Latin literature before Augustine's discussion of the theories of *On the commonwealth* in the *City of God*.

16. A contractarian interpretation of Scipio's formulation has sometimes been proposed: as for example by Zetzel 1995: 128–9, followed by Arena 2007: 50, and more recently by Brouwer 2017: 36–8.
17. On this interpretation, *iuris consensu* would function simultaneously both as the 'subjective genitive' construction usual with *consensus*, expressing the idea of belonging; and also as the much rarer 'objective genitive', for which the closest occurrence otherwise met in Cicero's writing would be *consensus et societas consiliorum et voluntatum*, 'consensus and partnership in deliberations and intentions' (*Planc.* 5), although here the genitives are doubtless primarily dependent on *societas*. See further Schofield *forthcoming 1*.
18. A recent treatment: Pelling 2002.
19. Quoted above, in Chapter 2, section 4 p. 44.
20. At one point Cicero goes so far as to incorporate in the argument translation and then paraphrase of a section of Plato's analysis (in Book 8 of the *Republic*) of the corruptions to which democracy is liable (*Rep.* 1.66–8). For Polybius, see Hahm 1995.
21. As noted in section 2 above, p. 68.
22. The lines of argument championing first popular rule and then aristocracy constitute a rhetorical pair, presented at arms' length (*Rep.* 1.47–53). They are sharply demarcated from the advocacy of kingship that completes the sequence (*Rep.* 1.54–64). There Scipio moves into a quite different mode: a conversation with Laelius in broadly Socratic style, in which he makes his own preference for kingship among the three emphatically clear (while reiterating his belief in the superiority of a mixed constitution to any of the primary forms: *Rep.* 1.54).
23. Richardson 1991: 4.
24. A passage on early Roman kingship in *On duties* (*Off.* 2.41–2; cf. 2.85), confirms that, as most translators (Rudd, Fott, the Loeb) explicitly suppose, equality of rights before the law is what is meant here. See further Chapter 2, section 3 pp. 37–40.
25. See above pp. 69–70 and n.22.
26. We might compare the use in Laelius's speech in Book 3 of the Aristotelian analogy of various forms of political rule with the different ways in which the mind rules the body and the appetites and emotions (see Chapter 4, section 5 pp. 132–3 and n.93).
27. In Republican Rome, political access to *imperium* ordinarily required not merely election to office (or, for example, appointment to a proconsulship, the way many military commands outside Roman territory were arranged), but validation by favourable auspices, the sign of divine favour, as well (Richardson

1991: 1–4). For the ascription of *imperium* to the Roman people itself, see Richardson 2008: 66–79.
28. Nicgorski 1991: 237–8.
29. The closest he comes to it is a remark near the end of Book 2. Here he states that while 'it was possible to define the best condition [of a *civitas*] without a model (*exemplum*)', he has used Rome's mixed constitution as such so that 'one can see concretely just what sort of thing reason and speech were describing' (*Rep.* 2.66).
30. See further Atkins 2013a: 69–72.
31. See section 6 pp. 87–90 below.
32. However, when Scipio speaks of the 'balanced' kind of constitution he will favour above any of the primary systems, the *auctoritas* vested in the *consilium* of the leading citizens indicates his view of where the principal responsibility for *consilium* should sit (*Rep.* 1.69, 2.57; similarly, and more emphatically, *Sest.* 137).
33. See section 4 p. 77 and especially section 5 pp. 81–3, and for full discussion of the distinction Chapter 2, section 2 pp. 33–5, where at pp. 34–5 n.31 it is noted that at Rome resolutions of the *plebs* came in time to achieve the standing of decisions of the *populus* as sovereign body.
34. Notoriously, ancient political theorists (and their successors in the Western tradition until recent times) were in general hostile to direct democracy, and to Athens as its paradigmatic embodiment. But Plato, despite his memorable attacks on Athenian politics in *Gorgias* and (if not by name) in Book 8 of the *Republic*, had subsequently recognized a law-governed as well as a lawless form of democracy in his *Statesman* (*Plt.* 302c–303b). Cicero follows suit. The evidence of the palimpsest gives out at a point where he might have been going to make it clearer at what period or periods he thought mob rule took over in Athens (*Rep.* 1.44).
35. On *dignitas*, see Chapter 2, section 2 p. 34 and nn.26 and 27, and for a recent brief discussion, Griffin 2017: 48–54 [= Griffin 2018: 722–5].
36. Pettit 1997: 288. However, Pettit's concern with policy relates to the question of what policy objectives should be pursued if non-domination is the overriding aim of republican politics. Cicero thinks it imperative to ensure that the capacity for deliberating policy (policy for stability rather than freedom) is put in the driving seat in the system in the first place.
37. In the same kind of context, we find in Aristotle the thought, similar to Scipio's point about behaviour in conditions of abundance, that humans congregate even when they have no need of mutual help (*Pol.* 3.6, 1279a17–21).
38. Cf. section 2, p. 96 n.11 above.

39. Fott 2014: 48 n.86. Zetzel 1995: 131 suggests that Cicero 'is not concerned here with universal causes for the formation of states, but with practical concerns of particular states'. According to Scipio, as Zetzel there notes, the prime focus of *consilium* needs to be durability (*Rep.* 1.41). But *contra* Zetzel, everything he says on the topic of durability in this context, and indeed in similar contexts elsewhere (e.g. *Rep.* 2.57), indicates insistence on a single theme: that the key to such stability consists in keeping a community bonded together in shared access to justice and advantage, under whatever specific constitution it is governed (cf. Büchner 1984: 125–6).
40. See section 4 of Chapter 2, pp. 44–6 above, for discussion of the 'equality' characterizing this structure.
41. See above section 3 p. 73 on the ambiguity in such a context of 'people' and its power.
42. See, for example, recent discussions by Hansen 2010, advocating abandonment of separation of powers and a return to mixed constitution thinking (as more realistic), and Calabresi, Berghausen, and Albertson 2012, who see the contemporary US polity as de facto a mixed constitution, and call for a return to a pure separation of powers regime.
43. *Rep.* 2.2–3. Accordingly, for that principled reason he will not (like Plato) 'make up' (*fingere*) a *res publica* of his own. Moreover, it will be 'easier' to give a historical account of the development of the Roman *res publica*, and of the solid and robust form into which it evolved (*Rep.* 2.2–3; cf. 2.21–2, where Laelius applauds him for doing so), than to follow a Platonic procedure (cf. Polyb. 6.48.7–10).
44. Interestingly Athens, with its frequent changes of constitution and many lawgivers, is acknowledged as in those ways an exception to the norm (*Rep.* 2.2).
45. Polybius, probably writing around the same time as Cato's work (now lost except for a few fragments), summarizes the Romans' achievement of their constitution in similar terms (Polyb. 6.10.13–14). Since Laelius is made to say that Scipio's historical account of its evolution has no Greek precedent (*Rep.* 2.21), Cicero is however presumably meaning to intimate that Polybius's account (now also mostly lost) was in fact preceded by Cato's work.
46. As suggested in Chapter 2 (section 4, pp. 45–6), Scipio certainly envisages the kind of constitutional structure that he is advocating as working like a Platonic harmony composed of dissimilar sounds (*Rep.* 2.69; cf. *R* 4.443c), rather than as a Polybian equilibrium of opposing forces; and as indicated in section 3 above, it will crucially give a guiding role to the wisdom and *consilium* Plato had

associated with philosopher rulers in the political theory of the *Republic* and he himself with kingship at its best (*Rep.* 1.60–3).

47. Cornell 2001: 56; see also the commentary in Zetzel 1995 on the first part of Book 2.
48. So, for example, Zetzel 1995: 178; cf. 2017a: 39 n.23. Fox 2007: 62–3, 98–104 reads this remark of Laelius, in what he takes to be its ironizing of history itself, as a key index of what he sees as Cicero's sceptical stance (undogmatic rather than negative) on the relationship between philosophy and history (and indeed practice) quite generally.
49. The rationale he gives (*Rep.* 2.5–11) is in fact an adaptation of the reason Plato gives in the *Laws* (4.704a–705b) for siting his no less fictional Cretan city of Magnesia where he does (see Zetzel 1995: 162–3).
50. But while idealized history is one thing, Scipio does have recourse to metaphysics. To understand the type of the best condition of something just in itself, one must use an image drawn from nature (*Rep.* 2.66, where the palimpsest gives out shortly after): perhaps the cosmos itself (cf. Ferrary 1984: 97–8), or more specifically the musical harmony (*Rep.* 2.69) of the heavenly spheres (*Rep.* 6.18–19).
51. The force in context of *quasi* (literally 'as if') is somewhat indeterminate (Zetzel 1995: 179), but intimating the impossibility of any absolute perfection in human affairs seems likeliest.
52. Cicero was or became well aware, however, that the exaggerations of his history writing could be accused of irony, since he makes that an explicit issue in his *Brutus* of 46 BC (*Brut.* 292–9; see Fox 2007: 192–203).
53. See Chapter 2, section 3 pp. 38–41.
54. On what Scipio calls *civilis prudentia*, 'political wisdom', see further section 5 pp. 81–3.
55. Translators diverge considerably in their renderings of *in quo*: 'in this situation' is closest to Rudd's 'in the matter'. The Latin translated by 'the very nature of politics' is *ipsa rerum publicarum natura*, following again Rudd (cf. Ferrary 1984: 95, Atkins 2013a: 98), taking that to be the best amplification of 'the very nature of things' (*natura rerum ipsa*). What Scipio has in mind must certainly include the natural cycle of constitutions (*Rep.* 1.45, 2.45). Yet that cycle is not inevitable, but subject to contingency. The translation 'commonwealths' (preferred by the Loeb, Fott, and Zetzel), although possible, seems a bit too restrictive, and not so obvious an amplification of 'the very nature of things'.
56. Further popular rights would be secured a few decades later, following more upheavals (*Rep.* 2.61–3; and see Chapter 2, section 3 pp. 39–40). But Cicero 'appears to have thought the constitution then remained stable

almost until the tribunate of Tiberius Gracchus in 133' (Zetzel 2017a: 55 n.81), even if there were some further popular rights secured during that period (Scipio gives examples: *Rep.* 2.60).
57. Mouritsen 2017: 166.
58. Cf. section 1 p. 63 above. This rendering of the Ennius quotation adapts that given by Rudd 1998: 81.
59. For discussion, see Gildenhard 2007: 109–30, and on virtues Chapter 5 below.
60. As we shall see below (section 7 pp. 92–3), he was to take up these matters in *On laws* (*Leg.* 3.10, 27–32), where he ends by indicating that the moral influence of the men who compose the senate had been discussed more thoroughly in *On the commonwealth*, presumably in sections now lost to us (but see *Rep.* 5.6–7, a fragment assigned to Book 4 in Zetzel 2017a: 80; cf. Zetzel 2017b: 468–9, 477–82, following Büchner 1984: 494–8).
61. Mouritsen 2017: 166.
62. Steel 2005: 131.
63. Wiseman 2010 serves as an illuminating commentary on this passage.
64. On the historical context Cicero is assuming, see Zetzel 1995: 6–8.
65. So Ferrary 1995: 54–5.
66. So Ferrary 1995: 57; cf. section 3 p. 69 above on Herodotus.
67. Philp 2007: 37–54; see also Bellamy 2018 (with useful bibliographical references). For the treatment of Cicero himself as exemplary leader in the later fifteenth-century humanist Martino Filetico, see Cox 2016: 52–3.
68. Zetzel 1995: 205–6 provides an excellent explication of the different terms Cicero employs in the description, and of their interrelationship.
69. Ferrary 1995: 51–3. See also Powell 1994, Zarecki 2014: 77–104 (which includes quite speculative elements).
70. For comment see Wood 1988: 133–6.
71. The legality (as also needless to say the acceptability) of such action on the part of a private citizen, or by a magistrate exceeding his constitutional powers, was in truth highly contentious, as Cicero well knew. Much of the political conflict of the final decades of the Republic focused on these and similar issues: see for example Wirszubski 1950: 31–65, Wiseman 2009: 177–210, Arena 2012: 169–243, Straumann 2016: 88–117.
72. The Roman office of dictator 'seems to have been conceived as a short-term magistracy with special powers, which could be created with the minimum of delay, since the man was simply nominated, not elected'. Originally it was usually to deal with some grave military threat that a dictator was called into service, as in the famous case of Fabius Cunctator, after Hannibal's victory over the Romans at Lake Trasimene in 217 BC. The office fell into disuse after

Hannibal's final defeat, but was revived for Sulla and Caesar in the first century BC for the 'grander function' of 'bringing stability to the political order' (Lintott 1999a: 109–13). Much about its history and conceptualization, however, is obscure and contested: see Straumann 2016: 63–88.

73. For discussion see Atkins 2013a: 71–9.
74. Seneca was subsequently to recast the idea, and so launch its career as the 'mirror of princes': a description of princely virtue in which a ruler could see himself as (optimistically) he truly was, or might at best become (*Clem.* 1.1.1; cf. Schofield 2015b: 68–70).
75. Wiseman 2009: 119–20 and 2010: 31 cites a passage from Varro's *On the Latin language* (a work dedicated to Cicero) against personal idiolects as some sort of echo of this Book 5 passage, a fragment numbered by most editors *Rep.* 5.8. It states (*Ling.* 9.6): 'As the helmsman ought to comply with reason, and each individual in the ship with the helmsman, in just that way the people should comply with reason, and each one of us with the people.' As Wiseman remarks, Varro is talking about linguistic usage, not politics, but one wonders whether there is a hint of wider resonances.
76. Lintott 1999a: 224; see further Zarecki 2014: 99–103, on Cicero's assessments of Pompey in February to April 49 BC as a whole.
77. See Steel 2017: 279–82 for argument for the importance of Pompey in all three dialogues of 55–1 BC, but especially *On the commonwealth* (see also the panegyric of Pompey in *Leg. Man.* 27–9, 36–50 (66 BC). Zarecki 2014: 71–2 collects a sequence of references to Pompey in Cicero's correspondence from the years 52–50 BC, describing him in July 51, for example, as an 'exceptional citizen, prepared in both spirit and *consilium* for all those contingencies which in the public sphere one must anticipate' (*Fam.* 2.8.2).
78. Dyck 2004: 5–7.
79. Dyck 2004: 30–4.
80. Only Books 1 to 3 survive as continuous manuscript text, with substantial lacunae particularly in Book 3. Otherwise we have only a few scraps, one specifically identified as a quotation from Book 5.
81. Whether that means he wrongly interprets the *Laws* of Plato as designing laws for the political system outlined in the *Republic* (as some interpreters suppose) seems to me unclear but unlikely. For a full recent discussion see Atkins 2013b.
82. Arena 2016: 85, 95.
83. Wiseman 2010: 29.
84. So Ferrary 1984.
85. Perhaps echoing Scipio's account of the *rector* (*Rep.* 2.51), Cicero here describes Pompey's action as that of the 'wise citizen'. Elsewhere he expresses admiration

for the government of Demetrius of Phalerum, the late-fourth-century BC ruler of Athens, who is described as 'a most public-spirited citizen, highly expert in safeguarding the citizen body' (*Leg.* 2.66; cf. 3.14). There seems to be no other reference to the *rector* in *On laws*, but there is no particular reason why we should expect discussion of the *rector* to have occurred in a treatment of the basic legal and constitutional structure of a *civitas*. Provision is made for a *dictator*, under the antique designation *magister populi* (*Leg.* 3.9; cf. *Rep.* 1.63, *Fin.* 3.75).

86. Scipio does speak with some enthusiasm of the aristocratic regime in place before the institution of the tribunate, when the nobles did not just exert authority but wielded real power (*potentia*: *Rep.* 2.56, 59; the choice of terminology may indicate power that is not formally authorized). But he is quick to point out that this situation, even though it was in accordance with reason that their *consilium* should be in control, was nonetheless unstable: once liberated from kings, the people were bound to claim more in the way of rights. Indeed, he takes this opportunity to repeat his prescription for a mixed constitution, incorporating liberty for the people: otherwise, he says, 'the unchanged condition of a commonwealth cannot be preserved' (*Rep.* 2.57, with comment in Zetzel 1995: 213–14, Atkins 2013a: 64–79).

87. See the useful discussion in Dyck 2004: 523–5. The secret written ballot had proved to be just as vulnerable to bribery as open oral voting. Dyck comments that although written ballots had done little to increase popular liberty, 'the appeal may have been the enhancement in dignity of the ordinary voter', although Cicero 'does not make that point'. On my reading, particularly of *species libertatis*, it is precisely his point, and consequently this is no 'pseudodebate', as Dyck complains.

88. In the surviving parts of the text of *On the commonwealth*, Scipio never explicitly discusses the question of how, in his balanced constitution, the deficit in 'communal deliberation' that he finds in aristocracy as a system is avoided: 'In aristocracies the mass of the population can scarcely have any share in liberty, when they are excluded from all communal deliberation and power' (*Rep.* 1.43). Perhaps he would say simply that the people will exercise the powers they possess wisely only if the leading citizens are obliged to share their own *consilium* with them in public addresses, whether in the *contio* or in some other forum.

89. The law is enunciated in the code itself at *Leg.* 3.10 (note also the provision that censors are to 'let no disreputable person to remain in the senate': *Leg.* 3.7).

90. See Chapter 2, section 2 p. 32.

91. Quite what Cicero means by giving decrees of the senate 'binding force' has been debated: Dyck 2004: 468–9. The likeliest interpretation is perhaps that

'they should be obeyed by magistrates without fail' unless vetoed by a tribune (Lintott 1999a: 230).
92. For a brief treatment, see Schofield 2017a: 47–9.
93. Pompey, by contrast, gets a good press in *On laws*: *Leg.* 1.8, 2.6, 3.22, 26.
94. See especially Chapter 2, section 5 pp. 50–2.
95. See, for example, Lintott 1999a: 232, on the lack on Cicero's part of any 'attempt to take into account the unification of Italy and the exponential growth of the empire as a whole'; Brunt 1988c: 240–80 (cited in Chapter 1, p. 24n.32), on unsatisfied demands for agrarian reform.
96. Brunt 1988b: 56–68.

4

Cosmopolitanism, Imperialism, and the Idea of Law

1. Cosmopolitanism

Diogenes the Cynic is one of those Greek philosophers people who have heard anything at all about the ancient Greek world tend to have heard something about. He is famous for his lifestyle: out in the open night and day, at all seasons of the year (he is notoriously said to have occupied a barrel for a period), wearing the minimum of clothing, begging for things to eat and drink, performing all natural functions in public without shame, and attacking every commonly accepted value and anything that could be regarded as mere convention, such as the institution of marriage and indeed the city itself. It is hard to imagine anyone more different from Cicero, renowned for their wit though both of them were. Yet in Cicero's writings on political philosophy we find a strong attraction to an idea that seems to have been originated by Diogenes, whether or not he really expressed it, as he is alleged to have done, by claiming to be *kosmopolitês*, a citizen of nowhere but the *kosmos*, the universe (D.L. 6.63). For in Cicero, too, for all his devotion to the *res publica*, there is also a strong vein of what one might call cosmopolitanism, in more than one version.[1]

Early on in Book 1 of *On the commonwealth*, for example, we get the following exchange between Laelius (portrayed as someone lacking patience with theoretical enquiry), who has just joined the gathering, and Philus (1.19):

LAELIUS: What was your topic, may I ask? What conversation did we interrupt?

PHILUS: Scipio had asked me what I thought about the appearance of two suns being accepted as a fact.[2]

LAELIUS: So we have got to the bottom of questions that concern our homes and the *res publica*, if the enquiry is to be about how affairs are in the heaven?

PHILUS: Don't you think it relevant to our homes to know how affairs are and what is happening at home? Our home is not the one bounded by our house walls, but this entire universe, which the gods have given us as a home and a country to be shared with them.

And for several more pages the astronomical theme is pursued. Eventually, however, Laelius will be asking why discussion had focused on the alleged astronomical phenomenon at a time of urgent political crisis. 'In a single *res publica*', he says there, 'there are two senates and now something close to two peoples'—thanks to the divisive effect of Tiberius Gracchus's death, and before that of his conduct of the tribunate (*Rep.*1.31).[3]

There are at least two dimensions to the exploration of a cosmic framework for *On the commonwealth*'s political theory. One (associated with Scipio) is more contemplative and mostly Platonic in character, the other (present most memorably in a speech from Laelius) more practically oriented and more Stoic.[4] To be sure, Scipio figures in the dialogue principally as a great statesman. In his first interventions in its conversation he is tellingly represented as expressing Socratic distrust of enquiry into nature and as regretting Plato's embrace of it under the obscurantist spell of Pythagoreanism (*Rep.* 1.15–16). But his stance subsequently becomes more nuanced.[5] Following an eloquent speech by Philus on Archimedes' construction of an orrery which could be used to predict solar eclipses, Scipio waxes lyrical on the usefulness of such knowledge for generals or political leaders needing to dispel popular superstition (*Rep.* 1.21–5).[6]

When the manuscript text resumes (following a missing leaf), he is launched on something more unexpected. Its theme is the microscopic insignificance of all human affairs—Rome's included, and more generally the pursuit of glory, wealth, and power—in comparison with eternity and the glory of the realms ruled by the gods. That perspective makes it impossible to think or talk of the possession of those objects of merely human aspiration as goods. True wealth and power belong to the person who is self-sufficient, and true happiness to someone who is free from mental disturbance. In that spirit, and calling into service anecdotes about not only Plato but his grandfather Africanus too, Scipio explains that he places a high value on science and learning, and on the exclusive intellectual focus on what is divine and everlasting that is distinctive of wisdom (*sapientia*) (*Rep.* 1.26–9).

Nor is this excursus on ultimate values merely a passing moment. Its main theme, and its apparently incidental references to Africanus and to Plato, are recapitulated in the dream of Scipio, the grand set piece with which the dialogue ends, and for centuries the only continuous stretch of *On the commonwealth* that anyone could read (*Rep.* 6.9–29). Here Scipio recounts his Platonic vision of what he says he was told and shown by his grandfather in a dream. As in the more fanciful mythical narrative told of the mysterious figure of Er with which Plato brought his *Republic* to an end, so the focus here too is on the fate of the soul after death, and Africanus too sets his account within a cosmic frame. Its core message is that 'for all those who have preserved, aided, or helped their country grow, there is a sure place marked out in heaven, where they may enjoy everlasting life in blessedness', designed to encourage Scipio to virtuous action and to the fulfilment of his political destiny (*Rep.* 6.13).[7] The dream accordingly ends with enunciation of a thoroughly Platonic statement of the immortality of the soul. Indeed, Cicero here incorporates (without acknowledgement) one of his favourite passages in all the Platonic dialogues, the *Phaedrus*' proof of its immortality (*Rep.* 6.27–8).[8]

'Be sure', Africanus then concludes, 'to employ it [i.e. the soul] in the best kinds of activities', which are identified as those of 'caring for the safety of one's country'. Then flight to its assigned place and its home above and detachment from the body will be swifter, the swifter still if it engages in contemplation of what lies beyond itself (*Rep.* 6.29).[9] In the central section of his discourse he directs such contemplation to the wonder of the astronomical structure of the cosmos,[10] and to the 'harmony of the spheres', a music too deafening for human ears according to Pythagorean theory (*Rep.* 6.15–19).[11] But the statesman Scipio keeps turning his eyes and mind back to earth, struck now by its comparative smallness, with the Roman empire 'no more than a dot on its surface' evoking his embarrassment (*Rep.* 6.17, 19). Africanus responds by telling him to scorn human glory. He should reflect on how parochial it is when one considers the empire's limited extent, and how evanescent it is over the whole span of time (*Rep.* 6.20–5).

Scipio's initial reflections in the dialogue on the limitations of the pursuit of merely human aspirations and on the proper focus of true wisdom

(*Rep.* 1.26–9), on the one hand, and the cosmic vision of his dream (*Rep.* 6.10–29), on the other, therefore together frame *On the commonwealth*'s entire discussion of politics and the political sphere. Politics is not thereby devalued, but placed firmly in a broader context. Cicero makes the conduct of statesmanship a necessity: not the merely necessary duty that it is for Plato's philosopher kings, but necessary duty now distinctively conceived (in decidedly unPlatonic and unAristotelian fashion) as the best of activities, and as such the fast track to immortality and the soul's truest home, especially however if not divorced from contemplation of what lies beyond politics (*Rep.* 6.16, 29; cf. 1.27). Cicero will frequently in subsequent writings weigh the comparative importance of the claims made on us by theoretical understanding and politics or more generally social obligation, on a final occasion at the end of Book 1 of *On duties* (*Off.* 1.153–8).[12] But one might argue that the use here in *On the commonwealth* of the resources of a political theology to tackle the question was the most intellectually elegant that he was ever to achieve.

Laelius's version of cosmopolitanism is very different. He too claims for it a theological basis. But its focus is on humans, and on how they should behave as humans. It is enunciated in a memorable section of the speech he is made to deliver in Book 3 of *On the commonwealth*, as the advocate of justice in the course of the debate Cicero stages there on whether justice is a genuinely objective value or not. Laelius says (*Rep.* 3.33):[13]

> True law is right reason in accord with nature, extending into us all [i.e. our minds], unchanging, everlasting. It calls to duty by its commands, it deters from wrongdoing by its prohibitions; but neither does it command or forbid the upright in vain, nor move the wicked by its commands or prohibitions.

> He goes on to stress that attempts to alter or repeal this law would amount to its violation, not within the powers of senate or people. It does not require expert exposition or interpretation, nor will it vary between Rome and Athens or between the present and the future. No, it is one law, everlasting and unchangeable, which will be valid for all nations and at every time, and there will be one common master and commander (so to speak) of all: god.

> He is the author, expounder, mover of this law. Anyone who should disobey it will be running away from himself. In scorning his nature as a human being, by this very deed he will pay the greatest penalties, even if he should escape all the other things that are generally considered punishments.[14]

In these words Laelius articulates the theological foundation for what we might describe in Kantian terms as the Stoic moral law within. In humans such law is 'the reason and mind of someone wise, as applicable to command and prohibition' (*Leg.* 2.8).[15] In his exposition of Stoic theology in *On the nature of the gods*, Cicero's Stoic speaker Quintus Lucilius Balbus explains a basic commonalty that the Stoics take to be shared by gods and humans, or at any rate the more rational members of the species (*ND* 2.154): 'They alone live according to justice (*ius*) and law (*lex*) by the use of reason.' In Book 1 of *On laws* Cicero appropriates these ideas on his own account. He cites the authority of 'the most learned men' (*Leg.* 1.18), which probably indicates in the first instance the unification of Stoic and Platonic (or more often in ethics Aristotelian) doctrine characteristic of his teacher Antiochus.[16] Law is 'the highest reason, rooted in nature, which commands the things that must be done and forbids the opposite'. He promises that the discussion which follows will specify 'the source of justice in nature' (*Leg.* 1.20). That promise is honoured with some Stoic-style syllogistic reasoning for the inference that to share in rationality on that basis is to form a citizen community (*Leg.* 1.23):

> Since nothing is better than reason, and this exists in both man and god, man's primary association with god is in reason. But those who have reason in common also have right reason in common. Since that is law (*lex*), we humans must also be reckoned to be associated with the gods in law. But further, those who have law in common have justice (*ius*) in common. But those who have these things in common must be held to belong to the same citizen body (*civitas*).

And as Cicero then goes on to state, in exercising right reason humans are obedient to the mind that is responsible for the celestial order of the universe.[17]

So the universe itself is the city that houses this community. The great Greek Stoic Chrysippus had maintained that it is the only true political community, i.e. the worldwide community of the properly rational. This view was taken to be the radical stance common to Stoics and Cynics alike by Cicero's contemporary, Philodemus, head of an Epicurean community in Herculaneum in the Bay of Naples: 'It is their view', he says (*On the Stoics* col.XX 4–6), 'that we should not think any of the cities or laws we know to be a city or a law'. Philus's invocation early in Book 1 of the idea of the cosmos as a home and country to be shared with the gods gave us the first intimation of the role that the Stoic doctrine might play in the arguments of *On the commonwealth* (*Rep.* 1.19).[18] Unsurprisingly, however, he is not made to claim like the early Greek Stoics that it is our only true country. Nor is such a line taken either in *On laws* or in later passages of *On the commonwealth*. In the preface to Book 2 of *On laws* Cicero proposes the idea of dual citizenship: of one's native township and of Rome and the *res publica*: two countries, not one (*Leg.* 2.5).[19] Apparently it does not occur to him even to allude here to the cosmic city. In *On the commonwealth*, it is suggested to Scipio in his dream that the heavens are the home where his soul belongs (*Rep.* 6.29), but only after insistence that 'nothing that happens on earth is more pleasing to that leading god who rules the whole world than those assemblies and gatherings of humans, formed through association in justice, which are called citizen bodies' (*Rep.* 6.13).

There are a number of reasons why we should not be too surprised by Cicero's attraction to the Stoic theory. Although the philosophical framework within which he develops his account of the best constitution in *On the commonwealth* owes most to Plato, Aristotle, and (still in mostly Platonic vein) the second-century BC Greek historian Polybius, Stoicism figured large in the philosophy to which Cicero had been exposed from an early age. He had a Greek Stoic named Diodotus living at his invitation in his own household throughout much of his adult life. Moreover to his mind the Stoic theory of law may well have looked to him (and indeed to the Stoics themselves) like a more developed version of the idea of law in Plato's own *Laws*. In *On laws* he simply calls it the 'view of the wisest', where law itself is characterized in the most general terms as 'something eternal that rules the entire universe through wisdom in command and prohibition' (*Leg.* 2.8).[20] Finally, Stoicism gave Cicero the resources for rebutting ethical relativism and upholding a realist view of moral values that he wanted to be able to have at his disposal.[21] That moral realism was already apparent in Scipio's conception of justice in Book 1 of *On the commonwealth* (Chapter 3, section 2 above); it will similarly emerge as a leitmotiv in various aspects of Cicero's treatment of law and justice throughout *On laws* (sections 2 to 4 below); and we shall return to the vigorous debate in Book 3 of *On the commonwealth* about its validity (section 5 below).

No less important for appreciating Cicero's embrace of a Stoic universalizing conception of law and community is reflection on the world he lived in. Rome was a citizen-state, a *civitas*. Yet as time went on the notion of citizenship (the core meaning of *civitas*) was complicated by the extension of more limited citizen rights to non-Romans, such for example as (pre-eminently) the inhabitants of Italy at large. Cicero could wax eloquent on Rome's inclusive approach to citizenship, as for instance in his defence of Lucius Cornelius Balbus in 56 BC (*Balb.* 31):

Without any doubt the thing that has done most to establish our empire and increase the renown of the Roman people is the precedent set by Romulus, leading founder of this city. By his treaty with the Sabines he taught us that this citizen body ought to be expanded by admitting even our enemies into it. Thanks to his authority and example the tradition of granting and sharing citizenship has never been broken by our forebears.

Rome had indeed gradually become a great imperial and imperializing power. Half a century or so later, the poet Ovid would write (*Fast.* 2.683–4): 'To other nations the earth is granted with fixed boundary: for Rome extent of city and world is the same.' In Cicero's day Roman rule was exercised through direct or indirect forms of control of various kinds over most of the territories clustered round the Mediterranean basin; and its reach stretched quite a bit further into Europe and the Near East. Roman courts became well used to adjudicating between the claims of Romans and non-Romans, and members of the political elite spent time abroad as governors of Roman provinces, where much judicial activity was expected of them. Cicero himself was reluctantly to take up such a post in Cilicia, the southern coastal region of modern Turkey, in early summer 51 BC—in fact not that long after completing *On the commonwealth*.[22]

There remains, however, an inevitable tension between regarding Rome and the *res publica* as one's principal community and seeing as fundamental membership of a cosmic city embracing all humanity. The text in which Cicero comes closest to addressing this issue is Book 1 of the later *On duties*, in a passage near the end of a discussion of the social virtues of justice and beneficence or liberality (*Off.* 1.50–8). There he discusses the whole range of communities to which a person will belong. He begins with the most comprehensive community existing between all humans as humans, and the obligations it implies. Then he works through the nation, the citizen body, the family, and the whole gamut of kinship relationships, before turning to friendship and the mutuality of exchange of services. But when these are finally ranked for their moral claims upon us, country and after country parents are given pride of place, with the *res publica* elsewhere in *On duties* ultimately accorded overriding importance: 'Without the *res publica* we could have no shared political, religious, legal or economic life.'[23]

The community of all humanity figures nowhere on the list. Perhaps this is because Cicero thinks all our social obligations, as the culminating argument of the main part of Book 1 suggests, are to be understood as preserving (in the words of its final sentence) 'the common bonding and associating together of the human race as a whole' (*Off.* 1.149). In short, the community of the human race might be viewed as the genus, all other social relationships its species. On the other hand, when it comes to contrasting obligations due to the *res publica* and to fellow human beings as such: 'The answer is briefly', in Margaret Atkins' summary, 'that our duties to the former are positive and manifold, while our duties to the enemy and the passing stranger are minimal and largely negative.'[24] We can give a stranger water or show him the way, provided that we can do it without suffering loss or trouble (*Off.* 1.51–2). Preventing visiting foreigners from using the city's facilities is, of course, inhuman (*Off.* 3.47). You must not break valid promises given to an enemy, particularly if made on oath (*Off.* 1.39–40). In sum, if there are thicker and thinner conceptions of cosmopolitanism, Cicero's is fairly thin—but not despite that ethically insignificant.

The universalism of Cicero's moral outlook is not restricted, however, to its bearing on the obligations of individual citizens. In *On laws* it is applied also to the legal regime that all 'good and stable peoples' (*Leg.* 2.35), and indeed 'free peoples' in general (*Leg.* 3.4), should adopt (section 4 below). And justice in conduct towards others is seen as something incumbent upon states and nations as well as individuals. Rome's obligations to its provinces and allies are the example that Cicero develops both in Laelius's speech in Book 3 of *On the commonwealth* and in Book 2 of *On duties*, seen as comparable with those that a government or its representatives must perform for its citizens (section 5 below). Such corporate responsibilities are conceived as much more substantial than those that individuals should exercise for passing strangers.[25]

2. Cicero's conception of law

Cicero proposes to fit the Stoic idea of a universal community of the rational to a legal code appropriate to a well-regulated constitution for a *res publica* (*Leg.* 1.20, 2.23; cf. 3.12). Of *On laws* only Book 2 (on religion) and in more fragmentary form Book 3 (on officers of state or 'magistrates', and in fact more broadly on government) survive, but these topics are stated to be most important (in that order) for that purpose (*Leg.* 2.69). One might well question whether the attempt at a fit is not simply some kind of muddle.[26] The difficulty has been and could be expressed in a variety of ways. For example, a legal code suitable for a particular form of *res publica* will require many quite specific provisions (as is certainly true of the surviving parts of the system proposed in *On laws*, which mostly mirrors or makes adjustments to the existing Roman constitution) that would be inapplicable to a universal community. Nor could such a code credibly claim universal validity—in fact, Cicero himself exempts the Eleusinian mysteries at Athens from the general ban he imposes on nocturnal religious rites (*Leg.* 2.35–7). Again, the right reason that governs the behaviour of the wise is an ideal, whereas Cicero accommodates within his system practices that he reckons not optimal, but something dictated by the need to be pragmatic—such as written ballots and the Roman tribunate (*Leg.* 3.19–26, 33–9)—if the constitution is to be appropriately regulated: not the best, but the necessary.[27]

The view that will be developed here is that Cicero's position on law and laws is for the most part coherent and defensible within its own terms. It may be that he does too little to explain just how the theory of Book 1 is envisaged as building into the elaboration of a legal code in Books 2 and especially 3, thereby prompting much of the puzzlement in which readers of the dialogue have found themselves.[28] But mostly the difficulty arises from not reading him with appropriate philosophical alertness and discrimination. The next three sections of this chapter deal with the matter. The present section discusses the way Cicero highlights the ethical demands of moral law as universally applicable to human beings. Section 3 examines the way he seeks to present the piety promoted by his laws on religion as complying with those demands, and how in a rather different manner he hopes to show the natural basis for proper exercise of *imperium* in the legislation proposed on magistrates. Section 4 considers how credibly he could deliver on his undertaking to make his legal code, which is confessedly presented as a variant of the traditional Roman constitution, appropriate for 'all good and stable peoples'.

In approaching Cicero's conception of law in *On laws*, two main things need initially to be borne in mind. First, though in the syllogism about law and reason that we looked at briefly earlier we get what one might call the

Stoic theory at full strength, the proof of the pudding is as usual in the eating. Cicero in effect exploits mainly those elements of the theory that will prove useful to his purposes. The key elements for him are, on the one hand, the idea that true law is in essence 'the reason and mind of someone wise, as applicable to command and prohibition' (*Leg.* 2.8; cf. 2.11)—the moral law within, to repeat the Kantian phrase; and on the other, the claim that the existence and force of such reason is rooted in the nature of things in a divinely ordered universe. In fact there is something literally divine in the wisdom of rationality (*Leg.* 2.8–10), with 'the starry heavens above' and all nature being ordered in the Stoic view (unlike Kant's) by the same reason as motivates moral action: the 'force, nature, reason, power, mind, sway (or whatever other word may express what I mean more plainly)' of the immortal gods (*Leg.* 1.21).

A second consideration follows from these points. Someone who thinks of law in this way is focusing on law as command, or on 'the *directive* aspect of law', 'not aiming to find universal rules which require and forbid actions independent of virtue'.[29] It is conceptualized not as itself a *system* of moral precepts, but rather as the rationality and ethical soundness inherent in any specific prescriptions or prohibitions that a person whose mind is properly guided by reason will articulate—whether in the context of legislative or judicial activity within some particular political community, or otherwise, as for example if a parent is trying to bring up children properly.[30] This conception of law requires, of course, that reason be understood not in Humean fashion as the mere instrument of the passions, but as a faculty designed to grasp substantive truths in every area in which it can be exercised.[31] But that assumption about reason is common ground in most ancient philosophy: in Platonism and Aristotelianism as well as Stoicism.[32]

The preface to Book 2 of *On laws* in fact makes it clear enough how such a conception of law as the prescriptions and prohibitions of right reason is envisaged as playing out in practice. No written law told Horatius to stand on the bridge over the Tiber alone when his two brothers had been killed as they tried with him to resist the forces that were attempting to reinstall Tarquin the Proud as king: it was the law and command (*imperium*) of courage. Tarquin's son Sextus may have been breaking no written law in raping Lucretia—but he certainly acted against eternal law (2.10). 'Law', as Cicero has said towards the end of Book 1, 'ought to correct vices and encourage virtues'—and so teach us how to live (*Leg.* 1.58). And as he now explains: before there was written law, 'there was reason, derived from nature, directing to right action and summoning away from crime.' It had its origin with that of the divine mind of the supreme god (*Leg.* 2.10).[33]

In other words, right reason as law always tells us to do what is morally right and not to do what is morally wrong. More specifically, right reason distinguishes between what is just and what is unjust in guiding us (2.13), because we are social animals (a key assumption in the Stoic theory, although not brought out explicitly by Cicero at this point). Law so understood is what should govern all human communities, not just the universal community of gods and humans (although to the extent that members of any specific human community comply with that law, they will thereby act as citizens of the universal community of the rational: a point implicit in the theoretical argument of Book 1: *Leg.* 1.28–32). Any actual legal code will therefore represent the law of right reason insofar as its provisions correctly deal with human behaviour. They will do that if they enjoin ethical conduct and prescribe what is just in our dealings with each other and within the divine order, and forbid the unethical and prohibit what is unjust, punishing the wicked while defending and protecting the good. If any specific law within a code fails the test, it cannot be regarded as law and should not even be called law (2.13–14). Nature is to function as 'the measure (*norma*) of law', determining what is a good or a bad law (*Leg.* 1.44; cf. 2.8: 'we must bring everything back to that [i.e. the nature of law]', echoing 1.20).[34]

If the true law of right reason (*Leg.* 1.18–19) is 'eternal' (*sempiterna*) (*Leg.* 2.10; cf. *Rep.* 3.33), does that suggest that Cicero regards as immutable the laws that he will go on to propose?[35] In the main body of Books 2 and 3, the line he takes on the status of his laws is quite differently based. Alterations to his code are conceived as likely to be needless, not as irrational deviations from eternally valid moral law. It is the excellence of the ancestral Roman constitution (as endorsed in *On the commonwealth*), or occasionally of older custom, that will make innovations on his own part mostly undesirable, even if he is able to extract extra benefit from discussions on the issues by learned Greeks (*Leg.* 2.23, 3.12–13). In the preface to Book 2, however, Quintus is represented as assuming that the laws of such a code as Cicero is envisaging would never be repealed. Does he think that might be so because the imperatives of moral law itself are (as Cicero has just said) intrinsically incapable of repeal or abolition (*Leg.* 2.14).

If so, that would look like a straightforward confusion of categories. There is a clear distinction flagged in the preface to Book 1 between the nature of law and justice, which is to be found by considering first human nature (presumably its capacity for rationality); then 'the laws by which citizen bodies ought to be ruled'; and finally 'the laws and decrees of peoples that have been put together and written down' (*Leg.* 1.17).[36] Piety is what in matters of religion the moral law itself invariably enjoins upon us; but it seems likely that there may be more than one reasonable way in which different societies might enact legislation for the practice of piety in any particular relevant sphere, and 'permanence is contingent in the human realm'.[37] Moreover, Quintus is seemingly presented as off target in various ways often enough in this dialogue, as for example in congratulating Cicero a little later on the unPlatonic cast of what is in truth a highly Platonic style of proem to the laws on religion (*Leg.* 2.17).[38] However Cicero here indicates assent to Quintus's assumption (*Leg.* 2.14). Does he do so because he really thinks that the laws he will propose, as expressions and applications of true law, are also intrinsically unalterable? So it is sometimes supposed.[39]

In fact Cicero qualifies his assent: 'provided that the two of you [i.e. Quintus and Atticus] accept them [i.e. the provisions of the legal code now to be proposed]' (2.14). Quite what we should make of this response is debatable. It seems unlikely that it is to be construed as a mere polite formality of dialogue convention, particularly given that Atticus and Quintus are not going to accept the laws on tribunes and voting by written ballot that Cicero puts forward (*Leg.* 3.19–26, 33–9). Perhaps he means here principally to indicate in Socratic style—as he does in different ways in others of his dialogues (for example, *Fin.* 5.95–6, *ND* 3.94–5)—that any conclusions reached can in philosophical dialogue claim no absolute validity of any kind. They are necessarily relative to the agreement of the participants.[40]

3. The law code

Soon after his opening general remarks on law in Book 2, we find Cicero writing in the style of Plato's *Laws* a 'proem' to the laws on religion that will follow, designed to persuade citizens that the theology he has been assuming requires them to take the obligations of piety with the utmost seriousness

(*Leg.* 2.15–16).⁴¹ The proem concludes with a sketch of some of the social and political benefits of having laws covering the need for piety in some principal specific areas of communal life:

Who would deny that such opinions are useful, when he understands how many things are secured by oaths, how much the religious guarantees underpinning treaties contribute to our security, how many people have been restrained from crime by the fear of divine punishment, and how sacred is the partnership of citizens with each other when the immortal gods are introduced, whether as witnesses or as judges?

The first of all the laws in the code now articulated, in traditional archaic language, reads (*Leg.* 2.19): 'They shall approach the gods in purity, they shall do so with piety, they shall set wealth aside.' In the highly selective commentary on the code which occupies the rest of Book 2, Cicero explains (*Leg.* 2.24): 'The law bids people to "approach the gods in purity", that is, with a pure mind. That embraces everything.' He thereby makes it crystal clear that all the detailed provisions which follow are to be understood as applications of right reason insofar as it requires of us proper reverence for the gods. Moreover, as Andrew Dyck emphasizes, he likewise makes it clear that their overall thrust will be to raise the bar above that set by Roman religion, even if most of the practices they specify are drawn from Roman law and practice or constitute variants of them (as Quintus is made to point out: *Leg.* 2.23). Their ethical imperatives will demand more than merely ritual purity, although it is stressed that such purity will also still be required.⁴²

The importance of setting wealth aside becomes a dominant theme in the commentary on the final three provisions of the religious code (*Leg.* 2.22), which in fact occupies a considerable portion of the entire book (*Leg.* 2.45–68). Cicero starts by translating a passage from Plato's *Laws* (*Laws* 12.955e–956b) prohibiting dedications to the gods in gold, silver, ivory, bronze, or iron, or any requiring time-consuming intricate workmanship (*Leg.* 2.45). Similarly, he cites with approval rules to control excess of any sort, whether of emotion, display, or expense, in funeral and burial practices. He endorses in the first instance provisions of the Roman Twelve Tables, but then Solon, Demetrius, and finally Plato's *Laws* again (*Leg.* 2.59–68). He is plainly here pursuing an agenda of reform.⁴³ 'It is entirely in keeping with nature', he says near the start of his discussion, 'that difference in fortune should be abolished in death.' His final verdict on the rules he cites from the Twelve Tables: 'they are certainly in accord with nature, which is the measure of law (*norma legis*)', although he allows that other provisions he goes on to mention are merely customary (*Leg.* 2.61–2). 'The measure of law' presumably indicates that it is the piety enjoined by the natural law of right reason which validates those rules against excess—a piety now conceived as expression of a pure mind, that finds no ultimate worth in anything other than right and wrong. Hence (*Leg.* 2.19): 'They shall set wealth aside.'

Book 2 of the dialogue therefore does a reasonably convincing job of producing a code of laws on religion which, at any rate in spheres that Cicero decides to present in his commentary as salient, can plausibly be argued to meet the test of nature as 'the measure of law' (*Leg.* 1.44; cf. 2.8).[44] With Book 3, on magistracies, which works out in practice as a discussion of the structure of government more generally, the code proposed seems to be related to true law rather differently. At its outset, Cicero makes the general point that 'nothing is so well fitted to justice (*ius*) and the requirements of nature as the power of command (*imperium*).' Without it no human community could exist—nor the universe itself. For the universe is obedient to god, seas and earth to it in turn, and human life is subject to the decrees of the highest law (*Leg.* 3.3; presumably he means by 'highest' the law that governs the universe as a whole). But with one dubious exception, that is the last we hear of nature either in the code or in what survives of Cicero's commentary (but much of that is lost) explaining its rationale. It is not invoked as 'the measure of law' (*norma legis*), as it was in Books 1 and 2.

The possible exception occurs in the closing section of Book 3 (or what is preserved of it). Atticus at that point asks Cicero to add some discussion of Roman law, and more particularly of the specific powers of magistrates. Since the main powers of the major magistracies are already spelled out in Cicero's code, with mostly minor variations on the Roman model itself, perhaps what is envisaged might be an account of those exercised by praetors in their judicial roles, not least in civil cases (*Leg.* 3.8).[45] According to the highly conjectural text that translators usually accept for want of anything better, Cicero replies by distinguishing a discussion of Roman law (which is what Atticus has requested) from the independent treatment of the 'law of nature' (*Leg.* 3.47–9). However, the manuscript text of the relevant sentence is, as they concede, heavily disturbed, in the judgement of the Oxford

Classical Text editor perhaps beyond redemption.[46] In any case, no further continued discussion of magistrates (if ever composed) now survives.

One might be tempted to conclude of Book 3 of *On laws* overall that in practice Cicero's '"philosophical approach" to the subject amounts', as Dyck puts it, 'to the superimposition of a hortatory/moralizing element upon a description of functions'.[47] But the need to conduct just wars and with justice (*Leg.* 3.9), one of the clauses of the code that Dyck cites in support of his verdict, hardly deserves being written off as 'moralization', given the massive impact of war, pretty well continually waged, on Roman political life. The requirement had already figured in Books 2 and 3 of *On the commonwealth*, and would be further discussed at some length in *On duties* (*Rep.* 2.31, 3.35, *Off.* 1.34–40).[48] No less importantly, another of the clauses of the code on magistracies cited in this same context by Dyck is the provision that the senatorial order is to be of unblemished behaviour, which receives such emphasis in Cicero's ensuing commentary, as what is crucial if the entire polity is not to sink into corruption (*Leg.* 3.29–32).[49] That provision can plausibly be seen as an application of moral law.

Nor is it the only such evidence of ethical concern, clearly present (for example) in those clauses of the code which articulate the duties of censors (*Leg.* 3.7). And no sooner does Cicero's commentary on the code get under way than we find considerations that are moral as well as political entering in there too. The tribunes' ability to curtail the rights of a consul was needed if consuls were not to seem 'too arrogant and violent' (*Leg.* 3.17). Last but not least, in the code itself, Cicero rules: 'for them [i.e. the principal magistrates] the people's safety is to be the ultimate law' (*ollis salus populi suprema lex esto*: *Leg.* 3.8). Unfortunately, the portion of the commentary which might have thrown further light on this principle came in the missing section. But when Cicero recurs to it in one of the *Philippics*, he treats it as natural, divine moral law, 'prescribing what is honourable, forbidding the opposite' (*Phil.* 11.28).[50]

Nonetheless, in general, Dyck's talk of superimposed moralizing might suggest a basic problem in relating the code on magistrates of Book 3 to natural law. Laws specifying principal officers and organs of state and their roles simply do not and could not have the primary function of 'directing to right action and summoning away from crime', to repeat one of the several different broadly equivalent formulae Cicero uses to characterize the injunctions of the true law of nature (*Leg.* 2.10). How could Cicero have thought otherwise? Something of a solution to the puzzle perhaps emerges if we distinguish the basis and form of law from its content. The content is described in such terms as 'directing to right action and summoning away from crime' (*Leg.* 2.10). But to articulate the basis and form of the law that the gods have given the human race, Cicero speaks simply of the 'reason and mind of a wise being, suited to ordering and deterring', owed ultimately to the 'wisdom in command (*imperandi*) and prohibition' which rules the universe as a whole (*Leg.* 2.8). When Book 3 launches its discussion of magistrates, it is *imperium*, in its core sense of 'command', that he associates with law, and again sees as governing not just the human sphere, but 'the entirety of the nature of things and the universe itself', in obedience to god (*Leg.* 3.3). It is the exercise of such command that is taken to give magistracy its function (*vis*: *Leg.* 3.2).

So what is natural is simply that there be wisdom in instituting positions with power to command and prohibit in a political society. In other words, in Book 3 it is in the first instance the basis (wisdom) and form (imperative) of law, not its moral content, that Cicero may have had in mind in conceiving of such political positions as natural and as expressions of law. On such an interpretation, the legal code of Book 3 overall, therefore, would have a quite different conceptual character from that of Book 2. Book 2 specifies morally oriented rules: those with which its citizens should comply in their relationship with the divine, and which because of that focus are given the precedence in the sequence of books in the dialogue.[51] With exceptions such as those noted above, a good number of Book 3's laws have no such orientation. In truth they fail for that reason to merit their denomination as 'laws' strictly speaking at all. Where they at any rate are concerned, Benjamin Straumann is right to say: 'Cicero is somewhat misleadingly using the term *leges* for "laws".'[52] As he suggests, the code they constitute specifies rather the fundamental structure of political authority and obedience within which society must operate.

What specific magistracies there should be, however, is not anything nature itself can determine. Nor *a fortiori* are the laws on magistracies that he will propose so determinable.[53] In fact, Cicero does not suppose that it is nature that decrees the need for *imperium* to be exercised through magistracies, rather than by some other form of rule. In the passage that follows his opening remarks on *imperium* as natural, he turns to things 'closer and more familiar to us'. He begins with a historical sketch of the ubiquity of kingship among ancient races, where this form of *imperium* was vested in those outstanding for their justice and wisdom. But after commenting on why kingship fell into disfavour, he refers to his task as that of legislating for 'free peoples', following the model of the best form of *res publica* established in *On the commonwealth* (*Leg.* 3.4; cf. 1.20, 2.23, 3.12).

The parameters of wisdom in legislating must therefore be in part a matter of contingency: what will be right for a monarchy will not be right for a 'free people'. For a free people, what is required is that form of wisdom that Scipio called *civilis prudentia*, 'political wisdom' (*Rep.* 2.45), a wisdom geared to the needs of a political society: a *civitas* or citizen body (*Leg.* 3.4).[54] Cicero goes on to amplify the sorts of consideration that he will bear chiefly in mind in drafting his laws on magistrates, given that the very existence of the citizen body as such depends on their wisdom and conscientiousness, and that the correct allocation of their powers is crucial for the 'calibration' (*moderatio*) of the *res publica* (*Leg.* 3.5,12). He insists also on the importance of instructing not just the magistrates in their exercise of *imperium*, but the citizens at large in their need to obey them. In a political society in which rulers and ruled change places, everyone needs to know the political behaviour expected of them in both roles (*Leg.* 3.5).[55]

So is Cicero's hope of fitting the general theory to the bodies of law on religion and on magistrates presented in Books 2 and 3 misconceived? I have suggested that in Book 2, for the laws governing religious observance, the idea of bringing Stoic moral law to bear on provisions designed to promote piety works well enough. In Book 3 Cicero's approach is rather different. Although he relies implicitly on moral law at various particular points of the main body of the text, a perfectly intelligible strategic recourse to nature of a different kind is made in the preface. Here it is the basis and form of *imperium* itself which, consistently with his general theory of law, is 'consonant with the justice and structure of nature' (*Leg.* 3.3). He had no need to make further reference to that in the rest of the book. Hence his silence on the topic there.

What guides the configuration of offices and the provisions specifying their powers and responsibilities that are set out and discussed in the main body of Book 3 is the need for them to be appropriate to the calibrated and equalized Scipionic constitution of *On the commonwealth* (*Leg.* 3.12; cf. 1.20), as for the laws governing religion in Book 2 also (*Leg.* 2.23). That optimal condition for a *res publica* was founded on the 'consensus of justice'. One might have hoped that Cicero would have indicated some connection between that essentially Aristotelian idea of political justice with his basically Stoic conception of moral law as the 'criterion (*regula*) of justice and injustice' (*Leg.* 1.19; cf. 2.13), given that it is to constitute the basis that 'humans have for living among one other, equal and common to them all' (*Leg.* 1.35; cf. 1.28–33). But in Books 2 and 3 the imperatives of law are mostly articulated in terms simply of commanding right behaviour and deterring from wrong, not as the glue that binds society together. So a connection, though in principle presumably feasible, is never explicitly worked out.

4. Laws 'for all good and stable nations'

When he gets down to the business of devising a legal code, Cicero represents his project as designed to have validity for 'all good and stable peoples' (*Leg.* 2.35) and for 'free peoples' in general (*Leg.* 3.4). This agenda is what he led his readers to expect, when in Book 1 he described that project as 'putting commonwealths on a firm footing, bringing stability to cities, maintaining every kind of people in a sound condition' (*Leg.* 1.37). He had said something congruent with that in the preface to Book 2, appealing to the agreement of unnamed theorists that 'laws were invented for the safeguarding of citizens, and the security of citizen bodies, and a peaceful and happy life for humans' (*Leg.* 2.11).[56] What he actually produces turns out to be more or less the same as the traditional Roman system, as Quintus is made to point out at the appropriate juncture in both Book 2 (*Leg.* 2.23) and Book 3 (*Leg.* 3.12). On each occasion Cicero replies that this is to be expected if the claims that Scipio made in *On the commonwealth* are correct about the 'calibration (*temperatio*) of the *res publica*' (*Rep.* 3.12). For it was precisely the constitutional design of *res publica* advocated there that on Scipio's view had maximum durability: on account of the optimization of justice (*Rep.* 2.69) that it achieved, through what he represented as an equal balance of power, deliberative capacity, and popular liberty (*Rep.* 1.69, 2.57).[57]

But as well as fulfilling the agenda that Cicero indicates, a legal code has to satisfy the crucial fundamental criterion of measuring up to the law of right reason. I take it that he would not pretend that there could be no true, just set of laws satisfying that criterion under any other valid constitutional system. It is rather that if the political requirement is to produce laws for free and *stable* peoples that satisfy the definition of a *populus* stipulated in the theory of *On the commonwealth*, then those laws will have to accord with the Scipionic calibrated constitutional system if they are to encapsulate justice in the appropriate form. And while there might be some scope for argument about detail, the delicacy of the balance to be achieved is not going to allow much room for manoeuvre over the shape and emphases of the code. So any people other than the Romans, wanting a legal code that will give them true law for a stable and just *res publica*, had better adopt Cicero's essentially Roman model, or something very like it (*tali descriptione*: *Leg.* 3.12).

Settling on the right laws to accept in any particular field of jurisdiction, given such constraints, is something where the judgement of rational persons about what is appropriate is called for. In exercising judgement—what Scipio calls 'political wisdom' (*civilis prudentia*, *Rep.* 2.45)—they will need to have regard not only to eternal verities, but in the present context to the requirements of the Scipionic constitution and its need to stay fine-tuned.[58] In Book 3 of *On laws* the way an existing constitutional settlement has evolved or might evolve is proposed as one kind of consideration that will need to be accommodated. The office of tribune is a democratic element in the Roman constitution that is not (in Cicero's eyes) ideal. But as he had had Scipio say in *On the commonwealth*, the 'very nature of commonwealths often overcomes reason'; and unless the people at large have some real say in government, the constitution will be liable to change (*Rep.* 2.57).[59] In *On laws*, as mentioned already, Cicero devotes a long section of Book 3 to the tribunate, arguing—although not persuading Quintus and Atticus—that the institution makes for the possibility of more responsible exercise of popular power than would be likely without it (*Leg.* 3.19–26). A wise citizen, he concludes, will regard the tribunate as necessary, even if not optimal, now that the Roman people have got familiar with tribunician power (*Leg.* 3.26). As usual he speaks of Rome: but as usual this is in truth intended as a prescription for all free peoples.

At this point one might begin to harbour the suspicion that Cicero's Rome is rather like the United States of the neoconservatives of the first decade of the present millennium, convinced of the perfection of the American constitution and of the transportability of democracy as the correct political recipe for every country on earth.[60] This is an outlook, one might find oneself reflecting, characteristic of conservative thinkers who belong to the elite of a great imperialistic state with global reach and ambition. There are at least two important differences. First, we should recall Cicero's remark that 'we are giving laws for free peoples' (*Leg.* 3.4). The status of a 'free people' was one with quite a history in the Greek world before the Romans found it a useful instrument of foreign policy. Crucial to it was the guarantee that—whatever the other limitations and insecurities to which 'free' cities might be subject, increasingly so as Roman imperialism became more dominant—they might 'use their ancestral laws', to quote a formulation in Polybius (Polyb. 18.46.5). Sicilian cities like Segesta (Cic. *2 Verr.* 3.13), and Greek cities like Athens or Rhodes (Cic. *Rep.* 1.47), were regarded as privileged on just this account.[61] Even if the principle was often honoured in the breach, it remained the principle. So for Cicero here to be ignoring it—in a work of political philosophy—would be unexpected. Second, we should not forget his constant insistence in *On the commonwealth* and *On laws* alike on the importance of custom and long historical experience in developing and maintaining the structures and institutions of a soundly based *res publica*. We may recall once more his quotation from Ennius in the preface to Book 5 of *On the commonwealth* (*Rep.* 5.1):[62]

On ancient customs and the men of old
Rome's commonwealth stands firm.

Those assets, he went on to propose, are essential prerequisites for founding and achieving stability for a *res publica*. So for Cicero the Roman model should in an important sense not be transportable. Unless other peoples can discover it for themselves and then grow into it organically, as it were, it could not—on his own premisses—be for them.

The universalism of the theory of *On laws* turns out very differently from what one might perhaps have expected from Cicero's appeal early on in Book 1 to the doctrine of the cosmic city: the community of all rational beings, divine or human, wherever they may be located in the cosmos (*Leg.* 1.23). What really interests him is still the *civitas* and *res publica* of *On the commonwealth*, with Rome and its laws and historic customs taken as the paradigm of the best constitution. The universal validity he claims for it as a model is due fundamentally to the difficulty of conceiving of any other type of system which will deliver for a free people the same stability over time as does the finely calibrated and equalized Scipionic constitution.[63] The assumption that that is universally the best system is, nonetheless, importantly underpinned by Stoic theory as mediated by Antiochus: Cicero was not wrong to think that it could supply foundations requisite for the reasonableness of such an assumption.

Two Stoic or Stoicizing theses articulated in Book 1 of *On laws* are what supply the need. These are, first, the thesis that justice is a natural, objective value, rooted in universal moral law—in right reason's basic moral prescriptions and prohibitions (*Leg.* 1.18–23, 35–48); and second, the thesis that human nature is everywhere the same: we are all born for justice, but our evil as well as our admirable tendencies are universally characteristic of humanity too (*Leg.* 1.24–34). Atticus helpfully summarizes as follows the main elements of the case that has been made for this second proposition (*Leg.* 1.35):

> These points have been thoroughly established: first, that we have been equipped and adorned by gifts of the gods, so to speak; secondly, that there is one basis (*ratio*) humans have for living among one other, equal and common to them all;[64] and finally, that all of them are held together by a kind of natural goodwill and kindliness among them, as well as by association in justice (*ius*).

The truth of the first Stoicizing thesis would preclude arguing that, while the Scipionic calibrated system may be suitable for Rome, quite different valid systems might be what better suit other free peoples if they conceive justice differently. The truth of the second would rule out any suggestion that some free peoples have a psychological make-up so different from the Romans that some other governmental system might be more appropriate for them.[65]

That might still look like Stoicism in effect used to legitimize Roman imperialism.[66] But Cicero tempers the recipe by the suggestion of a respect for historical particularity and for political and cultural individuality—as evidenced by his preparedness to endorse exceptionally the participation of women in nocturnal rites in the Eleusinian mysteries (*Leg.* 2.35–6)—that makes him stop short of that.[67] His justification of Roman imperialism, as the next section will demonstrate, runs along rather different lines.

5. Justice and imperialism

There is no doubting that in composing the dialogues we have been looking at, Cicero took very seriously the need to put the case for justice as an objectively valid imperative, with overriding claims upon us as social and political beings. Not only does he give over virtually the whole of the philosophical argument of Book 1 of *On laws* to this project. He decides to devote Book 3 of *On the commonwealth*, the first of the dialogue's two central books, to the topic of justice (the virtue *iustitia*). Whereas in the *Republic* Plato had turned in the middle books to epistemology and the metaphysics of the Form of the Good, Cicero takes up the issues about justice that Thrasymachus and Glaucon raise at the beginning of the Platonic dialogue—as though to suggest that they deserve to remain centre stage in any philosophical enterprise engaging with the foundations of politics.

He stages the discussion as a full-scale debate between Lucius Furius Philus and Gaius Laelius, the latter closest to Scipio of all his friends, before Scipio rounds off proceedings by recurring to the need for the requirement of 'consensus of justice (*ius*)' to be met if there is to be a proper *res publica*. Philus first puts the case for valuing wisdom and pursuit of advantage more highly than justice, and for thinking that it is injustice, not justice, that benefits a commonwealth (he is represented as anxious to make it clear that he advances it *argumenti causa*, not out of conviction: *Rep.* 3.8). In replying, Laelius insists that justice is part of the fabric of the world itself (*Rep.* 3.33),[68] and argues to the contrary that good government cannot be conducted without justice (*iustitia*), the thesis foreshadowed at the end of Book 2 (*Rep.* 2.69). Unfortunately, many leaves of the manuscript text of Book 3 are missing, and restoration of the sequence of those that remain a matter for conjecture and debate. Most of what we know of Laelius's side of the argument we owe to summary in Augustine and extracts quoted by him and other late authors. Much more of Philus' speech survives in the manuscript and also in quotations from it in Lactantius, who thought it a powerful demonstration that in this temporal world injustice does and must prevail.

One thing that may have prompted Cicero to present the issues in this agonistic form is Roman cultural memory of a famous occasion in 155 BC, 25 years before the dramatic date of the conversation of *On the commonwealth*. The Athenians had sent a diplomatic delegation to Rome, led by the heads of probably three of their philosophical schools. What transpired is differently reported in the several ancient sources which purport to inform us. The purpose of the embassy is not seriously in doubt.[69] It was to negotiate a way out of an unpaid fine imposed upon the Athenians for aggression against the border town of Oropos, a political football regularly kicked back and forth in disputes between Athens and Thebes. We are told that the fine ended up very significantly reduced.[70] However most of the sources are more interested in the displays of rhetoric which the philosophers are said to have given, when away from the negotiations.

But their accounts of those performances diverge considerably, both in level of generality and in such specifics as they supply. It seems likely that these descriptions derive ultimately from oral tradition short of hard information. Perhaps the most engaging and the most credible (if palpable embellishments of its basic narrative are ignored) is that by Plutarch, in his life of Cato the Censor, a dominant force in Roman politics and culture at the time of these events. He represents Cato as greatly disturbed by the corrupting influence that the Greek culture exhibited by the envoys, and by Carneades in particular, was likely to exert on Romans of the younger generation, and consequently as having argued in the senate that the issue at dispute should be settled as quickly as possible. Then the visitors could return home forthwith (Plu. *Cat. Mai.* 22).[71]

Cicero in *On the commonwealth* (as conveyed by Lactantius: *Inst.* 5.14.3–5 [= *Rep.* 3.9]) was much more specific about the performance of Carneades, the great Academic sceptic. It was represented as consisting of speeches on successive days, in which Carneades first argued for justice as guiding principle in life, and next day against it (so the reverse of the order in which Scipio's companions are made to speak). As Jonathan Powell has argued, it may well be that this complex scenario (choice of topic for the occasion included) is no more than a fiction, ingeniously designed by Cicero to provide himself with cover—exploiting the Academic sceptics' well known practice of arguing both sides of the case—for starting the discussion with a trenchant critique of morality, and (more specifically) a shameless defence of the immorality of Roman imperialism.[72]

That does not preclude a Carneadean basis for the content of Philus's speech in *On the commonwealth*: Philus is made to say explicitly that 'he will have to say things Carneades used in words [?to argue—the manuscript text breaks off before the verb or an epithet has been supplied] whatever might be expedient' (*Rep.* 3.8).[73] It may well be that suitable argumentative material originating with Carneades was in fact available for such use.[74] Carneades himself, however, never published a word on this or any other subject. What Philus's speech will have contained, I take it, is not really any sort of record of what might have been said in Rome, but Cicero's own elaboration, apparently at length, of some basic Carneadean lines of thought, doubtless as known from a relevant work by the usual source for such arguments, his voluminous pupil Clitomachus.[75]

The gist of what Carneades is alleged to have said is summarized as follows by Lactantius (*Inst.* 5.16.3 [= *Rep.* 3.21a]):

> Humans have ordained laws for themselves with a view to what is useful: varying, of course, to suit different customs, and within the same population often changed to suit changed times. But there is no natural justice (*ius*). Nature guides all—both humans and other living things—to whatever is useful for them. Accordingly there is either no such thing as justice (*iustitia*) or, if there were some such thing, it would be the height of stupidity, since one would only be harming oneself in trying to promote what is advantageous for others.

The first three sentences of this account certainly capture the lines of argument presented in the earlier sections of Philus's speech, as preserved in the manuscript text. He evidently began in a familiar cultural relativist vein, to the effect that variations in law and customs between different peoples (and changes over time in those at force in Rome itself) prove that there is no naturally valid universal principle of justice. Laws invariably reflect the interests of those who make them, which is why the Roman law governing legacies and inheritances for women are to the advantage of men but very unfair to women (*Rep.* 3.17; Cicero's own input is obvious here). After some material on what behaviour is actually natural to us (*Rep.* 3.18–19, 23), the sequence of the further passages that survive from the speech (whether in the manuscript text or elsewhere) is debatable. But they do focus for the most part—as Lactantius's final sentence indicates—on an opposition between justice and wisdom. That opposition seems in fact to have controlled the shape of the entire speech. It is already foreshadowed early in its course (*Rep.* 3.12), and is then introduced in a passage about Rome (again bearing Cicero's own fingerprints) in the cultural relativist section (*Rep.* 3.16).[76]

Lactantius's report itself omits, however, any indication of what was primarily at issue for Cicero, as confirmed by surviving material from the arguments of Philus and Laelius alike and (as we shall see) by Augustine: whether justice is indispensable for the conduct of government by a *res publica*. He does go on to say (referring particularly to Roman rule) that an argument about justice and empire was added as support for the case he ascribes to Carneades (*Inst.* 5.16.4 [= *Rep.* 3.21b]). But Lactantius completes his summary by reproducing in detail arguments dealing with the behaviour of individuals: clearly offered as the star weapons in Carneades' armoury

(*Inst.* 5.16.5–11 [= *Rep.* 3.29–30]). Here is the first of a second pair of examples that he cites:

> It is of course justice (*iustitia*) not to kill another human, and certainly not to lay hold of someone else's property. So what will the just person do, if he happens to be shipwrecked, and if someone physically weaker has seized a plank? Won't he push him off the plank, so as to get on himself, and by using it as support make his getaway—especially since there is no witness in mid-ocean?[77] If he's wise, he will do that. He will have to perish himself if he doesn't. But if he would rather die than lay a hand on another, then that person is just but stupid, given that he would not be sparing his own life while sparing another's.

Lactantius's overall concern in this context is with what counts as wisdom or folly for an individual: the Christian God wants virtue to be hidden in the guise of folly (*Inst.* 5.18.11).[78] For Cicero's Philus and Laelius, however, what matters above all is the *res publica*, and particularly its conduct of empire. The case for injustice developed by Philus may have owed its core theory and its sharpest formulations to Carneades—and, whether through Carneades or not, to arguments for the superior rationality of injustice put by Glaucon at the beginning of Book 2 of Plato's *Republic* (*Rep.* 3.23, 27; cf. Plato *R.* 2.358e–359b, 361a–d). But there seems little doubt that Cicero himself was responsible for what appears to have been its overall political cast. As Jean-Louis Ferrary commented: 'It is Cicero who, with Philus's speech, has written a text of astonishing vehemence against the Romans' pretentions that they were a just people.'[79]

A flavour of this strain in Philus's arguments can be savoured in Lactantius's brief report (*Inst.* 5.16.4 [= 3.21b]):

> All successful imperial peoples—including the Romans themselves, who have gained possession of the entire world—if they should wish to be just (that is to say, return property that belongs to others) would have to go back to living in huts and languishing in want and wretchedness.

In the manuscript text a short passage (*Rep.* 3.24) survives which begins in quite general terms:

> Wisdom orders us to increase our resources, to enlarge our wealth, to extend our boundaries..., to rule over as many people as possible, to enjoy pleasures, to be powerful, to rule, to be masters; but justice instructs us to spare everyone, to look after the interests of the human race, to render to each his own, to keep hands off things that are sacred or public or belong to someone else.

But just before the passage is truncated shortly afterwards, Philus has turned his attention specifically to Rome:

> Our own people, whose history from the beginning Africanus discussed in yesterday's conversation, whose rule now controls the whole world—do you think that it was through justice (*iustitia*) or wisdom that it grew from something tiny to be the greatest of all?[80]

What the Romans impose on others is in fact slavery. In what is quite likely the leaf of the surviving manuscript text closest to the end of Philus's speech, he begins the political application of its argument with the words (*Rep.* 3.28): 'There is no citizen body so stupid that it would not prefer to rule unjustly rather than to be enslaved justly.'[81]

Augustine, the one ancient author we know of to offer an overall summary of the dispute between the positions upheld by Philus and Laelius, confirms the emphasis on slavery. In Book 19 of the *City of God*, he reports as follows (*CD* 19.21 [= 3.36]):

> When the case was argued earlier on the side of injustice against justice and it was said that a commonwealth cannot exist and its affairs be conducted except through injustice, the following was laid down as the strongest support: that it is unjust for humans to be related to humans as those enslaved to masters[82]—yet without pursuing such injustice, no citizen body with imperial ambitions whose public affairs are on a grand scale can exercise empire over its provinces.

This is as naked and brutal version of Realpolitik as can be found anywhere in Thucydides. The force of the argument, as indeed of Philus's whole panoply of arguments, derives not just from its persuasiveness as an account of how agents often at least behave—the agents in this case being states—nor from the evident logic of the claim that, if maximizing advantage is the objective, such behaviour is what wisdom will recommend. It capitalizes, too, on the expectation that the reader will find the objectives and outcomes of the behaviour congenial or even admirable, and likewise the wisdom with which they are pursued and achieved. The Romans did glory in the deliberate acquisition of empire, as Polybius had pointed out a century before Cicero was writing (1.20.1–2; cf. 1.3.6, 1.63.9, 3.2.6, 15.9.2, 31.10.7),[83] and as is clear from Cicero's own public orations that bear on the theme.[84]

They were not shy of describing the imposition of their rule as slavery. In discussion of the threat of subjection to Rome, as the Gallic tribes perceived it, Caesar was quite explicit in explaining that it is human nature 'to desire freedom and hate the condition of slavery' (*BG* 3.10.3); and he makes the Gallic rebel Critognatus describe Roman imperialism in terms very similar to Philus's, when he denounces it for crushing Gaul 'with everlasting slavery' (*BG* 7.77.16), anticipating in spirit Tacitus's ascription to the Briton Calgacus of the notorious *cri de coeur*: 'where they make a desert they call it peace' (*Agr.* 30.5). Cicero, too, in his political oratory and in his correspondence quite often uses the vocabulary of slavery without embarrassment when talking of at least some of the peoples that have fallen under Roman rule.[85]

What Romans might well have found disconcerting, however, is acknowledgement that pursuit of empire so conceived cannot be conducted without injustice—which indeed is no mere acknowledgement, but the whole point of the argument at this point. The brazen frankness of the acknowledgement invests this entire treatment of imperialism with an ambiguity and an unease on which Cicero presumably relies in attempting to alienate the reader from it—the task to be undertaken expressly in the second of the two speeches on the subject that now follows. It is an ambiguity of which the Romans were perfectly well aware. They applauded the imperial project, but they knew that it brought with it all sorts of carnage, cruelty, and exploitation: one of Cicero's own great personal and political successes early in his career had been his successful indictment for extortion of Gaius Verres, governor of Sicily, in a court case of 70 BC. And they were apprehensive of the enormous wealth and personal power acquired through tenure of the extraordinary military commands to which figures like Pompey and Caesar were appointed in the years immediately preceding the writing of these Ciceronian dialogues.

As for the description of the Romans' conduct as actual injustice, there is evidence enough to show that the Romans did take the view that if they were to go to war, that would need ethical justification, even if that might consist only in assuring themselves that they had been wronged or were in imminent danger of being wronged.[86] On a famous occasion Cato the Censor argued successfully on a variety of ethical grounds that reprisals against Rhodes at the end of the third Macedonian war (171–68 BC) should not be pursued.[87] There was also institutional recognition that there were limits on how populations subject to Rome could be treated. The existence of a special extortion court, the *quaestio de repetundis* enabling provincials to sue for recovery of moneys from extortionate Roman officials, acknowledged rights on their side and collective obligations on the part of the Romans. Cicero describes the court as 'patron of the allies and friends of the Roman people' (*Div.Caec.* 65). More generally, as Miriam Griffin says, and as in particular Cicero's speeches and correspondence (not least during his time as a provincial governor) again bear out: 'We need not doubt that there was a Roman code of correct conduct towards enemies and subjects, adherence to which by the government and by individual governors and agents brought praise, and contravention of which brought blame, if not punishment.'[88]

Much less evidence survives of Laelius's reply to Philus in his speech defending the claims of justice. Courtesy of Lactantius, we possess a grandiloquent visionary statement of how one day there will be one law for Rome and for Athens: one unchangeable and everlasting law valid for all peoples and at every time (Lact. *Inst.* 6.8.6–9 [= *Rep.* 3.33]).[89] One thing more pertinent to our present concerns is clear, however: the line Philus had taken on imperialism was tackled head on. We can detect three principal elements in the reply. It looks as though Laelius's first move was to deny that there is always injustice in the subjection of humans to other humans. Augustine continues the report quoted above as follows (*CD* 19.21 [= 3.36]):

The reply on the side of justice was that it [viz. the institution of slavery][90] is just because for such humans [viz. the enslaved] enslavement is advantageous, and is instituted for their advantage, when it is rightly instituted:[91] that is, when the power and opportunity to commit injustices is removed from the wicked, and they will be better off being subjugated because they were worse off unsubjugated. And to bolster this reasoning a noble illustration is added, supplied—as one might say—by nature. It was articulated as follows: 'For why else does God rule over man, the soul over the body, reason over lust and anger and the other vicious parts of that same soul?'

Laelius's next move is preserved by Augustine once more, but in one of his other writings (his tract of AD 421 against the Pelagian bishop Julian). This time Augustine quotes verbatim from Cicero's text rather more extensively. The quotation evidently picks it up just at the point reached at the end of the previous one. For Philus's representation of imperial rule as the subjection of other nations to domination and appropriation of their territory amounting to enslavement, Laelius here substitutes an alternative picture (*Contra Julianum* 4.12.61):

Do we not observe that dominion has been granted by nature itself to everything that is best, to the greatest advantage to what is low-grade? For why else does god rule over man, the mind over the body, reason over appetite and anger and the other flawed parts of that same mind?...But different types of rule and being subject[92] must be recognized. The mind is said to rule over the body, and it is also said to rule over appetite. But it rules the body the way a king rules his citizens or a parent his children, whereas it rules appetite the way a master rules his slaves, in that it restrains and breaks it. The rule of kings and generals and magistrates and senators and peoples presides over citizens and allies in the same way that the mind rules bodies, whereas masters wear out their slaves in the way that the best part of that same mind, i.e. wisdom, wears out the flawed and weak parts, such as appetite, anger, and the other emotions.

In effect Laelius is saying: talk of masters and subjection or enslavement is well enough—but there are masters and masters, and *servire* is not a univocal term. This will be obvious to anyone who thinks about the different senses in which the mind rules over us; and we have to be clear what sort of master we are talking about if we so describe an imperial power. For in social relationships, too, the same kinds of distinction apply as in the case of human psychology.[93] In one category falls the relationship kings, generals, magistrates, senators, and peoples have with those they govern: these are specified as citizens and allies. In other words, rule over the subjects of empire ('allies') is assimilated to government of a citizen body: requiring obedience from the ruled comparable to the body's automatic response to the mind or a child's willing compliance with a parent's command (Augustine, *CD* 14.23 [= 3.37]).[94] Slave ownership is treated as a category entirely separate from that, distinguished from it by its forcible constraint of those of recidivist criminal disposition (*CD* 19.21 [= 3.36). At any rate in the extract quoted by Augustine, Laelius does not explicitly draw the corollary: that enslavement is in fact the wrong way to describe the rule properly exercised by agents in the first category. But his contrast has made the point for him.

Laelius wants us to think of the relation of an imperial power to those it governs as a paternalistic one. His third main point will be that Rome's allies 'need to be governed not because they are wicked or slavish and have to be broken, but because they are weak';[95] and defending them is the way the Romans have gained control over all the earth (*Rep.* 3.35 [from Nonius 498.16]). In other words, historically Roman imperial rule has been exercised with the justice Philus denied, and as government over something much more like citizen communities than slave colonies. The discussion of this theme was apparently the culminating chapter in Laelius's entire speech, and so of the whole debate about justice that Cicero stages in Book 3. It seems to have incorporated an articulation of the notion of a just war. Augustine says (*CD* 22.6 [= *Rep.* 3.34]):

> I know that in the third book (if I am not mistaken) of *On the commonwealth*, Cicero states that no war is undertaken by the best *civitas* except to maintain faith [*fides*; especially with allies][96] or for its own safety.

The point is confirmed by a verbatim report preserved by Isidore (*Etym.* 18.1 [= *Rep.* 3.35]):

> Those wars are unjust which are undertaken without justification. For aside from the justification of taking vengeance or of fighting off enemies there can be no conduct of a just war.

As it so happens, the only section of the speech that is preserved in the manuscript itself contains its concluding words. They constitute an attack on the populist politician Tiberius Gracchus, by now assassinated by another member of the Scipio clan, who is said to have 'neglected the rights and treaties of the allies and the Latins [i.e. the inhabitants of Italy]' (*Rep.* 3.41). Laelius expresses the apprehension that if this attitude becomes more widespread, Roman rule (*imperium*) 'will switch from justice (*ius*) to force (*vis*), so that those who up to now obey us willingly are kept doing so through fear' (ibid.). And he speaks darkly and with foreboding about his associated concerns over the 'immortality of the *res publica*' (ibid.).

These themes are pursued further in Cicero's last philosophical work, the *On duties* of 44 BC, where the nature of those forebodings becomes more explicit. Book 1 contains a section developing the theme of the just war (*Off.* 1.34–40).[97] And in an excursus in Book 2 devoted to Roman imperial behaviour (*Off.* 2.26–9), he looks back to a time when Roman rule was not so much *imperium* as *patrocinium*, a protectorate of the whole world, with magistrates and generals intent on defending and looking after the interests of provinces and allies 'with justice (*aequitas*) and repaying their trust (*fides*)'. Here Cicero exploits a model of the relationship between Rome and its subject peoples that was in its way as important in Roman imperialistic discourse as talk of enslavement.[98] The patron–dependant (*patronus-cliens*) nexus (like the notion of *tutela*, guardianship) seems to have been invoked particularly in rhetoric, for example when Cicero is excoriating the rapacity of a Verres or a Clodius, and in Roman diplomacy, at least as represented in Livy. But that idealizing vision of empire is now retrojected into the past. The rot set in with the dictator Sulla (back in the 80s BC),[99] when foreign peoples started being treated as so many repositories for valuables and real estate, to be sold off to the highest bidder.[100] The process is predictably represented as having gone much further under Julius Caesar's regime. But the interesting feature of the account is Cicero's further claim—and one not without contemporary resonance—that this kleptocratic development is what fuels autocracy and civil war: in other words, the corruption of imperial rule abroad inevitably undermines the *res publica* at home: 'justly are we being punished.'[101]

6. Conclusion

The binary contrast between good times (here effectively exemplifying Laelius's account of the Romans' acquisition of empire) and the bad present (fitting Philus's diagnosis), though a favourite one in the way the Romans told or were to tell their own history, found in Sallust (*Cat.* 6–13) and Livy too (1.9–12), is of course drastically oversimplified. Whatever may be deficient in his treatment of it, the way Cicero makes imperialism a central theme of *On the commonwealth* is nonetheless remarkable. A first indication appears in Scipio's extended discussion of Romulus's choice of location for Rome, which culminates in the suggestion that he seemed to divine that it would some day provide the 'seat and home for a supreme empire' (*Rep.* 2.10). Political philosophy can be apt to devote vast energy to theorizing the internal arrangements desirable for a state or a polity. It has been argued that in our own time the focus on these in Rawls' *A Theory of Justice* had the effect of impoverishing the range of issues, some more urgent, that those who work in the field have been alert to,[102] even if imperialism is now—perhaps belatedly—a topic of growing concern to political theorists.[103]

Readers who come to the political philosophies of Plato and Aristotle after their Thucydides sometimes have similarly disappointed reactions. Cicero wrote within the tradition of Plato and Aristotle, rather than Thucydides. But in the dimensions of his thinking in *On the commonwealth* and *On laws* that we have been looking at in this chapter, his horizons are undoubtedly wider than those that are most visible in theirs.[104] Here the precedent set by

Polybius, explicitly represented as having discussed political philosophy with Scipio (*Rep.* 1.34), may well have been important to the way Cicero approached his undertaking: Polybius had written his world history to explain 'how and by virtue of what sort of political system almost the whole of the known world was conquered and fell under the single rule of the Romans in a space of not quite 53 years' (Polyb. 1.1.5).

What is the relationship between the treatment in Book 3 of *On the commonwealth* of the question of the justice of global imperialism, and the ambition of *On laws*—more cosmopolitan in inspiration and in its Stoic philosophical underpinning—to work out what is effectively a version of Roman societal and constitutional norms which will be valid for all 'free peoples' with realistic aspirations to stability over time? In what survives of these two dialogues Cicero never poses the question.[105]

Notes

1. For a general critical account of Diogenes and early Greek cynicism, see Moles 2000. On his cosmopolitanism, see most recently Chin 2016: 131–4, Paone 2018. Another Greek tradition seems to have attempted to make Socrates the first cosmopolitan, but attributing to him the interestingly different expression *kosmios*, 'universien' (or *mundanus* when Latinized), to express the idea: Cic. *Tusc.* 5.108, Arr. *Epict. diss.* 1.9.1–6, Plu. *De exil.* 600f, with Chin 2016: 137–41.
2. A recently observed 'prodigy' that had been reported in the senate, and was subsequently interpreted as an omen of Scipio's death, which occurred soon after the dialogue's dramatic date, set early in 129 BC: *Rep.* 1.15, *ND* 2.14, with discussion in Zetzel 1995: 111.
3. See Chapter 3, sections 1 and 6 pp. 64, 85–6 above for more on the significance of Laelius's concerns within the dialogue's overall economy and trajectory.
4. But talk of distinction between Platonic and Stoic is often in Cicero's writing and thinking misleading, since much in the relevant passages is designed not as formal exposition of doctrine, but as rhetorical presentation of the common inheritance of philosophy, albeit with Plato often assumed to be its mainspring. See further p. 110 below.
5. Scipio appears to be represented throughout the dialogue, how faithfully to his historical original we cannot know, as the politician, whose attention can be engaged by speculative philosophy only fitfully.

6. Cicero was himself proud of having discovered in Sicily the neglected tomb of Archimedes (so he claimed) while holding the office of quaestor in 75 BC (*Tusc.* 5.64–6).
7. In referring to such patriots (*Rep.* 6.13), he uses again the expression *rector* (director), as well as *conservator* (preserver): see discussion in Chapter 3, section 6 pp. 87–90.
8. He refers back to this passage of *On the commonealth* in *Tusculan Disputations* (where he reproduces his translation with slightly different wording in places); and he gives a précis of Plato's argument in *On old age* (*Sen.* 78). The *Phaedrus* seems to have been a dialogue for which Cicero felt a particular affinity, otherwise most palpably evidenced in his other theoretical writings of the later 50s BC: for *On the orator*, see Mankin 2011: 19–23, and for *On laws*, Dyck 2004: 20–3.
9. There is a pre-echo of this strain of thought about the ultimate focus of a good statesman in Cicero's remarks about Marius in his speech of 63 BC defending Gaius Rabirius against a charge of treason (*Rab. Perd.* 29–30): see Gildenhard 2011: 377–8.
10. Here one catches an echo of the admiration Scipio had expressed for Archimedes' orrery in Book 1 (*Rep.* 1.21–2). In his account of Stoic theology in Book 2 of *On the nature of the gods*, Cicero was to put in the mouth of its proponent (Quintus Lucilius Balbus) one of the most sustained passages of high-flown eloquence that he ever composed, including once more a reference to Archimedes' orrery (*ND* 2.87–119).
11. See Aristotle *On the heaven* 2.9, 290b12–29.
12. See Chapter 5, section 3 pp. 160–1.
13. This passage is preserved not in the manuscript text of *On the commonwealth*, but by the Christian writer Lactantius in his *Divine Institutes* (*Inst.* 6.8.6–9). Lactantius judges it a perfect expression of true teaching, albeit articulated by someone 'far from knowledge of the truth'.
14. This distinction between law and god as its author and interpreter is not Stoic. It may have reached Cicero via his teacher Antiochus, syncretizing the Stoic idea of law with the theology of Plato's *Timaeus* (cf. *Tim.* 41e, with Horsley 1978: 42). The implication that the wicked are inevitably punished by mental torment or insanity is spelled out in more detail in Book 2 of *On laws* (*Leg.* 2.43–4), and constitutes a recurrent theme in the theology exploited in Cicero's oratory, not least in the 50s BC: see Gildenhard 2011: 104–16, 181–90, 322–6.
15. Whether Laelius is therefore being represented by Cicero as a committed Stoic may be doubted. Cicero tells us elsewhere that in his salad days he studied with the Stoic Diogenes of Babylon and later with Panaetius (*Fin.* 2.24; cf. *Fin.* 4.23,

Brut. 101), so it is fair to assume a degree of philosophical interest and competence on his part, even if for rhetorical effect he is credited at one point with acquiring his amiable manner from 'that same study as yours [i.e. the inflexible Stoic Cato's]' (*Mur.* 66). But here his role is to muster the strongest case he can make for justice as a genuinely objective value. When he has completed it, the compliment he receives from Scipio is for his eloquence (*Rep.* 3.42), for which he was indeed particularly famed (*Brut.* 83).

16. For the identification, depending on repetition of the phrase at *Leg.* 1.52, with a similar reference now made explicit, see for example Atkins 2013a: 165–9.
17. For full discussion of the Stoic theory, see Schofield 1991: 57–92, and on Cicero's use of it in *On laws* Asmis 2008: 3–11 (less persuasive speculation follows at Asmis 2008: 11–18). Straumann 2019: 15 n.7 proposes a radically reductionist interpretation of the right reason of the prudent man: as a 'metaphor' for the constitutional framework that he takes to be constituted by natural law—thus editing out the entire theological, metaphysical, and ethical basis of the theory, to which Cicero gives such prominence in both dialogues.
18. See p. 106 above.
19. On the dual citizenship that Italian communities obtained after the Social War of 91–88 BC, see Nicolet 1980: 37–47, Crawford 1992: 191–2, Dyck 2004: 255–60.
20. By the 'wisest' here he very likely has in mind the 'most learned' mentioned at *Leg.* 1.18 and 52 (see p. 109 n.16 above). Julia Annas draws attention to the many ways in which *On laws* exploits Plato's *Laws* both in major features and in the detail of the legislation it proposes (Annas 2013: 206–11, 2017: 169–72); so also Schofield 2017a: 57–60.
21. The importance of Stoicism as resource for moral realism is particularly well made by Annas 2013: 211–17, 2017: 172–80.
22. For fuller discussion of 'the construction of Roman universality', see Moatti 2015: 271–319 (especially 308–17 for Cicero's treatment of the idea in *On laws* and *On duties*), and more generally Edwards and Woolf 2006, Lavan, Payne, and Weisweiler 2016. We will be looking in section 5 at the prominence he gives to questions about the ethical defensibility of Roman imperialism in the discussion of justice in Book 3 of *On the commonwealth*.
23. Atkins 1990: 275, explaining, in the light of his remark that 'our country has on its own embraced all the affections of us all' (*Off.* 1.57), why its prime importance seemed so obvious to Cicero as to require no explicit defence. For the legacy of Republican patriotism in Western political thought, particularly as expressed in those words of Cicero in *On duties*, see Viroli 1995: 18–40.
24. Atkins 1990: 275. Her overall verdict (Atkins 1990: 277) is that with exceptions, such as respect for the laws of warfare, his talk of the society of the human

race is 'little more than empty rhetoric'. See also Griffin 2011: 318–19 [= Griffin 2018: 668–9]. A fuller but not dissimilar discussion: Nussbaum 2000.
25. See also pp. 110–11 and n.22 above.
26. Muddle is what it is often taken to be, as for example by Zetzel 2017a: xxv–vi; Powell 2001:34; Dyck 2004: 114–15, 410–11. Against that view see Annas 2013: 219–22, 2017: 180–6, to which the interpretation proposed here is much indebted.
27. See Chapter 3, section 6 pp. 91–2.
28. It has sometimes been supposed that Book 1 was composed after the rest of the work, and never properly integrated with it: see Dyck 2004: 6, Asmis 2008: 19 n.58.
29. Annas 2017: 185–6.
30. On the Stoic conception of the natural moral law see further Inwood 1999, Vogt 2008: Ch.4, whose interpretation I follow.
31. See Schofield 1991: 69–72, Frede 1994.
32. See Frede 1996.
33. These passages alone suffice to indicate that adherence to true law is what on Cicero's theory is responsible for virtuous behaviour. See also *Leg.* 1.37–52, where he purports to be putting lines of argument to that same effect which sit squarely within the mainstream of Greek ethical thought associated by him (following Antiochus) with the tradition of Plato's Academy and of Aristotle's school (as well as Stoicism). Girardet 1983: 60 and Straumann 2019: 4 downplay or ignore this major strain of thought in *On laws*. According to the former, there should be no expectation that the laws proposed in *On laws* should be oriented towards 'ethical norms'. The latter similarly writes: 'nowhere does Cicero indicate that obedience to his laws will produce ethical outcomes along these virtue-ethical lines.'
34. Cicero never gives a further specification of the relation of his law code to law as right reason. Atkins 2013a: 205–6 supposes that it is not only law itself that is 'modelled' (*expressa*) on nature, but 'particularly human law', comparing *Off.* 3.69 and Platonic paradigmatism. In the relevant passage of *On laws*, however, Cicero says only that properly constructed human laws are 'directed' (*diriguntur*) at nature (*Leg.* 2.13). Asmis proposed that he will have conceived them as specifying what the Stoics would have classified as 'intermediate actions' (Asmis 2008: 16–18, 21–2, 29–31). But although Cicero will invoke that concept in *On duties* (*Off.* 1.8), there is no trace of it in *On laws*.
35. It has sometimes been thought that Plato in his *Laws* envisages at least eventual immutability for the laws he has the Athenian Visitor propose in the dialogue. But while a conservative stance is undoubtedly adopted, as was common in ancient Greek political thinking and practice, the most general and reflective

comment in the *Laws* on the status of a legislator's work envisages that it will inevitably contain deficiencies that successor legislators will need to correct (*Laws* 6.769a–771a). Moreover, the *Laws*' Nocturnal Council is to devote time and energy to deliberating legislative problems—it being noted that 'correction' of laws and customs may be required, following comparative study of other societies (*Laws* 12.951a–952b). The issue is best discussed in Bobonich 2002: 395–408 and Bartels 2017: 152–88.

36. It will turn out that the laws in the third category traditionally in force at Rome are largely those that will be what is needed to populate the second.
37. Atkins 2013a: 207; cf. Annas 2017: 181–2. Later in Book 2 Cicero in effect recognizes that laws may need to be varied to reflect wholesome local tradition. Thus the general rule that women are not to be permitted to perform sacrifices at night is—following discussion with Atticus—to be subject to exception at Athens, to accommodate the Eleusinian mysteries, into which women as well as men were initiated (*Leg.* 2.35–6).
38. See Atkins 2013a: 162–4.
39. So for example Girardet 1983: 81–2, Ferrary 1995: 68–9.
40. See Atkins 2013a: 199–208 for further discussion of the issues at stake.
41. For Plato's conception of a legal proem or prelude, see briefly Schofield and Griffith 2016: 15–18; more fully Bobonich 2002: 96–119.
42. Dyck 2004: 324–5; cf. *ND* 2.71, where Stoic doctrine is being expounded.
43. He makes disapproving mention of the funerary monument of Gaius Figulus (probably the consul of 64 BC of that name), and of the magnificence of funerals and tombs prevalent in contemporary Rome, in contrast with the restraint of former times (*Leg.* 2.62, 66). The historian Keith Hopkins comments: 'My general impression is that rich Romans spent huge amounts of money, relative to the wealth available in their society, in order to create an enduring and ostentatious shelter for their dead' (Hopkins 1983: 206; in more detail Flower 1996: 115–26).
44. For a fuller argument for this conclusion, see Atkins 2017, who compares Cicero's treatment (to his general advantage) with Rousseau's attempt in *Le contrat social* (4.8) to institute a rational civil religion.
45. Dyck 2004: 552–3; cf. e.g. Lintott 1999a: 107–8. It has been suggested that the operation of trials in the civil law courts may have been the subject of the following fourth book (cf. *Leg.* 3.47).
46. Zetzel 2017a: 177 n.45, Fott 2014: 199 n.80, Powell 2006: 264 (even the word 'nature' is very insecurely attested, and its adoption into the text implausible: Dyck 2004: 554). Weight which it cannot therefore bear has sometimes been put on this passage as supporting Girardet's view that the laws of Cicero's code are understood by him as themselves the law of nature (e.g. Ferrary 1995:

COSMOPOLITANISM, IMPERIALISM, AND THE IDEA OF LAW   141

68–70; cf. Girardet 1983: 87–90). But even if the conjectural text were accepted, Cicero would need to be meaning no more than that the laws of the code meet the test of nature as 'the measure of law', despite its appropriation of much Roman law: not that his laws are themselves to be conceived as constituting a body of natural law.

47. Dyck 2004: 426–7.
48. See Barnes 2015, and below sections 4 and 5 pp. 123–5, 134 .
49. See Chapter 3, section 6 pp. 92–3.
50. See Chapter 6, section 4 p. 208.
51. On the first appearance of the idea of *ius naturae* in Cicero's surviving writings, it is characterized as at once inborn natural urge and (as the examples subsequently given indicate) moral imperative: 'something prompted by a sort of innate impulse (*vis*)'—with religion (*religio*), defined as the 'fear and awe of the gods', interestingly given as the first example (*Inv.* 2.65). None of the other examples gets anywhere close to magistrates or their *imperium*.
52. Straumann 2016: 45 (cf. 181). But this is not (as Straumann suggests) because they are not subject to the limitations of positive law, but because they have no intrinsic moral content.
53. *Contra* Straumann 2016: 45–6.
54. See further section 4 p. 122 and n.56, 123 with n.58 below.
55. A precept familiar in Greek political thought: see Dyck 2004: 435–6 for relevant passages, e.g. Arist. *Pol.* 3.4, 1277b11–13, 7.14, 1333a2–3.
56. Here we may recall Scipio's sketch of the aims proper to the 'calibrator' of the *res publica* (*Rep.* 5.8): see Chapter 3, section 2 p. 66. Atkins 2013a: 202–4 suggests that the account of the rationale for the invention of laws at *Leg.* 2.11 is understood by Cicero to be derived from and an application of Stoic natural law. But Cicero makes no such claim, nor is it obvious how law's ethical function of prescribing right action and forbidding crime could entail the political agenda he sees as the principal task of human legislation, even if moral law imposes a constraint on any laws governing the behaviour of individual citizens.
57. See Chapter 3, section 4 pp. 76–8.
58. See above, section 3 p. 121. In its focus on flexible judgement, Cicero's notion of political wisdom, well discussed by Ferrary 1995, resembles Aristotle's concept of practical wisdom, but even more strikingly the statesman's political knowledge in Plato's *Statesman*, in his ability to grasp the right moment (*kairos*) in the flux of events: on which see Lane 1998: 132–6, 143–6.
59. What reason would indicate is that those best equipped to exercise *consilium* should be those who guide the *res publica* (see Chapter 3, section 4 pp. 77–8; also on *Rep.* 2.57 Zetzel 1995: 213–14, and on its broader significance Atkins 2013a:

47–79, 96–119). Scipio's thought here is not dissimilar from the view expressed in Book 6 of Plato's *Laws* (*Leg.* 6.757d–758a), a passage Cicero may very well have had in mind, of the need to introduce the lot as a concession to the democratic idea of equality.

60. Rawson 1973: 343 observed in this context: 'The Romans had a tendency to suppose their patterns would fit anywhere: Pompey for one had recently imposed very Roman constitutions in Bithynia and elsewhere.'

61. For discussion of *civitates liberae* see Badian 1958: 33–54, 69–115; Sherwin-White 1973: 174–89; Lintott 1993: 36–40. We should also note Roman policy towards the local autonomy of Italian communities granted Roman citizenship after the Social War of 91–88 BC, which avoided interference in their political institutions or legal systems.

62. See Chapter 3, section 5 pp. 84–5.

63. For further exploration of a similar understanding of the universalism of *On laws*, see Moatti 2015: 315–19.

64. At *Leg.* 1.28–32 it has been argued that our evil as well as our admirable tendencies are universally characteristic of humanity: we share one and the same human nature.

65. We might note the contrast with Aristotle, who did hold that some populations (he specifies Asians) were psychologically apt for slavery, and so deserving of its imposition particularly through naval raiding by a power superior in intellectual and emotional capacity (*Pol.* 1.8, 1256b23–6, 7.6, 1327a41–b3, 1327b27–9).

66. Cf. Pagden 1995: 19–20, which makes an argument of this kind (although without reference specifically to *On laws*), expanded in Pagden 2000: 3–6, an article responding to Nussbaum 1997. Pagden's more recent article concludes with a discussion of Kant: as espousing a Stoic cosmopolitanism, which, while not imperialistic, is deeply imbued with a notion of a single true Kultur, and which in its implicit Eurocentricity cannot be 'detached from the history of European civilization' (Pagden 2000: 20).

67. See pp. 140 n.37 above. In this respect Cicero is more like the Kant presented—along with other anti-imperialist thinkers of the Enlightenment—in Muthu 2003, whose final theoretical chapter, conjuring with the possibilities for combining moral universalism with recognition of the ineluctability of cultural difference, is of special relevance for evaluating Cicero's stance in *On laws*.

68. See section 1, pp. 108–9 above.

69. But at the time he was composing *On the commonwealth*, Cicero may well have been unaware of it, since a letter of March 45 BC indicates that he still knew very

little of what prompted it, other than it may have involved Oropus (*Att.* 12.23.2).
70. For the reduction of the fine, see Paus. 7.11.5, with *Acad. Ind. Herc.* col.22.33–5 (lacunose: but '500 to 100' talents looks secure enough).
71. For full discussion of the evidence, see Powell 2013.
72. Plutarch makes no mention of a pair of orations nor of Carneades' topic. The other writer besides Lactantius who does so is Quintilian (*Inst.* 12.1.35). He like Lactantius evidently depends on Cicero.
73. Lactantius says that 'the whole speech' is Carneades' (*Inst.* 5.17.14). It seems unlikely that in Laelius's speech, on the other hand, arguments originating with Carneades were used. In Ciceronian sceptical dialogues of 45–4 BC, such as the *Academic books*, *On the nature of the gods*, and *On divination*, all cast in the same format of *pro* and *contra* argument, Carneades' name is consistently associated only with demolition of positive philosophical positions—in those contexts, usually Stoic.
74. There are two specific arguments in Philus's speech with which Carneades is credibly, and as most scholars think reliably, credited by Lactantius (*Inst.* 5.16.5–11 [= *Rep.* 3.29–30]): see below pp. 128–9.
75. So Ferrary 1988: 359–63.
76. The likely structure of later parts of Philus's speech remains uncertain, despite much discussion: see for example Ferrary 1977, Büchner 1984: 281–9, Powell 2006: ix–xi, Zetzel 2017c. Ferrary's treatment (largely echoed in Zetzel's) is perhaps the most penetrating, and his reconstruction is followed here.
77. The highlighting of the absence of witnesses suggests that this, like the other examples Lactantius instances here (cf. also *Fin.* 2.59), is conceived as refutation of the Epicurean argument (cited at *Rep.* 3.26; cf. Diog. Laert. 10.151)) that we should be just, not because justice is intrinsically good, but because of the fear that we can never be sure injustice will not be detected and punished. See Zetzel 2017c: 306–8.
78. So Zetzel 2017c: 312.
79. Ferrary 1988: 362.
80. The words 'grew...to be the greatest' (*maximus factus*) are supplied by editors.
81. He then refers—albeit not altogether pertinently—to incidents relating to the Romans' recent conflicts with Numantia (in northern Spain), which Scipio ended up destroying in 133 BC (cf. *Rep.* 1.17).
82. This is one of the rare instances in Greek and Roman texts where the very institution of slavery is regarded as unjust without qualification: Schofield 2017b: 115 n.10.

83. See Harris 1979: 107–17. For a more recent discussion of the interpretation of Roman imperial expansion under the Republic, see Eckstein 2007; and for sweeping new overviews Potter 2019, Scheidel 2019: 51–88.
84. Examples are too numerous to cite, but see Brunt 1978: 162–4. As he observes: 'Both Pompey and Caesar are lauded for making its [i.e. Rome's] boundaries coterminous with the *orbis terrarum*', listing for instance *Cat.* 3.26, *Sest.* 67, *Prov. Cons.* 30, 33, *Balb.* 64. According to Anchises in Virgil's *Aeneid*, Rome's imperial mission should and would be 'to impose the habit of peace, to spare those brought under subjection, and to inflict defeat in war on the arrogant' (*Aen.* 6.852–3).
85. See Lavan 2013: 82, 93–4, citing *Flac.* 6, *Q Fr.* 1.1.16, *Cat.* 4.22, *Verr.* 2.4.134.
86. See Riggsby 2006: 157–90. See below pp. 133–4 on the articulation of the idea of the just war in Laelius's reply to Philus.
87. See for example Riggsby 2006: 168–70.
88. Griffin 2008: 88 [= Griffin 2018: 264].
89. See above, pp. 108–9.
90. It is often assumed that the reference is rather to imperial rule over provinces, which Augustine's report of Philus's argument had just mentioned (so e.g. Ferrary 1988: 370–1; Pagden 1995: 20–2; Garnsey 1996: 38–41; Lavan 2013: 115–18). But the sequel shows that Laelius's reply began with much more general considerations about the nature of rule.
91. Augustine initially makes it sound as though Laelius was represented as claiming that all enslavement (or all the enslavement he has in mind) is advantageous. But as his report continues, it becomes clear that he held that it is advantageous—for both society at large and slaves themselves—only if it is rightly instituted.
92. The word translated 'being subject' is *servire*: translated as 'be enslaved' above in Augustine's report of Philus's argument. That is indeed the core meaning of the verb (see Lavan 2013: 75–80); but as Lavan notes (quoting the present passage, but referring to many other instances), it can be given the more general connotation of 'being subject', 'notably in the opposition between *servire* and *imperare* ("rule") that is so common in Roman discourse' (ibid. 78).
93. Cicero is adapting the Aristotelian theory of natural slavery, available to us and perhaps to him too at chapter 5 of Book 1 of the *Politics*, a work however nowhere mentioned in his surviving writings. He may have known it from the now lost *On Justice*, but more likely from an intermediary Peripatetic author such as Dicaearchus.
94. This has been taken to be a view of government that indicates 'un extraordinaire autoritarisme': Dumont 1983: 127. But *imperium* (the exercise of

executive power) is only one element in *On the commonwealth*'s highly participatory conception of good government: when it is exercised in a well-ordered political system, there is every reason for those subject to *imperium* to give it unquestioning even if not always uncomplaining assent (compare our own compliance with the law of the land).

95. So Atkins 2000: 495, whose interpretation I am following. The best alternative way of handling Augustine's evidence might be to suppose that Laelius distinguished between Roman rule over its allies (*socii*), as comparable with rule over citizens, and its control of its provinces (*provinciae*), as indeed a form of enslavement (so, for example, Ferrary 1988: 370–1, 376–7; Lavan 2013: 115–18). Certainly that kind of distinction between two sorts of imperial subjects is found elsewhere in Cicero: e.g. *Cat.* 4.22, *Verr.* 2.4.134 (cf. Lavan 2013: 93–5, 165–6). But nothing in the evidence for Laelius's speech suggests that he made any such distinction there; and when Cicero returns to the topic in *On duties* it is signally absent (see below). See further Schofield 2017b.
96. For talk of *fides* as the mark of the patron-client relationship Roman writers associate with the city's relation with her allies, see Lavan 2013: 186–90, 192–3, 200, 202–3.
97. See Barnes 2015.
98. For discussion see Lavan 2013: 176–210; on a Renaissance echo Woodhouse 2018.
99. Sallust—probably writing a little before or a little after Cicero—agreed: *Cat.* 11.4–7. It seems not unlikely that both authors reflect a view widely shared among the Roman elite of the time. It was notoriously and influentially echoed by Machiavelli (*Discorsi* 3.24): Armitage 2002.
100. But there is much evidence of Rome's unscrupulousness in its treatment of its friends as well as its enemies going back particularly in the second century BC. See Lintott 1972: 635–8, who concludes (ibid. 637): 'It was as often because of policy as through personal unscrupulousness that *fides* was disregarded.'
101. For discussion of the causal connection Romans of the late Republic saw between abuse of power abroad and corruption at home, see Lintott 1972, Griffin 2008: 99–109 [= Griffin 2018: 271–6]. The diagnosis has been echoed *mutatis mutandis* throughout the annals of debate about European imperialism (Bell 2011: 892): 'The European empires were hollowed out from within, and ultimately the costs—human, moral, geopolitical and financial—of sustaining them proved too much to bear, precipitating withdrawal, retreat, and often the reshaping of the imperial polities themselves. Albeit in modern form, the curse of the Romans returned to haunt their distant heirs.'

102. See for example Geuss 2005: 29–39.
103. See for example the collection edited by Sankar Muthu, especially the wide-ranging literature survey by Jennifer Pitts (Muthu 2012: 351–87).
104. Not that it would be true to say of either Plato or Aristotle that they wrote nothing of interest on imperialism. For example, on Plato's Atlantis, see Vidal-Naquet 1986, and on Aristotle's critique of Sparta, see Schofield 2018.
105. On the topics covered in his chapter, compare Atkins 2018: 160–91.

5

Republican Virtues

1. Civic virtue

The republican tradition always set a high premium on the cultivation of civic virtue. And as Quentin Skinner and others have shown, a powerful motor for the development of this mindset was absorption of the model of Republican Rome and the writings of its great republican authors—Cicero, Sallust, Livy. Not that it was thought that these Roman writers always got things right. At any rate Machiavelli begins Book 2 of the *Discorsi* with a critique of what he takes to be Livy's view (as well as Plutarch's) that Rome's acquisition of empire was due more to fortune than to virtue (cf. *The Prince* ch.25). Variants of the critique recur frequently in his pages. Machiavelli likes to appeal to heroic exemplars of the importance of virtue, rather than fortune, such as Camillus (to take just one instance: *Discorsi* 3.23, 31), 'second founder of Rome' (Plut. *Cam.* 1.1). He might have found Cicero's eulogy of Pompey a bit more to his taste than in this regard his reading of Livy. In a speech of 56 BC Cicero praised Pompey as a unique figure whose 'supreme good fortune so contested with supreme virtue that, in the opinion of all, more credit was due to the human being that he was than to the goddess [i.e. to Fortune]', as a preface to detailed itemization of his virtues at some length (*Balb.* 9–10).[1] Presumably the emphasis on virtue in the tradition that Cicero himself inherited was any way more or less inevitable. Sustaining a republican commonwealth requires the active participation of citizens, and of citizens so shaped in character as to be fiercely independent, yet restrained in what they think it reasonable to want for themselves, and imbued with a proper regard for each others' interests; able moreover to trust and cooperate with each other—to rely on each others' reliability; able, too, if elected to office to exercise good judgement on behalf of the commonwealth.

In short, citizens of a republic and their leaders will need something like the virtues prominent in a wide range of Ciceronian texts—the oratory, the letters, the philosophy—and not least in *On duties*, the main focus of this chapter. Philip Pettit comes to similar conclusions in spelling out the logic of his contemporary version of republicanism. He writes:[2]

> The laws that advance the aims of the republic, institutionalize its forms, and establish its regulatory controls need to be supported by republican civic norms— . . . by widespread civic virtue, by widespread civility—if they are to have any chance of being effective; the legal republic needs to become a civic reality.

And he goes on:[3]

> The achievement of widespread civility is equivalent to the achievement of a pattern of widespread personal trust— . . . supported by a belief in civility, of confident mutual reliance—and it means the establishment of a flourishing civil society.

In the authorial preface to *On the commonwealth*, Cicero for his part emphasizes the importance of the practice of virtue, especially in government. This is the claim he makes for it, early in the surviving text[4] (*Rep.* 1.2):

> Philosophers have nothing to say (at least nothing that may be said appropriately and honourably) which has not been brought into being and firmly established by those who drew up laws for citizen bodies. Where do piety and religion come from? Or the law, whether international or what we call our civil law?[5] Or justice (*iustitia*), good faith (*fides*), fairness (*aequitas*)? Or sense of propriety (*pudor*), restraint (*continentia*), avoidance of what brings disgrace, pursuit of praise and what is honourable? Or fortitude in hardship and danger? Why, from those who have firmly established some of them in custom and ordained others in law, given that they will have been inculcated by training.

The legislator, or as Cicero puts it shortly, the 'citizen who compels all by formal authority (*imperium*) and legal sanction (*poena*)' (*Rep.* 1.3), evidently exhibits virtue not least in requiring virtues of the other citizens.

At first sight the listing given of these virtues may look as though it resembles Greek philosophy's identification of justice, temperance (*sôphrosunê*), and courage as three of a canonical quartet; as for the fourth—wisdom, *sapientia*—those who 'govern cities by their counsel (*consilium*) and authority (*auctoritas*)' are subsequently said to have attained a superiority far outshining philosophers who have no experience of public business (*Rep.* 1.3).[6] But such mapping against the Greek quartet does not quite work. Thus in an important passage at the beginning of the *Tusculan Disputations* of 45 BC (*Tusc.* 1.2), Cicero reckons *fides* (good faith, loyalty) to be a specially Roman virtue, here reflecting the huge importance Romans attached to it in social and political relationships.[7] Certainly no Greek equivalent figures in Greek philosophers' discussions of justice. Again, sense of propriety, avoidance of disgrace, and pursuit of praise are all most readily construed as dispositions of what Plato took to be the spirited element in the psyche, which he suggested were typically associated with courage (*R.* 4.442b–c).[8] While restraint might in other contexts suggest temperance's inhibition of the appetites, it seems more likely that Cicero is here likewise thinking in the first instance of control of the emotions. Shame, as the sense of the imperative not to let oneself down primarily in the eyes of others (cf. Caes. *BCiv.* 1.67.4), is conceivably placed first in this group of virtues not only for stylistic reasons, but as a more generic disposition that motivates the next two, with the final item its positive motivational counterpart (cf. *Fam.* 5.16.4, where *pudor* stands at the head of a list of uniformly generic attributes and accomplishments).[9]

We do better to consider the function of this specification of virtues in its context. Clearly they are precisely those especially important for sustaining a political community against disruption of various sorts and from various sources—and for that reason a prime concern of the legislator. But they are not the only virtues Cicero sees as socially or politically crucial. The longest section of Book 1 of *On duties* (44 BC), itself his most extended surviving theoretical treatment of the virtues, is devoted to what he calls *decorum*: the salient feature of the disposition needed to ensure that our social behaviour both is and looks fitting. Elsewhere he introduces frequent talk of other mostly less intrinsically other-directed qualities, such as *gravitas* (moral weight, as well as 'gravity in the modern sense of the word, dignity, natural composure', as exhibited by someone of appropriate status, experience, achievement, and authority)[10] and *constantia* (constancy, steadfast reliability). These too he evidently takes to be pre-eminent personal attributes required to make 'Rome's commonwealth stand firm' (*Rep.* 5.1).

Readers familiar with Aristotle's *Politics*, and his discussion of the relationship between 'good citizen' and 'good man', might wonder whether Cicero ever makes a similar contrast. That kind of philosophical puzzle was not Cicero's métier. No such distinction is discussed in his pages. Nor was either concept a guiding principle or major ingredient in the configuration of his ethical thought, even if in his letters and his oratory the political groupings he regards as properly public spirited are regularly called the *boni*: 'the good', 'the sound people'.¹¹ At two points in *On duties* the good citizen (as so described) does, however, receive specific comment. The private individual should live on terms of 'fair (*aequo*) and equal (*pari*) rights' with the citizens and behave with civility, and he should want what is peaceable and honourable in public affairs: that is what we mean by talking of a 'good citizen' (*Off.* 1.124). This formulation is echoed but appropriately adapted to fit the statesman, in a subsequent description of the good citizen's reason and wisdom in 'not prizing apart the interests of citizens, but through fairness (*aequitas*) holding everyone together' (*Off.* 2.83). Part of the point here is that the truly great statesman will remember that he exercises his responsibilities as a citizen among citizens in a citizen body (*civitas*) (cf. QFr. 3.5.1).¹²

As for characterizing the good man as such, Cicero is well aware that the Stoics would count as good only human beings who have attained perfect wisdom. But both in *On duties* and in *Laelius*, his dialogue on friendship, written a little earlier in the same year, he makes it clear that he wants to work himself with a less demanding standard, which will recognize as good those who are ordinarily reckoned to be so 'in experience and common life' (*Lael.* 18; cf. *Off.* 3.13–17). He goes on to list the attributes to be expected of such a person. He proposes *fides* (trustworthiness), *integritas* (uprightness), *aequitas* (fairness), *liberalitas* (generosity); then freedom from *cupiditas* (greed), *libido* (lust), *audacia* (shamelessness); and great *constantia* (constancy). Such people we should consider deserving of being called 'good men', as they have been held to be (*Lael.* 19). They sound just the sort of people that Cicero's legislator would want as his citizens, although their attributes are not predicated specifically of citizenship.

When he makes his first mentions of the good man in *On duties*, where he is working explicitly within the framework of four cardinal virtues (*Off.* 1.11–17), Cicero sticks to just two of them—initially justice (*Off.* 1.31), and then temperance too—as those that 'seem more [than the impetuosity of courage] to attach themselves' to such a person, if we are thinking of someone who has not achieved the perfection of Stoic wisdom (*Off.* 1.46). He has quite a bit more to say about our everyday notion (*notio*) of a good man in Book 3, where he is not taking as his model any specific Stoic treatise as he does in Books 1 and 2. Here is where he tackles problem cases involving conflicting—or apparently conflicting—values. In the course of his discussion he draws *inter alia* on the pronouncements of Roman jurists who had put a concept of the good man to active use in developing principles of equity (*Off.* 3.68–82).[13] His own first shot is to say that the good man is someone 'who benefits everyone he can, while harming nobody unless provoked by injustice' (*Off.* 3.76)—in other words, an exemplar of justice and its twin virtue beneficence, as they have been characterized in Book 1 (*Off.* 1.20–60). Subsequently he mentions that Gaius Fimbria (consul in 104 BC), when sitting in court as judge, described a person who performs 'innumerable obligations and praiseworthy deeds' as fitting the idea of a good man (*Off.* 3.77). Cicero suggests that such a person would never dream of even thinking of doing something that he would not dare to own up to openly (*Off.* 3.77; cf. 3.81)—a standard reflecting the equitable principle of behaving in 'good faith' (*bona fides*) in disputes over legally binding contracts: that 'between good men there should be good dealing without deceit' (*Off.* 3.70).[14]

As this evidence from the arena of the law confirms, the Romans had recognized the need for civic virtue well before Cicero appropriated Greek philosophical theory in his own exploration of the topic in *On duties*.[15] Classical Latin in due course developed a rich and wide-ranging virtue vocabulary, whose shape and content in Cicero alone it would be difficult even to summarize in the space of a single chapter. So what follows is perforce very selective, and in Ciceronian spirit focuses mainly on some of his listings or groupings of virtues. Section 2 considers some of the principal constellations of virtues that Cicero identifies mostly in letters and speeches as particularly important for the health of the Roman *res publica*. Where the virtues are concerned, he gravitates, consistently if not invariably, to lists rather than to analysis. Section 3 is however devoted to the more theoretically based exploration of the virtues in *On duties*, and more particularly to justice, the social virtue par excellence. It has something to say about the relationship we should see between its approach to virtue and the configurations of qualities we meet in other texts. Section 4 presents observations on *magnitudo animi*, greatness of spirit, which as well as performing a starring role in *On duties* figures interestingly at various junctures in Cicero's oratory. Section 5 turns to *verecundia*, respect or considerateness, which Cicero evidently sees as crucial for preserving proper civility in a *res publica*. Section 6 offers a brief coda to the chapter.

2. Roman virtues

Cicero's preface to his *Tusculan Disputations* proposes a list of distinctively Roman virtues. This was a work by which he set particular store, to judge from the catalogue of his writings on philosophy and rhetoric that he prefaced to the second book of his *On divination* (which seems to have been composed or at any rate completed just after Caesar's assassination in March 44).[16] He gives a fuller account of its contents than for those of any other composition he mentions, and makes higher claims for it, too. Its five books are advertised as attempting nothing less than to 'explain the key prerequisites of a happy life', with the fifth covering 'the subject which sheds more light than any other on the whole of philosophy', and teaching 'that virtue is sufficient on its own for a happy life' (*Div.* 2.2). The prefaces to each of the five books develop eloquent variations on the nature of philosophy itself and its ethical importance. At the very outset Cicero makes it clear that his distinctive mission in them will be to supply something that has so far been lacking: philosophy written for Romans in a style adequate for the purpose, something he claims never to have been adequately achieved before (*Tusc.* 1.3–6).

The point is conveyed the more forcefully by the contrast with the Romans' great achievements in other spheres, on which he has expatiated in the two opening paragraphs (*Tusc.* 1.1–2). The implication is that there can be no intrinsic reason why they may not surpass the Greeks in philosophy, too, as well as in other key facets of life. The greater wisdom (*sapientia*) of the Romans in general, accordingly, is what Cicero begins with. It is illustrated first by the superiority of their mores, their conventions governing life, and their family and household arrangements, then by the superior laws and practices by which public affairs are regulated. In war they have excelled in *virtus* (here prowess or courage), but still more through better training (*disciplina*). The emphasis here is throughout on social acculturation.

Cicero goes on, however, to talk of something else: the Romans' natural advantages. It was superior natural endowment which enabled their ancestors to attain *gravitas, constantia, magnitudo animi, probitas,* and *fides*—and indeed outstanding *virtus* (now to be understood generically as moral excellence) of every kind.[17] The terms *gravitas, constantia,* and *magnitudo animi* carry no overt social implications. But that is not true of *probitas,* uprightness, which Cicero typically ascribes to those scrupulous in performing the commitments to others that they have undertaken.[18] Nor is it true of *fides*, the one attribute appearing on the list of virtues in *On the commonwealth* also: where it is associated particularly with justice, of course, as also in *On duties*.[19]

The list of virtues in the opening section of *Tusculan Disputations* is indeed strikingly different from those itemized at the beginning of *On the commonwealth*.[20] That is hardly surprising, given the quite distinct motivations for their construction. In *On the commonwealth* Cicero is arguing in general terms that it is legislators, rather than philosophers, who have laid the foundations of civic life, including the framework for the development of social virtues. The references at the start to piety and religion and to civil law carry particular Roman resonances, and the subsequent selection and description of the virtues are calculated to appeal to the self-image that would be cherished by his Roman readership. Nonetheless the argument itself remains general, applicable to any and every properly civilized society.

In *Tusculan Disputations* the explicit focus of Cicero's list, by contrast, is on the natural endowment that made the Romans of old special—and as he claims, surpassing any other people in every kind of virtue. When he claims that the virtues he singles out here were natural to them, he could be assuming, as Plato makes the priestess Diotima suppose in the *Symposium*, a special natural potential for virtue in some individuals—and then claiming that this is particularly prevalent among Romans (*Symp.* 209b).[21] Or perhaps he might be taken as meaning that Roman social acculturation was so strongly based and so effective that the relevant tendencies in all human nature seemed to develop and predominate naturally. In any event, it is not that the Roman virtues could be found only at Rome. It is rather that nowhere else have they flowered so strikingly and so consistently—like a natural growth in the right soil and environmental conditions.

Cicero's insistence on their natural development among Romans can be illustrated from some of his other writings. In *On behalf of Sestius* (56 BC), his most explicit political manifesto, and a speech studded with laudatory references to supporters of the republican cause who all helped his own return from exile, he couches those references in terms of various permutations of these particular virtue words. He goes so far as to claim that Rome is the actual birthplace of *gravitas* and *magnitudo animi* (*Sest.* 141). The suggestion that for Romans such qualities are a natural endowment is one made particularly strongly with respect to Cato. In *On behalf of Murena* (63 BC) Cicero includes one famous passage that purports to address Cato directly, as advocate for the prosecution. Before tearing into his adoption of Stoic casuistries, he pays him this tribute (*Mur.* 60): 'Nature herself has moulded you into nobility (*honestas*), *gravitas*, restraint, greatness of spirit, justice—in short in every field of virtue a person of towering stature.' And in *On duties* nearly twenty years later he will write of Cato (*Off.* 1.112; cf. 1.125): 'Nature had endowed him with unbelievable *gravitas*, and he had himself reinforced it with unswerving constancy (*constantia*), and always stuck to the purposes he had conceived and undertaken: so rather than having to look upon the countenance of the tyrant, death was the imperative.'[22] No doubt Cato was indeed born that way. But he himself would have seen it as required for living a good life as Stoicism had defined it. As Cicero has him put it in the exposition of the Stoic conception of the goal of life in Book 3 of *On moral ends*: 'choice constant (*constans*) and in agreement with nature' (*Fin.* 3.20).[23] The account of the virtues presented in Book 1 of *On duties*, following the Stoic Panaetius, makes constancy or consistency a hallmark of the fourth virtue, the home of *decorum*, the 'fitting' character of behaviour (*Off.* 1.14).[24]

After republican forces were defeated at the final battle of the civil war at Thapsus (in modern Tunisia) in April that year, Cato as their commander committed a famous Stoic suicide, rather than receive a pardon from Caesar.[25] Writing to Atticus soon after news of it reached Rome, Cicero comments on the difficulty he has been having in writing the (now lost) eulogy he started to compose, apparently at Brutus's instance (*Att.* 12.4.2; cf. *Orat.* 35, *Fam.* 6.7.5, *Att.* 12.40.1, 13.27.1, *Div.* 2.3):

> But with the *Cato* it is like trying to square a circle. I don't manage to write anything that your dinner-companions could read with pleasure, or at least without losing their temper. Even if I were to leave aside his votes in the senate, his whole attitude towards politics and his public counsels, and simply wish to praise his grave dignity (*gravitas*) and unswerving consistency (*constantia*), this alone would still be hateful to their ears.

Why would Caesarians like Aulus Hirtius and Gaius Vibius Pansa with whom Atticus liked to socialize have been so irritated by any references Cicero might have made to Cato's *gravitas* and *constantia*?

Conceivably it was in part a matter of class and of taste, intellectual and otherwise. Unlike the blue-blooded Cato, both these Caesarians were men of relatively humble origin; Pansa at least was Epicurean in philosophy, and Hirtius reputedly an epicure.[26] Perhaps such craggy superior virtues as *gravitas* and *constantia* were not for them. Moreover, Cicero often talked as though these attributes were the exclusive property of the optimate senators with whose conservative politics he himself—outsider that he was—increasingly identified. In his late dialogue *Laelius* on friendship (44 BC), for example, he says that even the ordinary person listening to a political harangue can tell the difference between a populist orator—an ingratiating, lightweight citizen—and one who is steadfast (*constans*) and sincere (*verus*) and dignified (*gravis*) (*Lael.* 95). At the beginning of the fifth *Philippic* he waxes lyrical over how much courage, *constantia*, and *gravitas* there is in the deliberations (*consilia*) of 'this order of ours' (*Phil.* 5.2).

Yet Cicero does not want this vocabulary to come across as narrow class or party talk. Hence the accents of regret in his comment on how it would be received by the likes of Hirtius and Pansa. Gaius Matius was also a Caesarian, and close in Caesar's counsels, although not a member of the senatorial class, and not someone who had pursued a political career. He had evidently been upset by rumours of criticisms made of him in the months after the Ides of March by Cicero, who writes to him in the summer of 44 BC trying to disabuse him and restore good relations.[27] Cicero tells his old friend of the qualities he most values in him (*Fam.* 11.27.6):

Everything about you appeals to me, but your most notable characteristics attract me most: loyalty in friendship (*fides in amicitia*), judgement (*consilium*), grave dignity (*gravitas*), steadfastness (*constantia*) on the one hand, charm (*lepos*), humanity (*humanitas*), your accomplishment in literature (*litterae*) on the other.

Telling Matius that he appreciates above all his signal *gravitas* and *constantia* is saying simultaneously: you are one of us, and your Roman virtues transcend any party divisions. More than that: he is telling him that in combining such virtues with charm and humanity he achieves something like human perfection. Praise of the difficult marriage of *gravitas* and *humanitas* is something that is intended to indicate Cicero's highest regard. It is accorded to Atticus (*Leg.* 3.1); and in *On behalf of Murena* he ends up remarking that, if Cato could sprinkle the affability (*comitas*) and approachability (*facilitas*) of his great ancestor Cato the Censor on his own gravity and severity, his excellent qualities would not be improved, but they would certainly be more agreeably seasoned (*Mur.* 66).[28]

Cicero's Roman virtues recur constantly in his political rhetoric at most stages of his career. The coupling of *gravitas* and *constantia*, heading the

Tusculan Disputations list, is particularly striking in its ubiquity. These qualities are very far from unique to Cato, even if in him they were perceived as present in exceptional strength. The forensic speeches from the very outset are littered with references to them in Cicero's frequent plaudits of his contemporaries. The early speech (quite how early is disputed) on behalf of the actor Q. Roscius says of one C. Cluvius (*Q Rosc.* 7): 'What sort of a person is he? Lightweight? No one of more dignified substance. Fickle? No one more steadfast.' (*quem hominem? levem? immo gravissimum. mobilem? immo constantissimum.*) Among the praises Cicero heaps on his provincial client in the peroration to *On behalf of Cluentius*, composed and delivered in 66 BC, ancestral Roman virtues are emphasized (*Clu.* 196): 'His regard for the distinction of his family, and for the ancestral position he has inherited from them, is such that it is ancestral dignity (*gravitas*) and steadfastness (*constantia*), kindness (*gratia*) and generosity (*liberalitas*) that he practices.' In more politically charged speeches of 56 BC, not long after his return from political exile, he makes a tribute to M. Bibulus, consul in 59 BC, when he resisted Caesar's legislative proposals, in the following terms (*Dom.* 39): 'Here today is a man of exceptional courage (*virtus*), steadfastness, dignity.'[29]

One prime context in which Cicero saw the need for the Roman virtues was in the conduct of empire: they are imperial, not just republican, attributes. In *On behalf of Balbus*, delivered in 56 BC, he has an extended passage extolling qualities of Pompey—the warlord on whom Cicero was usually pinning his hopes for the rescue of the Republic—in this regard. We hear of his *pudor*, sense of propriety, *integritas*, integrity, *religio*, conscience, *diligentia*, the pains he takes to get things right: in short, what the master list in *Tusculan Disputations* sums up as *probitas*. We hear of his moderation and uprightness, and of the respect all these qualities and what people say about them have earned him (*Balb.* 9–10). Naturally his courage and spirit in war are extolled, but also his piety and humanity and wisdom (*consilium*) in peace (*Balb.* 13). A decade earlier in 66 BC, when supporting the proposal to grant Pompey an exceptional military command to deal with an eastern threat, Cicero had likewise made a point of stressing Pompey's other *artes* ('accomplishments', as he there calls virtues besides the military ones: *Leg. Man.* 36): he mentions *innocentia* (incorruptibility), *temperantia* (restraint), *fides* (trustworthiness), and *facilitas* (accessibility), as well as his *ingenium* and *humanitas*, nicely rendered by the Loeb translation as 'what a brain and what a heart!'.[30] The oration is among other things an attack on the rapacity of much recent

Roman imperialism: 'Our forefathers (*maiores nostri*) desired that the roofs of our allies and friends should be a shelter against the weather, not a refuge for avarice' (*Leg. Man.* 39). In the speech for Balbus, he rounds off his praise of Pompey with a similar point, but now in what has become his vocabulary of prime choice: is a man like that—endowed with *gravitas, virtus, constantia*— the sort of person who would knowingly overlook, violate, or break a pact (*Balb.* 13)?[31]

When in a letter intended for public consumption Cicero is proffering his younger brother advice—no doubt unwanted—on how to govern his province around the end of 60 BC, he urges upon Quintus many of the same qualities: integrity and restraint; a sense of propriety throughout his entourage; caution and care in deciding what friends to cultivate, whether among Romans in the province or among the Greeks; and a dignified (*gravis*) and unwavering (*constans*) regime in his household. These will be the foundations of his *dignitas*, his authority and the respect in which it is held (Q Fr. 1.1.18). *Severitas* (strictness) in dispensing justice was evidently not something Quintus found difficult to practice, but nonetheless Cicero advises him to maintain *constantia* and *gravitas* in doing so (QFr. 1.1.19–20), and for good measure suggests that he combine these with approachability (*facilitas in audiendo*, something lauded in Pompey 6 years earlier: *Leg. Man.* 41); mildness (*lenitas*) in judgement; and conscientiousness in quizzing and giving satisfaction to those putting their cases to him (Q Fr. 1.1.21).[32]

Fides, the last item on the *Tusculan Disputations'* list of Roman virtues, indicates someone you can trust in whatever context. *Fides* in friendship was singled out in the letter to Matius (*Fam.* 11.27.6), and in the international sphere, as we were just seeing, it is held to be one of those qualities prized in Pompey by Rome's allies (*Leg. Man.* 42). The word is readily paired with *gravitas*, as in a letter of 56 BC where Cicero is complaining that the senior senators are untrustworthy and irresponsible in their attitude to him: they do not appreciate his *constantia* in public affairs (*res publica*)—they are irritated by his distinction (*Fam.* 1.7.7). In the twelfth *Philippic* he will speak of his own *fides* and *constantia* in service of the *res publica* (*Phil.* 12.30).

Latin writers attest numerous dimensions of Roman society in which *fides* plays an important role. Freyburger notes references, for example, to the 'good faith' of the citizens to which one of their number might appeal if in need of protection from officers of state, a procedure dating from very early, if Livy may be trusted (2.23.8, 3.41.3, 3.45.9),[33] or again to the 'good faith' of the Roman people or the *plebs* (2.55.6, 3.56.8; cf. Cic. *Brut.* 90).[34] Hellegouarc'h's comprehensive study of the political vocabulary of the Roman Republic takes *fides*—trust—to be the prime ingredient in the glue that held together all key Roman social and political relationships: as for example between patron and client, Rome and her allies (which as was noted in Chapter 4 could be assimilated to patronage), and friendship between individuals and peoples alike.[35] *Fides* is prominent also in Roman religion. 'The cult of the goddess Fides', he observes, 'of which one sees no trace among the Greeks, seems to have appeared at Rome in very earliest times.'[36]

Cicero for his part quotes the national poet Ennius: 'O winged and nurturing *Fides*, and oath sworn in Jupiter's name' (*Off.* 3.104), in discussion, in Book 3 of *On duties*, of Marcus Atilius Regulus's scrupulous observance of his famous oath to the Carthaginians, the climax to the whole book and indeed treatise.[37] In the philosophical writings, Cicero gives *fides* a starring role in his analysis of both friendship and justice. His *Laelius* looks above all for someone who in friendship will (like Matius) exhibit *gravitas*, *constantia*, and *stabilitas*, unchangeability; and what props up that *stabilitas* and *constantia*, he says, is *fides* (*Lael.* 64–5). According to *On duties*, *fides* is the foundation (*fundamentum*) of justice.[38] It is defined there as 'constancy (*constantia*) and truth in what is said and agreed' (*Off.* 1.23).

It has been hard in this book to move very far away from those lines of Ennius that Cicero quotes at the beginning of Book 5 of *On the commonwealth* (*Rep.* 5.1):

> On ancient customs and the men of old
> Rome's commonwealth stands firm.

The preface to *Tusculan Disputations* in effect works with the same dichotomy: the Romans have been a superior people on account of their mores, institutions, and training, but also because of their citizens' natural disposition to the Roman virtues (*Tusc.* 1.2). It will now have become clear why *gravitas*, *constantia*, *fides*, and—though it has figured only implicitly in the examples quoted—*probitas* (as scrupulousness in performance of commitments) are considered by Cicero in that light. These attributes (*magnitudo animi*, the other attribute mentioned in that preface, requires separate treatment)[39] form a mutually supportive cluster. Those—'the men'—who develop and exhibit them will have the determination and authority and commitment to carry through legitimate undertakings and mutual obligations that are required for an optimally functioning society.

3. Justice

While talk of the virtues is on Cicero's lips everywhere in his writings, it is not until his final philosophical work, *On duties*, composed towards the end of 44 BC, that he offers an extended theorized account.[40] *On duties*, like the other philosophical writings of 46–44 BC, is addressed to Romans. While elsewhere Cicero describes as one of their main objectives the education and instruction of young people (represented as service on his part to the *res publica*: *Div.* 2.4–5), here he is expressly offering his own son Marcus, currently studying philosophy in Athens, advice on the qualities he will need if he is to 'embark on an honourable life' (*Off.* 3.6).[41] Cicero means by that a life like his own, devoted to serving the *res publica*, which he apparently expects to revive in due course despite its current demise. But although the ultimate agenda is a Roman one, for an account of the qualities required of someone in public life, and of the *officia*, duties and obligations, associated with them, Cicero turns to Greek philosophy, and to what he thinks of as the Platonic and Aristotelian tradition in philosophy (*Off.* 1.1–6). He resorts specifically to a treatise of the second-century BC Stoic Panaetius, friend of Scipio and Laelius, on 'appropriate action' (*Off.* 1.7). He indicates that he will follow it using his own judgement and discretion (*Off.* 1.6).[42]

Philosophy had long since decided that it was best to think in terms of four primary or cardinal virtues. In *On duties* the theory has been radically reshaped by recourse to Stoic psychology. Virtues are now represented as the excellences of character achieved by any human being who manages basic impulses to perfection. Their dynamic and regulation are due to reason: reason is what above all else distinguishes humans from other animals. Cicero specifies impulses for reasoning and enquiry, for association with others, for pre-eminence and independence, for orderliness and control. The corresponding virtues are here identified as wisdom in its theoretical and practical modes (*sapientia* and *prudentia*); social virtue ('to ensure that the community and its cohesion are preserved': *Off.* 1.17), which subsumes justice and liberality or beneficence; greatness of spirit, or independence and a largeness of outlook that rises above the merely human (*magnitudo animi*)—it is seen as the mainspring of courage; and finally, regard for order and a fitting measuredness (*decorum*), which is similarly seen as the source of temperance and restraint, i.e. *sôphrosunê* in traditional Greek accounts of the virtues (*Off.* 1.11–17).[43] Cicero acknowledges that there is scope for potential and not readily resolvable conflict between the requirements of different among the virtues (notably at *Off.* 1.159). The demands of justice, with its focus on benefit and harm, and of the *decorum*, in its concerns for consistency and integrity, may run in contrary directions.[44]

It goes without saying that these are not presented here as specifically Roman virtues, even if Cicero will explain and illustrate them in ways designed to exhibit how thoroughly Roman it is to value them and to act in accordance with them; and even if in the specific case of *magnitudo animi* we shall need to consider how elsewhere he could claim that Rome is the birthplace of *magnitudo animi* as well as *gravitas* (*Sest.* 141).[45] *Gravitas, constantia, fides*: these are all mentioned as important qualities at particular junctures in the work. They do not have the prominence in the argument that one might perhaps have expected in a treatise written to educate young Romans. On the other hand, a stress on *gravitas* and *constantia* could not have resulted in much guidance on what specific sorts of behaviour are appropriate for the person embarking on an 'honourable life': i.e. on his *officia*.

Justice (*iustitia*) is what is given pride of place in Cicero's account. That might come as a surprise to the reader of the introduction to the theory of the virtues (*Off.* 1.11–17). Not only is reason's cognitive power and focus, and particularly its search for truth, listed first every time Cicero presents or runs over his list of natural human impulses. It is identified as what particularly differentiates humans from other animals. It is 'particularly suited to human nature' (*Off.* 1.13), or again 'most closely related to human nature' (*Off.* 1.18). We are programmed above all to have a passion for knowing the truth.[46] How, then, is the pre-eminence of justice in the treatment of our obligations to be explained or justified?

Cicero tackles the issue in the closing pages of Book 1 (*Off.* 1.153–8). Since we are also social animals, he argues, we cannot ourselves thrive, nor maintain proper relations with other humans or with the *res publica*, unless we perform the duties prescribed by justice and try to promote advantages for humanity. Even our preoccupation with understanding the truth would be diminished if not put to practical use. The battery of arguments employed includes a syllogism to which Cicero evidently attaches some importance. It has caused editors and commentators some difficulty. Perhaps the best interpretation comes from P.G. Walsh.[47] He notes that in this argument (at *Off.* 1.153), the concern is not with the impulse to knowledge, but with its perfection in the virtue of wisdom (*sapientia*), described as the 'leading' (*princeps*) virtue. Its scope is comprehensive. Cicero, adapting a common

Stoic formulation (cf. *Tusc.* 4.57, 5.7),[48] specifies its primary object as 'the community of gods and humans',[49] adding (presumably as implicit in that formula) 'and humans' social relations with each other'. Then he draws a conclusion: 'So the obligations that derive from community are the most important.' Evidently he assumes that if wisdom is the leading virtue, its primary and most comprehensive preoccupation with community must likewise be the most important of our human concerns—which justice will then impel us to foster.[50]

The discussion of justice in *On duties* constitutes one of Cicero's most interesting contributions to philosophy and political thought, and one of the most important theoretical treatments of the topic to reach us from classical antiquity. It has a number of highly distinctive features. In the first place, it belongs within the deeply considered account of the cardinal virtues just sketched, which endeavours to explain why and how—given that humans are motivated by the basic impulses that drive them—these qualities are fundamental. Nothing comparable in their treatment of virtues was offered by Plato or by the early Stoics, or indeed by any thinker before Panaetius known to us.[51] Again, justice is here coupled uniquely in ancient texts with liberality or beneficence, as the twin manifestations of a more generic virtue that builds up and safeguards society (*Off.* 1.20).[52] Finally, justice is presented as the 'mistress and queen of all the virtues' (*Off.* 3.28), to which the others are in different ways subordinate (as Book 1 proposes), and which itself needs to control our pursuit of wealth, glory, and other things that are to be considered beneficial if appropriately conceived (a key theme of Book 2), and to govern our most significant and difficult choices in life (the topic of Book 3).[53]

Cicero starts discussion of justice (*Off.* 1.20–41) by specifying what he takes to be its two core obligations. The primary obligation (*munus*), he says, is that nobody should harm another unless he has been provoked by injustice, i.e. unprovoked injury (*Off.* 1.20). The formulation is strikingly abstract, prescinding from the agent's perspective, and universal in scope. In Book 3 a Stoic rationale is supplied for this first *officium* of justice. Cicero there appeals to our natural sociability (*Off.* 3.27):

If nature prescribes that a human being should want to promote the interests of any human being, whoever they may be, for the reason that this is a human being, then necessarily, in accord with the same nature, there is a common interest shared by all. If that is so, then we are all constrained by one and the same law of nature; and if that also is true, then we are certainly forbidden by the law of nature from acting violently against another.

The thought is that we are programmed by nature to take concern for the interests of any other person whatever—and since that is true for *each* of us, we can be described as sharing a common interest in each other's welfare. As a minimum requirement, that prohibits us from committing unprovoked personal injury against anyone else.[54] Cicero points out (*Off.* 3.28) that that applies to our relationship with other citizens, not just our family and kin (otherwise there could be no civil society), and to foreigners as well as citizens (otherwise the 'common society of the human race' would be destroyed—and with that kindness, generosity, goodness, and justice). This is the strongest and clearest statement of a cosmopolitan ethics anywhere articulated in his philosophical writing.

With the second *officium* of justice the focus becomes more specific. This is the prescription that we should treat what is common as common, but what is private as one's own (*Off.* 1.21). On the one hand, this means contributing to the common good by mutuality in the performance of obligations, by giving and receiving expertise and effort and means, so binding together human with human in society. On the other hand, although nothing is anyone's private property by nature, justice here does not consist (as in earlier Stoicism) in according each person his worth or due (Stob. *Ecl.* 2.59.9–10): a potentially redistributive principle, applicable in any domain of value, including not least that of political office.[55] Now it is a matter of respecting the principle that each person should retain possession of whatever property has come his way, I take it via some not improper route.[56]

Cicero may have thought he could find authority for this maxim of justice about what is private in Panaetius, since it corresponds quite closely to a formulation already found in Panaetius's own teacher, Diogenes of Babylon. Apparently Diogenes suggested that sometimes 'worth/due' (*axia*) is the word we use when we mean 'what falls to' (*epiballei*) a person (Stob. *Ecl.* 2.84.13–17)). But that Greek expression (like the English 'falls to') carries varied nuances of meaning. Probably Diogenes intended 'what is fitting for' a role or status, retaining a connotation of valuation.[57] Cicero's Latin *quod cuique obtigit*, on the other hand, is simply 'what has fallen into anyone's possession', by one means or another. He comments on the various routes by which property can be acquired: by long occupation, by military conquest, by legal provision, by a settlement, by agreement, or by lot. He gives as examples places where he himself had an interest: his native Arpinum, Tusculum location of a favourite country villa.

Towards the end of Book 2 he will be insisting that the first responsibility laid upon those who manage the government of the *res publica* should be upholding the principle that 'everyone should hold on to what is his own', and ensuring that 'private individuals are never deprived of their goods by public acts' *Off.* (2.73). He will attack the *populares*, populist politicians, for promoting measures of land reform or debt cancellation that will have the effect of 'collapsing the foundations of the *res publica*' (*Off.* 2.78). He will go so far as to claim that 'commonwealths and citizen bodies have been constituted above all in order that people may hold on to what is their own' (*Off.* 2.73). Unsurprisingly, claims like these, buttressed by much evidence of Cicero's attachment to such ideas in his other writings and by his record of opposition to land redistribution in his political career, led Neal Wood, in a book of 1988, to interpret his entire political philosophy as motivated by a proto-Lockean 'enlightened economic individualism'.[58] 'Cicero', he wrote, 'is the first important social and political thinker to affirm unequivocally that the basic purpose of the state is the protection of private property.' He contrasted Cicero with Plato and Aristotle: 'Thereby he is the first, with some qualification, to offer a non-ethical conception of the chief end of the state.'[59]

At the same time, Wood did not deny that according to the definition of *res publica* in *On the commonwealth* (*Rep.* 1.39): 'The state is an association in justice for the common interest.' He had spelled out the implication: 'Without justice there could be no true state, and the common interest cannot exist without justice.'[60] Furthermore, recalling the equation there of *res publica* with *res populi*, 'the affairs and interests of the people', Wood went on to draw out as a further implication of the definition that 'the state is not only subordinate to the greater whole of the *populus* and the common interest, but also to the superior orb of the right and just.'[61]

It is hard to see how talk of a 'non-ethical' goal for the state could be compatible with the state's subordination to the 'superior orb of the right and just'.[62] Without reference to Wood's interpretation of Cicero's political thought, Margaret Atkins noted that in a reprise of the statement of the principal obligations of justice a bit further into Book 1 of *On duties*, there is reference in the formulation of the second of these only to serving the common interest, with no mention of private property or the need to ensure that 'everyone should hold on to his own' (*Off.* 1.31). As she comments, the obvious inference is that Cicero sees respect for the institution of private property as precisely what the fundamental dictates (*fundamenta*) of justice and the common interest require. 'A failure to observe this will destroy the *concordia* and *fides* that bind *societas*.' In other words, without security of private property, there can remain no sense of what matters above all if there is to be a proper *res publica*: that the common interest in the protection of everybody's interests is being sustained, and that citizens perceive there to be a just social order, and share a consensus on its being so.[63] It is certainly striking that, immediately after his initial defence of private property in Book 1, he quotes with approval a Platonic maxim: 'We are not born for ourselves alone', along with a similar Stoic doctrine. He draws from them the inference that we should make following nature so understood our guide in life, and do all we can by mutuality to bind human community together (*Off.* 1.22).[64]

We might also consider the matter another way. Let us suppose Cicero could have been persuaded that a more equitable redistribution of land and other property between rich and poor would serve justice and the common interest better than protecting existing tenures of these just as they are. Then the logical structure of his theory (whether in *On the commonwealth* or in *On duties*) would have left him compelled to opt for abandoning commitment to security of private property, not to justice and the common interest. One might take the view, as Peter Garnsey does, that Cicero would at that point simply have ignored theory, and stuck by his non-philosophical adhesion to entrenched Roman class values: 'Cicero used the Stoic notion of communality and sociability for as long as it served his interests; when it appeared to be going in the wrong direction, he dropped it.'[65] Alternatively, it might be that Cicero would have challenged the entire theoretical basis of the counterfactual supposition. Perhaps he would have wanted to argue that historical entitlement is a fairer basis for holding property than any redistributive system would be likely to achieve.[66]

Cicero's further exploration of justice in Book 1 sees him first affirming that it is *fides*, 'constancy and truthfulness in what has been said and agreed', that is the foundation of justice. But he then devotes much more space to the modes and motives for injustice. He identifies two forms of injustice:

inflicting unprovoked injury in the first instance; but also (something that is never mentioned by Plato or Aristotle in relevant contexts) failing to defend others against it or to resist such assaults upon them, when one can—that is just as bad as abandoning parents or friends or country (*Off.* 1.23). Some discussion of such failures to defend others follows a little later (*Off.* 1.28–9). Here Cicero runs through the various inadequate reasons that individuals offer in such circumstances for failing to act, or that might explain their behaviour. These significantly include those he takes Plato to endorse in the *Republic*, as absolving philosophers from undertaking any duty (which would have to include that of defending those who should be defended) other than not themselves inflicting injury.

He does not refer at this point to similar failures on the part of states in the political sphere. In his subsequent discussion of rights in the sphere of warfare, however, he refers to the way the Romans have observed the requirements of justice so fully as to act as patrons of those foreign states that have surrendered to them upon the assurance of good faith (*fides*) (*Off.* 1.35; cf. 2.27). We recall Augustine's report of the teaching of *On the commonwealth*: 'No war is undertaken by the best state (*civitas*) except to maintain faith or for its own safety' (*Rep.* 3.34).[67] Recognition of the duty of states to defend others to which they are bound by obligations and which have suffered or are threatened with injury had already been articulated by Thucydides. At the beginning of the speech he has the Corinthians make to the Spartans in the preliminaries to the Peloponnesian War (protesting against their inaction in the face of the Athenians' assault on their colony of Potidaea), there occurs the following indictment (1.69.1): 'The real agent is not the one who does the enslaving, but the one who could stop it but just looks on, even though he claims to be the liberator of Greece.' Cicero's own rationale for the primary obligation of justice (*Off.* 3.27) and his specification of the two forms of injustice (*Off.* 1.23) would many centuries later be invoked (along with the Thucydides passage) in the climactic passage of *Vindiciae, Contra Tyrannos*. This was a work published in 1579 by a pseudonymous Huguenot author, with many further editions and translations into several vernaculars over the following decades. In his hands the duty to defend another against injury constitutes a charter for intervention by one state in the affairs of another oppressed by tyranny, and for the obligation to restrain or even evict the tyrant: humanitarian intervention, in the contemporary phrase.[68]

It is in Cicero's discussion of motives that drive people to commit injustice themselves that applications to Roman politics and society become most explicit and pronounced. The fabulously rich Marcus Crassus is the first Roman notable to be mentioned by name, as someone with *maior animus*, i.e. great ambition, who wanted to be the leading figure (*princeps*) in the *res publica* and was gripped by *infinita pecuniae cupiditas*, 'limitless desire for money' (*Off.* 1.25). In the context, the implication is that scruples about its just acquisition were not uppermost in his mind. There is then an immediate explicit attack on Julius Caesar, presented in the first mention of him in *On duties* as one of the *maximi animi*, i.e. biggest personalities, and of the brilliantly talented, so ambitious for honour, *imperium*, power, and glory that he was completely oblivious of the requirements of justice. When that happens, preservation of the most sacred social bonds (*sancta societas*: once again Cicero quotes Ennius) becomes difficult in the extreme. Honour, *imperium*, and glory were of course major Roman values that Cicero himself recognized and celebrated, for example in congratulating the Romans for their ambition for these things (*Leg. Man.* 7–8, 41, 53). He does not and could not credibly reject the pursuit of glory.[69] And the importance of *magnitudo animi* is high on his own agenda.

4. *Magnitudo animi*

Magnitudo animi—an idea we keep meeting in various contexts—is looking increasingly problematic. It is one of the four virtues, but Cicero views Julius Caesar's *maximus animus* as a disaster for Rome. Its promotion to the status of cardinal virtue was apparently the work of Panaetius, but in other Ciceronian texts it figures as something quintessentially Roman, not anything learned from the Greeks. A brief look at its early career in Latin will be instructive here.

Despite Cicero's implication that it is a quality hallowed in Roman tradition, its first surviving appearance in the language comes in the passage already cited from *On behalf of Murena*. The context is a political attack on Cato in 63 BC, which nonetheless recognizes his great personal stature.[70] Thereafter the expression comes and goes in the letters, speeches, and philosophical writings. Seven years later, in *On behalf of Sestius*, Cato is again twice described in such terms. Cicero speaks first of his *gravitas, integritas, magnitudo animi* and *virtus* (here, I take it, courage), and then of his 'exceptional' *magnitudo animi* and 'amazing' *virtus* (*Sest.* 60, 62). With Ulrich Knoche, one may suspect that Cato himself was prone to emphasize the importance of *magnitudo animi*, defined by the Stoics as a settled ability to rise above universal human limitations, such as our vulnerability to pain and to fortune (Stob. *Ecl.* 2.61.15–17, Diog. Laert. 7.92).[71] Cicero elsewhere refers to the eloquence with which Cato talked of '*magnitudo animi*, self-control, death, virtue, the gods, love of country' (*Parad.* 3).[72]

But it would be wrong to think that Cato had exclusive rights in *magnitudo animi*. *On duties* itself supplies evidence that Cicero had to concede *magnitudo animi* to Caesar (*Off.* 1.26). And in a famous passage of his account of the Catilinarian conspiracy, Sallust in a comparison of Cato and Caesar portrays them as evenly matched in age, family, and a range of personal characteristics. They were equal, too, he says, in *magnitudo animi*, although in Caesar's case it found expression not in severity but in generosity, clemency, and a gentle manner (*Cat.* 54.1). As Hellegouarc'h suggests, it sounds as though the expression may have become a sort of catchword appropriated by politicians of every hue.[73]

In *On duties*, Cicero starts his sustained discussion of *magnitudo animi* (*Off.* 1.61–92) with an acknowledgement of how nothing seems more brilliant (*splendissimum*) than deeds performed with 'great and elevated spirit, and contempt for things human', above all those that bring military glory (*Off.* 1.61).[74] But he issues an immediate warning: *elatio et magnitudo animi* (elevation and greatness of spirit), when driven not by concern for the common security, but by wilfulness and an excessive desire for pre-eminence (or even sole pre-eminence) is not a virtue at all. Without justice, it cannot be anything honourable (*honestum*). It is then not bravery, but audacity. Deeds, not glory, are the test of 'true and wise *magnitudo animi*'. Nobody can be regarded as a great man if his 'greatness' depends on the folly of an ignorant mob (*Off.* 1.62–5). Caesar is again clearly in Cicero's sights.

Although in this section of the book Cicero never adverts to the idea of the unity and interdependence of the virtues, its importance for understanding *magnitudo animi* is made clear enough (*Off.* 1.66–9).[75] At the core of *magnitudo animi* as it should be are two things: knowledge that only the honourable and a fitting measuredness (*decorum*) are good, and the freedom from the passions that goes with that. Desire for money, characteristic of a narrow and petty spirit, cripples motivation for liberality and beneficence. Desire for glory robs people of liberty, which is what men of great spirit will compete to uphold. When someone of such a disposition experiences that impulse to excel in difficult and dangerous circumstances which is special to *magnitudo animi*, its supreme expression—given that humans are designed for community—will be in the conduct of great enterprises that will sustain the *res publica* and further the general interest (see especially *Off.* 1.67, 86, 92).

A.A. Long, the greatest modern scholar of ancient Stoicism, has written rewardingly about the treatment of glory in *On duties*. He reads *On duties'* assault on perverted *magnitudo animi*, and more generally its sustained critique in both Books 1 and 2 of 'false glory', as an attempt to promote a 'reformist ideology', a 'reform of the Roman honour code' which would 'turn glory into a co-operative value, grounded in justice'.[76] It might be better to speak of an assault by Cicero on the perversion of the pursuit of glory traditional in Roman public life. That was something traditionally conceived as part and parcel of a successful political life advancing the well-being of the *res publica*, as (for example) the Greek historian Polybius, writing in the mid-second century BC, attests (Polyb. 6.53–4).[77] Cicero's main target for attack is 'practice, not ideology'.[78] He sees the pursuit of glory at any price as one of the forces most destructive of a properly functioning public sphere. He tries instead to make pursuing glory something ultimately instrumental: useful in building a political career, and in giving you authority when transacting important public business (*Off.* 2.31). In the process of the attempt, something new in Roman discourse is being forged: a fully articulated distinction between meretricious and genuine glory.

There are three main routes to what Cicero calls supreme and perfect glory: the love or goodwill of the masses (*multitudo*); the trust (*fides*) you inspire in them; and the admiration for your qualities that lead them to honour you. Cicero has already made explicit his view that Caesar by contrast maintained his power by a regime of fear (*Off.* 2.23), something he accuses Mark Antony of misidentifying as the path to glory in the first Philippic (*Phil.* 1.33). Only real virtue and a well-founded reputation for virtue, and above all justice, secure goodwill, trust, and lasting admiration (*Off.* 2.32–8), and a glory that takes root and spreads its branches (*Off.* 2.43). Long judges this argument—that if you want real glory, you had better demonstrate real virtue—to be a pious failure.[79] People do in time tend, however, to see through power crazed or unscrupulous politicians who may glitter and achieve much for a while. Such glory does not equate to an honoured place in the history books. Ferdinand II of Spain, much admired by Machiavelli (*The Prince*, ch.21), has not had a good press for some time.

Beethoven notoriously cancelled his dedication of the Eroica symphony to Napoleon when liberator turned himself into emperor.

To find Cicero pursuing a truly reformist agenda, it might be best to focus not on his treatment of justice as the true road to *gloria*. It is in attacking particularly the assumption that war is the pre-eminent sphere for the display of *virtus* that he picks an argument with the entire Roman aristocratic tradition.[80] However he endeavours to claim that it is his own standpoint that is truly traditional, by representing his objective as restoration, rather than reform. From the time of the suppression of the Catilinarian conspiracy onwards, he and those public figures whose *magnitudo animi* he had praised had, as he represented it, practised true virtue and earned true praise. He returns as often to the superior claims of the public over the private life (*Off.* 1.69–73), and insists that statesmanship and government are more important spheres for the exercise of virtue than is war, with Roman as well as Greek examples (*Off.* 1.74–80). *Ratio* (reason) in settling disputes, when guided by calculation of *utilitas*, is more desirable than courage in fighting over the issue (*Off.* 1.80). Keeping one's head as a statesman is a form of courage and constancy that requires both 'a great and exalted spirit and one reliant on wisdom (*prudentia*) and counsel (*consilium*)' (*Off.* 1.81). And government has a greater scope and affects more lives than any other undertaking (*Off.* 1.92).

Magnitudo animi entered Cicero's vocabulary only when he was forced to think about Cato and what gave him his particular strength and authority as a public figure. But once it did, he was glad to appropriate it and associate it with others of the ancestral virtues he liked to celebrate in those devoted in their public life to the cause of the *res publica*: *fides, integritas, auctoritas*, for example, as well as *gravitas* and *constantia*. Devotion to the *res publica* and to Roman tradition (*instituta maiorum*) had been what motivated them. Their example proved that there was nothing intrinsically wrong with the Roman honour code. But what he perceived as the devastation produced during his lifetime by political ambition is now prompting Cicero to analysis of the temptations to which great powers and achievements are subject, and to extended examination of a quality such as *magnitudo animi*. So in *On duties* he accepts the need to develop an argument for and about *magnitudo animi*, which results in the analysis we have been examining.

The virtue has made a remarkable journey from its first appearance in his writings, back in *On behalf of Murena* (63 BC), to its now dominant role in Cicero's rearticulation of Roman republican ideology. Its absorption into

Roman political discourse—due of course to Cato and no doubt others as well as Cicero—is one of those cases where philosophy has made its mark on the wider vocabulary of a language.

5. *Verecundia*

Cicero introduces the fourth member of the quartet of canonical virtues as the one in which is seen '*verecundia* (respect or considerateness), and what one might call "life's finest clothing" (*ornatus vitae*), restraint (*temperantia*) and discretion (*modestia*), and total calming of mental agitations, and due measure in all things' (*Off.* 1.93).[81] His substantive treatment of the *officium* of the fourth virtue begins with advice on control of impulses, the need for judiciousness. We are to ensure, says 'the most infamous funster, punster, and jokester of classical antiquity', that even when we jest, 'something of the light of an upright character may shine out (*eluceat*)' (*Off.* 1.103).[82] This is mostly a matter of not letting oneself down (jokes need to be 'worthy', *dignus*, of a person). Perhaps this was a case of 'do as I say, not do as I do'. Plutarch's verdict (*Comp. Dem. & Cic.* 1.4): 'He was often carried away by his joking to the point of buffoonery, and when, to achieve what was needed in the cases he was pleading, he handled matters that deserved gravity with irony, laughter, and wit, he neglected decorum.'[83]

Subsequently the entire final sequence of the section on the fourth virtue (*Off.* 1.126–51) is given over to detailed advice about the behaviour to be expected of *verecundia* (cf. *Off.* 1.127, 128, 143).[84] In fact, this is where Cicero says most of what he has to say about the specific obligations that he associates with the fourth virtue in general. The section ends with what is sometimes treated by scholars as an 'appendix' (*Off.* 1.150–1), on occupations unsuitable for the style of life expected of a free person. The list of these starts with the jobs of customs officials and moneylenders, 'which incur expressions of loathing from people (*odia hominum*)'. Such loathing is precisely the kind of emotional response avoided by *verecundia*'s careful management of behaviour and lifestyle.

Having at the outset marked out the fourth virtue's territory, Cicero then states that the topic covers 'what can in Latin be called *decorum* ('the fitting')' (*Off.* 1.93).[85] The use of *decorum* as the term covering the province of the virtue whose most palpable presence is in *verecundia* comes as something of a surprise, and will deserve some discussion before we return to *verecundia* itself. One might antecedently have expected that moderation or restraint (corresponding to Greek *sôphrosunê*)—following wisdom, social virtue, and *magnitudo animi*—would have been named as fourth in *On duties'* quartet of virtues. In neither of Cicero's dialogues on ethics, however, does the main discussion of the canonical quartet settle on such a name for the fourth virtue. In Book 2 of *On ends*, where his treatment plainly relies on the same kind of material in Panaetius as it does in *On duties*, he associates it with order and moderation, but refers to it only as the 'fourth' virtue, giving it no name, and making no mention of *decorum* as such (*Fin.* 2.47; cf. *Off.* 1.15, 17).[86]

In *Tusculan Disputations*, Cicero expressly backs away from the terms he says he generally uses to translate *sôphrosunê*: sometimes 'restraint', sometimes 'moderation', occasionally 'discretion'. In searching there for the right word to indicate 'every kind of holding back and of *innocentia*' (in the etymological sense of 'not harming'), he ends up opting for *frugalitas* (Tusc. 4.36; cf. 3.17–18). He wants his readers to take *frugalitas* here as signifying comprehensive moral control, not in the usual narrow sense of 'being economical', 'good control of resources'. That choice sounds like a vain hope at best, repeated only once (probably very soon afterwards) by Cicero and never in any other Latin writer.[87]

What lies at the root of Cicero's nomenclature quandary? There were two problems. One is already apparent in the two ethical dialogues. Although he treats the fourth virtue as a species of the genus of virtue, he also wants a term for it or its province that indicates something nonetheless quite general about it, and which could indicate the way it is mutually implicated with the other three.[88] As he explains the point in *On moral ends* (*Fin.* 2.47): 'It dreads precipitate judgement, it does not have the effrontery to injure anyone by an insolent word or deed, it shrinks from doing or saying anything that might appear unmanly.' In other words, its impulses fuel and are fuelled by wisdom, justice, and courage respectively. But there was no obvious word in Latin for a virtue that constitutes a settled disposition for such an ordering motivation (in the way that Greek *sôphrosynê*, etymologically 'soundmindedness', could be so construed, as by Plato in the *Gorgias*: see *Grg.* 506d–507c).

A second additional element in the naming quandary relates to the need that Cicero, in writing *On duties*, evidently felt for a term which would indicate not only order and the harmonious state of the mind, but palpable appearance of order of a certain kind in our social behaviour. *Verecundia*, considerateness in behaviour, was to be the most important manifestation of the fourth virtue, guiding the articulation of many of the *officia* associated with it. Our behaviour must accordingly be consistently such as to avoid being perceived as offensive to others. Any more general name for the virtue from which such behaviour would flow should be capable of capturing that concern for social appearance, as well as signifying a source of ethical motivation.

But Latin vocabulary had, once more, no virtue word which could satisfy such requirements. Cicero finally decides to talk of *decorum*, 'the fitting', as the Latin word that best corresponds with Panaetius's Greek term (*prepon*), and which—thanks to its root sense of 'becoming'—simultaneously captures both fittingness and looking fine (as—somewhat archaically—of a woman's 'becoming new hairstyle').[89] But he does not suggest that the expression itself specifies a virtue. It functions rather as the most general term available for describing and commending what is characteristically exhibited both in the cluster of attributes he has listed (*verecundia, temperantia, modestia*), and in the style or appearance of the behaviours associated with them, too (*Off.* 1.93). He therefore has to work hard to try and show how *decorum* can serve the purposes he has in mind, since its basic sense in Latin was highly unspecific.

Perhaps the most helpful element in Cicero's attempt to do so consists in an analogy with its more usual role in the critical treatment of literature. He suggests that the way poets and dramatists have regard to *decorum* supports the account of the concept he wants to give (*Off.* 1.97–8). Indeed it is in Cicero's *Orator* (46 BC)—in effect mostly devoted to theory of literary style—that we first find him discussing the idea himself at some length (*Orat.* 70–4). In our *On duties* passage he contents himself with giving a single example, to drive home the obvious point that whatever the poet or dramatist makes a particular person say must fit their character. What would be in keeping for a bad person to utter would seem inappropriate in the mouth of someone like Minos or Aeacus (legendary figures who became judges in the afterlife). Or as we might put it, what is right for Mr Hyde to say would be wrong for Dr Jekyll. Cicero at once extracts the moral he wants drawn (*Off.* 1.97):

> However, whereas poets will assess what is fitting for each person on the basis of character (*persona*), nature herself has established for us a *persona* of great excellence that surpasses that of the other living creatures.

Poets, he comments further, deal with a great variety of *personae*, including villains, but we have been given by nature the role of constancy, moderation, restraint, considerateness. He adds, as premise to the line of thought he now develops (evidently with reference particularly to *verecundia*, considerateness): 'this same nature teaches us not to be careless in the way we behave towards other men' (*Off.* 1.98). In other words, just as an actor has to manage the way he presents the character he is playing, so considerateness involves managing the impression on others that we create. Only if we do that properly will we be achieving the order in our behaviour for which nature has given us the impulse. Only then will our virtue 'shine out' and 'arouse the approval of those with whom the life is lived, because of the order and constancy and moderation of every word and action' (*Off.* 1.98).

There is more to each of us than our universal human nature. Cicero will go on to develop a more elaborate theory of different *personae* that humans should or may develop in life, and of the specific *officia* attaching to them (*Off.* 1.107–25).⁹⁰ His discussion contains much of interest, including not least its specification of the duties of a magistrate or elected officer of state (*Off.* 1.124): 'to appreciate that he assumes the character and role (*persona*) of the citizen body, and is obliged to sustain its standing and its honour (*decus*), to preserve its laws, to dispense to people their rights, to be mindful of the things entrusted to his good faith (*fides*)'.⁹¹ But the treatment of *verecundia* in the final extended subsection of the treatment of *decorum* (*Off.* 1.126–51) does not make any explicit use of *persona* theory. It is in effect addressed to free citizens in general.

Here Cicero starts again with nature, understood now as our general physical make-up, and the claim that it has hidden those parts of the body which look ugly and dishonourable: human *verecundia* imitates nature. Dismissive treatment of the shamelessness of the Cynics, in contrast to the *verecundia* he is urging on his readers, then frames the rest of the main discussion (*Off.* 1.128, 148).⁹² The chief programmatic statement occurs at *Off.* 1.143: 'We have for some time been speaking of those virtues which pertain to *verecundia* and to the approbation of those with whom we live (cf. *Off.* 1.98), and it is what is appropriate to these that we should now be discussing.' Here is the tone set at the outset (*Off.* 1.128):

Let us follow nature and avoid anything that shrinks from the approval of eyes and ears. Let our standing, our walking, our sitting and our reclining, our countenances, our eyes and the movements of our hands, all maintain what I have called *decorum*.

There follows highly nuanced discussion of modes of speech and style of domestic accommodation, emphasizing now moderation, now what might be called the principle of 'horses for courses', in what moral philosophers might regard as a broadly Aristotelian vein. When Cicero turns at last to the substance of behaviour—what rather than how—he reiterates the importance of governing impulse (above all) and of appropriate judiciousness, but once again emphasizes the need to take care to control 'what pertains to the style and standing (*dignitas*) of a free person' (*Off.* 1.141; cf. 1.104).

Cicero's implicit contrast throughout is with the expectations one might have of a slave or of a slavish character. He had defined the relevant ethical sense of *decorum* earlier (*Off.* 1.96):[93]

What accords with nature in such a way that moderation and restraint are apparent in it, together with the style or look (*species*) characteristic of a free person (*liberalis*).

The unspoken assumption is that Marcus and Cicero's readership more generally are citizens of a free *res publica*. Translators generally make him talk of a 'gentleman' rather than a 'free' person. And it is certainly true that the style of behaviour he goes on to recommend in the detailed prescriptions of the *verecundia* section sound at points (notably the advice on housing: *Off.* 1.139–40) like nothing so much as etiquette for the diminishing number of Roman grandees left surviving the disintegrating republic.[94] Slavish behaviour for Cicero encompasses a great deal that in other societies would be regarded as perfectly compatible with the proper conduct of a free citizen—notably when it comes to his concluding list of occupations he regards as unsuitable (crafts, tax collecting, banking, retail, trade—except perhaps when on a large scale: *Off.* 1.150–1).[95] We can agree that Cicero's highly restrictive notion of the style of freedom is dramatically culture specific. Nonetheless a style of freedom is what it is a notion of. To quote Robert Kaster (writing about Roman republican culture more generally), *verecundia* 'animates the art of knowing your proper place in every transaction and binds the free members of a civil community'.[96]

The approbation of respected peers (*fama bonorum*) was something by which Cicero set store (*Att.* 9.1.3, 9.7.6, 11.7.3), even if he often felt they did not merit respect (*Fam.* 1.9.17, *Att.* 9.1.3, 9.2a.3, 9.12.3). Registering its importance was a way of retrospectively (in autumn 46 BC) representing one component, at least, in his eventual decision to join the Pompeian forces in the Civil War (*Fam.* 6.6.6). He writes to Varro, also in retrospect (May 46 BC), that the two of them had shown more *verecundia* than those who had never stirred from home (*Fam.* 9.5.2).[97] His prescriptions for *verecundia* in *On duties* are likewise emphatically, despite a different focus, not mere etiquette, nor does his treatment of *decorum* represent the awkward imposition of an aesthetic category on to ethical subject matter, as commentators have complained. They might better be viewed as a charter for civility (*mos consuetudoque civilis*: *Off.* 1.148). Cicero is writing as a Roman citizen to other Roman citizens of his own class—not least, of course, his son Marcus. So his prescriptions are naturally not universalizable as they stand, and none the worse on that account.

More importantly, such prescriptions are not in principle universalizable, except where there is talk in the most general way about our duties to others as citizens and as members of the human race, and indeed thereby our obligation to preserve mutual human association (*Off.* 1.149: a striking example of *decorum* within the sphere of another virtue: justice). How you manage the impression you make on others—and what impression it should be—depends both on who you are and on who the relevant others are. If contemporary moral philosophers were to be asked to specify what for us would be the behaviour appropriate to consideration for others rooted in discretion and restraint, they would rightly cast it in terms often highly specific to the world as it is in the early twenty-first century—terms unavoidably more complex than Cicero's, given the multicultural societies that many people across the globe live in now.⁹⁸

6. The republican citizen

A picture is forming. It constitutes a portrait of the ultimately reliable and honest republican citizen as exemplar of virtue. This figure will command the authority and display the determined commitment to carry through such legitimate undertakings and mutual obligations as are required for the *res publica* to function as it should. Understanding and fulfilling those obligations will require of him above all the social virtues needed to ensure that civic community and its cohesion are peaceably preserved. Justice is his basic imperative, which in positions of political responsibility he must ensure not only within the *res publica*, but beyond its frontiers when Rome's allies are being unjustly treated by other powers. Action possible only for those endowed with *magnitudo animi* is the supreme expression of virtue, exhibited in the conduct of great enterprises conferring glory. But that will count as virtue and true glory only when designed to sustain the *res publica* and to further the general interest, and when unmarred by the vices of ambition for power and inordinate moneylust, pursued with no regard for justice, that Cicero associates with warlords like Crassus and Caesar. Finally, the good citizen must manage and control the civility of his self-presentation, by the discretion he exercises in the respect and considerateness he consistently shows in his relations with other citizens.

Living images of that good citizen recur in the speeches Cicero made after Caesar's assassination and as *On duties* was being completed, when once more he mounted the public stage. Their salience is marked in the series of speeches (the 'Philippics') that he launched against Mark Antony, now standard-bearer of the Caesarian cause, from September 44 well into the following year. He hymns the virtues exemplified by those he sees as champions of the *res publica*. Gaius Vibius Pansa, consul in 43, is portrayed as a man of *magnitudo animi, gravitas* and *sapientia* (*Phil.* 7.7); Cassius the tyrannicide—in words which seem to echo *On duties* (*Off.* 1.81)—is equal in *magnitudo animi* and in wisdom (*consilium*) (*Phil.* 11.28). Everybody knows the *consilium, ingenium, humanitas, innocentia* and *magnitudo animi* displayed by Cicero's friend Trebonius in liberating the country (from Caesar's tyranny) (*Phil.* 11.9). Most grandiloquent of all is the roll call of virtues exemplified in their liberation of the Roman people by the three commanders Pansa, Hirtius, and Octavian, as Cicero describes them on the last page of the last of the *Philippics*: *imperium, consilium, gravitas, constantia, magnitudo animi*—and (a surprise—we were thinking *magnitudo animi* was as so often to be the crowning item) *felicitas*: good luck (*Phil.* 14.37).[99] There are multiple ironies here. Pansa and Hirtius, who would be dead by the end of the year, were in all likelihood prime examples of those dinner companions of Atticus who could not have borne to hear talk of *gravitas* and *constantia*; Octavian is going to turn into the Emperor Augustus; and Cicero's own luck is going finally to run out.

Notes

1. See further section 2 pp. 156–7 below. But Cicero certainly thought that military commanders needed luck—*fortuna* or *felicitas*—as well as attributes of mind and character: *Leg. Man.* 28 (with section 6 pp. 176 n.99 below).
2. Pettit 1997: 280.
3. Pettit 1997: 281.

4. The dialogue's opening pages are lost.
5. By 'what we call' (*dicitur*), Cicero presumably means to imply that use of the term 'civil' (*civile*) to connote private law (as at Rome it standardly did) indicates that it is that part of law whose scope is relations between citizens.
6. So Powell 2012: 19.
7. See Hellegouarc'h 1963: 23–35; in greater detail Freyburger 1986: 99–225. *Fides* (and the passage from *Tusculan disputations*) are further discussed below, in section 2.
8. See Cooper 1984: 12–17. But of course Cicero distinguishes shame and restraint and associated behaviours from fortitude, which is no doubt being conceived here primarily as a military virtue.
9. On the uses of *pudor* in Caesar's *Civil War*, see Grillo 2012: 46–51. Hellegouarc'h 1963: 283 summed up its use in political contexts as expressing 'the attitude of a politician who does not dare infringe the limits of what he considers his duty'. In a succinct more general discussion, Kaster 1997: 5 draws attention also to *pudor*'s interiority: 'People feel *pudor* not only because they are seen, or fear being seen, by someone else, but also because they see themselves and know that their present behaviour falls short of their past or ideal selves.' Brunt 1986: 16, commenting on Cicero's explanation of his conduct in the Civil War, likewise interprets *pudor* as 'self-respect', rather than regard for the opinion of others. Kaster 2005: 28–65 offers a comprehensive taxonomy and analysis of the word's usage. See further section 5, on *verecundia*.
10. See the full discussion in Hellegouarc'h 1963: 279–90 (quoted words: 280). As he comments, the core literal sense, 'heaviness' or 'weightiness', seems to have retained its influence on the word's use to designate a personal quality: 279 with nn.2–4.
11. See further Chapter 6, section 3 p. 198.
12. See Chapter 3, section 1 p. 61, on 'the best *civitas*' and 'the best citizen' as the twin subjects of *On the Commonwealth*.
13. See also Chapter 6, section 2 p. 196.
14. See further Chapter 6, section 2 p. 199; also Griffin 2013: 107–14 [= Griffin 2018: 701–5], comparing Cicero's stance with Seneca's.
15. See Earl 1961: 18–27.
16. The catalogue (*Div.* 2.2) describes the *Tusculans* as the next work composed after *On moral ends*, which was being finished off around the end of June 45: *Att.* 13.12.3, 19.4, 21a.1.
17. For a recent study of the profile of the word *virtus* in Latin (confirming the two primary meanings here identified), and particularly of its slipperiness in Cicero's usage, see Balmaceda 2017: 14–47.
18. See Hellegouarc'h 1963: 285–6.

19. See Atkins 1990: 268, commenting on *Off.* 1.23 and 2.84 (cf. also section 1 p. 148 and n.7 above). Cicero was not to be alone among Latin authors in hymning Roman superiority in virtue. It becomes a constant theme in later writers. Here, for example, is the elder Pliny a century later (*NH* 7.130): 'Of the peoples across the entire globe, the Roman nation is unquestionably the one most pre-eminent of all in virtue.'
20. The contrast is noted and interestingly discussed in Gildenhard 2007: 118–30. He argues that a crucial element in its explanation is time of composition: *On the commonwealth* in the last days of the Republic, *Tusculan Disputations* under Caesar's dictatorship—where the possibility of meaningful political participation has disappeared. Hence—Gildenhard proposes—Cicero lists there only the virtues which would support individual apolitical self-sufficiency, not for example justice. But since *fides* is grouped with justice and fairness in *On the commonwealth*'s list, and indeed according to *On duties* is the foundation of justice (*Off.* 1.23), it looks as though justice is in effect not altogether excluded from his purview at *Tusc.* 1.2. The reference to *gravitas* and *constantia* might (as Gildenhard suggests) put readers in mind of Cato (see below p. 153–4) and his heroic republican resistance to tyranny. Yet why they should infer from that a subtext of resort specifically to apolitical self-sufficiency, in a passage celebrating the Romans' communal heritage, would be hard to fathom. As will become apparent, these and the other qualities on the *Tusculans* list in fact for the most part mark out someone who is eminently reliable in dealings with others.
21. The Stoics built this notion of 'good natural potential' (*euphuïa*) into their theory of ethical development: see Schofield 1991: 32 with n.18, 115–18.
22. Tyranny is how Cicero habitually thought first of Caesar's ambitions and then of his rule. For more on tyranny (especially with reference to Caesar), see Chapter 6, sections 4 to 6.
23. It is then summed up in the word offered as translation of the Greek *homologia*: *convenientia*, 'agreement' or 'consistency' (*Fin.* 3.21).
24. Elsewhere he will associate *gravitas*, too, with the practice of philosophy. Epicurus speaks of living honourably, wisely, with justice. Nothing could be more dignified (*gravius*), more worthy of philosophy, did he not make pleasure their focus (*Tusc.* 5.26). Cicero is at pains to give the *gravitas* of the philosopher a more venerable pedigree. He had earlier contrasted 'these pleasure-seeking philosophers' with 'those serious philosophers of old' (*Tusc.* 3.40). In *On laws* Plato is described as the 'weightiest, most dignified (*gravissimus*) of all philosophers' (*Leg.* 2.14). For more on the *decorum*, see section 5 p. 171–4 below.
25. On Cato's suicide, see Griffin 1986 [= Griffin 2018: 402–19].
26. Benferhat 2005: 234–47.
27. On Cicero's exchange with Matius, see Chapter 6, section 5.
28. See Hellegouarc'h 1963: 288–9.

29. On Cicero's economy with the truth in the story he liked to tell of the circumstances of his exile, and on the 'late republican morality play' he would like to have seen made of it (*Fam.* 5.12), see Kaster 2009.
30. See Earl 1961: 11–12 on Sallust's similar treatment of non-military virtues as *bonae artes*.
31. See Morrell 2017: 22–97, 204–36 for a recent analysis and assessment of what the author takes to be Pompey's initiatives in improving provincial governance.
32. Cicero will eventually congratulate Quintus's province of Asia on its good fortune in having someone with the attributes of a Platonic philosopher ruler as its governor, before turning to practical advice on how to deal with the awkward issue of its tax farmers (*QFr.* 1.1.29–31).
33. Freyburger 2002.
34. Freyburger 1986: 118.
35. Hellegouarc'h 1972: 23–35.
36. Hellegouarc'h 1972: 26. A full discussion: Freyburger 1986: 229–98. But in other spheres Greek valuation of *pistis* and Roman of *fides* seem to run parallel: Gruen 1982; a major recent study is Morgan 2015: 36–122.
37. On Regulus and oaths, see further Chapter 6, section 2 pp. 194–5.
38. See Atkins 1990: 268, 279. Yet the requirement to honour one's promises (for example) is not treated as absolute by Cicero: *Off.* 1.31–2. For discussion of the difficulty of reaching any determinate and generally applicable principles or decision procedures requiring or authorizing particular actions within the ethical framework of *On duties*, see Chapter 6, section 2 p. 196.
39. See section 4 below.
40. Griffin and Atkins 1991: ix–xxviii supply an excellent introduction to *On duties*. Woolf 2015: 170–200 offers a reflective philosophical evaluation of its ethical stance.
41. *On duties* is not a dialogue, but formally more akin to an extended letter, notably in the openings of each book and in its final sentence bidding the younger Marcus farewell, who is frequently addressed as recipient throughout the text—though its advice is clearly applicable to teenagers or very young men (*adulescentes*) generally (*Off.* 2.44–51). See the discussions of Dyck 1996: 10–16, Gibson and Morrison 2007: 9–13.
42. Quite how much of *On duties* is likely to be owed to Panaetius has been much debated. A minimalist view: Lefèvre 2001; a maximalist: Brunt 2013b. For the cautious view that Cicero follows Panaetius (in Books 1 and 2: no Panaetian model was available for Book 3) in the main overall structure of his own treatise, if not always in much of the detail, see Griffin and Atkins 1991: xvi–xxi. As they point out, it is clear that Panaetius's work contained a strong political vein. So (*contra* Lefèvre) the general presence of a political focus, most marked in the Panaetian Books 1 and 2, cannot be regarded as entirely Cicero's

own distinctive contribution (see also Griffin 2011: 320–3 [= Griffin 2018: 670–2], Brunt 2013b: 213, 217–18).
43. There can be little doubt that Cicero here reproduces the general shape at least of Panaetius's theory of virtue. On natural impulses as the key distinctive element in the theory, see Clem. Al. *Strom.* 2.129, with the discussion of Dyck 1996: 85–6. Probably thanks to Panaetius, the treatment of *decorum* at *Off.* 1.14 (or as he puts it there, *quid sit quod deceat*) is reminiscent of a specific Platonic passage (*Laws* 2.653d–654a). Cicero cites Plato explicitly (*Phdr.* 250d) in the exposition soon afterwards (*Off.* 1.15).
44. See especially Woolf 2007: 335–44.
45. *Magnitudo animi* had, of course, figured in the listing of Roman virtues given in the preface to *Tusculan Disputations* (*Tusc.* 1.2): see section 2 of this chapter.
46. A practical focus for cognitive reason is not entirely absent. Cicero ends his main treatment of it with the clause (*Off.* 1.11): 'He [i.e. a human being] visualizes with ease the whole course of life, to prepare whatever is necessary for living it.' Such concerns are more strongly emphasized at the end of the dedicated discussion of the impulse to knowledge (*Off.* 1.19). He had of course already had much to say about the practical excellences of *civilis prudentia* and *consilium* in *On the commonwealth*: see Chapter 3, sections 4, 5 and 6. Nor is mention of these entirely lacking from *On duties*, e.g. at *Off.* 1.75–6, 123, 156, 2.83, 3.71, 117.
47. Walsh 2000: 155–6.
48. See Brouwer 2014: 7–18.
49. Presumably to be understood as 'the cosmic city' of gods and humans (*ND* 2.154); cf. Schofield 1991: 64–92.
50. Accordingly, after a brief discussion of the pursuit of knowledge early in Book 1 (*Off.* 1.18–19), Cicero turns to the much more extensive treatment of the other three virtues.
51. Aristotle does not nominate any set of virtues as the core group, even though it is evident from the organization of his two works on ethics that he does accord pride of place to the four Plato had explicitly presented as such.
52. The rationale is presumably an isomorphism in their respective functions. The just person refrains from taking from another what is not his own, whereas the liberal person gives to another something that is his own. If Panaetius looked to any philosophical precedent, he might have found one in Aristotle: see *EN* 4.1, 1120a15–23. The ensuing substantive treatment of beneficence and liberality (*Off.* 1.42–59, 2.52–85) is shaped mostly by insistence on the need to keep within one's means, and to take account of the character and situation of intended recipients and of the existing connection with them that one may have (cf. *Off.* 1.42, 45).

53. For further discussion of the distinctiveness of Cicero's treatment of justice as the overarching virtue in *On duties*, and of the way he works through the idea over its three books, see Atkins 1990, to which this section of the chapter is much indebted.
54. For further discussion of Cicero's argument in this extract from Book 3, see Chapter 6, section 6 pp. 215–16.
55. As in Aristotle: *EN* 5.3, 1131a24–9, *Pol.* 3.12, 1282b23–30, 5.2, 1302b11–14 (see Schofield 1996: 848–55). But elsewhere in *On duties* Cicero insists on the importance of the principle in this original form—indeed, as the 'foundation' of justice (*Off.* 1.42, seeming here to treat beneficence not as a sibling, but as a species of justice, which is what it was in the standard Stoic classification: Stob. *Ecl.* 2.62.3).
56. See p. 164 n.66 below.
57. So Inwood and Gerson 1997: 215. Cf. e.g. Arist. *Pol.* 1.13, 1260a17-20. For Stoic use of *epiballein*, see e.g. Stob. *Ecl.* 99.16–19, Plut. *Stoic. rep.* 1034d (Cleanthes), Stob. *Flor.* 4.508.14 (Antipater).
58. See especially Wood 1988: 111–15. He had earlier in the book spoken of Cicero's 'moral, economic, and political individualism—possibly in part reflective of the social atomism of his age' (Wood 1988: 12). Raphael Woolf in his more recent book on Cicero suggests (Woolf 2015: 7): 'If there is a core philosophical motive in Cicero's work, it is, I believe, to uphold the metaphysical reality and ethical importance of individual agency.' The theme becomes particularly salient in the account he offers of *On duties*: see especially Woolf 2015: 173–85. But Woolf is not speaking of economic individualism.
59. Wood 1988: 132 (at this point he referred to the monumental work of de Ste. Croix 1981: 426), having earlier (ibid. 11) spoken 'with reservations' of 'a central non-moral purpose' for the state.
60. Wood 1988: 129, rendering *res publica* as 'state' (but see Chapter 2, section 5 pp. 47–50).
61. Wood 1988: 138.
62. Wood made it clear that he took the conception of justice and right in play to have a strong moral dimension, e.g. Wood 1988: 129 with n.42. Perhaps he meant only to be pointing out that, unlike Plato (at any rate in the *Laws*) and Aristotle, Cicero in *On duties* does not make the 'achievement of true moral virtue' the goal of the state—it is not for him 'primarily a school in ethics' (Wood 1988: 130; cf. 132). But see Chapter 4, section 2 pp. 36–8 on the conception of law in *On laws*, geared to the promotion of virtue.
63. Atkins 1990: 267 n.12. Barlow 2012 offers an extended critique of Wood's treatment of Cicero along these same lines.

64. The Platonic text in question comes in fact from a pseudonymous letter: *Ep.* 9.358a.
65. Garnsey 2009: 165; cf. Garnsey 2007: 113. 'The senatorial aristocracy, blinded in part at least by short-term views of its own political and economic advantage, failed by timely concessions to satisfy the needs or aspirations of the Italian allies, the best-organized Equites, the urban plebs, the peasantry, and the soldiers' (Brunt 1988b: 81; cf. Brunt 1988c).
66. A modern parallel for such a stance might be Nozick 1974: 149–231. Annas 1989: 170 (with n.25) suggests that Cicero had 'no criterion for deciding whether an entitlement is just'. But the default assumption should be that the routes listed by which entitlements are established—long occupation, military conquest, legal provision, a settlement, agreement, or lot (*Off.* 1.21)—are meant reasonably enough to indicate legitimacy. Presumably military conquest (the one item on the list treated as obviously unjust by Annas) might as the outcome of a just war be regarded as legitimate.
67. See Chapter 4, section 5 pp. 133–4 above.
68. See Garnett 1994: li-liv, 181–5. The author also cites a famous tag from Terence: 'I am a human being: I think nothing human alien to me', echoed by Cicero in a similar Stoicizing context elsewhere (*Leg.* 1.33), and (for example) engraved on one of the beams of Montaigne's study.
69. The pursuit of *gloria* was a major priority for aristocratic Romans. See the evidence assembled from early surviving texts in Earl 1961: 18–27, and for Cicero's own stance Long 1995: 224–33. In the summer of 44 BC he composed a work in two books, complete by July of that year (*Att.* 15.27.2, 16.2.6, 16.3.1), but now lost, *On glory* (*Off.* 2.31). The question of its proper pursuit commands a good deal of attention in Book 2 of *On duties* itself.
70. See section 2 153–4 above. Cicero there describes him as 'in the virtues a person of towering stature'. For the Stoic credentials of *magnus et excelsus homo*, note in Stobaeus's account of Stoic ethics (with Knoche 1935: 56): 'The virtuous person is big and powerful and tall and strong' (*Ecl.* 2.99.12–14; these seemingly physical attributes are then all explained in terms of moral psychology in the sequel: *Ecl.* 2.99.14–19).
71. Knoche 1935: 56. The self-sufficiency of *megalopsuchia* (*magnitudo animi*) for achieving such elevation of mind is in a report of Diogenes Laertius associated particularly with the Stoic Hecato, pupil of Panaetius (Diog. Laert. 7.127).
72. As noted by Knoche 1935: 46.
73. Hellegouarc'h 1972: 293.
74. How would such feats of prowess exemplify 'contempt for things human' (the formulation is several times repeated: *Off.* 1.13, 67, 72)? Cicero's discussion (*Off.* 1.72–3) suggests that great spirits are free from anxiety about what will

happen to them or about what resources they have in life. In other words, they despise not human life and activity itself but the preoccupations which usually dominate people's minds. Unlike other people, they 'appreciate the frailty of things human and the variability of fortune', as Panaetius is quoted as saying, and are unimpressed by them (*Off.* 1.90).

75. The interdependence of the virtues was mentioned—as an assumption not needing argument or comment—in the prefatory section of Book 1 (*Off.* 1.15).
76. Long 1995: 230, 224, 233. For the distinction between true and false glory in *On duties*, see especially *Off.* 2.43, and among other Ciceronian texts where it is drawn at least implicitly *Sest.* 139, *Tusc.* 3.3–4, *Phil.* 1.29, 33.
77. See Earl 1961: 18–27 (particularly on epitaphs of early members of the Scipio clan), Griffin 1996: 278–90 [= Griffin 2018: 492–3] (against Long's construal of Cicero's project as 'reform of the Roman honour code'); also Griffin 2011: 323–6 [= Griffin 2018: 673–5].
78. Griffin 2011: 325 [= Griffin 2018: 674].
79. Long 1995: 230.
80. On Rome's exceptional militarism and its structural rationale, see Scheidel 2019: 51–88.
81. There is a helpful note on this prospectus in Griffin and Atkins 1991: 37 n.1. *Verecundia* is associated with *pudor* at *Rep.* 5.6–7 (a section more probably assigned to Book 4: Büchner 1984: 394–8, Zetzel 2017b: 477–82) and *Leg.* 1.50. Kaster 2005: 61–5 provides a helpful treatment of the differentiated semantic behaviour typical of the two terms. *Rep.* 5.6 makes *verecundia* a natural 'fear of not unjust censure', borrowing a Greek definition of *aischunê* ('shame') recorded in Gell. *NA* 19.6.3, and presents it as something foundational for the functioning of human society which the 'calibrator' (*rector*) of commonwealths or public affairs (*rerum publicarum*) will seek to reinforce as a bulwark against crime (see Kaster 2005: 174 nn. 121 and 125).
82. The description of Cicero the humourist is due to Beard 2014: 100.
83. As translated (with adaptations) in Beard 2014: 102, who like Cicero (*Off.* 1.93) is rendering the Greek *prepon* as 'decorum'.
84. Kaster 1997: 14 n.30 makes the strangely mistaken claim that *verecundia* is not treated by Cicero as 'important to his argument'. Kaster 2005: 16 sees it as an 'emotional disposition'. But Cicero's account treats *verecundia* on Stoic lines as a rationally developed and controlled capacity for managing behaviour, precisely attuned to avoidance of provoking socially undesirable emotional responses in others. Little in Kaster's detailed discussion of *verecundia* in Cicero or other authors (Kaster 2005: 13–27) in truth does much to support its interpretation as itself an 'emotional' disposition.

85. Cicero is explicit that he is translating Greek *prepon*, doubtless as he found it in Panaetius (*Off.* 1.93).
86. See Dyck 1996: 85, arguing that the very close similarities between this passage and *Off.* 1.11–14 suggest that Cicero is using the same Panaetian source text in the two cases. It was no doubt from Plato again that Panaetius himself found guidance and inspiration in developing the theory of *decorum* as implicated in the other three virtues: see *Grg.* 506d–507c.
87. In a forensic speech delivered towards the end of the same year of 45 BC before Caesar as judge, in defence of Deiotarus, king of Galatia in Asia Minor (*Deiot.* 26; cf. *Fam.* 9.12.2). He explains *frugalitas* there as equivalent to *modestia* (discretion) and *temperantia* (restraint).
88. *On duties* gives voice to the same conception: it 'is observed in each single kind of virtue' (*Off.* 1.98; cf. 1.96: it 'pertains to the individual parts of *honestas*'). On mistaken attempts to emend the text of these passages, see Schofield 2012: 51–3.
89. Although the fourth virtue is discussed along with the other three in the opening passage of Book 1's treatment of the virtues (*Off.* 1.11–17), the word *decorum* does not figure until it is formally introduced at the beginning of the section devoted to its exploration (*Off.* 1.93).
90. On the theory of *personae* and its Panaetian credentials, see Gill 1988. On appeal in Epictetus's ethics to the obligations attaching to particular roles, see Long 2002: 232–44, Frede 2007.
91. Also quoted earlier: Chapter 3, section 6 p. 88.
92. For the Cynics see Chapter 4, section 1 p. 105 and n.1.
93. For fuller discussion see Schofield 2012: 50–3.
94. Luxurious building was a common target of moralizing disapproval on the part of Roman writers: see Edwards 1993: 137–72. She quotes Cicero in *On behalf of Murena* (*Mur.* 76): 'The Roman people hate private luxury, but love public magnificence.'
95. The sort of list a Plato or an Aristotle might have constructed: for discussion of its provenance see Brunt 1973: 26–34 [= Brunt 2013a: 172–8].
96. Kaster 2005: 27.
97. See Brunt 1986: 16 [= Brunt 2013a: 250].
98. Appiah 2006 perhaps gives a flavour of how contemporary *verecundia* might look.
99. *Felicitas* was often ascribed to successful military commanders, and is counted by Cicero as one of key four attributes (along with military expertise, courage, and *auctoritas*) that they should combine: *Leg. Man.* 28. References to Julius Caesar's *felicitas* were particularly frequent in the literature contemporary with his ascendancy: see Murphy 1986.

6

Republican Decision-making

1. Citizen decision

In her book *The Morality of Happiness*, Julia Annas introduces ancient philosophical ethics with a basic contrast:[1]

> Its leading notions are not those of obligation, duty and rule-following; instead of these 'imperative' notions it uses 'attractive' notions like those of goodness and worth. Ancient ethical theories do not assume that morality is essentially demanding, the only interesting question being, how much does it demand; rather, the moral point of view is seen as one that the agent will naturally come to accept in the course of a normal unrepressed development.

That characterization perhaps does not quite fit Cicero or Roman ethics. Book 1 of *On duties* certainly makes it as clear as in any surviving work of ancient philosophy that humans are conceived as naturally endowed with a variety of impulses, which when managed to perfection, with a focus always on what is honourable (*honestum*) or morally admirable, develop into the virtues. Choosing the honourable course when practical decisions are called for is what will eventually become second nature to the virtuous person. The 'moral point of view' of *On duties* is accordingly well captured by Annas's characterization of ancient ethics in general. But Cicero's treatise is, after all, titled *On duties* (or, in an alternative translation of the Latin expression *de officiis*, *On obligations*). *Officium* is in fact a Roman moralizing transformation of the Greek *to kathêkon*, 'what it belongs to us to do', or 'what accords with our nature'. The transformation accordingly makes behaving virtuously also a matter of performing those actions that are *required* of us—precisely by the form of the honourable represented in the disposition characteristic of the virtue or virtues, as may be needed in some particular context: in short, a matter of doing our duty (as a requirement conceived in that way). The discourse of 'ought' is not banished from

Cicero's pages. If obligation is not their leading notion, it is certainly a major preoccupation.

While one's virtuous impulses might be well developed, identifying what actually is the right and honourable thing to do—what one ought to do—can still be problematic. So far as concerns action within the public sphere, Cicero is insistent in *On duties* (as pervasively throughout his writings as a whole) on the overriding claims upon citizens of obligations to the *res publica*—which should come 'naturally' to us, to be sure. 'No social relation', he says in Book 1, 'is weightier or commands more affection than the relation each one of us has with the *res publica*' (*Off.* 1.55). We recall his profession back in 56 BC of 'incredible and unparalleled love for the *res publica*' as what has involved him in calamity (*de Or.* 3.13).[2] But even when the *res publica* is in good health, what action is called for to promote its interests can be debatable. When it is in trouble, as frequently during his own public career, and when civilized order is either unstable or broken down completely, then it may become entirely opaque whether any action at all that a citizen might take could properly or effectively promote the well-being of the *res publica*. Indeed, *On the commonwealth* argues that under tyranny or oligarchy, or in conditions of mob rule, there cannot actually be any *res publica*, since these are regimes where the *populus* no longer possesses any *res* over which it can exercise rights.[3] For Cicero, citizen and statesman in turbulent and dangerous times, such issues were as much existential as theoretical, with the potential to destabilize theory too, as sections 3 and 4 of this chapter will vividly illustrate.

The third book of *On duties*, which will be a main focus in its first two sections, is where philosophical attention is given to problem cases for decision on action. It tackles conflicts or supposed conflicts between the honourable and the advantageous, or indeed also as it transpires between the honourable and the honourable. Section 1 will discuss some of the examples Cicero presents. It is sometimes thought that he thinks such matters can be settled by invoking rules of conduct. He does indeed explicitly invoke the notion of a rule (*regula*) at one point (*Off.* 3.81). But section 2 will argue (with Brad Inwood and Raphael Woolf) that closer examination reveals him as in fact for the most part much more of a situationist in ethics. Then from the theorizing of *On duties* we turn to the practical thinking, deeply informed by philosophical ethics, in which he engaged on critical questions of duty in his correspondence with friends. Section 3 considers the options for decision on public duty that he deliberated as civil war loomed in 49 BC. In section 4 his responses to questions of duty as they arise for the citizen under the rule of a tyrant are reviewed: in this case theoretical questions, but pressing (Cicero does not pretend otherwise) in the immediate practical context of that time. Section 5 tackles the obligations of the friends of those who achieve or aspire to autocracy, as these are raised in (and by) a famous exchange of letters between Cicero and his old friend Matius in the summer of 44 BC, in the aftermath of Julius Caesar's assassination. Finally, in section 6 the chapter turns attention to the justification of tyrannicide attempted in *On duties*. The problems and solutions he explores in his theoretical writings emerge as intimately related with those debated in his correspondence, as matters of urgency in his political life.[4]

Cicero takes the scheme of *On duties* as a whole from the Greek Stoic philosopher Panaetius, who never himself however composed the portion of his own treatise that would have dealt with such conflicts (*Off.* 3.7–8; cf. *Att.* 16.11.4).[5] One might initially be surprised at how little attention is paid by Cicero to the whole range of mutual obligations that glued Roman society together, and that were to be of much interest to other Roman writers. In Books 1 and 2 conduct of public life is the dominating preoccupation.[6] In Book 3, by contrast, much of the detailed discussion of specific instances of conflict concerns business or other private financial transactions, often with legal dimensions or resonances that clearly much interested Cicero (notably at *Off.* 3.50–78).[7] Yet behaviour impacting directly on the public sphere and the *res publica* is once again what is mostly scrutinised in later sections of the book (*Off.* 3.79–89, 99–115).[8] These will be the focus in what follows.

Here is a hypothetical case of this latter sort that Cicero invites us to consider (*Off.* 3.90):

Q Suppose one's father were to be stealing treasures from temples, or tunnelling into the treasury building: is his son to denounce him to the magistrates?

A *That* is an act of impiety.[9] Instead he should speak in his father's defence if he is charged.

Q Does one's country not, then, take precedence among all the duties one has?

A Yes, certainly. But it actually assists the country itself to have citizens who revere their parents.

Q And if the father tries to seize a position as tyrant, or to betray his country, will the son keep silent?

A He will certainly beg his father not to do it. If he makes no headway, he will take him to task, he will go so far as to make threats. In the last resort, if things point to the ruin of his country, he will put the country's safety before the safety of his father.

Decision-making is often a conflicted business, as this scenario illustrates. Different verdicts on what would be right here seem possible. Miriam Griffin notes that when Cnaeus Calpurnius Piso was condemned posthumously for treason, the Emperor Tiberius took the view that his younger son 'could not be blamed for *supporting* (not merely keeping quiet about) his father's activities, because he had to obey his father' (Tac. *Ann.* 3.17.1).[10] Montaigne would engage with Book 3 of *On duties* in the essay on the useful and the honourable with which he launched the third volume of *Essais*, not least with the passage quoted above. He deftly adjusts the Ciceronian original to make it say something quite different, 'as a proper lesson for our times'. He simply drops the question mark, leaving us rather with the assertion: 'country does not take precedence among all other duties, and it assists the country itself to have citizens who revere their parents.'[11]

Book 3's official aim is to show that any such conflict must be merely apparent: our true interest must always lie in taking the honourable path. Some of the instances of conflict Cicero offers are actually not so readily shoehorned into that framework. The example just presented is a case in point. It is taken from a collection of puzzle cases assembled (as he tells us: *Off.* 3.89) from the sixth book of a work on duties by Panaetius's pupil Hecato, who evidently did tackle the subject his teacher failed to address. At any rate as Cicero reports them, his puzzles were a distinctly varied lot. As presented, not all of them can readily be seen as pitting apparent advantage against what is honourable. The scenario pictured in the extract quoted above (one of two of the problems where duty to the *res publica* is a consideration) might more easily be read as posing a question about the relative ranking to be assigned in the last resort to interests of family and to those of one's country.[12] Or again, it might well be seen as posing a choice between honourable behaviour relative to a parent and that owed to country. Cicero himself would think that these two alternative formulations might in the end add up to the same thing. From the beginning of Book 3, he has taken the line that 'nothing is advantageous'—truly advantageous— 'that is not honourable' (*Off.* 3.11). If killing a tyrant, even though he may be a friend, is truly beneficial for the *res publica*, then 'honourableness has followed upon advantage' (*Off.* 3.19), and it could be said that advantage must be 'regulated' (*derigenda*) by the honourableness of the patriotic deed (*Off.* 3.83).[13] On that understanding of the advantageous and the honourable, although 'these two seem discordant verbally, they seem in substance to sound a single note' (*Off.* 3.83).

As in most of the first batch of cases that Cicero cites from Hecato (*Off.* 3.89–90), he indicates the verdict that Hecato passed upon the son's problem with a criminal or traitorous father.[14] Cicero's own general stance on the prioritization of the obligations demanded of citizens by justice would commit him to agreeing that duty to the *res publica* ranks highest. Interestingly, in the section of Book 1 devoted to the topic, his summing up does not distinguish country and parents in its ranking (*Off.* 1.58):

Were there a comparison, or competition, as to who ought to receive the greatest share of our dutiful service (*plurimum offici*), our country and our parents would be foremost, for we are obliged to them for the greatest benefits (*beneficia*). Next would be our children and our whole household (*domus*), which looks to us alone and can have no other refuge. Then our relations (*propinqui*) with whom we are on good terms and with whom even our fortunes are generally shared. Therefore: whatever is necessary to support life is most owed to those I have mentioned.

Then he turns to friendship (on which more in section 5 below) as what is most important for the activity of 'shared life and living': 'counsel and conversation, encouragement, comfort, and sometimes even reproofs'. But he has already ruled that it is the *res publica* that demands our greatest devotion: 'our native country on its own embraces all the affections of us all' (*Off.* 1.57).[15]

What exactly might be the particular circumstances, however, in which such a duty trumps all other considerations of family or friendship, or indeed of what other virtues might require of us, is not thereby determined. Hence some of the particular interest of Hecato's scenario. Cicero does allow that some of those less highly ranked obligations may on occasion change priority among themselves, or indeed with other obligations not included in the ranking. The common bonds created by mutual *beneficia*, kindnesses given or help rendered to one another, for example, had already been given brief recognition (*Off.* 1.56; the Greeks by contrast wrote whole treatises on this subject, and Seneca was to devote to the obligations of such *beneficia* a work in seven books). Cicero allows that they may sometimes trump family ties. 'You should, for example, assist your neighbour in gathering in the harvest sooner than your brother or a friend', to whom you would ordinarily expect to give precedence, as notably if help with a lawsuit were required (*Off.* 1.59). But he does not for his own part indicate here whether he thinks duty to the *res publica* might sometimes need (as Hecato envisaged) to cede its pre-eminence, e.g. to filial duty, albeit filial duty conceived as in general itself beneficial to the *res publica*.[16]

In Book 1, however, Cicero argues that there are some things so repulsive, so criminal, that a wise person would not perform them even to save his country. His older contemporary the Stoic philosopher Posidonius, he tells us, had collected a large number of such actions. When he was composing *On duties* he may well not have been in a position himself to look at the collection, and does not mention particular examples, saying by way of justification that some are so grisly or indecent that it seems dishonourable even to mention them.[17] Not only will the wise person not undertake them for the sake of the *res publica*, but the *res publica* will not consent to such action on its behalf. Here the dictates of social virtue have to yield place to the requirements of restraint and moderation (*Off.* 1.159).

Not dissimilar is Cicero's treatment in Book 3 of an example which explicitly offsets morally admirable behaviour against dishonourable action apparently beneficial for Rome. A deserter from the camp of the supposedly unprovoked aggressor Pyrrhus, the Romans' great adversary, comes to the consul Gaius Fabricius. In return for a reward he will return to camp and encompass Pyrrhus's death by poison. The apparent benefit for the Romans is obvious: 'one lone deserter would have put paid to that great war and to a serious opponent of our empire.' But Fabricius has the deserter returned to Pyrrhus, an action commended by the senate. It 'would have been a great disgrace and a scandal to have overcome by crime and not by valour someone with whom the contest was for glory' (*Off.* 3.86; cf. 1.38). In other words, what might have seemed advantageous was not really so, since the Romans would actually have lost what they were really fighting for: honourable victory.[18]

Cicero then (*Off.* 3.87) goes on to try the alternative supposition that it is naked power itself that is being sought, through any means whatever. He pronounces the rather less convincing verdict that, in that event, power acquired at whatever the price still cannot be advantageous 'since it comes with notoriety'. Perhaps sensing the weakness of the reasoning, he bolsters the argument with another example designed to clinch the point that advantage purchased at the cost of notoriety (or worse) is no advantage. He takes an episode from more recent Roman history, in which some of Rome's allies were subjected to an unfairly reimposed regime of taxation: 'Can hatred and notoriety be advantageous to any empire, which ought to be reliant on glory and on the goodwill of its allies?' Would any member of the Roman elite really want to discount the attraction of glory? As for goodwill, we might catch an echo of the arguments of Book 2 on how best to secure the vital advantage of support from people. It is to cultivate their admiration and above all their goodwill, which he there counts first among the ways in which glory is achieved (*Off.* 2.20–2, 31–8).

Before he turned to Fabricius, Cicero had discussed a number of other significant Roman statesmen, beginning with Gaius Marius, a dominant figure at the turn of the second and first centuries BC, and ending with Pompey (very briefly but—unusually in *On duties*—scathingly dealt with) and an extended broadside against Caesar, neither of these latter two identified by name (*Off.* 3.79–86).[19] Marius, a dominant figure in Roman politics at the turn of the second and first centuries BC, and his nephew Marcus Marius Gratidianus are presented as of interest because they both first achieved high political standing by underhand methods, whose infraction of fairness seemed relatively minor. Even so: 'Is there anything of such great value, or any advantage so worth winning', Cicero asks (*Off.* 3.82), 'as to get you to shed the lustre and repute of a good man?'

That question indicates something fundamental to his moral outlook in *On duties*. Just before his presentation of these examples, he had reverted for a moment to the memorable tale of Gyges, as discussed particularly in Plato's *Republic* (*R.* 2. 359c–360d), to which he had devoted more extended presentation earlier in the book (*Off.* 3.38–9, 78). Gyges had acquired a magic ring with which he could make himself visible or invisible at will, giving him virtually infinite power of wrongdoing, which will remain undetected by gods and humans for ever. It is philosophically crass, Cicero argues, to dismiss this scenario as impossible. The point is: suppose it possible for someone, but suppose, too, that we could require them to admit that they would use the ring to do anything whatever to advance their own desires for wealth, power, or sexual gratification. What that shows, as Raphael Woolf observes, is that to pursue evildoing as advantageous comes at a price: you cannot expect to have normal relations with other humans if you could not answer such a question without branding yourself as thoroughly anti-social, and so (given that humans are essentially social animals) as inhuman.[20]

The treatment of Julius Caesar is particularly elaborate and highly rhetorical (*Off.* 3.82–5). Cicero focuses on what is represented as his ambition—successfully achieved—to be king of the Roman people.[21] He poses a dilemma. Anyone who thinks that honourable is out of his mind: 'he justifies the extinction of laws and liberty, and counts their subjugation—something hideous and abominable—as glorious.' Anyone who admits that ruling as king in a citizen body that was and should be free is not honourable, but claims that it is advantageous for the person who can do so, is in effect turning a blind eye to the worst kind of murder: parricide of the country which fathered him. How could being a parricide be an advantage for anyone, even if a cowed population called him 'Father'—i.e. of the country.[22] To that consideration another trope is added. How can someone who has obtained such eminence by unjust means not labour under the disadvantage of constant anxiety and fear of treachery and danger, and again of his own uneasy conscience?[23]

The final example in the whole work is developed on a scale of major proportions, evidently conceived as the grand finale to the entire treatment of alleged conflict between the honourable and the advantageous (*Off.* 3.99–115). This is the case of Marcus Atilius Regulus, on which Cicero lavishes an extended and highly argumentative discussion.[24] Regulus had been taken prisoner by the Carthaginians, but had been released on parole by them—in fact under oath—so that he could undertake a mission to Rome and put the case for repatriation of Carthaginian prisoners of war (as he duly did) in exchange for his own release. Remaining at home with his wife and family once returned to Rome (with no loss of status) might have seemed the expedient thing to do, if the Romans rejected the arguments for repatriation of the prisoners: as on Regulus's own advice they subsequently did.[25] Cicero sees off a whole battery of objections to the effect that, in these circumstances, that would not have been wrong. Regulus is presented as a paradigm of the superior claims of the honourable, with the initial focus in this case on his *magnitudo animi*, towering spirit, and *fortitudo*, courage, in returning to Carthage and thereby going to certain death, as it transpired by 'exquisite torture' (*Off.* 3.100; cf. 110).²⁶ Cicero concludes the entire extended section with the point that Regulus could have taken the apparently easier course only with a timid, craven, dejected, and broken spirit: nobody would want to live with that (*Off.* 3.115).

What made this the honourable course in the first place was its conformity with justice and *fides*, good faith.²⁷ Regulus demonstrated his sense of justice through respecting the rules of war and the sanctity of oaths, in making that subsequent return to Carthage in accordance with them. It was also shown in his patriotism and fulfilment of his *officium* to the *res publica*, by his successfully advising the senate not to accede to the Carthaginian proposal that he duly conveyed to them. For him to have done otherwise, says Cicero, would in fact not have been wise or advantageous: how could something disadvantageous to the *res publica* be advantageous for any of its citizens (*Off.* 3.101)? He states it as his view that giving such advice was what in particular made Regulus's conduct admirable (*Off.* 3.110–11). That verdict comes at the end of a substantial part of the Regulus section dealing with arguments against such a high valuation of oaths, particularly as made with reference to his situation (*Off.* 3.102–10). Cicero claims that nothing in Regulus's time, and in former times more generally, was taken more seriously than the obligation of justice and good faith generated by an oath.²⁸ So that he stuck by his own oath is not especially remarkable. It was his judgement about what would not be advantageous for his country, and his decision that it would accordingly be the honourable thing to give such advice accordingly to the Romans, and to suffer himself the consequences of doing so, which makes him stand out (*Off.* 3.111).

2. Principles, rules, and the casuistry of exceptions

An oath of the kind sworn by Regulus was a form of promise, or perhaps rather a form of guarantee that the promise he made would be honoured without fail. It is particularly striking, however, that quite early in his treatment of justice in Book 1 of *On duties*, immediately after initial discussion of the basic forms of justice and injustice, we find Cicero explaining why promises need not always and sometimes should not be kept (*Off.* 1.31–2). Altered circumstances can change into the opposite what might ordinarily appear to be *officia* that most befit the good and just person. In Book 3, in the section following presentation of Hecato's puzzles, Cicero returns to the topic, and to some of the same examples, as for instance (*Off.* 3.95):

> If a man who has deposited money with you were to make war on your country, would you return the deposit? I believe not, since you would be acting contrary to the *res publica*, which should be what is most dear to you.

'Many things that seem honourable by nature become through circumstances honourable no longer', he says, summing up. He articulates the relevant consideration in terms of changed advantage: 'To keep promises, to stand by agreements, to return deposits become no longer honourable, if advantage changes.' In the Book 1 section on promises, Cicero had begun by recalling the two basic rules of justice, which are both formulated in terms of harm and benefit: no harm is to be done to anyone, the common advantage is to be served. In circumstances where there is a change in how one or other of these needs to be realized, *officium* changes too (*Off.* 1.31).[29]

Promising something on oath is treated very differently, in a distinct and unconnected section of Book 3, and with altogether other considerations. The force of the guarantee that an oath confers on a promise is its status as a religious affirmation, an act of piety. What stops the person making the affirmation from violating the oath is not fear of divine wrath (generally agreed to be bad theology), but its having been made 'as though god were its witness': 'in putting oneself before the divine, one thereby enters the realm of the normative.'[30] Violation would be a violation of *fides*, good faith, here represented as a divine being (*Off.* 3.104).[31] In short, the divine places a different and higher constraint upon us than does the human order of things.

But can the validity of an oath vary with circumstances? What determines that is not what was said but what was really intended (*Off.* 3.107; cf. 1.40): 'If an oath has been sworn in such a way that the mind grasps that it ought to be done, it should be kept; if not, there is no perjury if it is not done.' 'In such a way' is not meant to leave the matter to arbitrary decision. The expression must be taken as implying 'in such an external context'. If the oath was sworn to an enemy of one's country (as in Regulus's case), then it has to be taken as genuinely intended, and the laws of war require that it be honoured. But if you agree the price of a ransom with pirates holding you captive, who are 'the common enemy of all', so that your oath can properly be interpreted as not really meant, failure to pay the ransom involves no deceit.

It looks as though Cicero might envisage the possibility of two grades of promise, with different degrees of *fides* attaching to them. There will be those promises to be regarded as defeasible, should circumstances make it disadvantageous to the person to whom the promise was made, or else to the one who gave it (*Off.* 1.31)—or to the *res publica* (*Off.* 3.95). There will by contrast be those given on oath, to be honoured without fail if properly intended, although presumably these too would be subject to the general proviso that the promise has not been made through forcible intimidation or trickery (*Off.* 1.32, 3.92; cf. 3.110).[32]

A consideration which might tell against such a distinction is raised by Raphael Woolf. He suggests that since 'Regulus' sticking to his promise, and the serving of the common good, are treated as pulling in the same direction', it is more likely than not that had they not done so, there would in Cicero's view have been 'sufficient reason to break the promise'.[33] So despite the rhetorical intensity of his talk of divine witness to an oath, he would really regard such promises as no less defeasible than any other. It is hard to evaluate the force of such a counterfactual interpretative proposal. But as Mary Beard remarks: 'The religious sphere at Rome cannot easily be distinguished from the political.'[34] In this case stringent laws of warfare were also at stake, which Cicero clearly thought beneficial to all parties observing them, whatever the outcomes on any particular occasion.

In any case, he is explicit that when Regulus's advice to the Romans was accepted (presumably whether wisely or not), he had no option but to honour his oath (*Off.* 3.111; cf. 3.108).[35] It is implied that oaths were once observed more scrupulously than they are in his own time. Nonetheless, the laws of war still 'often' require that fidelity to oaths sworn to the enemy must be observed (*Off.* 3.107; cf. 1.39). The sequel indicates that this is mandatory if an oath is sworn with a true intention to perform it, as when the hostilities are being conducted with a 'just and legitimate enemy' (presumably, one who similarly abides by the rules of war). With such an enemy 'there are many shared rights' (*Off.* 3.108).[36]

It is difficult to find other principles of similar generality articulated or adumbrated in *On duties*, however, that impose the absolute and straightforward demand of a sincerely meant oath uttered in an appropriate context. One candidate, perhaps, might be thought to be the *formula*, or rule of procedure, introduced by Cicero for guidance on dealing with cases of conflict between the honourable and the apparently advantageous (*Off.*

3.19–21). We are not to further our own advantage by causing another disadvantage.[37] But application of the rule is not invariably straightforward, as a debate he stages in due course between the Stoics Diogenes and Antipater illustrates (*Off.* 3.50–7).[38] Otherwise, as Andrew Dyck comments, there is little use of the *formula* as such in the treatment of problem cases that occupies the main body of Book 3.[39]

In general, the advisory rules (*praecepta*) specifying our obligations that Cicero promises (*Off.* 1.7) prove to be susceptible of exceptions, or to carry implications which will change when circumstances change. Terry Irwin helpfully suggests that for ancient ethics we should distinguish between *principles*, such as 'give everyone his due' (specifying what justice always requires of us), and *rules* that exemplify the principles, such as 'pay your debts' and 'keep your promises', which apply generally, but in particular circumstances may be defeasible.[40] The general validity of the 'no harm' and 'common benefit' rules of justice, as a framework for ethical decision, plainly turns on a more fundamental notion of fairness which has an independent force of its own. But for the practical application and the assessment of the relative weight of these and other rules, as required on particular occasions, we need to be 'good calculators of our duties', working out what different needs there are, and which of them can or cannot be achieved without our involvement (*Off.* 1.59). There are rules designed to guide doctors, army commanders, and public speakers. But such practitioners cannot achieve anything worthwhile without experience and practice. The same goes for the application of rules on the massively important topic of obligation (*Off.* 1.60).[41]

Cicero much approved of a relatively recent development in civil law, whereby litigants made statements before a judge of contractual disputes 'in good faith' (*ex fide bona*), it being assumed that both were *boni*, 'honest people'. This was designed to achieve greater transparency in what was at stake in (for example) the buying and selling of property (*Off.* 3.65–72).[42] But Cicero's early mentor (*Brut.* 306) the jurist Quintus Mucius Scaevola, an important advocate of this practice, commented that it called for a judge of real stature to determine what information each party ought to provide for the other, especially because in most cases there were rival assessments to consider (*Off.* 3.70).[43] In other words, the requirements of *fides* itself were seldom transparent.

3. Civil war

In the bulky collections of Cicero's surviving correspondence is a particularly rich and absorbing sequence of his letters to Atticus, dating from just before the civil war between the forces of Pompey and Caesar went live in 49 BC.[44] They run from autumn 50 BC, as he is making his way home in the hopes of promoting concord (*concordia*), following the year he spent in Cilicia as governor of the province, through the early months of 49 BC as Caesar and Pompey start squaring up for the conflict that duly ensued, to June of that year, when we find him writing from Pompey's camp at Dyrrachium on the east coast of the Adriatic. Cicero uses Atticus as sounding board for his seemingly endless indecision about what he should do: 'I talk with you as if with myself': *Att.* 8.14.2 (cf. *Lael.* 22), and sometimes finds that calming (e.g. *Att.* 7.11.5, 7.12.3, 9.4.1, 9.10.1 and 10). He apologizes for writing so often, sometimes on a daily basis (e.g. *Att.* 7.12.3, 8.14.1). He begs him for advice (e.g. *Att.* 8.3.1 and 7).[45] Atticus replies fairly consistently: stay put, wait and see (*Att.* 9.10, where that was the theme Cicero at any rate chose to take as most salient). Prompted by Atticus (*Att.* 7.1.2–3), Cicero wants to remain on good terms with both the protagonists, and above all he wants peace: 'Even an unjust peace', he writes near the end of January (*Att.* 7.14.3; echoed in a letter to an old friend after the conflict: *Fam.* 6.6.5), 'is more advantageous (*utilis*) than the most just of wars with one's fellow citizens.'

Realistic prospects of any kind of rapprochement between the two warlords ebb away, however, and Cicero is left with a decision, as he and Atticus see it, between staying put (at least until it becomes clearer how events may play out) or joining Pompey's entourage. This then mutates in time into a choice between staying in Italy, without necessarily committing to Caesar, or crossing the Adriatic to join the Pompeian forces. On 17 February, he is still for remaining (*Att.* 8.2.4): leaving Italy (if that is the course Pompey takes) he thinks advantageous neither for him nor for the *res publica*, nor for his son and nephew, and moreover neither right (*rectum*) nor honourable (*honestum*). He reminds himself that Socrates 'never put a foot outside the gates' of Athens during the regime of the thirty tyrants.

But by the beginning of March (*Att.* 8.15.2) he is saying that what is influencing him most away from his initial temporizing is not the prospect of Pompey's anger, nor learning that the consuls are on their way to join him.

It is debating in my mind *officium* (duty, obligation) that tortures me and has tortured me all along. The warier course is certainly staying, the more honourable is thought to be making the crossing. Sometimes I feel as though I had rather be thought to have acted unwarily by many than dishonourably by a few.

This concern for what the few 'sound' or 'honest' men (*boni*) think, principally senators committed to the republican cause, recurs more frequently from this point on (e.g. *Att.* 9.1.3, 9.6.4, 9.7.6, 9.10.9), even though he often expresses contempt for the spinelessness of those he refers to in those terms or as the 'best element' (*optimates*) (e.g. *Att.* 7.7.5, 8.16.1, 9.5.3, 9.13.6).[46] In the end, he does decide to leave Italy for Pompey.

Why? Solely, he says in letters early in March, for Pompey ('what moves me is one man alone' (*Att.* 8.14.2)), and for the particular obligations (*officia*) he has incurred or for what he owes (*debemus*) to someone who is after all claiming to be defending the public cause (*Att.* 9.1.4, 9.5.3; cf. 8.3.2).[47] But he does so with no hope of an outcome beneficial to the *res publica*, and not before he has poured out several times his disgust and fury at the way both Pompey and Caesar have behaved, and at what they may be planning (*Att.* 8.3, 8.9a, 8.11, 10.4, 10.14). People have hopes of Caesar, but fear Pompey (*Att.* 8.16.2). Pompey, in particular, has fallen desperately short of the ideal of a statesman articulated in Book 5 of *On the commonwealth* (*Att.* 8.11.1).[48] Also in *On the commonwealth*, he had articulated the view (as Atticus reminds him) that nothing is good except what is honourable, nothing bad except what is dishonourable. But Pompey and Caesar alike have always put the safety of the country and the respect due to it (*dignitas*) in second place after their own domination (*dominatio*) and their private advantage (*domestica commoda*) (*Att.* 10.4.4).[49]

The whole sequence exudes the obsessiveness of anxiety to a high degree. The anxiety is multidimensional. Cicero agonizes not just about what he is to do and whether his behaviour hitherto has been pragmatically and ethically justifiable (*Att.* 9.10 is a particularly defensive and self-torturing example).[50] He constantly frets, too, and no less importantly, over his relationships with both Caesar and Pompey, and over the public perception of his conduct. It is an extraordinary human document.[51] For our purposes, one of its chief interests is what it tells us about the way one Roman republican conceptualized the dreadful dilemma he faced. A whole battery of binary oppositions is deployed: the just and the advantageous, spun at the end of January in favour of the benefit of an unjust peace; the honourable and the advantageous, both in mid-February seen as best satisfied by a decision to remain in Italy; the honourable and the wary (*cautum*), where in early March he 'sometimes' feels himself more drawn by what some think the honourable course of joining Pompey; national security against individual domination, respect for country against private convenience; the few and the many; what is so and what is thought to be so.[52] We encounter the idea of a just war, already introduced by Laelius into his argument in Book 3 of *On the commonwealth* for the thesis that the *res publica* cannot be conducted without justice (*Rep.* 3.34–5), with its preconditions to be further developed in *On duties* (1.34–40).[53] And the notion of *officium* itself is accorded a focal role.

Cicero's reliance on the contrasting categories of the honourable (or the just) and the advantageous in a way anticipates the structuring of *On duties*, composed five years later, with that very same opposition.[54] But the categories were not proprietary to Stoicism. They had general currency in philosophical discourse.[55] Moreover, Cicero's treatment of the concepts in the letters of 49 BC operates with an understanding of their relationship that is not obviously Stoic, if we take the authentically Stoic view to be the doctrine (*Off.* 3.11), echoed in *On the commonwealth* as Atticus reminded him (*Att.* 10.4.4): 'Whatever is honourable is advantageous, and nothing is advantageous that is not honourable.'

These letters often appear to make the more usual, common-sense assumption that consideration of the honourable and the advantageous may point us in contrary and irreconcilable directions. Cicero plainly supposes an unjust peace to be something that conveys no honour on those who settle for it. But in January 49 he thought such a peace more advantageous than conducting 'the most just of wars' against one's fellow citizens, and throughout continued to regret that a settlement with Caesar had not been achieved. Advantage is in fact what seems uppermost in his mind in the letters of early 49: his own and his family's, and that of the *res publica* and the military forces (principally Pompey's) mustered in its defence. It sounds as though it may have been in part this primary focus on advantage which prompted Atticus to remind him occasionally of 'what I had done, said, and even written' (*Att.* 8.2.2, his letter of 17 February). As again in mid-April (*Att.* 10.4.4), Atticus evidently had in mind *On the commonwealth*'s Stoic formulation of precisely the inseparability of advantage from the honourable, with a reference to what was worthy of someone who had achieved Cicero's political pre-eminence. Cicero supposed more active and overt support for Pompey was meant (out of keeping with what he had been taking to be the general tenor of Atticus's advice up to that point). He replied rather sharply that Atticus seemed to have a different view from him of what would be honourable for him to do, given Pompey's deplorable conduct.[56]

The rhetorical effectiveness of binary logic such as the opposition between the honourable and the advantageous possessed and still possesses strong appeal. It certainly had Cicero in its thrall. At the same time, even as he deployed it in these letters, it is hard to think that he would not have considered active concern for what was advantageous for family and *res publica* to be something itself an honourable impulse natural to us (indeed in one letter we have seen him saying pretty much just that: *Att.* 8.2.4);[57] or that in that connection he would not have agreed with the words he was to write in *On duties* five years later: 'while these two seem discordant verbally, they seem in substance to sound a single note' (*Off.* 3.83).[58] His problem was that resistance to the injustice of Caesar's violation of the norms of republican public life was what justice would demand, and as such also an honourable course to take, albeit one that would precipitate civil war and so bring little or nothing in the way of advantage. Joining Pompey's forces, as resistance seemed to require, would also however enable him to act on an honourable impulse by discharging his obligations of friendship (as he represented their relationship). And there was also the problem of sustaining his own *dignitas* in the eyes of the 'sound' republicans—the *boni*—who were joining Pompey: another matter of personal honour.

Cicero's capacity for resolution in those early months of 49 BC might be regarded as having been 'sicklied o'er with the pale cast of thought'. However as long as full-scale war could not be regarded as quite unavoidable, the balance of both the honourable and the advantageous might well have seemed to favour the policy of waiting and seeing, as Atticus was recommending. The irresolution of waiting and seeing meant detachment, however, with disturbing psychological consequences. Cicero's impulse for doing what is honourable may not have left him, but its frustration triggers anomie and a deeper existential Angst. In a particularly interesting letter of 28 February 49, he yet again requests Atticus's advice on what he should do. He starts in defensive mode, justifying his fence-sitting conduct as 'quite uncompromised' (*integra*). For anything that he might be thought to have failed to do, his proffered explanation begins in philosophical mode. He has a line of 'excuse that is not merely persuasive (*probabilem*)' (persuasiveness being sufficient for an Academic such as Cicero), but 'wise (*sapientem*)': it has the invulnerable security attainable by a Stoic sage. He then rehearses his responses to recent approaches by both Caesar and Pompey. After requesting Atticus to spell out more fully his opinion on these points, he puts to him the following request (*Att*. 8.12.4):

> Please take a look into the future, and sketch the sort of figure it is and looks right (*deceat*) for me to be, and where you think I could most be useful to the *res publica*— is any kind of peacemaking role (*persona*) required, or is it all a matter of the fighting man (*bellator*)?

He adds: 'I measure everything by duty (*officium*).'

Here the dense accumulation of terms which will recur in the *decorum* theory of *On duties*—the verb *deceat*, *persona*, and *officium* itself—inevitably suggests that he is already thinking within Panaetius's Stoic framework about what he should be and do, and conceivably expects that to be recognized by Atticus, too.[59] Casting his question in those terms enables Cicero at once to crystallize his dilemma as crucial to his own identity, and in effect to give himself the reason why he could never adequately resolve it. He is already aware that the chances of a negotiated peace have pretty well evaporated. He knows that he will never be a credible 'fighting man' (and as it fell out, although in the end he joined Pompey's camp, he was never himself to participate in the action). He has lost the *persona* which enabled him to organize honourable impulses into effective action.

Cicero immediately qualifies the request for guidance that he is making, however. Despite the reference to the *officium* proprietary to a particular *persona*, he shifts ground at once by recalling Atticus's advice ten years before that he should respond positively to overtures to fall in with schemes Pompey and Caesar (then allies) were wanting to implement, and how to his own regret and eventual humiliation in exile he had rejected what was proposed, as threatening republican liberty.[60] Now he wants more of Atticus's 'calculations' (*calculos*), to permit him to make use of advice not just focused on glory (which might result from pursuing the honourable course of *officium*), but also a bit more geared to what will be 'salutary' (*paulo salubrioribus*: *Att*. 8.12.5). One constant has been his concern for keeping his family from danger. It is significant that, in the dilemma that ends a list of issues for political deliberation that he writes out for Atticus's consumption two weeks later in a Greek rhetorical exercise, the second alternative—the last option mentioned in the whole sequence—is being allowed just to think of himself and his family (*Att.* 9.4.2).[61]

The crux of the matter is surely that it was so difficult for him to see how he could realistically serve the *res publica* at all any more. The warmongering of Caesar and Pompey has effectively all but destroyed it. Civil war could never be the best option for the *res publica*; and though the cause of Pompey and the *boni*, the optimate senators who have joined him, may be just, it is clear well before the major conflict begins that Caesar was likely to prevail. These are the circumstances in which Cicero prevaricates, with the whole scheme of values within which he could take decisions in danger of collapse, and his sense of his own identity fracturing. The Roman public sphere in which he had exercised his role is at worst finished and at best in suspension, for who knows how long. Cicero has therefore effectively lost his *persona*, which is to say much of his identity. He is alienated from others and himself alike. Just a week before, he had written that because of Pompey's actions, he has to lose not only all he owns, but *memet ipso*, 'my very self', or as Shackleton Bailey translates, 'what I was' ('what I am' might be better) as well as 'what I had' (*Att.* 8.7.2).

In letters early in March, when Cicero is starting to try and take the plunge and join Pompey, the thing he says is pulling him in that direction is his *officium* to a friend and benefactor (*Att.* 8.14.2, 9.1.4, 9.5.3, 9.6.4).[62] And this is the version he would later publicize in *On behalf of Marcellus*, a speech delivered in Caesar's presence in 46 BC (*Marc.* 14). In truth, he was never then or earlier on particularly friendly terms with Pompey; and though he had supported Pompeian causes, and for his part owed his return from exile in 57 BC largely to Pompey's support, he did not disagree when Atticus pointed out that he exaggerated the help he had received from that quarter (*Att.* 9.13.3). Nonetheless it would doubtless have been clear to all observers that he was politically indebted principally to Pompey and that his broad political sympathies were with the *boni*.

Perhaps what seems most indicative in the letters is Cicero's growing sense of having disgraced himself when Pompey and the consuls have (as he thinks) left Italy (*Att.* 9.6.4, composed on 11 March 49). He feels himself to be now in Caesar's clutches and at the mercy of that *peithananke*, compulsion masquerading as persuasion, in which Caesar engages (*Att.* 9.10.2, 9.13.4). He has lost his bearings (books, writing, philosophy mean nothing, he says in a letter of 18 March in which he likens himself to a 'caged bird': *Att.* 9.10.2).⁶³ What really pushed him in the end to opt for Pompey? In subsequent years, he would say to old friends to whom he felt he owed explanations: *officium* (obligation, presumably to Pompey), or my reputation with sound men (*boni*), or being overcome by shame (*pudor*) (*Fam.* 6.6.6, to Aulus Caecina in 46 BC); or again shame (note its repeated prominence), or obligation, or fortune (*fortuna*)—that was just the way the cookie crumbled (*Fam.* 11.26.4, to Gaius Matius, in 44 BC).⁶⁴ Even if we take due account of Cicero's inability to resist a rhetorical tricolon, it sounds as though he is admitting that he cannot really explain himself in terms that could satisfy him. The fact is that he was a figure prominent in public life: that was inevitably his *persona*. Active political participation was what he and everyone else expected of him. He had to jump one way or another. But he could really find only motives of personal obligation and status for doing so. He could not convincingly represent his action as what his 'incredible and unparalleled love for the *res publica*' (*de Or.* 3.13) impelled him to do.⁶⁵

4. Tyranny

Philosophy is in these letters seldom far away from Cicero's mind. His own *On the commonwealth* gets referred to a number of times (cf. *Att.* 7.3.2, 8.2.2, 8.11.1, 10.4.4). He compares the staying put option with Socrates' behaviour under tyranny, as we have seen. But still stuck in Italy on 18 March he feels as Plato did when he was held under virtual arrest at the court of the Sicilian tyrant Dionysius: like a caged bird longing to fly away (*Att.* 9.10.2). A few days later he quotes verbatim in the Greek something Plato wrote in the same connection in the Seventh Letter: 'The requests of tyrants, as you know, have an element of compulsion', what he for his part calls *peithananké*, 'persuading compulsion' (*Att.* 9.13.4).⁶⁶

Less than two weeks before that, he had sent Atticus one of the more curious compositions in the entire Ciceronian corpus. Cicero had received what he construed as the *peithananké* of a short letter from Caesar expressing the hope that he could soon benefit from Cicero's advice and authority and help across the board (*Att.* 9.6a). On 12 March, he reports to Atticus that he has been formulating sequences of questions, framed in the style of those typically subjects of a rhetorical exercise, and indicating the pros and cons of different courses of action—allegedly to keep his thoughts off his immediate troubles. He sets down a sample—in Greek, again (*Att.* 9.4.2):

[A] Should a person stay in his country if it is under tyrannical rule? [B] Should he take steps to overthrow tyranny by every means, even if on account of that the city is going to be comprehensively endangered? [C] Should he be wary of the overthrower, in case he seizes power for himself? [D] Should he try and support his country, if it comes under tyrannical rule, by exploiting opportunity and by argument rather than through war? [E] [i] Should a statesman drop out of public life and retire somewhere, if the country is under tyrannical rule, or [ii] should he take every conceivable risk for the sake of liberty? [F] Should he make war against its territory and blockade it if it is under tyrannical rule? [G] Should he enlist with the party of the best elements even if he does not approve of overthrowing the tyranny by war? [H] Should he be prepared in politics to share in the risks taken by benefactors and friends, even if he thinks the general policy they have worked out is not well conceived? [I] [i] Should someone who has performed great services for his country and on that very account suffered irreparable damage, and is the victim of malevolence, voluntarily incur danger for the sake of his country, or [ii] should he be permitted to put thought into looking after himself and his family, giving up political opposition to those in power?

Cicero employs the Greek term *theseis* in referring to these questions (*Att.* 9.4.1, 9.9.2), or in Latin *consultationes* (*Att.* 9.4.3), which we might render as 'deliberative enquiries' (cf. *de Or.* 3.109, where the notion is first identified by the standard rhetorical term *quaestio infinita*: 'question not relating to a particular set of circumstances').[67] He calls them 'political' (using as often the Greek term), by which he means general issues for discussion in political philosophy.[68] Here very likely he reflects the categorization of the modes of philosophical discourse introduced by his early teacher in philosophy, Philo of Larissa (Stob. *Ecl.* 2.7, pp. 41.7–16), head of the Academy.[69] He tells Atticus that he debates such questions pro and contra, a rhetorical exercise he says elsewhere is distinctive of the Peripatetics and Academics (*de Or.* 3.17, cf. 3.67–8; *Tusc.* 2.9).[70]

Such an exercise gives him an intellectual resource for decision-making other than the consideration of the honourable and the advantageous otherwise prominent in their correspondence. General in form though the questions he itemizes may be, Cicero's letter is up front in acknowledging that they are topical as well as 'political'. In this particular instance, the basic *thesis* he proposes for consideration is presumably [A}, with those that follow regarded as more specific and pointed versions or redraftings of the general issue it raises. Indeed, the two closely related alternative questions [E] and [I} become rather specific, predicated not of any citizen whatsoever, but more particularly of a statesman, and then even more particularly of a distinguished benefactor of his country. It might perhaps be debatable whether strictly speaking they should count on Philo's reckoning as belonging to political philosophy at all. Topicality has eventually taken over more or less completely here. In his treatment of *theseis* in *On the orator*, however, Cicero had made his leading speaker Crassus claim that illuminating some particular concern at hand was a key benefit of debate about the general issues they get us to consider (*de Or.* 3.120; cf. *Brut.* 322).

Cicero tells Atticus that he debates the kinds of topic that he lists, now in Greek, now in Latin. Nonetheless his extended use of Greek on this occasion, at unprecedented length, is significant. It is not just that code-switching into Greek is a hallmark of the intimacy of his relationship with Atticus.[71] As Sean McConnell argues, the Greek language of tyranny helps to stress just how alien are the circumstances in which he finds himself: 'being subject to a tyrant is a typically Greek rather than Roman situation.' The references to Socrates' position during the regime of the thirty and to Plato's virtual imprisonment by Dionysius emphasize the disjunction from the norms of Roman Republican public life.[72]

Cicero's was an orator of incomparable powers, well able to construct a persuasive case for or against any and all of the options. In one guise or another all figured in the agonizing of other letters to Atticus in the early months of 49. It is indicative that the two alternative questions in the sequence here—[E] and [I]—are close to being identical, with the difference that second time round, in the very last option proposed, Cicero invests the dilemma with a freight of fierce personal resentment. And though the dilemmatic form symbolizes his own irresolution, he reverses the order in [I] from [E], indicating (I take it) that the second alternative—looking after himself and his family—is above all what he would like to be able to conclude. But one thing he does not possess is any easy decision procedure. Referring back to this letter a few days later (17 March), he himself says of his *theseis*: 'Some of them are very hard to judge' (*Att.* 9.9.2). Presumably he means primarily: 'hard to find decisive philosophical grounds for judging'. Yet since he wanted an ethical basis for guiding his own conduct, what he says no doubt indicates the difficulty he felt in making the practical choice. The choice he eventually made in the spring of 49 seems to answer most to [H] ('Should he be prepared in politics to share in the risks taken by benefactors and friends, even if he thinks the general policy they have worked out is not well conceived?').

These questions were to be answered by or rather mostly for Cicero in a different way once Caesar's supremacy was finally secured in the spring of 46 BC (after the uncertainties of the months immediately following Caesar's victory over Pompey in August 48, at the battle of Pharsalus in Thessaly, were resolved). Having concluded at once for his part that attempting to fight on would be pointless and needlessly destructive, Cicero effectively replied to the basic question [A] in the affirmative, at any rate for himself. Staying in his own country, even though it was now under tyrannical rule, was the right course. In August 46 he encouraged Marcus Marcellus, a prominent republican and blue-blooded aristocrat of considerable stature (he had been consul in 51), to think the same (*Fam.* 4.8.2). If there was to be some form of *res publica*, Marcellus should be a leading figure (*princeps*) in it, albeit yielding necessarily to circumstances; if not, this was still the most suitable place for spending one's exile:

After all, if liberty is our object, where is there a place exempt from domination (*dominatus*)?[73] But if we are merely looking for some place or other, what is pleasanter than hearth and home?

It was now for Cicero the statesman to 'drop out of public life and retire somewhere' ([E] [i]) under what he and many of his class perceived to be tyranny. He had to keep his mouth shut, more or less—*hêsuchazein*, in the Greek:[74] which implies both literal quietness and the 'quiet' life of what the Romans called *otium*, the leisured existence made possible by withdrawal, voluntary or otherwise, and temporary or more lasting, from public life (e.g. *Fam.* 4.4.4, from autumn 46: 'honourable *otium*, my only solace in adversity').[75]

This did not mean that he had lost all political influence. Caesar and the Caesarians closest to him clearly went out of their way to treat Cicero with respect and friendliness, chief among them Pansa.[76] There survives a sequence of letters dating to late summer and early autumn 46 written to various friends, mostly not of the highest political status, who had fought for Pompey in the civil war, and were hoping for amnesty from Caesar (e.g.

Fam. 4.13, 6.6, 6.10, 6.12, 6.13, 6.14). With all due caution, Cicero gave reassurances of differing strength, and promised that he would do his best for them. In such contexts, he went so far as to ascribe to Caesar not only *magnitudo animi* (*Fam.* 4.4.4), *humanitas* (*Fam.* 4.13.2), and *clementia* (*Fam.* 6.6.8), but *gravitas*, justice or fairness (*iustitia*), and wisdom (*Fam.* 6.6.10).[77] When on occasion he did utter in public, unsurprisingly he felt obliged to address the dictator in similarly positive terms, as in the speech for Marcellus (the surviving *On behalf of Marcellus*) that he gave in autumn 46 also.

Cicero also found another way of making what he considered a significant intervention in the public sphere. There was a further option on his rhetorical list of possibilities that had positive appeal for him, at any rate if given an interpretation he had perhaps not envisaged when he articulated it. This was the idea of 'supporting his country by exploiting opportunity and by argument or in speech (*logos*)' [D]. This effectively enabled him to forge a variant of the *persona* he had forged in public life. The extensive developing programme of writing about rhetoric and philosophy, into which he threw himself from 46 onwards, he came to perceive increasingly not just as a recipe for whiling away enforced leisure, but as itself an important contribution to the *res publica* and the civic education of Romans. The alternative to 'dropping out of public life'—that is, 'taking every conceivable risk for the sake of liberty' [E] [ii]—never however seems to have been on the cards so far as he was concerned. Nor was Cicero to be invited to join the relatively large group of conspirators who brought the dictatorship to an end in 44 on the Ides of March.

Once Caesar was dead, Cicero applauded the assassination. In letters, it is greeted as a straightforward and indeed glorious act of liberation from tyranny, provoking few moral questions: 'our heroes have achieved what was in their own power to achieve most gloriously and magnificently' (*Att.* 14.4.2).[78] In the second Philippic, he compares the deed to his own action in putting down the Catilinarian conspiracy (*Phil.* 2.28), and recalls similar feats hallowed in the annals of republican freedom (*Phil.* 2.26). He does not ask by what right the conspirators carried out their act. The theory of the statesman—the *rector*—that he had worked out in *On the commonwealth* was available as an answer. The *res publica* may have to rely at times of crisis on men of exceptional insight and courage, who though holding no public office will seize the moment and act on its behalf (like Lucius Junius Brutus who had led the revolt against the Tarquin kings).[79] In writing to Decimus

Brutus (one of Caesar's assassins) in December 44, Cicero says accordingly (*Fam.* 11.7.2):

> Something which I want you to grasp and remember with special care is that in safeguarding the liberty and safety of the Roman people, you must not wait for the authority of a Senate which is not yet free. If you did, you would be condemning your own act. For you did not liberate the *res publica* relying on any public decision, a fact which makes the business even greater and more glorious.

In *On laws* he had in a different context enunciated the famous principle *salus populi suprema lex esto* ('the people's safety is to be the ultimate law': *Leg.* 3.8). In one of the later Philippics (delivered in late February 43), he has recourse to just such a principle, identifying the requisite sort of law as a divine law of nature, 'commanding what is honourable, forbidding the opposite'.[80] That is what authorizes the liberators in taking up otherwise unauthorized military commands for the safety of the *res publica* (*Phil.* 11.28).

5. Friendship

Cicero's old friend Gaius Matius took a very different view of Caesar's murder. He was evidently one of Caesar's closest confidants (*Att.* 9.15a, *Fam.* 6.12.2, 11.27.5), and grieved at the death of a friend (*Fam.* 11.28.2, 4, 6, 7). Very soon after the Ides of March, Cicero on 7 April 44 broke a journey to stay overnight at Matius's house. From there he wrote to Atticus about Matius's reaction to what had happened: that Rome was beyond salvation, its problems insoluble. 'If he [i.e. Caesar], with all his genius, could not find a way out', Cicero recorded him as saying, with relish (*Att.* 14.1.1), 'who will find one now?' Further letters followed in which Cicero expresses irritation with Matius's stance (*Att.* 14.4 and 5). At some later point in that year, Cicero wrote to Matius to rebut a complaint he had been making (as Cicero was informed by an intermediary). Various aspects of Matius's conduct since March were being criticized, and he had gathered that Cicero had gone along with them, or at any rate failed to support him. Cicero assured him of his long and continuing warm affection for him and appreciation of his many acts of support, and of his high esteem of his personal qualities (*Fam.* 11.27).[81] In replying, Matius professed himself relieved and reassured. But for good measure he presented a sustained justification not only of his recent conduct, but also of his alignment with Caesar in the period of the civil war (*Fam.* 11.28).

Much in this pair of letters and in their intellectual and other contexts is not our present concern.[82] Above all, however, they constitute both a disturbed enactment of friendship and an argument about its obligations. In different ways both Cicero (with more qualification) and Matius want to insist on how friendship can transcend politics: in Cicero's case, mainly his friendship with Matius, whereas what preoccupies Matius is exclusively and angrily his own with Caesar. Both letters address issues relating to prioritization of *officia* that are central to the business of this chapter. They are both stiffly formal, quite unlike the relaxed style of many of the letters to Atticus, and both have an element of the disingenuous.[83]

To begin with Cicero's letter: it falls into three distinct parts, with the third a section that introduces a philosophical quandary. Cicero begins with a long review of the course of his friendship with Matius over many years. He stresses his appreciation for Matius's attentions at moments of great stress and uncertainty, advice on dealings with Caesar both before and after the civil war, and companionship in the period of the dictatorship. Then he turns to deal, too briskly to carry full conviction, with the complaints against him that he chooses to treat as most salient. Lastly, he writes as follows (*Fam.* 11.27.8):

But to a person of your philosophical knowledge (*hominem doctissimum*) it is obvious that, if Caesar was king (as it seems certainly to me), your own obligation (*officium*) can be argued either way. Either the side I for my part always take, that your loyalty (*fides*) and humanity (*humanitas*) in loving a friend even after his death are thoroughly praiseworthy. Or the side that quite a number of people take, that the liberty of the country needs to be ranked above the life of a friend. I only wish the arguments I put in these discussions had been conveyed to you. At any rate, no one recalls more readily and more often than I the two things which above all redound to your honour: yours was the weightiest influence both against embarking on a civil war and in favour of exercising moderation in victory. I have found no one who did not agree with me.

This is Cicero putting diplomatically what he takes to be a hard truth that Matius needs to face. People are naturally querying Matius's recent behaviour, given that Caesar had made himself king (a claim Matius will not explicitly challenge in his response).[84] Cicero's own main message, in the context of the letter as a whole, is that citizens have to be able to withstand the broader scrutiny of political philosophy, despite all that friendship means to him as well as to Matius. That scrutiny for Cicero means debate, posing questions rather than answers, in true Academic style, and indeed here somewhat reminiscent of the dilemmas formulated in the rhetorical exercise he reported himself as conducting back in March 49 (*Att.* 9.4.2).[85] His final comment indicates that Matius passes this particular test. At the time of the great crisis of 49, Matius's was the greatest and most influential voice for peace, and then subsequently for moderation in victory. His political activity in those years has been his most admirable and admired contribution to public life.

Cicero must have hoped that the evaluation would be taken to heart by its recipient: Matius would presumably not have been unaware of Cicero's own conviction that a peaceful settlement between Caesar and Pompey would have been infinitely preferable to civil conflict, and conceivably also of his hope that he himself might broker it. At the same time, he does his best to emphasize how in controversies about Matius's conduct, he has been constant in defending Matius's constant commitment to his friend. He had already put loyalty in friendship head of the list of attributes he signalled that he most appreciated in Matius (*Fam.* 11.27.6).[86]

The alternative of ranking the liberty of one's country over the life of a friend is represented as what its numerous proponents take to be the view of his obligation that Matius should accept. It perhaps makes most sense as such if we suppose that he had been actively criticizing the assassins and their republican supporters, but was in their view failing to prize the liberty that motivated them and that they had now restored. This interpretation gets some support from the letter he wrote in reply to Cicero. 'Very well', he treats those he terms the 'authors of liberty' ('self-styled', *ut quidem ipsi dictitant*) as saying to him (*Fam.* 11.28.3), 'you shall be punished for daring to disapprove of our action.' Cicero in effect distances himself from these critics. But is he not somewhat disingenuous in doing so?

He himself had been and remained emphatic in his praise of these authors of liberty.[87] Moreover, when not long after his letter to Matius he turned in *On duties* to the problem of whether the honourable and the advantageous truly understood ever conflict, at the outset he gives killing a tyrant who is also a close friend as an example that may prompt doubt on the matter (*Off.* 3.19). Is not murdering another human being, especially a friend, the greatest of crimes? Not when that action is more aptly described as tyrannicide, at least in the opinion of the Roman people as Cicero represents it (an exaggeration, to the say the least). He plainly means to endorses that view. Here, he says, 'honourableness has followed upon advantage' to the *res publica*.[88]

Nor was that the first occasion in his theoretical writings of 44 on which Cicero had given consideration to friendship and tyranny in the aftermath of Caesar's assassination. In *Laelius*, the dialogue on friendship he composed at some point in the summer of that year (whether before or after the exchange with Matius is not known), he includes a substantial section devoted to a related question (*Lael.* 36–44).[89] Should the friend of someone who is attempting a coup to establish himself as king, or intent upon some other dishonourable action damaging to the *res publica*, be obliged to support him in the attempt? The answer given is firmly in the negative. The first law of friendship is to ask of friends what is honourable and to do what is honourable on their behalf: that is, nothing dishonourable in either case.[90] A similar line is taken in Book 3 of *On duties*. There Cicero begins a section on friendship by remarking (*Off.* 3.43): 'Another area where duties are greatly confused is friendships.' But among the items of 'brief and not difficult advice' he goes on to give is this: 'The good man will never, for the sake of a friend, act contrary to the *res publica*, to s sworn oath, or to good faith.'

Matius's present *officium*, however, is in fact another matter. The *persona* theory Cicero was to take over from Panaetius in Book 1 of *On duties* could have provided a philosophical basis for the line he says he himself took about that issue.[91] Next after the *persona* constituted by our universal human nature, he specifies the one appropriate to the nature individual to each of us, and then discusses it at considerable length (*Off.* 1.107–114). We are to 'follow our own nature, so that even if other pursuits may be weightier and better, we should measure our own by the criterion (*regula*) of our own nature' (*Off.* 1.110). In a later comment on the need to weigh natural bent against changing circumstance, Cicero says (*Off.* 1.120):

When someone has adopted a plan of life entirely in accordance with his own nature (assuming it is not a vicious nature), let him then maintain constancy—that, most of all, is what *decorum* consists in.

Cato's unfailing constancy and exceptional *gravitas* made suicide the right choice for him, when defeated by Caesar in North Africa early in 46, as it would not have been for those republicans of more flexible and easy-going natures (*Off.* 1.112). Since Matius was in Cicero's eyes someone distinguished especially by his constancy in friendship, it is entirely credible that Cicero really did think him right to give priority to his loyalty to Caesar, rather than to the better cause of liberty.

Matius' letter in reply, 'in spite of the persona of bluff simplicity that he adopts, is itself a masterpiece of rhetoric.'[92] He tackles in robust terms the charges against him that he perceives, taking first as most potentially damaging the issue Cicero had raised last (*Fam.* 11.28.2):

> I am well aware of the criticisms which people have levelled at me since Caesar's death. They present it as a fault in me that I take hard the death of a person with whom I was on close terms, and resent it that someone I loved has been done away with. They say that country should be ranked above friendship, as if they have already proved that his demise was advantageous for the *res publica*. But I am not going to argue fine points—I acknowledge that I have not yet got to that level of philosophical understanding. It was not Caesar that I followed in the civil discord, but a friend. The whole business stuck in my throat, but I did not desert him. I never approved of the civil war, nor indeed the cause of the discord, which I put all my energies into putting out, at the time it was still just smouldering.
>
> Accordingly, when a person with whom I was on close terms emerged victorious, I was not captivated by the lure of office or money, prizes of which others, whose influence with him was less than mine, took immoderate advantage. In fact, my own estate was reduced by a law of Caesar, a law whose beneficial effects have meant that most of those people who rejoice at Caesar's death have stayed within the citizen body. I have struggled to have citizens on the losing side spared as I would have done for my own survival.

Three points perhaps stand out as of particular interest for political philosophy. First, Matius makes it clear that he well recognizes that Cicero's articulation of the question of the decision between friendship and country is couched in philosophical mode. He rejects that way of looking at his *officium*. He sticks by his friends. He has no aspirations to higher insights, and certainly not to philosophical understanding (*sapientia*: the wisdom of the Stoic sage). Second, and in any case, the assumption that the *res publica* was best served by the death of his friend is just that: an assumption, not something proven, as its advocates take for granted. The sequel proved him right. What followed was fifteen more years of civil war, followed in its turn by autocracy.

Third, Matius is insistent that his allegiance was to his friend, not to Caesar and his political cause, for which he did not have much sympathy. Nor did he exploit his closeness to that friend to secure political position or financial gain. His own political activity was restricted to efforts to prevent war, and then to support of citizens on the losing side when it was over (Cicero had, of course, highlighted these contributions in his own letter). In short, he has done his best to act as an ordinary citizen of the citizen body of the *res publica*. At the end of his letter he stresses again the modesty (*modestia*) of the life he has lived (*Fam.* 11.28.8), or in other words his choice of a life forswearing the political ambition which Cicero acknowledges has taken them in different directions, and kept them mostly apart physically (*Fam.* 11.27.2).

How convincing is this third element in Matius's defence? 'The advent of one-man rule', it could be said, 'meant that public and private could no longer be separated, even to the extent that they could be under the Republic'.[93] Although Matius does not expressly contest the suggestion that Caesar was 'king', the way that he responds overall implies an alternative assumption.[94] In the *res publica* (the alternative line of argument might go), at any one time there are citizens who exercise great power in whatever office they hold, and it is for their friends in the citizen body to advise and seek to influence them on matters public as well as private (accordingly Matius need not be interpreted as representing all his efforts as undilutedly private). Friends who exercise such functions—the thinking might continue—do not thereby sign up to all or any of the political projects or ventures that the leader in question embarks upon, and indeed may entertain grave misgivings about those. It was not Matius's activity alone that could be so construed. That was presumably the basis which Cicero himself in spring 49 might have thought was implicit in his decision in the end to join Pompey, to the extent that he took himself thereby to be discharging his *officium* to Pompey alone (in reciprocation for the help and friendship he had received from him). But he, like Matius, was evidently to some degree compromised.

Whether the friendship between Cicero and Matius survived, we can only speculate.[95] What does seem clear is that the issue which they argued between them concerning the limits of friendship, when the well-being or survival of the *res publica* is at stake, was a matter of much wider debate. When Cicero implies that he has frequently been party to such discussions, that seems only too likely. The likelihood that the letters to and from Matius are the tip of an iceberg is confirmed by the emphasis Cicero gives to the question in both *Laelius* and *On duties*. The uncertain political environment which the Roman elite inhabited in the months following the Ides of March doubtless made such controversy well-nigh inevitable. As Peter Brunt pointed out, some of Caesar's assassins had long been adherents of his, others had held important positions under his regime, and others again (notably Decimus Brutus) he had treated as favourites. Brunt continued:[96]

> They were reproached for disregarding the obligations of friendship and betraying their leader.... It must be borne in mind that their enterprise was dangerous.... It is not plausible that they risked so much simply 'in envy of great Caesar'.... At worst, it might be said of them that, like Caesar himself, they set their own *dignitas*, which his 'tyranny' subverted, above the public good, but in fact they did not distinguish it from the liberty of the Republic.

6. Tyrannicide

In *On duties*, as Miriam Griffin has written, Cicero 'never misses an opportunity to castigate Caesar, by name or anonymously [in fact mostly the latter], for his unlawful ambitions (1.26, 3.36, 3.83), his demagoguery (1.64, 2.21, 2.78), his resultant rapacity towards men of property (1.43, 2.29, 2.83–4, 3.36), and his harsh treatment of Rome's enemies and subjects (1.35, 2.28, 3.49).'[97] As for his murder, Cicero had no problem in judging that violent action (whether claiming some sort of official endorsement or not) against a tyrant, or against someone regarded as clearly aspiring to similar power, was justified if 'safeguarding the liberty and safety of the Roman people' required it.[98] As he put the point in defending Sestius in 57 BC, Sestius had wanted to employ *ius* (law), but since that had become impossible had to resort to *vis* (violence) (*Sest.* 92).[99]

In Book 3 of *On duties*, Cicero first insists that the Roman people consider as the most handsome of all glorious deeds the act of someone who kills a tyrant (he is using the term *tyrannus*), even if the tyrant was his friend. We should not say that it was advantageous but dishonourable. The advantage (that is, for the *res publica*) made it honourable (*Off.* 3.19). It is Caesar's assassination that plainly occasions introduction of the topic of tyrannicide here at the very beginning of the main argument of Book 3. But as mostly elsewhere in *On duties*, it is significant that the issues are deliberately not personalized, but presented in terms of general moral or psychological truths, owned as such in Roman tradition or in Roman popular sentiment.

Cicero plants that remark about the view taken by the Roman people, however, as his cue for developing a more theoretical defence of tyrannicide, articulated in terms of Stoic universalism. He proposes what he calls a *formula*, for enabling secure determination of just when it is that what we call advantageous conflicts with what we regard as honourable (*Off.* 3.19–20). But the arguments relating to the *formula* that follow (*Off.* 3.21–32) are arguments working through a conception specifically of justice in relation to advantage. The idea of the honourable never figures as such in this section. When preoccupation with conflicts between the honourable and the apparently advantageous resurfaces (starting at *Off.* 3.33), precious little use of the *formula* is made.[100] Its function is in truth restricted to its use in explaining the basis of human society, and (in the final argument that Cicero advances in this context) why the tyrant can have no part in it.[101]

The term *formula* is borrowed from Roman law. It is explained by Griffin as follows:[102]

In civil cases the praetor (or other magistrate), after hearing the parties to a dispute, set out the question of fact for the judge to establish and the legal decision which would follow depending on the facts. Similarly, the *formula* tells us what facts need to be determined before we can make a correct decision about how to act where apparent benefit is concerned.

Here is how Cicero formulates his own rule of procedure for determining acceptable advantage, which he rightly says is in line with Stoic teaching (*Off.* 3.21):[103]

For one human being to deprive another of something, and to further his own advantage by the other human's disadvantage, is more contrary to nature than death or poverty or pain or anything else that may befall the body or external possessions.

Over the next few paragraphs, Cicero marshals a battery of considerations in support of the rule, beginning with the argument that such action undoes 'what is most of all in line with human nature'. It undermines human society and common life itself. Its fundamental basis in human nature is argued subsequently, in Stoic syllogistic style, in a paragraph later in the sequence (*Off.* 3.27):[104]

If nature prescribes that a human being should want to consider the interests of a human being, whoever they may be, for the very reason that this is a human being, it is necessary, according to the same nature, that there is a common advantage shared by all. If that is so, then we are all constrained by one and the same law of nature; and if that also is true, then we are certainly forbidden by the law of nature from acting violently against another. But the first claim is true. Therefore the last is true.

Cicero's explanation of his *formula*, as epitomized in these extracts, makes plain two things important for grasping the tack he is taking with it. The first is that it is in reality nothing but a more detailed articulation of the 'no harm' principle of justice stated back in Book 1. The second is the way that principle is related to the 'common advantage' principle also stated there (*Off.* 1.20, 31). As interpreted here, the 'common advantage' principle, although presented only second in Book 1, supplies at any rate one way of arguing for the 'no harm' injunction, prohibiting injustice (*Off.* 3.26), which was clearly treated as the primary rule when first introduced. In other words, Cicero wants to emphasize the social import of the 'no harm' principle.

He argues at the outset that violation of the *formula* would resemble some limb or other bodily organ deciding it could best flourish by appropriating the strength of the neighbouring organ, thereby bringing about the enfeeblement and death of the whole body. This is how he puts the point (*Off.* 3.21–2):

Injustice destroys the common life and society of humans. For if we are so minded that any person will use theft or violence against another for his own profit, then necessarily the thing that is most of all in accordance with nature will be shattered, the society of the human race. Suppose that each limb were disposed to think that it would be able to grow strong by taking over to itself its neighbour's strength: necessarily the whole body would weaken and die. In the same way, if each one of us were to snatch for himself the advantages other men have and take what he could for his own profit, then necessarily society and community among humans would be overthrown.   (Trans, Atkins, adapted)

The metaphor or analogy of the body was a favourite trope of Ciceronian comment on the state of the *res publica*, found as early as 66 BC, in his speech *On behalf of Cluentius*. There the rule of law is portrayed as the mind that controls the sinews, blood, and limbs of the *civitas* or citizen body (*Clu.* 146).[105] It frequently recurs thereafter in both his speech making and in his correspondence—but mostly to portray the *res publica* as having become diseased, and needing amputation of infected organs.[106] Its application here more generally to 'the society of the human race' (*humani generis societas*) is a novelty in his writings, and indeed in Greek and Roman political thought more generally. Nor do we encounter elsewhere in Cicero the conceit of a counterproductive attempt by one limb to gain in vigour by drawing off strength from another.[107]

After a number of further arguments for the rule specified in the *formula*, Cicero puts a counter-argument, modelled upon (or at any rate strongly resembling), one of Hecato's problem cases (*Off.* 3.90). If a good or wise person will otherwise die from hunger or cold, may he not steal from someone else? The answer: certainly not—at any rate, not if it were solely for his own advantage, though if he would thereby be preserved to benefit the *res publica* and human society, that is a different matter—always assuming that he is wary of self-interested pretence. In these circumstances, theft is permitted, but because it is now in the interests of society at large, it does not breach the rule specified in the *formula* (*Off.* 3.29–31). And if the someone else were the standard example of the paradigmatically cruel tyrant Phalaris? That is a different matter again: there is no community between us and tyrants but complete estrangement, and one would be justified in robbing someone it is honourable to kill. At this point, Cicero reverts to the analogy of the body. Tyrants as monsters in human form should be expelled from the community of mankind.[108] They must be excised from what one might call the body of humanity in which we share,[109] just as limbs that become bloodless and lifeless are amputated (*Off.* 3.32).

One might have expected a justification of tyrannicide to have been given a political basis. It might have been argued, for example, that someone who suppresses the rights of a free people must be overthrown 'by whatever means', to use the language of Cicero's rhetorical exercise back in 49 BC (*Att.* 9.4.2).[110] But that would have fitted better into the conceptual world of *On the commonwealth*. Here he operates within the very different framework of *On duties*' Stoic universalist conception of what humans owe to each other. The treatment of tyrannicide that he offers here is rather artificially engineered into a discussion otherwise focused on appropriation *in extremis* of another's property. It looks as though Cicero could not for his specific purpose find readymade philosophical reasoning associated with Stoic universalism. So his recourse in the first instance was to apply the theft quandary to the case of the tyrant. In that context, he introduced as a premise the thesis that killing a tyrant is an honourable act (so *a fortiori* robbery is not against nature). Through reuse of the body analogy, he could then attempt what is in effect an explanation of why tyrannicide is honourable—why there is in fact a moral imperative to remove the tyrant from human society as an inhuman monster (to whom the terms of the *formula* therefore do not apply at all). The tyrant is like a terminally diseased limb which threatens the health of the other parts, and therefore needs amputation.

In truth, the analogy does all the work, with the theft quandary supplying no more than a peg on which to hang it. Crucial for the plausibility of the reasoning is the assumption that the tyrant is a monstrous being masquerading as human. By Cicero's day, there was a well-established ideological conception of the tyrant as someone in the grip of every kind of uncontrollable appetite and correspondingly unrestrained in satisfying them.[111] Hence the treatment of Phalaris as typical of tyranny. Phalaris was a Sicilian tyrant of the sixth century BC, notorious for bestial cruelty. Often instanced (as by Pindar early in the fifth century, already as a well-known story: *Pyth.* 1.95–6) was his reputed practice of roasting victims alive in a hollow bull made of bronze.[112] He serves as the extreme (and heavily mythologized) particular case which is represented as the norm for a tyrant.[113]

Cicero's argument is therefore general. But it is Caesar that he has in his sights in this section of Book 3, beginning with the claim that the Roman people think killing a tyrant honourable (even if he is a friend), and culminating in argument from amputation of a diseased limb (*Off.* 3.19–32). As early as in January 49, at the start of the civil war, Cicero and Atticus talk of Caesar in the language of Greek tyranny. Caesar's military actions have nothing honourable about them, says Cicero. He has no constitutional authority for seizing the citizens' towns to make easier invasion of our native country, and (slipping into Greek) cancellation of debts and recall of exiles (the typical actions of Greek revolutionaries), besides hundreds of other villainies—with the melodramatically described goal (in Greek again, from Euripides) 'of possessing tyranny, the greatest of gods' (*Att.* 7.11.1). Atticus in his reply evidently agreed, for Cicero in his next letter to him says (*Att.* 7.12.2): 'As for the man whose "Phalarism" you dread, I expect nothing but atrocities from him.'

Ingo Gildenhard makes an apt comment on the first of these letters:[114]

> In all, the Greek themes and citations in Cicero's letter amount to the suggestion that Caesar, in crossing the Rubicon, underwent a metamorphosis. He turned from a fellow-senator and *civis Romanus* into a *monstrum*, an unnatural entity in the Roman order of things. . . . Far from being driven by any concerns for his constitutional rights, Caesar's actions manifest the perverse and perverted psychology of the tyrant.

Yet Cicero knew that not all tyrants were like that. Only two weeks later (5 February 49), he observed that it was uncertain whether Caesar would imitate Phalaris or Peisistratus, the autocrat who ruled Athens for substantial periods in the middle years of the sixth century BC, and came to be regarded as having been a benevolent despot (*Att.* 7.20.2). A month later (on 4 March) he referred to 'this Peisistratus' (*Att.* 8.16.2), although in the weeks that followed there was little stability in the view he was to take of Caesar. After the civil war, the correspondence of 46 cited above makes it clear that Caesar's behaviour as dictator, on Cicero's own evidence, bore little resemblance to that of a Platonic tyrant.[115] In one of his rare public speeches, when pleading in 45 before Caesar for a client, he stated that 'we think him not only not a tyrant, but most merciful in victory' (*Deiot.* 34).

It is hard to resist the conclusion that Cicero found himself hard put to find an appropriate defence of tyrannicide within the philosophical framework of *On duties*. He ended up falling back upon the metaphor of the body politic (applied to the universal community of mankind), and on his favourite image of Phalaris as paradigmatic tyrant, with the crucial but entirely uncritical implication that the paradigm is true of any and every autocrat. Hobbes would not have been impressed.

Notes

1. Annas 1993: 4.
2. See Chapter 1, section 5 p. 20.
3. See Chapter 2, section 5 pp. 50–2.
4. See Chapter 1, section 4 pp. 17–19.
5. On Panaetius's treatise, see Dyck 1996: 17–29, Veillard 2014; also Chapter 5, section 3 p. 159 and n. 42 and pp. 159–60 n.43 above.
6. Griffin 2011 [= Griffin 2018: 662–75], expanding on Griffin and Atkins 1991: xxiii–xxv.
7. See Schofield 1999 for discussion of the first and longest example that Cicero presents.
8. Dyck 1996: 495 comments that Book 3 'contains the most sustained political commentary' [i.e. continuous commentary] of the whole treatise.
9. 'Impiety' translates *nefas*. The Greeks and still more the Romans conceived of piety, being a sacred duty, as owed to one's parents as well as to the gods. Virgil's expression *pius Aeneas* might well be translated 'filial Aeneas'.
10. Griffin 2011: 315–16 and n.13 [=Griffin 2018: 666 and n.13].
11. See Thompson 2018: 103–8. The contemporary author of the Dutch tract *Political Education* (1582) (on whom see section 2 p. 197 n.35 below) quoted and endorsed the argument in its original Ciceronian form: van Gelderen 1993: 224.

12. Hecato makes the standard assumption that tyrants have regard only to their own interest, ruining their country in doing so.
13. Some editors and commentators cannot believe that Cicero wrote *honestas utilitatem secuta est*: see, for example, Dyck 1996: 519. But there are similar remarks elsewhere in Book 3: e.g. *Off*. 3.40 ('The thing that was advantageous, namely to consider the interests of the country, was for that reason honourable'), where Cicero explains that the advantageous 'took its strength' or 'had its impact' (*valuit*) from honourableness; also *Off*. 3.88.
14. Quite how much in Hecato's own approach here and elsewhere Cicero would have endorsed is doubtful (see also n.16 below), particularly in the light of reservations expressed both about the treatment of the general topic of the honourable and the advantageous by philosophers writing since Panaetius (*Off*. 3.34), and specifically about the approach that Hecato took on another particular problem case (*Off*. 3.63). A second batch of examples follows (*Off*. 3.91–2), summarizing what Hecato represented as a sequence of disputes between the second century BC Stoics Diogenes of Babylon and Antipater (whose position gets Cicero's own vote: *Off*. 3.56–7), expounded and discussed more fully earlier in Book 3 (*Off*. 3.50–7). See in general Dyck 1996: 557–60, 612–3, Schofield 1999.
15. See Chapter 4, section 1 p. 111.
16. Dyck 1996: 613 and Griffin 2011: 315 [= Griffin 2018: 666] assume that the passage gives us Cicero's views as well as Hecato's. But as Walsh 2000: 107 points out, one would expect Cicero to have regarded temple robbery with rather more concern. Obligation to the immortal gods is ranked highest of all at the end of Book 1 (*Off*. 1.160), and *On laws* ruled that anyone stealing or snatching anything consecrated or entrusted to a consecrated place was to be regarded as a parricide (*Leg*. 2.22).
17. Griffin and Atkins 1991: 62 n.1 and Dyck 1996: 487 (with some subsequent retraction: e.g. 512) speculate on material in Book 3 that might derive from Posidonius. But on 5 November 44 a book by him was still awaited (also, presumably in case that was not forthcoming, an abstract of it made by the Stoic Athenodorus) which discussed conflict cases, perhaps in a section on 'duty in special circumstances' (*Att*. 16.11.4). On whatever basis of information, in *On duties* itself Cicero expresses surprise that, despite the importance Posidonius attached to the topic, he merely touched upon it in 'some of his treatises' (*Off*. 3.8).
18. The Fabricius episode has already figured much more concisely in Book 1, as illustrating the Romans' historic exercise of justice in dealings with their enemies (*Off*. 1.40). That Book 1 passage is omitted in one branch of the

manuscript tradition, and likewise excised by some modern editors. For discussion and a defence of its authenticity, see Dyck 1996: 150–3.
19. Crassus, third of the warlords who dominated the politics of the final decades of the Republic, receives unfavourable treatment in connection with the forgery of a will a little earlier (*Off.* 3.73–5).
20. Woolf 2015: 195–7, in a section he entitles 'The ethics of openness'.
21. Everything to do with the ambitions and agenda of the principal protagonists in the politics of the final years of the Roman Republic was the subject of alternative narratives (see Chapter 2, section 1 p. 28, on liberty, which Caesar for his part claimed he was acting to restore: *B Civ.* 1.22.5). In composing the second of his Philippic orations against Mark Antony (October 44), not long before Book 3 of *On duties* (November 44), Cicero himself had written—to Antony's discredit—of how Caesar caused it to be put on public record that he had been offered kingship by order of the people, but had refused it (*Phil.* 2.87, with the account of the incident in Wiseman 2009: 170–5).
22. See Dyck 1996: 605, citing *Fam.* 12.3.1 (October 44), where Cicero exclaims to Cassius on Mark Antony's erection of a statue of Caesar with the inscription 'Father of the Country'; cf. *Phil.* 2.3.
23. The classic predecessor text for this line of argument is Plato's treatment of the tyrant in Book 9 of the *Republic* (*R.* 9.579b–e). Gildenhard 2011: 101–13, 185–90, 349 documents Cicero's exploitation of the idea of the criminal's guilty conscience, which occurs in both his oratory and his philosophical writing: e.g. *Leg.* 2.43, *Pis.* 43. For comment on its use here: Wiseman 2009: 206–7.
24. Regulus, like Fabricius, had already made an appearance in Book 1 (*Off.* 1.39), as an illustration of the need for *fides* in honouring promises, even when made to the enemy in the course of a war.
25. Dyck 1996: 623, 634 summarizes reasons for thinking that more likely the Romans would have extradited him back to Carthage, or at any rate downgraded his status, as in similar cases presented by Cicero himself at *Off.* 3.109–10 (discussed by Dyck 1996: 631–3).
26. Deprivation of sleep by some means or other was a salient component, according to the not wholly concordant available accounts (Dyck 1996: 625–6).
27. See Griffin and Atkins 1991: xxvi, Dyck 1996: 490–1.
28. Plato was more outspoken than Cicero on contemporary disregard for oaths (e.g. *Laws* 10.908c, 11.917b), and would on that account reform their use in legal proceedings (*Laws* 12.948b–949b). Cicero took a more traditional line in his own *On laws*: *Leg.* 2.16 (translated in Chapter 4, section 3 p. 117), 22, 41.
29. Here what is honourable is clearly to be determined by advantage. But while we are irresistibly drawn to advantage, we cannot find it anywhere except in

what is praiseworthy, handsome, honourable—our primary and highest aims (*Off*. 3.101).
30. Woolf 2007: 329.
31. See Chapter 5, section 2 pp. 157–8.
32. Cf. Dyck 1996: 135–6 on *Off*. 1.39.
33. Woolf 2007: 330.
34. Beard 1994: 731.
35. The author of the anonymous Dutch tract *Political Education* (1582), calling on the States General of the Netherlands to swear a new oath to forswear allegiance to the King of Spain, had on his title page as a motto Cicero's words (*Off*. 3.111): 'It was the will of our ancestors that no bond should bind good faith more tightly than a sworn oath.' He makes extensive use of Book 3 of *On duties*: see Van Gelderen 1993.
36. Going to war was a solemn business, and the requirements of religious observance which were at any rate traditionally attached to its initiation by the provisions of the Romans' 'fetial' code (*Off*. 1.36, 3.108), constituted a non-negligible dimension of its solemnity and legitimacy. On the fetial code, see Harris 1979: 166–75, Dyck 1996: 134–5, Barnes 2015.
37. See further section 6 below, pp. 217–18, for articulation and discussion of the *formula*. Something like an alternative formulation of the rule is given at *Off*. 3.72.
38. See Annas 1989, Schofield 1999. It is in the summing up of this debate (at *Off*. 3.57) that we find the one fairly explicit example of its use, couched in terms of concealment to another's disadvantage for one's own advantage: see Griffin and Atkins 1991: 121 n.1.
39. Dyck 1996: 525. There are a quite a few cases presented in which it could have been invoked without difficulty (for example, Romulus's murder of his brother: *Off*. 3.41, or Gratidianus's cheating of his colleagues: *Off*. 3.81). But Cicero seems generally content in most such instances to appeal explicitly or otherwise to the need to eschew anything apparently advantageous that is dishonourable or ignoring what a relevant virtue would require.
40. Irwin 2014: 114–15.
41. See Inwood 1999: 120–6, Woolf 2007: 318–34, on the mainly particularist cast of the ethics of *On duties*. Annas 1993: 7 suggests that in ancient ethical theorizing as a whole 'there is not much to be said in general about hard cases.'
42. See also Chapter 5, section 2 pp. 150–1 above.
43. See Griffin and Atkins 1991: xxvi–xxvii, 9 n.1, Dyck 1996: 584–5, Griffin 2013: 106–14 [= Griffin 2018: 700–5].

44. Rawson 1975: 183–202 and Lintott 2008: 281–300 provide full interpretative accounts. Brunt 1986 [=Brunt 2013a: 243–74] offers a wide-ranging study of the sequence focused on the role in his decision making of Cicero's conception of his *officium*. McConnell 2014: 62–114 presents a selective discussion (with useful bibliographical references) arguing that much of the energy expended in these letters is devoted to construction of 'a positive story of Cicero's political conduct', particularly through its Platonic allusions.
45. Giving and receiving advice was widely regarded as one of the duties of friendship: see White 2010: 117–36. In his dialogue on friendship Cicero stresses the need for candour in giving it, and where appropriate for rebuke: *Lael.* 44, 88–9.
46. See also p. 204 below, and Chapter 5, section 1 pp. 149–50. White 2010: 130–3 goes so far as to suggest that expression of this concern indicates the question 'underlying' much of what preoccupies Cicero in these letters, as in those he writes to other correspondents over the years. But at the same time, he allows that the problems under consideration were often conceived as those of 'moral action', treated however in what he categorizes as terms of 'sententious abstraction'. A passage such as the exercise in Greek quoted below from *Att.* 9.4 (section 4 p. 206) shows just how ethically and politically complex and concrete were the issues with which Cicero was seriously grappling in the conceptual vocabulary available to him—on that occasion from the resources supplied by Greek history, philosophy, and oratory.
47. Cicero was, from the beginning, of the belief that by retaining his army once the formal limit of his command had expired, Caesar had breached the fundamental rules governing the conduct of the *res publica* (e.g. *Att.* 7.7.6, composed in December 50), still more so when on leaving his province he entered the territory of Rome itself under arms (e.g. *Att.* 7.11.1, from mid-January 49). Resistance to him was therefore the just cause, even if it was not wise to prosecute it, and although, as Cicero writes on 6 March 49, Pompey had conducted it timidly, and for the future would do so 'without scruple (*improbe*)' (*Att.* 9.1.4; cf. 10.4.3).
48. Quoted in Chapter 3, section 5 p. 90.
49. A chronological narrative focused on Cicero's assessment of Pompey judged against *On the commonwealth*'s ideal of the 'calibrator' of the *res publica* is supplied by Zarecki 2014: 94–104. Hutchinson 1998: 148–62 provides a detailed study of *Att.* 8.3, a letter in which a litany of the shortcomings of Pompey's conduct is launched with the general complaint that his 'proceedings have throughout been destitute alike of wisdom and courage'—not to mention his disregard of Cicero's *consilium* and *auctoritas* (*Att.* 8.3.3).

50. McConnell 2014: 78 points out that Atticus is implicitly encouraged at the end of the letter to make his repeated advice to Cicero on caution more widely known, presumably in an attempt to manipulate Cicero's public image (*Att.* 9.10.10).
51. 'During this period', wrote Shackleton Bailey 1994: 88, 'the correspondence is rich and copious as never before or after, reflecting every change of mood, every reaction to incoming news and rumors. To read it is almost to live under the same roof.'
52. This use of polar categories is well discussed in Leonhardt 1995, who considers that most of them reflect a contrast between the *honestum* and the *utile*.
53. See Chapter 4, section 5, pp. 133–5.
54. See section 1 above, pp. 188–9.
55. In the *Gorgias*, Plato's Socrates works with a contrast between the beneficial or the pleasurable with the morally admirable (*kalon*) (*Gorg.* 474c–475e); Aristotle is credited by Stobaeus with classifying the objects of desire under these three heads (*Ecl.* 2. 51.18–52.1 W-H).
56. But at the end of month, after he had decided to join Pompey, he was writing to two other correspondents that while it looks as though what is honourable and what is most expedient might diverge, 'the only thing for the people we should be is to judge nothing expedient that is not right and honourable', and act accordingly (*Fam.* 4.2.2; cf. 5.19.1).
57. Above p. 199.
58. See section 1 p. 189 above.
59. For the theory, see Chapter 5, section 5 pp. 170–3.
60. See Shackleton Bailey 1965: 17–18, with *Att.* 2.17–19.
61. See section 4 p. 205.
62. On friendship as a factor in Republican politics, see Brunt 1988e, with section 5 below. Interestingly, in the ranking of our prime obligations that Cicero proposes in *On duties* (see Chapter 4, section 1 p. 111, with *Off.* 1.57; cf. 1.160), those to friends find no place, despite his stress on the importance and strength of that relationship between good men (*Off.* 1.55–6). Elsewhere in the work, however, he highlights obligations to friends along with those to the *res publica* (e.g. *Off.* 1.123, 2.4).
63. See section 4 p. 203.
64. On *pudor*, 'shame', see Chapter 5, section 1 pp. 148–9.
65. The treatment of Cicero's decision and of the relevant letters to Atticus and others offered here largely follows that in Brunt 1986: 15–17 [= Brunt 2013a: 248–51]. But Brunt inclined to the view (at odds with everything Cicero actually said in the evidence examined above) that 'in reality Cicero's final

decision was influenced still more by his conception of what was due to the commonwealth than by his ties with Pompey.' Writing to a correspondent in the time of Caesar's dictatorship, he claimed he drew consolation from his having anticipated back in 49 that a victory by Pompey's forces would have been followed by *caedes*, vindictive mass slaughter, whereas if Caesar prevailed, *servitus*, slavery, would be the outcome (*Fam.* 4.14.1–2).

66. For the echoes of Greek tyranny noted here, see Gildenhard 2006, McConnell 2014: 62–114.
67. For discussion of *thesis* as it figures in Hellenistic rhetorical theory see Clarke 1951, Reinhardt 2000. As something put forward for consideration, it functions quite differently from Aristotle's specification of *thesis* as something posited as a fundamental starting point for demonstration (*An. post.* 1.2, 72a14–16).
68. See Swain 2002: 156–7.
69. See Brittain 2001: 289–90, 341–2.
70. He adopts the pro and contra format for his own most characteristically Academic philosophical dialogues of 45–4 BC: *Academic books, On ends, On the nature of the gods, On divination.*
71. Swain 2002: 146–62.
72. McConnell 2014: 103; cf. Gildenhard 2006. The tropes of Greek rhetoric on tyranny had however long been absorbed into Roman discourse, and Cicero himself had been free with accusations that opponents were behaving as *tyranni* (Latinized), from his speeches against Verres in 70 BC onwards: Dunkle 1967: 160–5. But the term was not used by him of figures in Republican history such as Spurius Maelius and Tiberius Gracchus, who were perceived as aiming at kingship in the hostile Roman tradition to which he subscribed. Wiseman 2009: 184 comments: 'The *tyrannos* was a figure specific to Greek politics', but then notes that: 'the *tyrannos* soon did come to be part of Roman political discourse, no longer an alien phenomenon.' See further Gildenhard 2011: 85–92.
73. For the connotations of *dominatus*, see Chapter 2, section 1 p. 28 and n.3.
74. Socrates is memorably presented by Plato as asserting defiantly at his trial that he never has practised quietness and never would: *Ap.* 36b-e, 37e–38a (with Schofield 2006: 19–30).
75. 'Honourable *otium*' was the way of life Cicero had predicated fifteen years before of the apolitical Atticus, in contrast with his own enthusiasm for political honours (*Att.* 1.17.5; cf. *Off.* 1.69–73); in his own case, in very different circumstances, it has a bitter flavour (cf. Balsdon 1960: 49–50). In Greek philosophy, the choice of lives became a regular topic for debate, from Plato's *Gorgias* onwards. The 'quiet life' found philosophical advocates, notable among them Epicurus (followed by Cicero's Roman contemporary Lucretius: see Lucr.

2.1–19), as well as opponents (Cicero attacks the choice of the 'quiet' over the political life in the preface to On the commonwealth: Rep. 1.4–11).
76. Already encountered in Chapter 5, section 2 pp. 154–5.
77. Caesarians would speak of his *lenitas* and *clementia* in victory (B.Afr. 86, 92), although Caesar himself—writing again in March 49—preferred words like *misericordia* and *liberalitas* (Cic. Att. 9.7C; echoed in Sallust's talk of his *beneficia* and *munificentia*, his *mansuetudo* and *misericordia*: Cat. 54.2), no doubt because they sounded less monarchical than *clementia*. On the political subtleties of the vocabulary of mercy at Rome during the civil war and its aftermath see Griffin 2003 [= Griffin 2018: 570–86].
78. The evidence is collected and eloquently presented in Wiseman 2009: 201–2.
79. See Chapter 2, section 1 pp. 27–8, and Chapter 3, section 5 pp. 88–9.
80. See Chapter 4, section 2 p. 119.
81. See Chapter 5, section 2 p. 155.
82. See above all the penetrating study by Griffin 1997 [= Griffin 2018: 495–509] of Cicero's letter to him and his reply.
83. For comment and analysis of the registers in which they are composed, see Hall 2005. On their disingenuousness, Lintott 2008: 359–62.
84. See also below p. 213.
85. See above section 4 p. 204. Griffin 1997: 96–101 [= Griffin 2018: 500–4] makes the case for interpreting both Cicero and Matius (in his reply) as understanding these arguments articulated for and against the superior claims of friendship in roughly the same way. Both take them to have been framed as a dispute turning on philosophical considerations.
86. See Chapter 5, section 2 p. 155 for a rendering of the relevant passage, together with discussion of Cicero's general treatment of *fides* and *constantia* in both friendship and public life.
87. See above section 4 pp. 207–8.
88. See section 1 pp. 189–90 with n.13 above, and for further discussion section 6 pp. 214–17 below.
89. *Laelius* was composed and made public before *On duties*, which refers to it at Off. 2.31.
90. At Lael. 61 it is allowed that one ought to assist the wishes of a friend that are 'less just' if his life or reputation is at risk, and to deviate then from the straight and narrow path, provided that utter disgrace would not ensue. It is unclear quite how this concession might or might not bear on the earlier treatment of plans on the part of a friend to commit an act deeply damaging to the *res publica*. But it sounds as though something on a lesser scale than that may be what is

envisaged. After all, the focus is on someone trying to get out of a tricky personal situation rather than attempting radical political action.
91. For a general sketch of the theory, see Chapter 5, section 5 pp. 171–3.
92. Lintott 2008: 362.
93. Griffin 1997: 101 [= Griffin 2018: 504].
94. See also section 1 p. 192 and n.21 above.
95. Heldman 1976: 98 n.114 records a diversity of conflicting scholarly opinion. He himself is sure that the bond between them was 'not just loosened, but severed'.
96. Brunt 1988e: 380. Wiseman 2009: 203 passes a less sympathetic verdict: 'It may seem frivolous to suggest that Caesar was killed because the *optimates* liked things to be at their own convenience, but something like that must be near the truth.' Among other supporting observations, he goes on to cite the comments Matius makes on the arrogance of his critics (*Fam.* 11.28.3) in developing this general diagnosis.
97. Griffin and Atkins 1991: xii.
98. See section 4 pp. 207–8 above for the formulation.
99. See Lintott 1999b: 52–66. In Cicero's scheme of values, *vis* is the antithesis of *ius*, whose primacy in civil society he constantly championed in speeches (e.g. *Caec.* 5, 33, 76) and theoretical writings (e.g. *Leg.* 3.42): so Frier 1985: 118–20.
100. See above section 2 p. 196 nn. 37 and 38.
101. For this interpretation of *Off.* 3. 19–32, see Dyck 1996: 519–20.
102. Griffin and Atkins 1991: 107 n.3.
103. See also section 2 pp. 195–6 above on the *formula*.
104. Quoted also in Chapter 5, section 3 pp. 162–3. It is discussed in Schofield 1995b: 199–201.
105. The preceding sentences in the passage are quoted in Chapter 2, section 4 p. 43.
106. See Gildenhard 2011: 127–32 (which gives particular attention to its use in Cicero's first speech against Catiline: *Cat.* 1.30–1), Wiseman 2012. The metaphor had been long entrenched in Greek political imagery, not least in Plato: see Brock 2013: 69–82.
107. A fable along similar lines (recounted in Livy) was allegedly told by Menenius Agrippa, sent by the senate as an envoy to the *plebs*, in a successful attempt to bring to an end their 'secession', at an early phase of the 'Struggle of the Orders' (2.32.8–12). Shakespeare was to put a rendering of it in Menenius's speech in the opening scene of *Coriolanus*. The story might well have been already current in Cicero's day.
108. He talks of *feritas et immanitas beluae*, 'the savagery and monstrousness of a beast': language that he had applied to Verres in his pamphlet speeches

twenty-five years before: *Verr.* 2.2.51, 2.5.109, making him 'resemble a tyrant from the tragic stage' (Gildenhard 2011: 91).

109. This expression translates *communi* . . . *humanitatis corpore*, an early and widely (but not universally) accepted emendation of the manuscript reading.
110. See [B] in the passage quoted in section 4 p. 204.
111. See Gildenhard 2011: 85–92 for an overview of the development of the notion of tyranny and its reception at Rome.
112. Cicero uses Phalaris as an example very frequently, often instancing the brazen bull: *Verr.* 2.4.73, *Rep.* 1.44 (as a classic tyrant), *Fin.* 4.64, 5.85, *Tusc.* 2.18, 5.75, *Off.* 2.26.
113. That model is most fully worked out in Plato's *Republic* (*Rep.* 9.571a–580a, appetites; 588b–590b, bestiality). Cicero's brief characterization of Tarquin the Proud clearly fits this same profile (*Rep.* 2.45–6).
114. Gildenhard 2006: 199 (with discussion of 'Phalarism' in particular, at 200–2).
115. See section 4 pp. 206–7.

7
Epilogue: Philosophical Debate and Normative Theory

1. Introduction

In his essay 'Making the world safe for utilitarianism',[1] the political philosopher Jonathan Wolff highlights a contrast between the credit rating of utilitarianism—or of what he calls maximizing consequentialism—in philosophical ethics, and its standing in Western democratic systems where decision-making in matters of public policy is concerned. 'Utilitarianism', he comments, 'has been out of favour in philosophy for some time.' Certainly there are a number of alternative approaches to ethics which attract greater interest and more support in contemporary philosophy, all typically occasioning subtle and vigorous debate in the journals and on the conference scene. On the other hand: 'while philosophers have turned away from maximizing consequentialism, public policy decision making it has embraced it. Many areas of public policy are dominated by cost-benefit analysis, which at least in its purest form is a particularly crude form of consequentialism: consequentialism of money.' Philosophers, Wolff suggests, should find this worrying; 'some', he goes on, 'have duly reported themselves worried.'[2] However what he himself concludes (and there are similar remarks in others of his writings) is that 'while there are plenty of more appealing approaches to personal morality, we do not seem to have many candidate alternatives for public policy decision making.'[3]

A similar phenomenon can be found in the philosophical writings of Cicero, precisely in his treatment of the political sphere and in a much-discussed passage of *On laws*.[4] More generally, we find in him a tension between a conception of philosophy and of philosophical ethics as in its very nature a debate, and the idea that the point of doing philosophy is to find and advocate a sound basis for living our lives. To amplify a little, as Cicero sees it some views in ethics have more going for them, some less, but to the mind of the Academic sceptic that he is, none has established itself as beyond serious further intellectual challenge. To do ethics properly means understanding the main ethical systems which have been or could be proposed, and getting involved in the intricate and apparently unending debate over their merits and demerits.[5] However, if philosophy is to deliver on its main function—to supply foundations both for our common existence and for our lives as individuals—it looks as though we must settle for embracing some particular ethical position, despite our recognition that doing so must be problematic.

The general point can conveniently be illustrated from the *Tusculan Disputations* (45 BC). Here Cicero speaks of philosophy itself in contrasting modes. On the one hand, in the preface to Book 2 he says that while in the *Academic books* (written earlier in the same year) he has set out the case for Academic scepticism with all due precision, nothing would be more welcome than some counter-argument. The characteristic activities that gave Greek philosophy its vitality were the disputes and disagreements of thinkers who really understood the subject (*Tusc.* 2.4). On the other hand, the preface to Book 5 assures us that philosophy is the guide for life, the explorer of virtue, the expeller of vice: human life is dependent on it (*Tusc.* 5.5). The five books of the work taken together 'have made apparent the things most necessary for living happily' (*Div.* 2.2). Or as Book 3 of *On ends* (another of the dialogues of 45 BC) had put it, philosophy is the *art* of living a life (*Fin.* 3.4; cf. *TD* 1.1, *Off.* 2.6).

The tension between the two ideas is obvious. If philosophy is to guide us, it must tell us something definite and convey at least the appearance of definitiveness: that death is something that should not trouble us, or that virtue is uniquely sufficient in itself to give us happiness. But if philosophy is to work out answers to the questions people ask about these and similar topics, it needs to debate them vigorously and to welcome challenges to any conclusions it may reach—without the debate it will lose its vigour and thereby its capacity to guide us. But the definiteness and definitiveness philosophy needs if it is to provide people with firm ethical guidance will be hard to come by if debate brings—as it characteristically does—disagreement, still more irreconcilable disagreement.

It is not just that this tension in Cicero's discussions of philosophy and philosophical ethics is apparent to us his readers. He was himself acutely aware of the difficulty, articulates it in different ways at different points in his writings, and develops different strategies—explicitly or implicitly theorized as such—for coping with it in different contexts. One place where Cicero's sense of the problem emerges with special clarity is in the *Lucullus* (again 45 BC), in the course of a long critique of the discussions of dogmatic philosophers that constitutes the final main section of the sceptical reply to the Stoicizing epistemology which had been developed in the first main part of the dialogue. A particularly good example is the treatment, developed in a characteristic stretch of distinctively Ciceronian philosophical rhetoric, of divergences between Stoic and the essentially Peripatetic ethics of Antiochus of Ascalon (*Luc.* 133–4):[6]

The Stoics hold that all moral errors are equal, but with this Antiochus most forcefully disagrees. Then please may *I* be allowed to consider which of the two views I should follow? 'Cut it short', he says. 'Do for once decide on something or other.' Even given that the arguments on either side appear to me acute and of equal weight? . . . Here's an even bigger disagreement. Zeno thinks the happy life is found in virtue alone. What does Antiochus say? 'Yes', he says, 'the happy life, but not the happi*est*.' . . . I am torn. Sometimes one view seems more persuasive to me, sometimes the other. Yet unless one or other of them is right, I think that virtue lies utterly prostrate.

And so it goes on for several pages more, even if at one point Cicero owns to finding it not easy to tear himself away from Antiochus's Peripatetic conception of the ends of life—'I haven't to date found anything more persuasive' (*Luc.* 139). Antiochus took the more common-sense view that there are goods of the body (such as health) and external goods (such as wealth) as well as virtue as the good of the soul. Virtue was for him, as for Zeno and the Stoics, sufficient for happiness. But the happiest life required things like health and wealth too.

Perhaps the most succinct and explicit statement of the problem Cicero faces, given his own sceptical philosophical outlook, comes in the preface to Book 2 of *On duties* (*Off.* 2.7):

An objection is brought against me—by educated men, indeed—who ask whether I think my behaviour is altogether consistent. For although I say that nothing can be known for certain, nonetheless I am in the habit of holding forth on various subjects, and on this occasion I am engaged in formulating advice (*praecepta*) about our obligations.

One way of dealing with such a problem might be to consign scepticism to the philosophy seminar, leaving a philosopher with more scope for developing positive teaching elsewhere. That is more or less the policy adopted in Book 1 of *On laws*, to which we may now turn.

2. Silencing debate

One of the most intriguing moments in all Cicero's philosophical writing comes in Book 1 of *On laws*. It occurs at a point where, following the first main sequence of argument in the dialogue (*Leg.* 1.16–34), Cicero says that he is now going to make some remarks on his principal thesis: that justice (*ius*) is rooted in nature. The other discussants—his brother Quintus and his close friend Atticus—consider this completely unnecessary. The arguments they have just been given by Cicero have already convinced them of the truth of the thesis; and Atticus briefly recapitulates them in explaining why (*Leg* 1.35). Cicero replies that though they are right to think the conclusion follows from those arguments, he is going nonetheless to pursue the scholastic method favoured by some philosophers (doubtless he means the Stoics: cf. e.g. *Tusc.* 5.18–19), and dedicate a separate treatment to the topic.

Atticus exclaims (*Leg.* 1.36):

I take it your own freedom as to how to discuss things has gone missing—or else you are the sort of person not to follow your own judgement in a debate, but to submit to the authority of somebody else.

In other words, Atticus is accusing Cicero of abandoning—temporarily or permanently—the freedom the Academic sceptic claims to consider any philosophical question on its merits and as he judges best, in contrast to adherents of the other schools. Other philosophers are standardly represented in the dialogues as required to tackle them only by the methods sanctioned in their schools, and only on the doctrinal basis accepted by them. 'We alone are free', Cicero will say in Book 5 of the *Tusculan Disputations*, whereas others are subject to 'laws imposed on the way they debate' (*Tusc.* 5.33). The echo of Academic sceptic talk in Atticus's intervention here, and its confirmation that Cicero is already an Academic sceptic at the time of writing, were not often picked up by scholarship until

Woldemar Görler pointed out what he rightly called this 'massive indication' in a notable article of 1995.[7] Once noticed, it is indeed decisive for interpretation.

Cicero does not altogether deny Atticus's charge, although he makes it clear that he is not abandoning Academic independence of judgement as a general policy (*non semper*). Why, then, does he bow to authority (to the extent that he does) on this occasion? Because he is embarked on a specific project in applied political theory, which has the *practical* aim of 'putting commonwealths on a firm footing, bringing stability to cities, maintaining every kind of people in a sound condition' (*Leg.* 1.37). That requires in the first instance positing basic principles that are aptly supplied and have been assiduously investigated (*bene provisa et diligenter explorata*). Such a stipulation in fact impeccably parallels Academic methodology, although Cicero does not emphasize the point. The testing of impressions that Academics insist on when the stakes are high requires 'meticulous consideration' (*accurata consideratio*) and 'most assiduous exploration' (*diligentissime circumspexerit*: *Luc.* 36). The importance of the political project he articulates is presumably what dictates the need for just such a careful and dedicated treatment of its ethical foundations.

So how does one do that? Here Cicero's policy will be to identify principles which commend themselves (*probentur*) to those who think that what is morally admirable is either the only good or an incomparably great good—i.e. the Stoics or the Platonists and Aristotelians (*Leg.* 1.37–8)—whose differences on that issue are subsequently to be treated as verbal, not substantive, in line with the view of the non-sceptical Academic Antiochus (*Leg.* 1.54–5). Yet here, too, is another echo of Academic sceptic methodology. Such Academics do not claim certain knowledge. What can command their assent is whatever line of thought seems most *persuasive* or *deserving of approval* (*probabile*) or seems *nearest* the truth. But there is in the present case a crucial variation—constituting the degree of surrender of his own judgement that Cicero is admitting. As we have seen, identifying a theory of justice that will support construction of a good constitutional system requires acknowledgement that we are to be concerned with the public sphere, and with practice as well as theory. Once this thought is registered, it will not suffice for Cicero and his interlocutors to agree (or disagree) among *themselves* about what seems most probable or nearest the truth: that would be too fragile a basis for the enterprise. The theory to be proposed should have the approval of a broad swathe of thinkers who all accept that what is good or in itself desirable is the morally admirable alone, or incomparably more so than anything else.

In other words, the right thing is to make sure one has *their* approval, not—as standardly in Academic scepticism—simply to make one's own mind up. That said, however, as Jed Atkins has pointed out, we should recall that it was precisely the mutual corroboration of witnesses required in the determination of important legal cases to which Carneades appealed in explaining the Academic method: a method described as the rigorous testing of impressions that we engage in 'in matters that contribute to happiness', to ensure so far as we can that they are 'undiverted and thoroughly explored' (Sextus *M* 7.184). Moreover, as Atkins also observes, Cicero does *choose* to take this approach, and thus 'in a manner of speaking' exercises his free judgement.[8] Indeed, in a rather similar context in the preface to *On duties*, he insists (*Off.* 1.6) that in relying on the same philosophical tradition as is called in aid here, he does so 'using my own judgment and discretion' (*iudicio arbitrioque nostro*).[9]

There is a further and more unsettling dimension to the stance Cicero is adopting. He next tells us (*Leg.* 1.39) not merely that it means rejecting— unsurprisingly—the views of the Epicureans, whose hedonistic conception of the good and pursuit of pleasure leaves them (he insinuates) without any understanding of what involvement in the public sphere entails, and who had better stay away from it. More startlingly, those views must be rejected in this context *even if true:*– even if they *say* (*dicunt*, indicative mood) what is true, and not (as we might have expected) if they *were to be saying* what is true (though editors have proposed emending to get the subjunctive *dicant*). The passage echoes one in *On the orator* (55 BC) where a similar treatment is accorded to Epicureanism in the context of enquiry 'not into what is the truest philosophy, but the one most closely tied to the orator'. We should warn Epicureans to keep quiet about their doctrine—'as if it were a holy secret'—that there is no role in public affairs for the wise person, 'even if it is (*est*: once again some editors substitute the subjunctive, *sit*) absolutely true (*verissimum*)' (*de Or.* 3.64). This might be regarded as Cicero's version of Plato's Noble Lie, or more particularly of the variant in Plato's own *Laws*, where after a stretch of dialogue developing the case for thinking that the just life is pleasanter than the unjust, the Athenian Visitor proposes that even if that weren't the case, any lawgiver who was even the slightest use—

assuming he was prepared for a good purpose to lie to the young—could devise no more profitable or persuasive *falsehood* (*Laws* 2.663d–e).

The final price to be paid by Cicero the Academic in launching into the serious political project which he is undertaking—and the final stage in the surrender of his own judgement—is that he will have also to ask the sceptical Academy of Arcesilaus and Carneades to 'stay silent': they throw all these matters into total confusion (*Leg.* 1.39). In other words, what would be totally unhelpful would be for the statement of principle underpinning the political project he is undertaking to be met by a classic Academic counter-argument, e.g. to the effect that wisdom dictates pursuit of self-interest, not what is alleged to be 'natural' other-regarding justice. Not wanted, in short, would be any repeat of Carneades' reputed delivery on successive days at Rome in 155 BC of speeches first for and then against justice. That episode would already be familiar to the reader of *On laws*, from Book 3 of *On the commonwealth* (54–2 BC), where it is replicated after a fashion in the debate between Philus and Laelius that Cicero makes the centrepiece of that whole dialogue, and to which we shall be returning shortly.[10] All the same, says Cicero, 'I would like to conciliate it [sc. the new Academy]. I don't dare push it aside' (*Leg.* 1.39). For of course, Academic sceptics aren't *committed* like Epicureans to *doctrines* incompatible with those which the *On laws* project is to take as its basis. It is open to them to approve whatever in the end seems to them most probable or persuasive or nearest the truth (cf. e.g. *Div.* 2.150, *Off.* 3.20).

In this manner Cicero concludes a remarkable passage of philosophical writing. To summarize, he here temporarily abandons full-blooded Academic scepticism to undertake a practical project in applied political theory: establishing a philosophical foundation—the doctrine of the natural basis of justice—for 'putting commonwealths on a firm footing, bringing stability to cities, maintaining every kind of people in a sound condition'. Such an enterprise requires observance of a number of constraints:

- *Pragmatism*: the foundational principle need not be true, but must be fit for purpose.
- *Authority*: the appropriate principle must be accepted on the authority of philosophers who have shown it to be carefully considered.
- *No debate*: dissent or query regarding the principle is to be 'silenced'—these form no part of the relevant methodology.

There is an evident similarity with Jonathan Wolff's attitude towards utilitarianism and cost–benefit analysis in the article of his with which this chapter began.

However Wolff stresses that he is defending utilitarianism and cost–benefit analysis in public policy decision-making as decision procedures rather than as moral theories, and as decision procedures 'only under certain highly constrained conditions'.[11] Elsewhere in discussing risk management he talks of laying the groundwork 'so that the moral questions appear in clear focus', not of offering answers to those questions, or of articulating 'the normative framework' for the enterprise.[12] Cicero might have found those statements somewhat pusillanimous. If utilitarianism is what public policy decision-making is principally to rely on, other conflicting stances in philosophical ethics are to that extent being put aside. So even if utilitarianism is called in aid only because it enables the adoption of a decision procedure which can be claimed to be objective, plausibly enough for the purpose of achieving a result that will gain a measure of public acceptance, it is hard to see how it is not effectively being treated as its 'normative framework'.

At the same time, Cicero has his own ways of indicating the theoretical limitations of the approach to political theory he is advocating in this *On laws* passage. The account of its content just given above shows him not only flagging up his marginalization of Epicurean and Academic sceptic stances, but conceding the possibility that there may in truth be greater validity in what they claim or argue than in the position he is embracing. As Raphael Woolf puts it: 'One might say that to announce loudly that one is closing down debate is itself to initiate a debate.' Woolf goes on to add a further apt comment:

Cicero, I suggest, is using the notion of uniformity of outlook to illustrate a crucial feature of the theory he is advocating. The idea of natural law is precisely the idea that there is a universal set of normative principles applicable in all contexts. If this idea is correct, then there is indeed no room for divergence of opinion about what justice is.[13]

It is also significant that Cicero makes the Epicurean Atticus his principal interlocutor in Book 1 of *On laws*.[14] *On laws*, after all, is a dialogue, indeed one of Cicero's liveliest dialogues, not a treatise propounding its proposals dogmatically. Nor does Cicero simply ignore Atticus's own philosophical commitments. When he invites him to sign up to a basically Platonic and Stoic thesis on the rule of all nature by god or mind or some other power, Atticus makes it clear that he does so for the sake of the argument to be developed on its basis, and explicitly brackets his own Epicureanism (*Leg.* 1.21–2). As I point out elsewhere,[15] when he offers a summary of that argument, he does so in terms which abstract from its specifically Stoic commitments (*Leg.* 1.35). And when in the sequel to the passage we have been considering, Cicero mounts against cultural relativist versions of legal positivism a defence of the view (couched in essentially Stoic terminology) that 'there is only one justice, which constitutes the bond among humans, and which has been constituted by the one law, which is right reason in commands and prohibitions' (*Leg.* 1.42–8), he has already clearly been attacking the Epicurean view of justice in some detail (*Leg.* 1.40–1, where the manuscript text resumes after a lacuna). Atticus is not made to offer any direct comment on Cicero's extended assault on other views such as these when eventually it is brought to a close (*Leg.* 1.52). Perhaps trying to rekindle a sense of genuine dialogue at this point, Cicero announces that the next topic will be the dispute between the Old Academy and the Stoics on the good. Urbanity and a different perspective are not however restored until Atticus's next intervention: a sardonic anecdote about disagreement in philosophy, which was told him—he says—by Phaedrus: tellingly enough, an Epicurean, like himself (*Leg.* 1.53).

One might suggest at this point something that could appear to pose a more troublesome objection both to Cicero's procedure and to the conclusions he draws from its employment. If his objective is the achievement in practice of a consensus on foundations for a stable and sound political settlement, it might be argued, does he not need to persuade citizens at large of his proposals? Finding a cluster of good philosophical schools with whom they would meet with approval is one thing. Getting them actually implemented is quite another. For a reply to this purported difficulty that we could offer to Cicero, it will suffice to distinguish between the basis on which his political recipe is recommended (its principles would be approved by a consensus of the soundest philosophers in the Platonic and Aristotelian tradition) and the audience to whom it is being recommended. That audience consists of the non-philosophers Atticus and Quintus within the frame of the dialogue, but as the projected readership of its text he is addressing the Roman political elite. Conceivably Cicero hoped that if sufficient numbers of his peers took its proposals to heart, whether immediately or at some future date, a consensus on their implementation might—in some form or to some extent—emerge among those best placed and equipped to bring about political reformation.

3. Full-throttled debate

Cicero sometimes writes as though political theory—discussion of the best form of *res publica* or of what laws and customs are beneficial—belongs within the intellectual province of the experienced statesman, whereas treatment of what is good or bad, of obligation, and of how we should live (*bene vivendi ratio*) is for the philosopher to work at and then carry through into practice (*de Or.* 1.209–13, *Div.* 2.9–12).[16] He credits Carneades with this division of labour (*Div.* 2.9), which belonged within a broader survey of professions that is executed in Socratic style. Such a survey was designed for use in sceptical critique of overweening pretensions entertained by some one among them. One thing clear about the contrast is that it is not to be construed as a sharp division between theory and practice. The assumption is rather that experience needs to inform political theory, and that philosophical findings can and should shape our lives.[17] Another thing obvious enough (cf. *de Or.* 1.214–18) is that there is no reason in principle why someone might not become equipped with capacities for both political theory and for philosophy, and achieve accomplishment in each. Then again, doing good political theory might require good philosophical reflection: as Cicero clearly indicates in his treatment of justice in Book 1 of *On laws*, and especially in his explicit references to philosophical schools and traditions at *Leg.* 1.37–9 (discussed in section 2 above).

But does the philosophy called in aid of political theory necessarily have to exclude debate (as in that *On laws* context)? The evidence of the companion dialogue *On the commonwealth* suggests that Cicero thought otherwise. Book 3 of that dialogue (now fragmentary) had contained full-throttled debate about justice, explored already in Chapter 4.[18] For our purposes, all that we need to note is that the material Cicero included in those arguments contained a good deal of philosophical argumentation on ethical fundamentals. To quote a recent summary of one reading of Philus's case, offered by James Zetzel:[19]

> ... moving from the grandest idea of law and justice being identical, through the more cautious Aristotelian idea of justice as another's good—already rejected by Thrasymachus in *Republic* 1—to the vulgar consequentialism of the Epicureans, ending with the picture of a world in which only a fool would pay any attention to moral standards, and in which ... a monarch is no better than a brigand.

By contrast:

> Laelius starts from this utter negation of morality and reverses it: by the time he is finished, we can again believe in justice, this time as a transcendent moral standard independent of any human failings.

So presentation of philosophical debate can be as important in Ciceronian political theorizing as in every other area of his philosophical enquiries. How then to account for its presence at the very heart of *On the commonwealth* but its exclusion from *On laws*? The obvious and simple answer is that the two dialogues constitute examples of two different genres. While neither excludes philosophy (as understood in the terms referred to at the beginning of this section), *On the commonwealth* is a work primarily of political theory as theory, whereas *On laws* works out a practical legislative project. Here Cicero replicates in his own fashion a salient difference between Plato's *Republic* and *Laws*, very much the models for *On the commonwealth* and *On laws*.

The philosophical debate between Thrasymachus and Socrates in Book 1, together with the challenge reformulating Thrasymachus's stance thrown down to Socrates by Glaucon and Adeimantus at the beginning of Book 2, is what fuels the entire trajectory of the *Republic*, whose main purpose is in fact not to develop a political theory but to illuminate the nature of justice and the good. The *Laws*, by contrast, is shaped by the legislative project to which it gradually works its way round. The conversation represented in the dialogue is dominated by an anonymous Athenian Visitor, who more resembles a Solon than a Socrates, even if his identity as an Athenian thinker is crucially shaped by Socratic ethics. It contains plenty of theoretical reflection, but virtually no philosophical debate. There is occasional and not insignificant disagreement on topics such as tolerance by society of drinking, and again of homosexual practices, and in Book 4 we get an echo of Socrates' debate with Thrasymachus in Book 1 of the *Republic*. It is true that argument from time to time against other philosophical views is of crucial importance in enabling the Athenian to set out fundamental ideas governing the whole framework of the project. His critique of a militarist conception of the proper goal for a *polis* at the beginning of Book 1 is what is made to trigger his account of the values that will inform his own view of its proper goal. The attack on atheism in Book 10 provides argument for the religious structure that shapes the life of the good city that he delineates, and its constitutional, institutional, and legislative provisions. Nowhere, however, is there two-sided philosophical debate.

A picture begins to form. In the sphere of politics, debate is called for when discussion is at any rate primarily conducted at the level of theory. But when political theory is to be applied in a practical project of legislation, debate will be unwelcome, as liable only to muddy the waters or blunt the message.

4. Final thoughts

It is not only when developing the basis for a practicable legislative project for the *res publica* that Cicero thinks it best to eschew debate. Philosophical debate is for the most part and of set purpose excluded in *On duties*. Guidance, untrammelled by any promise to engage with the disagreements between the philosophical schools over its subject matter (cf. *Off.* 1.6), is uncomplicatedly what it is. We might ask: is there then anything that marks it out as a work of *Academic* philosophy—for which debate is the best way to get at the truth or the best approximation to it—in any sense at all?

To this question the answer is an unequivocal 'Yes'. Here the preface to the whole work is a key text. For while it does not launch any debate between the philosophical schools about the questions Cicero will be engaging with, he sets the scene by *recalling* his own staging of such debates elsewhere (he means principally *On ends* and *Tusculan Disputations*). He dismisses the views of Epicureans and similar schools out of hand, although in the last pages of the work he will judge it prudent to line up some arguments against them, presumably just in case Marcus might feel tempted to waver from the instruction with which he has now been supplied (*Off.* 1.5, 3.116–19). Then he proposes that the business of giving advice is best regarded as the territory of the Stoics, Academics (here he means the Old Academy of Speusippus, Xenocrates, and Polemo: *Leg.* 1.38), and the Peripatetics,[20] ruling out minor figures (as he regarded them) such as Ariston, Pyrrho, and Erillus, whose views simply leave no scope for that kind of philosophizing (cf. *Fin.* 2.43, 5.73). In the event he will in what follows be presenting a Stoic treatment of the issues—as it quickly transpires, largely in Panaetius's version.[21] But he will do so not slavishly as a translator, but 'as I am used to doing, drawing on those sources according to my own judgment and decision (*iudicio arbitrioque nostro*), to the extent and in the manner that will seem best' (*Off.* 1.6; cf. 1.7–10).

These last remarks indicate to the reader that this *is* to be a work by Cicero the Academic sceptic. He refers to his usual practice, in terms that recapitulate elements of the classic statements of Academic methodology in the dialogues (*ND* 1.11–12, *Div.* 2.150). That he should find a Stoic presentation of the subject most appealing will not surprise readers of his ethical dialogues, nor that he likes Panaetius's version best, while allowing that either a Peripatetic or a Stoic basis for the business in hand would suffice (*Off.* 3.33). Book 4 of *On ends* had concluded with praise of Panaetius as a Stoic who in style and doctrine alike was close to the Old Academy and the Peripatetics (*Fin.* 4.79). The way Cicero puts the point, however, makes it clear that he himself is by no means to be perceived *as* a Stoic now, a message reinforced in the prefatory sections of Books 2 and 3.

That is in effect the kind of reply he makes explicitly at the beginning of Book 2 to the objection that back in our introductory section we saw him registering. Contrary to the objection, he says, Academic sceptics are not left with no views, or no practical options for living. Academics say that some things are persuasive (*probabilia*), some not, even if certainty is unavailable. And there is no reason why he should not go for what seems persuasive to him, while avoiding the arrogance of flatly asserting or denying things. At this point he refers to a fuller discussion to his *Academic books* (*Off.* 2.7–8). For now what is more important is that the kind of philosophical guidance attempted in *On duties* can best proceed having given just a few mentions of debate, now recollected in tranquillity.

From *On laws* and *On duties* together, we might draw the moral that in the practical sphere it is important to achieve as much consensus as possible if philosophy as such is to speak with authority. Our examination of these writings suggests that Cicero would have wholeheartedly agreed with

Jonathan Wolff: 'Philosophers find it hard to compromise.... Without pure philosophical reflection, and the dogged pursuit of what may seem to others crazy ideas, intellectual discussion would be flat and static.' But he would also have agreed with Wolff's assessment of philosophy's best strategy for moving the development of policy forward in matters of applied moral and political theory: 'to draw more people into a consensus view, so that policy can be more widely endorsed, even if different people's reasons for the policy differ'. Kantians and utilitarians can 'agree that it is wrong to murder innocents when no good could come of it' (although presumably a Kantian would not for preference put the point that way).[22]

Cicero's social and intellectual world was very different from our own. Yet he raised a good question when he asked whether philosophy's need for ongoing debate is compatible with the requirements of guidance on policy and practice, if there is to be any prospect of its being usefully applied in that context.

Notes

1. Wolff 2006a.
2. Wolff 2006a: 2–3.
3. Wolff 2006a: 19.
4. The same general issue is interestingly pursued, particularly with reference to politics and to this same passage of Book 1 of *On laws*, in Nicgorski 2016: 15–58.
5. For the Academics' encyclopedic method, see for example Algra 1997.
6. Antiochus was a member of the Academy active in the late second and early first centuries BC, with whom Cicero studied in Athens in 79 BC (*Brut.* 315), and someone he forever after greatly admired. Antiochus had come to believe that its scepticism was a betrayal of the Academy's true philosophical tradition, as represented by Plato's early successors, who for him constituted the 'Old Academy'. His own teaching was effectively a synthesis of the views of the Old Academy and the Peripatetics (the school founded by Aristotle), and in epistemology the Stoics, whose position on the good however he rejected. See further Allen 2018; more comprehensively Sedley 2012.
7. Görler 1995: 103 [= Görler 2004: 257–8].
8. Atkins 2013a: 183–5.
9. See further section 4 pp. 240–1.

10. See Chapter 4, section 5, and section 3 below.
11. Wolff 2006a: 3.
12. Wolff 2006b: 410, 427.
13. Woolf 2015: 117.
14. So Woolf 2015: 116–17.
15. Schofield forthcoming 2.
16. This Carneadean division of labour was already noted in Chapter 1, section 4 pp. 14–15. It here gets some fuller exploration.
17. We might compare the opening pages of *On duties*, where its topic of obligation is said to involve two kinds of question: one relating to the criteria for what things are good (*finis bonorum*: see Allen 2014 for the explanation of this expression, frequently employed by Cicero), the other to rules of guidance (*praecepta*) (*Off.* 1.7).
18. See Chapter 4, section 5 pp. 126–34.
19. Zetzel 2017c: 318.
20. See p. 231 n.6 above.
21. See Chapter 5, section 3 p. 159.
22. Wolff 2011: 4–5.

Bibliography

Algra, K. (1997). 'Chrysippus, Carneades, Cicero: the ethical *divisiones* in Cicero's *Lucullus*', in B. Inwood and J. Mansfeld (eds.), *Assent and Argument in Cicero's Academic Books*. Leiden: Brill, 107–39.

Algra, K., Barnes, J., Mansfeld, J., and Schofield, M. (eds.) (1999). *The Cambridge History of Hellenistic Philosophy*. Cambridge: Cambridge University Press.

Allen, J. (2014). 'Why there are ends of both goods and evils in ancient ethical theory', in M.-K. Lee (ed.), *Strategies of Argument: Essays in Ancient Ethics, Epistemology and Logic*. Oxford: Oxford University Press, 231–54.

Allen, J. (2018). 'Antiochus of Ascalon', in *The Stanford Encyclopedia of Philosophy* (Summer 2018 edn.), E.N. Zalta (ed.), URL = https://plato.stanford.edu/entries/antiochus-ascalon/

Ando, C. (2010). '"A dwelling beyond violence": on the uses and disadvantages of history for contemporary republicans', *History of Political Thought* 31: 183–220.

Annas, J. (1989). 'Cicero on Stoic moral philosophy and private property', in M. Griffin and J. Barnes (eds.), *Philosophia Togata: Essays on Philosophy and Roman Society*. Oxford: Clarendon Press.

Annas, J. (1993). *The Morality of Happiness*. Oxford: Oxford University Press.

Annas, J. (2013). 'Plato's *Laws* and Cicero's *de Legibus*', in M. Schofield (ed.), *Aristotle, Plato and Pythagoreanism in the First century BC: New Directions for Philosophy*. Cambridge: Cambridge University Press, 206–24.

Annas, J. (2017). *Virtue and Law in Plato and Beyond*. New York: Oxford University Press.

Appiah, K. A. (2006). *Cosmopolitanism: Ethics in a World of Strangers*. London: Allen Lane.

Arena, V. (2007). '*Libertas* and *virtus* of the citizen in Cicero's *De Republica*', *Scripta Classica Israelica* 26: 39–66.

Arena, V. (2012). *Libertas and the Practice of Politics in the Late Roman Republic*. Cambridge: Cambridge University Press.

Arena, V. (2016). 'Popular sovereignty in the late Roman Republic: Cicero and the will of the people', in R. Bourke and Q. Skinner (eds.), *Popular Sovereignty in Historical Perspective*. Cambridge: Cambridge University Press, 73–95.

Armitage, D. (2002). 'Empire and liberty: a republican dilemma', in M. van Gelderen and Q. Skinner (eds.), *Republicanism: A Shared European heritage*. Vol. 2: *The*

Values of Republicanism in Early Modern Europe. Cambridge: Cambridge University Press, 29–46.

Asmis, E. (2004). 'The state as a partnership: Cicero's definition of *res publica* in his work *On the State*', *History of Political Thought* 25: 569–98.

Asmis, E. (2008). 'Cicero on natural law and the laws of the state', *Classical Antiquity* 27: 1–33.

Astin, A. E. (1967). *Scipio Aemilianus*. Oxford: Clarendon Press.

Atkins, E. M. (1990). '"Domina et Regina Virtutum": justice and *societas* in *De Officiis*', *Phronesis* 35: 258–89.

Atkins, E. M. (2000). 'Cicero', in C.J. Rowe and M. Schofield (eds.), *The Cambridge History of Greek and Roman Political Thought*. Cambridge: Cambridge University Press, 477–516.

Atkins, J. W. (2013a). *Cicero on Politics and the Limits of Reason*. Cambridge: Cambridge University Press.

Atkins, J. W. (2013b). 'Cicero on the relationship between Plato's *Republic* and *Laws*', in A. Shepherd (ed.), *Ancient Approaches to Plato's Republic*. London: BICS Supplement 117, 15–34.

Atkins, J. W. (2017). 'Natural law and civil religion: De legibus Book II', in O. Höffe (ed.), *Ciceros Staatsphilosophie: Ein kooperativer Kommentar zu 'de Re Publica' und 'de Legibus'*. Berlin & Boston: De Gruyter, 167–86.

Atkins, J. W. (2018). *Roman Political Thought*. Cambridge: Cambridge University Press.

Badian, E. (1958). *Foreign Clientelae, 264–70 B.C.* Oxford: Clarendon Press.

Bailyn, B. (1967). *The Ideological Origins of the American Revolution*. Cambridge, MA: Harvard University Press.

Balmaceda, C. (2017). *Virtus Romana: Politics and Morality in the Roman Historians*. Chapel Hill: University of North Carolina Press.

Balsdon, J.P.V.D. (1960). '*Auctoritas, dignitas, otium*', *Classical Quarterly* 10: 43–50.

Baraz, Y. (2012). *A Written Republic: Cicero's Philosophical Politics*. Princeton: Princeton University Press.

Barlow, J. (2018). 'Scipio Aemilianus and Greek ethics', *Classical Quarterly* 68: 112–27.

Barlow, J. J. (2012). 'Cicero on property and the state', in W. Nicgorski (ed.), *Cicero's Practical Philosophy*. Notre Dame, Indiana: University of Notre Dame Press, 212–41.

Barnes, J. (2015). 'Cicero and the just war', in his *Mantissa: Essays in Ancient Philosophy IV*. Oxford: Clarendon Press, 56–79.

Barnes, J., and Griffin, M.T. (eds.) (1995). *Philosophia Togata II: Plato and Aristotle at Rome*. Oxford: Clarendon Press.

Bartels, M. L. (2017). *Plato's Pragmatic Project: A Reading of Plato's* Laws. Stuttgart: Franz Steiner Verlag.

Beard, M. (1994). 'Religion', in J. A. Crook, A. Lintott, and E. Rawson (eds.), *The Cambridge Ancient History*, Volume 9 (2nd edn.). Cambridge: Cambridge University Press, 729–68.

Beard, M. (2014). *Laughter in Ancient Rome: On Joking, Tickling, and Cracking Up*. Berkeley, Los Angeles, London: University of California Press.

Beard, M., and Crawford, M. (1985). *Rome in the Late Republic*. London: Duckworth.

Bell, D. (2011). 'Empire and imperialism', in G. Stedman Jones and G. Claeys (eds.), in *The Cambridge History of Nineteenth-Century Political Thought*. Cambridge: Cambridge University Press, 864–92.

Bellamy, R. (2018). 'The paradox of the democratic prince: Machiavelli and the Neo-Machiavellians on ideal theory, realism, and democratic leadership', in M. Sleat (ed.), *Politics Recovered: Realist Thought in Theory and Practice*. New York: Columbia University Press, 166–93.

Benferhat, Y. (2005). *Cives Epicurei: Les épicuriens et l'idée de monarchie à Rome et en Italie de Sylla à Octave*. Brussels: Editions Latomus.

Bobonich, C. (2002). *Plato's Utopia Recast. His Later Ethics and Politics*. Oxford: Clarendon Press.

Brittain, C. (2001). *Philo of Larissa. The Last of the Academic Sceptics*. New York: Oxford University Press.

Brock, R. W. (2013). *Greek Political Imagery from Homer to Aristotle*. London: Bloomsbury.

Brouwer, R. (2014). *The Stoic Sage*. Cambridge: Cambridge University Press.

Brouwer, R. (2017). '"Richer than the Greeks": Cicero's constitutional thought', in O. Höffe (ed.), *Ciceros Staatsphilosophie*. Berlin/Boston: Walter de Gruyter, 33–46.

Brunt, P. A. (1973). 'Aspects of the social thought of Dio Chrysostom and of the Stoics', *Proceedings of the Cambridge Philological Society* 19: 9–34 [= Brunt 2013a: 151–79].

Brunt, P. A. (1978). '*Laus imperii*', in P. D. A. Garnsey and C. R. Whittaker (eds.), *Imperialism in the Ancient World*. Cambridge: Cambridge University Press, 159–91.

Brunt, P. A. (1986). 'Cicero's *officium* in the Civil War', *Journal of Roman Studies* 76: 12–32 [= Brunt 2013a: 243–74].

Brunt, P. A. (1988a). *The Fall of the Roman Republic*. Oxford: Clarendon Press.

Brunt, P. A. (1988b). 'The fall of the Roman Republic', in Brunt 1988a: 1–92.

Brunt, P. A. (1988c). 'The army and the land in the Roman revolution', in Brunt 1988a: 240–80.

Brunt, P. A. (1988d). '*Libertas* in the Republic', in Brunt 1988a: 281–350.

Brunt, P. A. (1988e). '*Amicitia* in the late Roman Republic', in Brunt 1988a: 351–81.
Brunt, P. A. (2013a). *Studies in Stoicism*. Oxford: Oxford University Press.
Brunt, P. A. (2013b). 'Panaetius in *De Officiis*', in Brunt 2013a: 180–242.
Büchner, K. (comm.) (1984). *M. Tullius Cicero: De Re Publica*. Heidelberg: Carl Winter Universitätsverlag.
Calabresi, S. G., Berghausen, M. E., and Albertson, S. (2012). 'The rise and fall of the separation of powers', *Northwestern University Law Review* 106: 527–49.
Chin, T. T. (2016). 'What is imperial cosmopolitanism? Revisiting *kosmopolitēs* and *mundanus*', in M. Lavan, R. A. Payne, and J. Weisweiler (eds.), *Cosmopolitanism and Empire: Universal Rulers, Local Elites, and Cultural Integration in the Ancient Near East and Mediterranean*. Oxford: Oxford University Press, 128–52.
Clarke, M. L. (1951) 'The *thesis* in the Roman rhetorical schools of the Republic', *Classical Quarterly* 1: 159–66.
Cooper, J. M. (1984). 'Plato's theory of human motivation', *History of Philosophy Quarterly* 1: 3–21. Reprinted in J. M. Cooper, *Reason and Emotion*, Princeton: Princeton University Press, 1999: 118–37; and in G. Fine (ed.), *Plato 2: Ethics, Politics, Religion, and the Soul*, New York: Oxford University Press, 1999: 186–206.
Cornell, T. J. (2001). 'Cicero on the origins of Rome', in J. G. F. Powell and J. North (eds.), *Cicero's Republic*. London: BICS Supplement 76, 40–56.
Cornell, T. J. (2005). 'The value of the literary tradition concerning archaic Rome', in K. A. Raaflaub (ed.), *Social Struggles in Archaic Rome*. Malden/Oxford/Carlton: Blackwell Publishing, 47–74.
Cox, V. (2016). 'Cicero at court: Martino Filetico's Iocundissimae disputationes', in G. Manuwald (ed.), *The Afterlife of Cicero*. London: BICS Supplement 135, 46–66.
Crawford, M. H. (1974). *Roman Republican Coinage*. Cambridge: Cambridge University Press.
Crawford, M. H. (1992), *The Roman Republic* (2nd edn.). London: Fontana Press.
Crawford, M. H. (1996). *Roman Statutes*. London: Institute of Classical Studies, University of London.
de Ste. Croix, G. E. M. (1981). *The Class Struggle in the Ancient Greek World: From the Archaic Age to the Arab Conquests*. London: Duckworth.
Drummond, A. (1995). *Law, Politics and Power: Sallust and the Execution of the Catilinarian Conspirators*. Stuttgart: Franz Steiner.
Dubin, N. (2016). 'The Catiline conspiracy and the credibility of letters in French Revolutionary art', in G. Manuwald (ed.), *The Afterlife of Cicero*. London: BICS Supplement 135, 177–98.

Dugan, J. (2005). *Making a New Man: Ciceronian Self-Fashioning in the Rhetorical Works*. Oxford: Oxford University Press.
Dugan, J. (2013). 'Cicero's rhetorical theory', in C. Steel (ed.), *The Cambridge Companion to Cicero*. Cambridge: Cambridge University Press, 25–40.
Dumont, J. C. (1983). 'Conquête et esclavage chez Cicéron: De Republica, III, 36-37', *Ktema* 8: 113–28.
Dunkle, J. R. (1967). 'The Greek tyrant and Roman political invective of the late Republic', *Transactions of the American Philological Association* 98: 151–71.
Dyck, A. R. (1996). *A Commentary on Cicero's De Officiis*. Ann Arbor: The University of Michigan Press.
Dyck, A. R. (2004). *A Commentary on Cicero's De Legibus*. Ann Arbor: The University of Michigan Press.
Earl, D. C. (1961). *The Political Thought of Sallust*. Cambridge: Cambridge University Press.
Eckstein, A. M. (2007). 'Conceptualizing Roman imperial expansion under the Republic: an introduction', in N. Rosenstein and R. Morstein-Marx (eds.), *A Companion to the Roman Republic*. Oxford: Blackwell, 567–89.
Edwards, C. (1993). *The Politics of Immorality in Ancient Rome*. Cambridge: Cambridge University Press.
Edwards, C., and Woolf, G., eds. (2006). *Rome the Cosmopolis*. Cambridge: Cambridge University Press.
Fantham, E. (1973). '*Aequabilitas* in Cicero's political theory and the Greek tradition of proportional justice', *Classical Quarterly* 23: 285–90.
Fantham, E. (2004). *The Roman World of Cicero's De Oratore*. Oxford: Oxford University Press.
Feeney, D. C. (2007). *Caesar's Calendar: Ancient Time and the Beginnings of History*. Berkeley/London: University of California Press.
Ferrary, J.-L. (1977). 'Le discours de Philus (Cicéron, De re publica, III, 8–31) et la philosophie de Carnéade', *Revue des Études Latines* 55: 128–56.
Ferrary, J.-L. (1984). 'L'Archéologie du *de re publica* (2, 2, 4–37,63)', *Journal of Roman Studies* 74: 87–98.
Ferrary, J.-L. (1988). *Philhellénisme et impérialisme. Aspects idéologiques de la conquête romaine du monde Hellénistique*. Rome: École française de Rome.
Ferrary, J.-L. (1995). 'The statesman and the law in the political philosophy of Cicero', in A. Laks and M. Schofield (eds.), *Justice and Generosity. Studies in Hellenistic Social and Political Philosophy*. Cambridge: Cambridge University Press, 48–73.
Flower, H. (1996). *Ancestor Masks and Aristocratic Power in Roman Culture*. Oxford: Clarendon Press.

Fott, D. (trans.) (2014). *Marcus Tullius Cicero. On the Republic and On the Laws*. Ithaca and London: Cornell University Press.

Fox, M. (2007). *Cicero's Philosophy of History*. Oxford: Oxford University Press.

Frede, D. (1989). 'Constitution and citizenship: Peripatetic influence on Cicero's political conceptions in the *De re publica*', in W. W. Fortenbaugh and P. Steinmetz (eds.), *Cicero's Knowledge of the Peripatos*. New Brunswick and London: Transaction Publishers, 77–100.

Frede, M. (1994). 'The Stoic conception of reason', in K. J. Boudouris (ed.), *Hellenistic Philosophy: Volume 1*. Athens: International Center for Greek philosophy and culture, 50–63.

Frede, M. (1996). 'Introduction', in M. Frede and G. Striker (eds.), *Rationality in Greek Thought*. Oxford: Clarendon Press, 1–28.

Frede, M. (2007). 'A notion of a person in Epictetus', in T. Scaltsas and A. S. Mason (eds.), *The Philosophy of Epictetus*. Oxford: Oxford University Press, 153–68.

Freyburger, G. (1986). *Fides: étude sémantique et religieuse depuis les origines jusqu' à l'époque augustéenne* (2nd edn.). Paris: Les Belles Lettres.

Freyburger, G. (2002). 'La *fides* civique', in S. Ratti (ed.), *Antiquité et citoyenneté*. Bésançon: Presses universitaires Franc-Comtoises, 341–7.

Frier, B. W. (1985). *The Rise of the Roman Jurists: Studies in Cicero's Pro Caecina*. Princeton: Princeton University Press.

Garnett, G. (ed. and trans.) (1994). *Vindiciae, Contra Tyrannos*. Cambridge: Cambridge University Press.

Garnsey, P. (1996). *Ideas of Slavery from Aristotle to Augustine*. Cambridge: Cambridge University Press.

Garnsey, P. (2007). *Thinking about Property: From Antiquity to the Age of Revolution*. Cambridge: Cambridge University Press.

Garnsey, P. (2009). 'Cicero on property', in J. Carlsen and E. Lo Cascio (eds.), *Agricultura e Scambi nell'Italia Tardo-Repubblicana*. Bari: Edipuglia, 157–66.

Geuss, R. (2005). *Outside Ethics*. Princeton & Oxford: Princeton University Press.

Gibson, R. K., and Morrison, A. D. (2007). 'Introduction: what is a letter?', in R. Morello and A. D. Morrison (eds.), *Ancient Letters: Classical Ancient Letters: Classical and Late Antique Epistolography*. Oxford: Oxford University Press, 1–16.

Gildenhard, I. (2006). 'Reckoning with tyranny: Greek thoughts on Caesar in Cicero's *Letters to Atticus* in early 49', in S. Lewis (ed.), *Ancient Tyranny*. Edinburgh: Edinburgh University Press, 197–209.

Gildenhard, I. (2007). *Paideia Romana: Cicero's Tusculan Disputations*. Cambridge: Cambridge Philological Society.

Gildenhard, I. (2011). *Creative Eloquence. The Construction of Reality in Cicero's Speeches*. Oxford: Oxford University Press.

Gildenhard, I. (2013). 'Cicero's dialogues: historiography manqué and the evidence of fiction', in S. Föllinger and G. M. Müller (eds.), *Der Dialog in der Antike*. Berlin/Boston: De Gruyter, 235–74.
Gill, C. (1988). 'Personhood and personality: the four *personae* theory in Cicero, *De officiis* I', *Oxford Studies in Ancient Philosophy* 5: 169–99.
Girardet, K. M. (1983). *Die Ordnung der Welt. Ein Beitrag zur philosophischen and politischen Interpretation von Ciceros Schrift De Legibus*. Wiesbaden: Franz Steiner Verlag.
Görler, W. (1995). 'Silencing the troublemaker: *De Legibus* I.39 and the continuity of Cicero's scepticism', in J. Powell (ed.), *Cicero the Philosopher*. Oxford: Clarendon Press, 85–113.
Görler, W. (2004). *Kleine Schriften zur hellenistisch-römischen Philosophie*. Leiden: Brill.
Griffin, M. T. (1986). 'Philosophy, Cato, and Roman suicide', *Greece & Rome* 33: 64–77, 192–202 [= Griffin 2018: 402–19].
Griffin, M. T. (1994). 'The intellectual developments of the Ciceronian age', in J. A. Crook, A. Lintott, and E. Rawson, *The Cambridge Ancient History*, Volume 9 (2nd edn.). Cambridge: Cambridge University Press, 689–728 [= Griffin 2018: 432–60].
Griffin, M. T. (1995). 'Philosophical badinage in Cicero's letters to his friends', in J. G. F. Powell (ed.), *Cicero the Philosopher*. Oxford: Clarendon Press, 325–46 [= Griffin 2018: 461–74].
Griffin, M. T. (1996). 'When is thought political?', *Apeiron* 29: 269–82 [= Griffin 2018: 486–94].
Griffin, M. T. (1997). 'From Aristotle to Atticus: Cicero and Matius on friendship', in J. Barnes and M. T. Griffin (eds.), *Philosophia Togata II: Plato and Aristotle at Rome*. Oxford: Clarendon Press, 86–109 [= Griffin 2018: 495–509].
Griffin, M. T. (2003). '*Clementia* after Caesar: from politics to philosophy', in F. Cairns and E. Fantham (eds.), *Caesar against Liberty? Perspectives on his Autocracy*. Papers of the Langford Latin Seminar 11. Cambridge: Francis Cairns (Publishing), 157–82 [= Griffin 2018: 570–86].
Griffin, M. T. (2008). '*Iure plectimur*. The Roman critique of Roman imperialism', in T. C. Brennan and H. I. Flower (eds.), *East & West: Papers in Ancient History presented to Glen W. Bowersock*. Cambridge, Mass. & London: Harvard University Press, 85–111 [= Griffin 2018: 263–76].
Griffin, M. T. (2011). 'The politics of virtue: three puzzles in Cicero's *De Officiis*', in B. Morison and K. Ierodiakonou (eds.), *Episteme, etc.: Essays in Honour of Jonathan Barnes*. Oxford: Oxford University Press, 310–27 [= Griffin 2018: 662–75].
Griffin, M. T. (2013). 'Latin philosophy and Roman law', in V. Harte and M. Lane (eds.), *Politeia in Greek and Roman Philosophy*. Cambridge: Cambridge University Press, 96–115 [= Griffin 2018: 693–706].

Griffin, M. T. (2017). 'Dignity in Roman and Stoic thought', in R. Debes (ed.), *Dignity: A History*. Oxford: Oxford University Press, 47–66 [= Griffin 2018: 722–31].

Griffin, M. T. (2018). *Politics and Philosophy at Rome: Collected Papers*. Oxford: Oxford University Press.

Griffin, M. T., and Atkins, E. M. (trans.) (1991). *Cicero. On Duties*. Cambridge: Cambridge University Press.

Griffin, M.T., and Barnes, J. (eds.) (1989). *Philosophia Togata: Essays on Philosophy and Roman Society*. Oxford: Clarendon Press.

Grillo, L. (2012). *The Art of Caesar's* Bellum Civile: *Literature, Ideology, and Community*. Cambridge: Cambridge University Press.

Gruen, E. (1982). 'Greek *pistis* and Roman *fides*', *Athenaeum* NS 60: 50–68.

Hahm, D.E. (1995). 'Polybius' applied political theory', in A. Laks and M. Schofield (eds.), *Justice and Generosity: Studies in Hellenistic Social and Political Philosophy*. Cambridge: Cambridge University Press, 7–47.

Hall, J. (2005). 'Politeness and formality in Cicero's letter to Matius (*Fam.* 11.27)', *Museum Helveticum* 62: 193–213.

Hansen, M. H. (2010). 'The mixed constitution versus the separation of powers: monarchical and aristocratic aspects of modern democracy', *History of Political Thought* 31: 509–31.

Harries, J. (2006). *Cicero and the Jurists*. London: Duckworth.

Harries, J. (2007). *Law and Crime in the Roman World*. Cambridge: Cambridge University Press.

Harris, W. V. (1979). *War and Imperialism in Republican Rome, 327–70 B.C.* Oxford: Clarendon Press.

Heldman, K. (1976). 'Ciceros *Laelius* und die Grenzen der Freundschaft', *Hermes* 104: 72–103.

Hodgson, L. (2017). *Res Publica & the Roman Republic*. Oxford: Oxford University Press.

Hopkins, K. (1983). *Death and Renewal: Sociological Studies in Roman History, Volume 2*. Cambridge: Cambridge University Press.

Horsley, R. A. (1978). 'The law of nature in Philo and Cicero', *Harvard Theological Review* 71: 35–59.

Hellegouarc'h, J. (1972). *Le Vocabulaire latin des relations et des partis politiques sous la République* (2nd edn.). Paris: Les Belles Lettres.

Hutchinson, G. O. (1998). *Cicero's Correspondence. A Literary Study*. Oxford: Clarendon Press.

Inwood, B. (1999). 'Rules and reasoning in Stoic ethics', in K. Ierodiakonou (ed.), *Topics in Stoic Philosophy*. Oxford: Clarendon Press, 95–127.

Inwood, B., and Gerson, L. (trans.) (1997). *Hellenistic Philosophy: Introductory Readings* (2nd edn.). Indianapolis/Cambridge: Hackett Publishing Company.

Irwin, T. H. (2014). '*Officia* and casuistry: some episodes', *Philosophie Antique* 14: 111–28.

Kaster, R. A. (1997). 'The shame of the Romans', *Transactions of the American Philological Association* 127: 1–19.

Kaster, R. A. (2005). *Emotion, Restraint, and Community in Ancient Rome*. Oxford: Oxford University Press.

Kaster, R. A. (2009). 'Some passionate performances in late republican Rome', in R. Balot (ed.), *A Companion to Greek and Roman Political Thought*. Malden, MA, and Oxford: Wiley-Blackwell, 308–20.

Kempshall, M. S. (2001). '*De Re Publica* I.39 in medieval and Renaissance political thought', in J. G. F. Powell and J. North (eds.), *Cicero's Republic*. BICS Supplement 76: London, 99–135.

Keyes, C. W. (ed. and trans.) (1928). *Cicero: De Re Publica, De Legibus*. Cambridge, MA and London: Harvard University Press and W. Heinemann (Loeb Classical Library).

Knoche, U. (1935). *Magnitudo Animi: Untersuchungen zur Entstehung und Entwicklung eines römischen Wertgedankens*. Philologus, Supplementband 27, Heft 3. Leipzig: Dieterich.

Laborde, C, and Maynor, J. (eds.) (2008). *Republicanism and Political Theory*. Malden, MA, London, Carlton: Blackwell Publishing.

Lane, M. S. (1998). *Method and Politics in Plato's 'Statesman'*. Cambridge: Cambridge University Press.

Lavan, M. (2013). *Slaves to Rome. Paradigms of Empire in Roman Culture*. Cambridge: Cambridge University Press.

Lavan, M., Payne, R. A., and Weisweiler, J. (eds.) (2016). *Cosmopolitanism and Empire: Universal Rulers, Local Elites, and Cultural Integration in the Ancient Near East and Mediterranean*. Oxford: Oxford University Press.

Lefèvre, E. (2001). *Panaitios und Ciceros Pflichtenlehre: vom philosophischen Traktat zu politischen Lehrbuch*. Stuttgart: Franz Steiner Verlag.

Leonhardt, J. (1995). 'Theorie und Praxis der *deliberation* bei Cicero: der Briefwechsel mit Atticus aus dem Jahre 49', *Acta Classica Universitatis Sceientiarum Debreceniensis* 31: 153–71.

Lintott, A. W. (1972). 'Imperial expansion and moral decline in the Roman Republic', *Historia* 21: 626–38.

Lintott, A. W. (1993). *Imperium Romanum. Politics and Administration*. London and New York: Routledge.

Lintott, A. W. (1999a). *The Constitution of the Roman Republic*. Oxford: Clarendon Press.

Lintott, A. W. (1999b). *Violence in Republican Rome* (2nd edn.). Oxford: Oxford University Press.

Lintott, A. W. (2008). *Cicero as Evidence: A Historian's Companion*. Oxford: Oxford University Press.

Long, A. A. (1995). 'Cicero's politics in *De officiis*', in A. Laks and M. Schofield (eds.), *Justice and Generosity: Studies in Hellenistic Social and Political Philosophy*. Cambridge: Cambridge University Press, 213–40.

Long, A. A. (2002). *Epictetus: A Stoic and Socratic Guide to Life*. Oxford: Clarendon Press.

Long, A. A., and Sedley, D. N. (1987). *The Hellenistic Philosophers*, 2 volumes. Cambridge: Cambridge University Press.

Mackie, N. (1992). '*Popularis* ideology and popular politics at Rome in the first century B.C.', *Rheinisches Museum für Philologie*: 135: 49–73.

Mankin, D. (2011). *Cicero: De Oratore Book III*. Cambridge: Cambridge University Press.

McConnell, S. (2014). *Philosophical Life in Cicero's Letters*. Cambridge: Cambridge University Press.

McCormick, J. (2011). *Machiavellian Democracy*. Cambridge: Cambridge University Press.

Millar, F. G. B. (1998). *The Crowd in Rome in the Late Republic*. Ann Arbor: University of Michigan Press.

Moatti, C. (1997). *La Raison de Rome. Naissance de l'esprit critique à fin de la République (IIer-Ier siècle avant Jésus Christ)*. Paris: Éditions du Seuil.

Moatti, C. (2015). *The Birth of Critical Thinking in Republican Rome*. Cambridge: Cambridge University Press. A translation of Moatti (1997).

Moatti, C. (2017). '*Res publica, forma rei publicae*, and *SPQR*', *Bulletin of the Institute of Classical Studies* 60: 33–48.

Moles, J. L. (2000). 'The Cynics', in C. J. Rowe and M. Schofield (eds.), *The Cambridge History of Greek and Roman Political Thought*. Cambridge: Cambridge University Press: 415–34.

Morgan, T. (2015). *Roman Faith and Christian Faith: Pistis and Fides in the Early Roman Empire and Early Churches*. Oxford: Oxford University Press.

Morrell, K. (2017). *Pompey, Cato, and the Governance of the Roman Empire*. Oxford: Oxford University Press.

Morstein-Marx, R. (2004). *Mass Oratory and Political Power in the Late Roman Republic*. Cambridge: Cambridge University Press.

Morstein-Marx, R. (2013). '"Cultural hegemony" and the communicative power of the Roman elite', in C. Steel and H. van der Blom (eds.), *Community and Communication: Oratory and Politics in Republican Rome*. Oxford: Oxford University Press: 29–47.

Mouritsen, H. (2001). *Plebs and Politics in the Late Roman Republic.* Cambridge: Cambridge University Press.

Mouritsen, H. (2017). *Politics in the Roman Republic.* Cambridge: Cambridge University Press.

Murphy, P. R. (1986). 'Caesar's continuators and Caesar's *felicitas*', *The Classical World* 79: 307–17.

Muthu, S. (2003). *Enlightenment against Empire.* Princeton: Princeton University Press.

Muthu, S. (ed.) (2012). *Empire and Modern Political Thought.* Cambridge: Cambridge University Press.

Nicgorski, W. (1991). 'Cicero's focus: from the best regime to the model statesman', *Political Theory* 19: 230–51.

Nicgorski, W. (2016). *Cicero's Skepticism and his Recovery of Political Philosophy.* New York: Palgrave Macmillan.

Nicolet, C. (1970). 'Cicéron, Platon et le vote secret', *Historia* 19: 39–66.

Nicolet, C. (1980). *The World of the Citizen in Republican Rome.* London: Batsford.

Nozick, R. (1974). *Anarchy, State, and Utopia.* New York: Basic Books.

Nussbaum, M. (1997). 'Kant and cosmopolitanism', *Journal of Political Philosophy* 5: 1–25.

Nussbaum, M. (2000). 'Duties of justice, duties of material aid', *Journal of Political Philosophy* 8: 176–206.

Oakley, S. P. (1997). *A Commentary on Livy: Books VI–X. Vol. 1, Introduction and Book VI.* Oxford: Clarendon Press.

Ogilvie, R. M. (1965). *A Commentary on Livy: Books 1–5.* Oxford: Clarendon Press.

Pagden, A. (1995). *Lords of All the World. Ideologies of Empire in Spain, Britain and France c.1500–c.1800.* New Haven and London: Yale University Press.

Pagden, A. (2000). 'Stoicism, cosmopolitanism, and the legacy of European imperialism', *Constellations* 7: 3–22.

Paone, C. (2018). 'Diogenes the Cynic on law and world citizenship', *Polis* 35: 478–98.

Parker, H.T. (1937). *The Cult of Antiquity and the French Revolutionaries.* Chicago: University of Chicago Press.

Paulson, L. (2017). *Voluntas.* PhD thesis submitted to Université Paris-Sorbonne.

Pelling, C. (2002). 'Herodotus' debate on the constitutions', *Proceedings of the Cambridge Philological Society* 48: 123–58.

Pettit, P. (1997). *Republicanism. A theory of Freedom and Government.* Oxford: Oxford University Press.

Pettit, P. (2012). *On the People's Terms: A Republican Theory and Model of Democracy.* Cambridge: Cambridge University Press.

Philp, M. (1996). 'Republicanism and liberalism: on leadership and political order – a review', *Democratization* 3: 383–419.
Philp, M. (2007). *Political Conduct*. Cambridge MA and London: Harvard University Press.
Pitts, J. (2012). 'Political theory of empire and imperialism: a postscript', in S. Muthu (ed.), *Empire and Modern Political Thought*. Cambridge: Cambridge University Press, 351–87.
Potter, D. (2019). *The Origin of Empire: Rome from the Republic to Hadrian*. Cambridge MA: Harvard University Press.
Powell, J. G. F. (1994). 'The *rector rei publicae* of Cicero's *De Republica*', *Scripta Classica Israelica* 13: 19–29.
Powell, J. G. F. (ed.) (1995). *Cicero the Philosopher. Twelve Papers*. Oxford: Clarendon Press.
Powell, J. G. F. (2001). 'Were Cicero's *Laws* the laws of Cicero's *Republic*?', in J. G. F. Powell and J. North (eds.), *Cicero's Republic*. London: BICS Supplement 76, 17–39.
Powell, J. G. F. (ed.) (2006). *M. Tulli Ciceronis: De Re Publica, De Legibus, Cato Maior De Senectute, Laelius De Amicitia*. Oxford: Clarendon Press.
Powell, J. G. F. (2012). 'Cicero's *De Re Publica* and the virtues of a statesman', in W. Nicgorski (ed.), *Cicero's Practical Philosophy*. Notre Dame, Indiana: University of Notre Dame Press.
Powell, J. G. F. (2013). 'The embassy of the three philosophers to Rome in 155 BC', in C. Kremmydas and K. Tempest (eds.), *Hellenistic Oratory: Continuity and Change*. Oxford: Oxford University Press, 219–47.
Raaflaub, K. A. (1996). 'Equalities and inequalities in Athenian democracy', in J. Ober and C. Hedrik (eds.), *Dêmokratia*. Princeton: Princeton University Press, 139–74.
Raaflaub, K. A. (2003). 'Caesar the Liberator? Factional politics, civil war, and ideology', in F. Cairns and E. Fantham (eds.), *Caesar against Liberty? Perspectives on his Autocracy*. Papers of the Langford Latin Seminar 11. Cambridge: Francis Cairns (Publishing), 35–67.
Raaflaub, K. A. (ed.) (2005a). *Social Struggles in Archaic Rome: New Perspectives on the Conflicts of the Orders* (2nd edn.). Malden/Oxford/Carlton: Blackwell Publishing.
Raaflaub, K. A. (2005b). 'The conflict of the orders in archaic Rome: a comprehensive and comparative approach', in K. A. Raaflaub (ed.), *Social Struggles in Archaic Rome*. Malden/Oxford/Carlton: Blackwell Publishing, 1–46.
Rahe, P. A. (1994). 'Cicero and republicanism in America', *Ciceroniana* 8: 63–78.
Rawson, E. D. (1973). 'The interpretation of Cicero's *De legibus*', *Aufstieg und Niedergang der Römischen Welt* I.4: 334–56.

Rawson, E. D. (1975). *Cicero: A Portrait*. London: Allen Lane.
Rawson, E. D. (1985). *Intellectual Life in the Late Roman Republic*. London: Duckworth.
Reinhardt, T. (2000). 'Rhetoric in the Fourth Academy', *Classical Quarterly* 50: 531–47.
Reinhold, M. (1979). 'Eighteenth-century American political thought', in R. R. Bolgar (ed.), *Classical Influences on Western Thought*. Cambridge: Cambridge University Press, 223–43.
Reinhold, M. (1994). 'The influence of Cicero on John Adams', *Ciceroniana* 8: 45–51.
Rich, J. W. (2005). 'Valerius Antias and the construction of the Roman past', *Bulletin of the Institute of Classical Studies* 48: 137–61.
Richardson, J. S. (1991). '*Imperium Romanum*: empire and the language of power', *Journal of Roman Studies* 81: 1–9.
Richardson, J. S. (2008). *The Language of Empire*. Cambridge: Cambridge University Press.
Riggsby, A. M. (2006). *Caesar in Gaul and Rome: War in Words*. Austin, TX: University of Texas Press.
Rudd, N. (trans.) (1998). *Cicero: The Republic and the Laws*. Oxford and New York: Oxford University Press.
Scheidel, W. (2019) *Escape from Rome: The Failure of Empire and the Road to Prosperity*. Princeton: Princeton University Press.
Schofield, M. (1991). *The Stoic Idea of the City*. Cambridge: Cambridge University Press (Chicago: Chicago University Press [2nd expanded edn. 1999]).
Schofield, M. (1995a). 'Cicero's definition of *res publica*', in J. G. F. Powell (ed.), *Cicero the Philosopher*. Oxford: Clarendon Press, 63–83.
Schofield, M. (1995b). 'Two Stoic approaches to justice', in A. Laks and M. Schofield (eds.), *Justice and Generosity: Studies in Hellenistic Social and Political Philosophy*. Cambridge: Cambridge University Press, 191–212.
Schofield, M. (1996). 'Sharing in the constitution', *The Review of Metaphysics* 49: 831–58.
Schofield, M. (1999). 'Morality and the law: the case of Diogenes of Babylon', in his *Saving the City*. London and New York: Routledge, 160–77.
Schofield, M. (2006). *Plato: Political Philosophy*. Oxford: Oxford University Press.
Schofield, M. (2008). 'Ciceronian dialogue', in S. Goldhill (ed.), *The End of Dialogue in Antiquity*. Cambridge: Cambridge University Press, 63–84.
Schofield, M. (2009). 'Republican virtues', in R. Balot (ed.), *The Blackwell Companion to Greek and Roman Political Thought*. Oxford: Wiley-Blackwell, 199–213.
Schofield, M. (2012). 'The fourth virtue', in W. Nicgorski (ed.), *Cicero's Practical Philosophy*. Notre Dame, Indiana: University of Notre Dame Press, 43–57.

Schofield, M. (2015a). 'Liberty, equality, and authority: a political discourse in the later Roman Republic', in D. Hammer (ed.), *A Companion to Greek Democracy and the Roman Republic*. Chichester: Wiley-Blackwell, 113–27.
Schofield, M. (2015b). 'Seneca on monarchy and the political life: *De Clementia, De Tranquillitate Animi, De Otio*', in S. Bartsch and A. Schiesaro (eds.), *The Cambridge Companion to Seneca*. Cambridge: Cambridge University Press, 68–81.
Schofield, M. (2017a). 'Cicero's Plato', in T. Engberg-Pedersen (ed.), *From Stoicism to Platonism*. Cambridge: Cambridge University Press, 47–66.
Schofield, M. (2017b). 'Cicero on imperialism and the soul', in R. Seaford, J. Wilkins, and M. Wright (eds.), *Selfhood & the Soul*. Oxford: Oxford University Press, 107–24.
Schofield, M. (2018). 'Aristotle's critique of Spartan imperialism', in P. Cartledge and A. Powell (eds.), *The Greek Superpower: Sparta in the Self-Definition of Athenians*. Swansea: University of Wales Press, 215–34.
Schofield, M. (forthcoming 1). '*Iuris consensu* revisited', in M. Graver, N. Gilbert, and S. McConnell (eds.).
Schofield, M. (forthcoming 2). 'Atticus in *De Legibus* and *Brutus*', in G. M. Müller (ed.).
Schofield, M. (forthcoming 3). 'Debate or guidance? Cicero on philosophy', in F. Leigh (ed.), *Themes in Plato, Aristotle, and Hellenistic Philosophy: Keeling Lectures 2010–18*. London: BICS Supplement 141.
Schofield, M. (ed.), and Griffith, T. (trans.) (2016). *Plato: Laws*. Cambridge: Cambridge University Press.
Sedley, D. N. (1997). 'The Ethics of Brutus and Cassius', *Journal of Roman Studies* 87: 41–53.
Sedley, D. N. (ed.) (2012). *The Philosophy of Antiochus*. Cambridge: Cambridge University Press.
Sellers, M. N. S. (2010). 'Revolution, French', in A. Grafton, G. Most, and S. Settis (eds.), *The Classical Tradition*. Cambridge, MA and London: Harvard University Press (Belknap Press), 822–6.
Shackleton Bailey, D. R. (ed.) (1965). *Cicero's Letters to Atticus*, vol. I. Cambridge: Cambridge University Press.
Shackleton Bailey, D. R. (1971). *Cicero*. London: Duckworth.
Shackleton Bailey, D. R. (1994). 'A Ciceronian Odyssey', *Ciceroniana* 8: 87–92.
Sherwin-White, A.N. (1973). *The Roman Citizenship* (2nd edn.). Oxford: Clarendon Press.
Skinner, Q. (1989). 'The state', in T. Ball, J. Farr, and R. L. Hanson (eds.), *Political Innovation and Conceptual Change*. Cambridge: Cambridge University Press, 90–131.

Skinner, Q. (1990). 'The republican ideal of political liberty', in G. Bock, Q. Skinner, and M. Viroli (eds.), *Machiavelli and Republicanism*. Cambridge: Cambridge University Press, 293–309.
Skinner, Q. (1998). *Liberty before Liberalism*. Cambridge: Cambridge University Press.
Skinner, Q. (2002). *Visions of Politics*. Cambridge: Cambridge University Press.
Skinner, Q. (2009). 'A genealogy of the modern state', *Proceedings of the British Academy* 162: 325–70.
Sommer, M. (2013). 'Scipio Aemilianus, Polybius, and the quest for friendship in second-century Rome', in B. Gibson and T. Harrison (eds.), *Polybius and his World: Essays in Memory of F.W. Walbank*. Oxford: Oxford University Press: 307–18.
Steel, C. (2002–3). 'Cicero's *Brutus*: the end of oratory and the beginning of history?', *Bulletin of the Institute of Classical Studies* 46: 195–211.
Steel, C. (2005). *Reading Cicero: Genre and Performance in Late Republican Rome*. London: Duckworth.
Steel, C. (2017). '*Re publica nihil desperatius*: salvaging the state in Cicero's pre-civil war philosophical works', in G. M. Müller and F. M. Zini (eds.), *Philosophie in Rom—Römische Philosophie? Kultur-, literatur- und philosophiegeschichtliche Perspektiven*. Berlin & Boston: De Gruyter, 269–82.
Strasburger, H. (1966). 'Der "Scipionenkreis"', *Hermes* 94: 62–70.
Straumann, B. (2016). *Crisis and Constitutionalism: Roman Political Thought from the Fall of the Republic to the Age of Revolution*. New York: Oxford University Press.
Straumann, B. (2019). '"The laws are in charge of the magistrates": reply to Edelstein, Sullivan and Springborg', *Global Intellectual History*, DOI: 10.1080/23801883.2019.1569750.
Swain, S. (2002). 'Bilingualism in Cicero? The evidence of code-switching', in J. N. Adams, M. Janse, and S. Swain (eds.), *Bilingualism in Ancient Society: Language Contact and the Written Text*. Oxford: Oxford University Press, 128–67.
Syme, R. (1939). *The Roman Revolution*. Oxford: Clarendon Press.
Tan, J. (2008). '*Contiones* in the age of Cicero', *Classical Antiquity* 27.1: 163–201.
Tatum, W.J. (1999). *The Patrician Tribune: Julius Clodius Pulcher*. Chapel Hill and London: University of North Carolina Press.
Thomas, Y. (1991). 'L'institution de la majesté', *Revue de Synthèse* 112: 331–86.
Thompson, D. I. (2018). *Montaigne and the Tolerance of Politics*. New York: Oxford University Press.
Thonemann, P. (2018). 'A lover and a fighter', *Literary Review* 466: 14–15.
Ungberg-Steinberg, J. von (2005). 'The formation of the "Annalistic tradition": the example of the Decemvirate', in K. A. Raaflaub (ed.), *Social Struggles in Archaic Rome*. Malden/Oxford/Carlton: Blackwell Publishing, 75–97.

van der Blom, H. (2016). *Oratory and Political Career in the Late Roman Republic.* Cambridge: Cambridge University Press.

Van Gelderen, M. (ed.) (1993). *The Dutch Revolt.* Cambridge: Cambridge University Press.

Veillard, C. (2014). 'Comment definer son devoir? Le *Peri kathekontos* de Panétius', *Philosophie Antique* 14: 71–110.

Vidal-Naquet, P. (1986). 'Athens and Atlantis: structure and meaning of a Platonic myth', in his *The Back Hunter: Forms of Thought and Forms of Society in the Greek World*, Baltimore and London: Johns Hopkins Press, 263–84.

Viroli, M. (1995). *For Love of Country.* Oxford: Clarendon Press.

Vogt, K.M. (2008). *Law, Reason, and the Cosmic City: Political Philosophy in the Early Stoa.* Oxford: Oxford University Press.

Wallace-Hadrill, A. (1997). '*Mutatio morum*: the idea of a cultural revolution', in T. Habinek and A. Schiesaro (eds.), *The Roman Cultural Revolution.* Cambridge: Cambridge University Press, 3–22.

Wallace-Hadrill, A. (2008). *Rome's Cultural Revolution.* Cambridge: Cambridge University Press.

Walsh, P. G. (trans.) (2000). *Cicero. On Obligations.* Oxford: Oxford University Press.

White, P. (2010). *Cicero in Letters: Epistolary Relations of the Late Republic.* New York: Oxford University Press.

Williamson, C. (2016). 'Crimes against the state', in P. J. Du Plessis, C. Ando, and K. Tuori (eds.), *The Oxford Handbook of Roman Law and Society.* Oxford: Oxford University Press, 333–48.

Wirszubski, C. (1950). *Libertas as a Political Idea at Rome during the Late Republic and Early Principate.* Cambridge: Cambridge University Press.

Wiseman, T. P. (1979). *Clio's Cosmetics: Three Studies in Greco-Roman Literature.* Leicester: Leicester University Press.

Wiseman, T. P. (2009). *Remembering the Roman People. Essays on Late-Republican Politics and Literature.* Oxford: Oxford University Press.

Wiseman, T. P. (2010). 'The two-headed state: how Romans explained civil war', in B. W. Breed, C. Damoc, and A. Rossi (eds.), *Citizens of Discord. Rome and its Civil Wars.* New York: Oxford University Press, 25–44.

Wiseman, T. P. (2012). 'Cicero and the body politic', *Politica Antica* 2: 133–40.

Wolff, J. (2006a). 'Making the world safe for utilitarianism', in A. O'Hear (ed.), *Political Philosophy*, Royal Institute of Philosophy Supplementary Volume 58: 1–22.

Wolff, J. (2006b). 'Risk, fear, blame, shame and the regulation of public safety', *Economics and Philosophy* 22: 409–27.

Wolff, J. (2011). *Ethics and Public Policy: A Philosophical Inquiry*. London: Routledge.
Wood, G. S. (1969). *The Creation of the American Republic 1776–1787*. Chapel Hill: The University of North Carolina Press.
Wood, N. (1988). *Cicero's Social and Political Thought*. Berkeley/Los Angeles/London: University of California Press.
Woodhouse, A. (2018). 'Subjection without servitude: the imperial protectorate in Renaissance political thought', *Journal of the History of Ideas* 79: 547–69.
Woolf, R. (2007). 'Particularism, promises, and persons in Cicero's *De officiis*', *Oxford Studies in Ancient Philosophy* 33: 317–46.
Woolf, R. (2015). *Cicero: The Philosophy of a Roman Sceptic*. London and New York: Routledge.
Yakobson, A. (2006). 'Popular power in the Roman Republic', in N. Rosenstein and R. Morstein-Marx (eds.), *A Companion to the Roman Republic*. Oxford: Blackwell, 383–400.
Zarecki, J. (2014). *Cicero's Ideal Statesman in Theory and Practice*. London and New York: Bloomsbury Academic.
Zetzel, J. E. G. (ed.) (1995). *Cicero: De Republica. Selections*. Cambridge: Cambridge University Press.
Zetzel, J. E. G. (2001). 'Citizen and commonwealth in *De Re Publica*, Book 4', in J. G. F. Powell and J. North (eds.), *Cicero's Republic*. London: *BICS* Supplement 76, 83–97.
Zetzel, J. E. G. (2013). 'A contract on Ameria: law and legality in Cicero's *Pro Roscio Amerino*', *American Journal of Philology* 134: 425–44.
Zetzel, J. E. G. (trans.) (2017a). *Cicero. On the Commonwealth and On the Laws* (2edn.). Cambridge: Cambridge University Press.
Zetzel, J. E. G. (2017b). 'Cicero on the origins of civilization and society', *American Journal of Philology* 138: 461–87.
Zetzel, J. E. G. (2017c). 'The attack on justice: Cicero, Lactantius, and Carneades', *Rheinisches Museum* 160: 299–319.

Index of Passages

Note: References in **bold** indicate passages translated into English

ACADEMICORUM
  PHILOSOPHORUM INDEX
  HERCULANENSIS
  col. 22.33–5   143n.70
APPIAN
  Bella Civilia
  2.7   28
  Epicteti Dissertationes
  1.9.1–6   136n.1
ARISTOTLE
  Analytica Posteriora
  1.2, 72a14–16   225n.67
  de Caelo
  2.9, 290b12–29   137n.11
  Ethica Nicomachea
  4.1, 1120a15–23   180n.52
  5.3, 1131a10–b24   45
  5.3, 1131a24–9   181n.55
  Politica
  1.8, 1256b23–6   142n.65
  1.13, 1260a17–20   181n.57
  3.4, 1277b11–13   141n.55
  3.12, 1282b23–30   181n.55
  4.14, 1298a3–5   42
  5.2, 1302b11–14   181n.55
  6.2, 1317a40–1318a10   56n.53
  7.6, 1327a41-b3   142n.65
  7.6, 1327b27–9   142n.65
  7.14, 1333a2–3   141n.55
AUGUSTINE
  Civitas Dei
  2.21   50, 64
  6.2.48   25n.42
  14.23   133
  19.21   64, 133
  22.6   **133**
  Contra Julianum
  4.12.61   **133**
AUGUSTUS
  Monumentum Ancyrum
  1.1   **30**
  34.2   33

AULUS GELLIUS
  Noctes Atticae
  11.10.1   56n.54
  19.6.3   183n.81
CAESAR
  Bellum Africum
  86   226n.77
  92   226n.77
  Bellum Civile
  1.5.3   33
  1.7.7   54n.26, 74
  1.9.2   54n.26, 74
  1.22.5   221n.21, **30**
  1.67.4   148
  Bellum Gallicum
  3.10.3   130
  7.77.16   130
CICERO
  Academica
  1.9   12
  ad Atticum
  1.17.5   225n.75
  1.17.8   95n.5
  1.18.2   95n.5
  2.1.8   85
  2.17–19   224n.60
  4.16.2–3   61
  4.18.2   95n.5
  5.12.2   61
  7.1.2–3   197
  7.3.2   61, 203
  7.7.5   198
  7.7.6   223n.47
  7.11.1   218, 223n.47
  7.11.5   197
  7.12.2   218
  7.12.3   197
  7.14.3   197
  7.20.2   218
  8.2.2   199, 203
  8.2.4   197, 200
  8.3   223n.49
  8.3.1   197

CICERO (cont.)
  8.3.2 198
  8.3.3 222n.39
  8.3.7 197
  8.7.2 202
  8.9a 198
  8.11 198
  8.11.1 198
  8.11.1 203, **89–90**
  8.12.5 201
  8.14.1 197
  8.14.2 197, 198, 202
  8.15.2 197
  8.16.1 198
  8.16.2 198, 218
  9.1.3 174, 198
  9.1.4 202, 223n.47
  9.2a.3 174
  9.3.3 198
  9.4 223n.46
  9.4.1 197, 204
  9.4.2 201, 209, 217
  9.4.3 204
  9.5.2 95n.5
  9.5.3 198, 202
  9.6.4 198, 202
  9.6a 203
  9.7.1 95n.5
  9.7.6 174, 198
  9.7C 226n.77
  9.9.2 204–205
  9.10 197–8
  9.10.1 197
  9.10.2
  9.10.9 198
  9.10.10 197, 224n.50
  9.11.4 203
  9.12.3 174
  9.13.3 202
  9.13.4 202
  9.13.6 198
  10.4 198
  10.4.3 223n.47
  10.4.4 198, 203
  10.14 198
  11.7.3 174
  12.4.2 154
  12.23.2 142n.69
  12.40.1 154
  13.12.3 177n.16
  13.19.3–5 23n.26
  13.19.3 62
  13.19.4 177n.16
  13.21a 177n.16
  13.27.1 154
  14.1.1 208
  14.4 208
  14.4.2 207
  14.5 208
  16.11.4 187, 220n.17
pro Balbo
  9–10 147, 156
  13 156
  31 32
  64 144n.84
Brutus
  1–10 9
  2–6 18
  7 17
  83 137n.15
  90 157
  102 137n.15
  212 88
  292–9 100n.52
  306 8
  309 8
  313–16 26n.52
  315 8
  322 204
  329–33 9
pro Caecina
  5 227n.99
  33 227n.99
  70 38
  76 227n.99
in Catilinam
  1.3 88
  1.30–1 227n.106
  3.26 144n.84
  4.10 23n.16
  4.16 29
  4.22 144n.85, 145n.95
pro Cluentio
  146 43, 216
  196 155
pro rege Deiotaro
  26 184n.87
  34 218
Divinatio in Caecilium
  65 131
de Divinatione
  2.2 177n.16, 230

2.3 61-2, 154
2.6-7 6
2.9-12 238
2.9 238
2.10-12 14
2.11 159
2.150 235, 241
de Domo Suo
24 35
39 155
110 28
ad Familiares
1.7.7 157
1.8.3 36, 74
1.9.12-17 93
1.9.17 174
3.7.5 55n.39
4.4.4 206
4.8.2 206
4.13 206
4.13.2 206
4.14.1-2 224n.65
4.14.1 74
5.12 179n.29
5.16.4 148
6.6 206
6.6.5 197
6.6.6 202
6.6.8 206
6.6.10 206
6.7.5 154
6.10 206
6.12 206
6.12.2 208
6.13 206
6.14 206
8.1.14 61
9.5.2 174
9.12.2 184n.87
11.27 208
11.7.2 208
11.26.4 202
11.27 208
11.27.2 212
11.27.5 208
11.27.6 157, 210, **155**
11.27.8 209
11.28 208
11.28.2 208
11.28.3 210, 227n.97
11.28.4 208

11.28.6 208
11.28.7 208
11.28.8 212
12.3.1 221n.22
14.1-2 224n.65
de Finibus
2.3-4 65
2.24 137n.15
2.43 240
2.47 170-1
2.59 143n.77
3.4 230
3.20 153
3.21 178n.23
3.75 102n.85
4.23 137n.15
4.64 228n.112
4.79 241
5.11 86
5.67 74
5.73 240
5.85 228n.112
5.95-6 116
pro Flacco
6 144n.85
17 54n.29
66-7 54n.29
de Inventione
2.53 58n.70, 66
2.65 141n.51
2.166 54n.26
2.168-9 96n.12
Laelius
14 62
18 150
19 150
22 197
25 62
36-44 211
44 223n.45
61 226n.90
64-5 158
88-9 223n.45
95 154
de Lege Agraria.
2.3-4 4
2.6-7 35
2.10 35
2.12 35
2.20 34
2.29 31

CICERO (cont.)
  2.81 35
 de Lege Manilia
  7–8 166
  27–9 102n.77
  28 176n.1, 184n.99
  36–50 102n.77
  36 156
  39 156
  41 157, 166
  42 157
  53 166
 de Legibus
  1.8 90, 104n.94
  1.15 15, 47
  1.16–34 232
  1.17 116
  1.18–23 125
  1.18–19 115
  1.18 109, 138n.20
  1.19 121
  1.20 15, 90, 109, 112, 115, 120, 121, 216
  1.21–2 236
  1.21 113
  1.22 163
  1.23 124, 109
  1.24–34 125
  1.28–33 121
  1.28–32 115, 142n.64
  1.31 163, 216
  1.35–48 125
  1.35 121, 232, 236
  1.36 232
  1.37–52 114
  1.37–9 238
  1.37–8 233
  1.37 122
  1.38 240
  1.39
  1.40–1 236
  1.42–8 236
  1.44 115, 118
  1.48 68
  1.50 183n.81
  1.52 138nn.16, 20, 236
  1.53 236
  1.54–5 233
  1.58 114
  1.69 122
  2.5 109

  2.6 90, 104n.94
  2.8–10 113
  2.8 109–10, 113, 115, 118
  2.10 119
  2.11 113, 141n.56
  2.13–14 115
  2.13 121, 139n.34
  2.14 47, 90, 178n.24
  2.15–16 116
  2.16 221n.28, **117**
  2.17 116
  2.19 117
  2.22 117, 220n.16, 221n.28
  2.23 90, 112, 115, 117, 120, 122
  2.24 117
  2.30 92
  2.35–7 112
  2.35–6 125, 140n.37
  2.35 112, 122
  2.41 221n.28
  2.42 28, 90
  2.43–4 137n.14
  2.43 221n.23
  2.45–68 117
  2.57 122
  2.59–68 117
  2.61–2 140n.43
  2.66 102n.85, 140n.43
  2.69 112, 122
  3.1 155
  3.2 119
  3.3 118–19
  3.4 112
  3.5 121
  3.7 103n.89, 119
  3.8 119, 208
  3.9 102n.85, 119
  3.10 101n.60, 103n.89
  3.12–13 115
  3.12 112
  3.14 102n.85
  3.17 119
  3.19–26 112, 116, 123
  3.19–22 33, 91
  3.21–2 215–16
  3.22 90, 104n.94
  3.23–6 91
  3.24 46, 91
  3.25 91
  3.26 54n.24, 90–1, 104n.93, 123
  3.27–32 101n.60

3.27–8 92, 215–16
3.29–32 119
3.29–30 93, 112, 116
3.32 93
3.33–7 91
3.33 91
3.38–9 91
3.42 227n.99
3.47 140n.45
Lucullus
36 233
133–4 231
139 231
pro Marcello
14 202
pro Murena
60 154
66 25n.51, 155
76 184n.94
de Natura Deorum
1.7 9
1.11–12 241
2.14 136n.2
2.87–119 137n.10
2.154 180n.49
3.94–5 116
de Officiis
1.1–6 159
1.3 16
1.5 240
1.6 159, 234, 240
1.7–10 240
1.7 159, 196, 243n.17
1.8 139n.34
1.11–17 150, 159–160, 184n.89
1.11–14 184n.86
1.11 180n.46
1.13–17 184n.89
1.13 160
1.14 153, 180n.43
1.15 74, 171, 180n.43, 183n.75
1.17 159, 170
1.18–19 180n.50
1.18 160
1.19 180n.46
1.20–60 150
1.20–41 161
1.20 161
1.21 162, 182n.66
1.22 163

1.23 158, 165, 178nn.19, 20
1.25 166
1.26 167, 214
1.28–9 164
1.31–2 179n.38
1.31 163, 195
1.32 195
1.34–40 119, 134, 198
1.35 165, 214
1.36 222n.36
1.38 190
1.39–40 112
1.39 221n.24, 222n.32
1.40 194, 220n.18
1.42–59 180n.52
1.42 180n.52
1.43 214
1.45 180n.52
1.46 150
1.50–8 111
1.51–2 112
1.55–6 206
1.55 186
1.56 189
1.57 138n.23, 189, 224n.62
1.58 189
1.59 189
1.61–92 167
1.61 167
1.62–5 167
1.66–9 167
1.67 167
1.69–73 169, 225n.75
1.74–80 169
1.76 88
1.80 169
1.81 169, 176
1.85 53n.18
1.86 167
1.88 37
1.92 167, 169
1.93 172, 183n.83, 184nn.85,89,93
1.96 174, 184n.88
1.97–8 172
1.97
1.98 172–3, 184n.88
1.103 170
1.104 173
1.107–25 173
1.107–14 211
1.110 211

CICERO (cont.)
  1.112 211, **153**
  1.120 211
  1.123 180n.46, 224n.62
  1.124 37, 43, 149
  1.125 153
  1.127 170
  1.126–51 170, 173
  1.128 170, 173
  1.139–40 174
  1.141 173
  1.143 173
  1.148 173 –4
  1.149 112, 175
  1.150–1 170, 174
  1.153–8 107, 160
  1.153 160
  1.156 180n.46
  1.159 159
  1.159 190
  1.160 220n.16, 224n.62
  2.4 224n.62
  2.6 230
  2.7–8 241
  2.7 231
  2.20–2 190
  2.21 214
  2.23 168
  2.26–9 134
  2.26 228n.112
  2.27 165
  2.28 214
  2.29 214
  2.31–8 190
  2.31 168, 226n.89
  2.32–8 168
  2.41–51 55n.41
  2.41–2 97n.24
  2.41
  2.43 183n.76
  2.44 179n.41
  2.52–85 180n.52
  2.73 163
  2.78 163, 214
  2.83–4 214
  2.83 149, 180n.46
  2.84 178n.19
  2.85 37, 68, 97n.24
  3.6 159
  3.7–8 187
  3.8 220n.17
  3.11 188, 199
  3.13 150, 186
  3.19–32 218, 227n.101
  3.19–21 195
  3.19–20 215
  3.19 188, 210, 214
  3.20 235
  3.21–32 215
  3.21–2 216
  3.21 215
  3.26 216
  3.27 165, **161, 215**
  3.28 161–162
  3.29–31 217
  3.32 1, 217
  3.33 241
  3.34 220n.14
  3.36 214
  3.38–9 191
  3.40 220n.13
  3.41 222n.39
  3.43 211
  3.47 112
  3.49 214
  3.50–78 187
  3.50–7 195, 220n.14
  3.56–7 220n.14
  3.57 222n.38
  3.63 220n.14
  3.65–72 196
  3.68–82 150
  3.70 150, 196
  3.71 180n.46
  3.72 222n.37
  3.73–5 221n.19
  3.77 150
  3.78 191
  3.79–89 187
  3.79–86 191
  3.81 150, 222n.39
  3.82–5 192
  3.82 191
  3.83 214
  3.86 190
  3.87 190
  3.88 220n.13
  3.89–90 189
  3.89 188
  3.90 217, **187**
  3.91–2 220n.14
  3.92 195

3.95   193, 195
3.99–115   192
3.99–105   187
3.100   192
3.101   193, 221n.29
3.102–10   193
3.104   158, 194
3.107   195, **194**
3.108   222n.36
3.109–10   221n.25
3.110–11   193
3.110   192, 195
3.111   193, 222n.35
3.115   192
3.116–19   240
3.117   180n.46
Orator
  10   72
  35   154
  70–4   172
de Oratore
  1.2–3   17
  1.5   26n.52
  1.6–8   18
  1.26   17
  1.34   18
  1.35–8   18
  1.209–13   238
  1.210–13   14
  1.211   64
  1.224–18   238
  3.1–12   9, 17
  3.13   17, 20, 186, 202
  3.17   204
  3.28   16
  3.63   87
  3.64   234
  3.67–8   204
  3.69   139n.34
  3.86   72
  3.109   204
  3.120   204
Paradoxa Stoicorum
  3   166
Orationes Philippicae
  1.29   183n.76
  1.33   168, 183n.76
  1.36   57n.68
  2.3   221n.22
  2.26   27, 207
  2.28   207

2.87   221n.21
4.5   33
5.2   154
6.19   30
7.7   176
10.23   33
11.9   176
11.28   119, 176, 208
12.30   157
13.33   33
13.47   33
14.37   176
in Pisonem
  6   28
  43   221n.22
pro Plancio
  5   97n.17
  33   38
  88   88
de Provinciis Consularibus
  30   144n.84
  33   144n.84
pro Rabirio Perduellionis Reo
  29–30   137n.9
ad Quintum Fratrem
  1.1.16   144n.85
  1.1.23   25n.51
  1.1.18   157
  1.1.19–20   157
  1.1.21   157
  1.1.29–31   179n.32
  2.13.1   61
  3.4.1   95n.5
  3.5.1–2   61
  3.5.1   89, 150
de Re Publica
  1.2   148
  1.4–11   211
  1.3   148
  1.10   88
  1.1–12   63
  1.12   15
  1.13   15
  1.14–18   62
  1.14   85
  1.15–20   95n.7
  1.15–16   106
  1.17   143n.81
  1.19   109, **105–6**
  1.21–5   106
  1.21–2   137n.10

CICERO (cont.)
    1.26–9 106
    1.27 107
    1.31–3 85
    1.31–2 193
    1.31 106, 150
    1.33 15, 47, 65
    1,34–7 81
    1.34 16, 65, 78, 95n.6, 135
    1.36 16
    1.37 16
    1.38 65
    1.39 42, 47, 56n.55, 57n.65, 64, 65, 76, 96n.11, 163
    1.41–2 73
    1.41 87
    1.42 68–71, 74, 76, 87
    1.43–4 69
    1.43 44, 71, 74, 98n.32
    1.44 59n.80, 70, 74–75, 98n.34, 228n.112
    1.45 69, 74, 79, 86, 100n.55
    1.46–64 69
    1.47–53 97n.22
    1.47 71, 87, 123, **41**
    1.48 42
    1.49 67, 74, **42**
    1.52 73
    1.53 57n.60, 74, 87
    1.54–64 97n.22
    1.54 79, 97n.22
    1.60 72
    1.61–3 72
    1.61 72
    1.63 102n.85
    1.65–8 86
    1.65 69, 85
    1.66–8 97n.20
    1.68 69
    1.69 44, 69–70, 93, 96n.11, 98n.32
    1.70–1 62
    1.70 79
    1.75–6 180n.46
    2.2–3 99n.43
    2.2 79, 99n.44
    2.3 62, 78
    2.5–11 100n.49
    2.10 135
    2.15 79, 87
    2.18–19 79
    2.21–2 16, 62, 79, 99n.43
    2.21 88, 99n.45
    2.22 80
    2.23–5 46
    2.24 80
    2.27 80
    2.28–9 80
    2.30 80, 92
    2.31 46, 119
    2.33 46, 87
    2.35 46
    2.37 80, 96n.11
    2.38 46
    2.39–40 80
    2.41 15, 65
    2.42 44
    2.43 65, 74, 80
    2.45–6 228n.113
    2.45 100n.55, 121, 123
    2.46 88
    2.50 74
    2.51 65, 88, 102n.85
    2.52 62, 77, 79
    2.53 96n.11
    2.55–9 91
    2.56 77, 91, 103n.86
    2.57 44, 98n.32, 99n.39, 103n.86, 122, 141n.59
    2.59 82–83, 103n.86, 122
    2.60 100n.56
    2.61–3 100n.56
    2.62–3 43
    2.62 44, 55n.44
    2.65 15
    2.66 98n.29, 100n.50
    2.67 81, 89
    2.69 45, 76–**77**, 89, 99n.46, 100n.50, 122, 126
    2.70 62
    3.8 126–27
    3.9 127
    3.12 122, 128
    3.13 68
    3.16 128
    3.17 128
    3.18–19 128
    3.21a 128
    3.21b 128
    3.23 68, 76, 128, 129, **37**
    3.24 129
    3.26 143n.77
    3.27–8 92

3.27 129
3.28 130
3.29–30 129, 143n.74
3.33 92, 115, 126, 132
3.34–5 198
3.34 134, 165
3.35 119, 133
3.36 130, 133
3.37 133
3.38–9 92
3.41 134
3.42 16, 137n.15
3.43–8 65
3.43 68, 96n.14
3.45 67
3.46 41, 44
3.48 56n.51
5.1–2 12
5.1 149
5.2 63
5.5 87
5.6–7 101n.60, 183n.81
5.6 87
5.8 102n.75, 141n.56
6.1 87
6.8 62
6.9–29 107
6.11–12 24n.28
6.12–16 63
6.12 85, 88
6.13 67, 107, 109
6.15–19 105, 107
6.17 107
6.18–19 100n.50
6.19 107
6.20–5 107
6.27–8 107
6.28–9 63
6.29 107, 109
pro Roscio comoedo
7 155
de Senectute
78 137n.8
pro Sestio
60 166
62 166
67 144n.84
92 214
96 35
98 94
103 35

104–19 35
137 36, 98n.32
139 183n.76
141 153, 160
Tusculanae Disputationes
1.1–2 152
1.1 230
1.2 84, 148, 158, 178n.20, 180n.45
1.3–6 152
1.7 16
2.4 230
2.9 204
2.18 228n.112
2.27 47
3.3–4 183n.76
3.17–18 171
3.40 178n.24
4.36 171
4.51 88
4.57 160
5.5 230
5.7 160
5.18–19 232
5.26 178n.24
5.33 232
5.75 228n.112
5.64–6 137n.6
5.108 136n.1
in Verrem
1.1.2 57n.68
2.2.51 227n.108
2.3.13 123
2.4.73 228n.112
2.4.134 144n.85, 145n.95
2.5.109 227n.108
2.5.163 5
CLEMENT OF ALEXANDRIA
Stromateis
2.129 180n.43
DIO CASSIUS
38.17.6 28
DIOGENES LAERTIUS
5.44 86
6.63 105
7.92 166
10.151 143n.77
DIONYSIUS OF HALICARNASSUS
Antiquitates Romanae
5.67.3 49
5.67.5 49
5.68.1 49

DIONYSIUS OF HALICARNASSUS
(*cont.*)
5.68.3 49
5.68.5 49
6.38.3 49
6.68.3 49
6.71.3 33
6.74.3 33
6.85.1 33
7.50.4 33
HERODOTUS
3.80–2 41, 69
ISIDORE
Etymologiae
18.1 134
ISOCRATES
Areopagiticus
21 57n.66
LACTANTIUS
Institutiones Divinae
5.14.3–5 127
5.16.3 128
5.16.4 128
5.16.5–11 143n.74
5.17.14 143n.73
6.8.6–9 132, 137n.13
LIVY
1.9–12 135
1.17.7–11 46
1.22.1 46
1.32.1 46
1.35.6 46
1.41 46
2.15.3 30
2.23.8 157
2.32.8–12 227n.107
2.55.7 157
3.31.7 38
3.37.5 39
3.41.3 39
3.41.4 157
3.45.9 157
3.49.3 39
3.55.2 39
3.55.3–7 39
3.56.1 39
3.36.8 157
LUCRETIUS
2.1–19 225n.75
MACROBIUS
In Somnium Scipionis
1.4.2–3 88

NEPOS
Cato
3.3 78
NONIUS
498.16 133
ORATORUM ROMANORUM
    FRAGMENTA (H. Malvocati, 4
    edn.)
21.32 70
OVID
Fasti
2.683–4 111
PAUSANIAS
7.11.5 143n.70
PHILODEMUS
de Stoicis
col.XX 4–6 109
PINDAR
Pythian Odes
1.95–6
PLATO
Epistulae
9.358a 182n.64
Gorgias
474c–475e 224n.55
506d–507c 171, 184n.86
508a 45
Phaedrus
237b–c 65
250d 99n.43
Leges
2.653d–654a 180n.43
2.663d–e 234
4.704a–705b 100n.49
6.757d–758a 141n.59
6.769a–771a 139n.35
10.908c 221n.28
11.917b 221n.28
12.948b–949b 221n.28
12.951a–952b 139n.34
12.955e–956b 117
Politicus
296d–297b 72
297e–298e 72
302c–303b 98n.34
Respublica
1.332d–e 72
2.358e–359b 68, 129
2.359c–360d 191
2.361a–b 129
4.442b–c 148
4.443a 45

INDEX OF PASSAGES   273

    4.443c–444a 57n.64
    6.489b–c 72
    8.557a–558c 56n.53
    9.571a–580a 228n.113
    9.579b–e 221n.23
    9.588b–590b 228n.113
  Symposium
    209b 153
  Timaeus
    41e 137n.14
PLINY
  Naturalis Historia
    7.117 14
    7.130 178n.19
PLUTARCH
  Camillus
    1.1 147
  Cato Maior
    22 127
  Comparatio Demosthenis et Ciceronis
    1.4 170
  Comparatio Dionis et Bruti
    2.1–2 22n.1
  Dio
    22.1 22n.1
  de Exilio
    600f 136n.1
  Pelopidas
    34.5, 22n.1
  Philopoimen
    1.3–4 22n.1
    2–3 1
  Romulus
    13.4 33
  de Stoicorum Repugnantiis
    1034d 181n.57
POLYBIUS
    1.1.5 135
    1.3.6 130
    1.20.1–2 130
    1.63.9 130
    3.2.6 130
    6.4–9 74
    6.8.3 49
    6.9.10–14 69
    6.10.6–11 45
    6.10 69
    6.10.13–14 99n.45
    6.15–17 45
    6.18 69
    6.48.7–10 99n.43

    6.53–4 168
    15.19.2 130
    18.46.5 123
    31.10.7 130
QUINTILIAN
  Institutio Oratoria
    12.1.35 143n.72
SALLUST
  Epistulae ad Caesarem Senem
    2.11.2–4 55n.39
  Bellum Catilinae
    6–13 135
    6.7 29
    11.4–7 145n.99
    38.3 92
    54.1 167
    54.2 226n.77
  Bellum Iugurthinum
    31.1 34
    31.2 34
    31.7 34
    31.26 34
    33.30 29
    41.2 33
    41.5 33
  Historiae
    3.38 40
    3.48.1–6 41
    3.48.1 34
    3.48.3 55n.32
    3.48.6 34
    3.48.8 34
    3.48.15 34
    3.48.16 34
    3.48.24 34
    3.48.28 34
SENECA
  de Beneficiis
    2.20 1
  de Clementia
    1.1.1 102n.74
SEXTUS EMPIRICUS
  Adversus Mathematicos
    7.184 234
STOBAEUS
  Eclogae
    2.41.7–16 204
    2.51.18–52.1 224n.55
    2.59.9–19 162
    2.61.15–17 166
    2.62.3 181n.55

STOBAEUS (cont.)
    2.84.13–17 162
    2.99.12–14 182n.70
    2.99.14–19 182n.70
    2.99.16–19 181n.57
  Florilegium
    4.508.14 177n.7
SUETONIUS
  Divus Iulius
    40.1
TACITUS
  Agricola
    30.5 131

Annales
    1.1.1 30
    3.17.1 188
    3.27 39
THUCYDIDES
    1.69.1 165
VARRO
  de Lingua Latina
    6.18.1 34
    9.6 102n.75
VERGIL
  Aeneid
    6.852–3 144n.84

General Index

Note: This index captures most names mentioned in the main text of the book, and many of its most salient general terms. However ubiquitous names such as 'Cicero' and 'Rome' (with its associated adjective) are not listed except in particular connections, nor are similarly ubiquitous general terms such as 'politics' and 'society' (or associated expressions), againother than in particular kinds of application.

For the benefit of digital users, indexed terms that span two pages (e.g., 52–53) may, on occasion, appear on only one of those pages.

Academy, Academic 7–8, 127, 200, 204, 209, 229–30, 232–6, 240–1
acculturation 152–3
Adams, J. 22nn.5–6
Adeimantus 239
advantage
  and the honourable 186, 188, 190–5, 197–200, 204, 210, 214–15
  common advantage 52, 162–3, 215–16
  determination of acceptable advantage 215–17
  in debate of Book 3 of *On the commonwealth* 126, 128, 130, 132
  sharing in advantage 50, 65, 71, 76, 96n.12
  vs. justice 197
Aelius Tubero 85
aequabilis, aequabilitas 16, 37–8, 44–5, 57n.60, 71, 77
aequitas 37–8, 43, 55n.41, 68, 134, 148, 149–50
aequus 37, 55n.41
Africanus, P. Scipio 106–7
agrarian reform 17, 24n.32, 163–4
Ahala, C. 52n.2
allies 94, 112, 131, 133–4, 156–7, 175, 190
ambition 166, 175, 214
Ancus Martius 46
Ando, C. 31
Annas, J. 185
Antiochus of Ascalon 8, 109, 124, 230–1, 233
Antipater 195
appetite 72, 133, 148, 218
Arena, V. 37
Arcesilaus 235
Archimedes 106

aristocracy 40–2, 44, 46, 64, 69–71, 73–4, 82–3, 90–1, 93
Ariston 240
Aristotle 1–2, 7, 41, 63, 66, 69, 74, 107, 109–10, 114, 121, 135, 159, 163–4, 173, 233, 237, 239
  ensuring constitutional stability 75
  experience in approach to ethics and politics 81
  good man and good citizen 149
  scope of public deliberation 42
  test of a correct constitution 52
Arpinum 4, 162
artes, accomplishments 156
Asmis, E. 66
assassination 186, 207, 213
assembly 10, 29, 31, 39, 46, 80, 82, 109
association 29, 42–3, 49–50, 64, 71, 109, 109, 121
astronomy 106–7
atheism 239
Athenian Visitor 234, 239
Athens 41–2, 44, 74, 82, 112, 123, 126, 132, 165, 197, 218
Atkins, J. 234
Atkins, M. 163
Atticus 61, 89–91, 93, 116, 118, 123, 125, 154, 176, 197–203, 209, 218, 232–3, 236–7
Augustine 47, 61, 64, 126, 128, 130, 132–3
Augustus 6, 30, 33, 94, 176
  See also Octavian
Aulus Gellius. 42
austerity 83–4
authority, *auctoritas*
  best citizen's 79
  Cicero's personal political 27, 203

authority, *auctoritas* (cont.)
    Cicero's vocabulary of praise 169
    good citizen's 18, 175
    in government 20, 148
    in public business 168
    leading citizens', in Cicero's mixed
        constitution 44–5, 81–3, 89,
        91–2, 120
    of the *boni* 92
    of wisest and bravest, in early Rome 81
    philosophical 232–3, 235, 241
    provincial governor's 157
    reason's (displacing custom's) 12
    Roman senate's 32–4, 94, 208
autocracy 47, 134, 186, 212, 218–19

Beard, M. 11–12, 195
Beethoven 168
benefaction 83
benefactor 202, 204–5
beneficence, kindness 111, 150, 159, 161,
    162, 167
beneficia 189
benefit 14, 159, 161, 189, 194, 215, 238
body 1, 107, 132–3, 173, 216–19
boni 149, 174, 196, 198, 200, 202
bravery 81, 83, 167
Brunt, P. 10, 24n.32, 30–2, 36–7, 40, 46, 94,
    213–14
Brutus, D. 27, 207, 213
Brutus, L. 27, 30, 88, 207
Brutus, M. 1, 27–8, 154

Caelius, M. 61
Caesar
    aristocratic ambition and status 14,
        93, 166
    assassination 1, 6, 27–8, 30, 152
    Cicero attacks in *On duties* 191, 214
    civil war 6, 19–20, 89, 197–203, 209–10
    conduct of Caesarians 154–5, 176, 206
    cultural reforms 13–14
    dictatorship 6, 63, 134, 206
    his cupidity 175
    his *magnitudo animi* 166–7
    his valuation of *dignitas* 53n.6, 74, 214
    his view of Cicero 14, 35, 203, 206
    Matius's loyalty 186, 208–11, 212–13
    military commands 93, 131
    political activity under the Republic
        5, 155

    on Gauls' perception of Roman
        aggression 130
    on *senatus consultum ultimum* 33
    rule characterized as tyranny 1, 168, 203,
        214, 218
Calgacus 130
calibration, *moderatio, temperatio* 46, 66, 79,
    81–5, 87, 89–91, 94, 121–2, 124–5
Camillus 147
Carneades 127–9, 234–5, 238
Carthage 192–3
Cassius 6, 176
Catiline 5, 22n.8, 28–9, 35, 93, 167, 169, 207
Cato the Stoic 6, 9, 85, 153–5, 166–7,
    169, 211
Cato the Censor 78–9, 127, 131, 155
censor 92–3, 119
chance 80
Chrysippus 109
Cicero, M.
    son 159, 174, 240
    writings 4–7, 14
        Academic books 12, 23n.26, 230, 241
        On behalf of Balbus 156
        Brutus 9, 16–18
        On behalf of Caecina 38
        Cato (the lost eulogy) 154
        On behalf of Cluentius 155, 216
        On the commonwealth 5, 7, 12, 14–16,
            18–20, 24n.28, 36, 40–6, 61–93, 105,
            116, 120, 125, 148, 152–3, 158, 164,
            186, 198, 207, 217, 235, 238
        On divination 152
        On duties 6–7, 134, 148–51, 152–3,
            158–70, 176, 185–93, 210–11,
            213–14, 214, 231, 240
        Laelius 154, 158, 211, 213
        On laws 5, 64, 90, 112–22, 208, 229,
            232–8, 241
        Lucullus 230
        On behalf of Marcellus 206
        On behalf of Milo 85
        On moral ends 170–1, 230, 240–1
        On behalf of Murena 153, 155, 166, 169
        On the nature of the gods 9, 109
        Orator 72, 172
        On the orator 5, 9, 17–18, 20, 64, 72,
            87–8, 204, 234
        Philippics 6, 27, 30, 33, 154, 168, 176,
            207–8
        On behalf of Sestius 94, 153, 166

Tusculan Disputations 16, 84, 152,
  152–3, 155–8, 171, 230, 232, 240
Against Verres 39
Cicero, Q. 19, 33, 61, 90–1, 93, 115–17,
  122–3, 157, 232, 237
Cilicia 5–6, 111
citizen, citizens, citizenship
  audience of *On laws* 237
  best citizen 19–20, 61–2, 86–7, 89,
    93, 149
  Cicero's conception of citizenship 20, 37,
    43, 68, 117
  civic virtue 147
  democratic conception of citizenship
    42–3
  good citizen 18, 37, 149, 175–6
  Hobbes vs. neo-Roman thinkers on
    liberty of citizens 29
  problems in determining duties of
    citizens 21, 112, 186–8, 193,
    212–13
  republican citizenship 176
  Roman citizens 10, 16, 18, 34, 46, 157
  Roman citizenship 31, 36, 39–40, 93,
    110–11
  rule over citizens 121, 133
  verecundia and free citizens 173–5
city 2, 109
civic life 152–3
civil law 148, 153
civil society 3, 68, 148, 162, 174
civil war 6, 17, 19–20, 63, 89, 134, 154,
  174, 186, 197, 209–10, 212, 218
civility 148, 151, 174–5
civitas 9, 15, 31, 40, 42, 45, 47, 56n.57, 61,
  67–8, 76–7, 80, 87, 96n.11, 109–10,
  116, 121, 122, 134, 173, 216
  as citizenship 110
  best *civitas* 61, 85, 89, 149
  civitas liber 28
clementia 80, 206
Clitomachus 127
Clodius 28, 30, 35, 90, 93, 134
comitas 155
command and prohibition 108–10, 113–14,
  119–21, 208, 236
common advantage/benefit/interest 49, 52,
  161–3, 194–6, 216–17
commonwealth 5, 14–15, 18, 28, 30, 32, 34,
  47, 49–50, 84, 87, 89, 122–3,
  158, 233

community
  human 111–12, 115, 125, 159–60,
    161–3, 175, 215,
    216–17, 219
  rational beings (gods and humans) 112,
    115, 124, 160
  see also commonwealth
concordia, concord 77, 168, 197
conflicting values 150, 185–214
conscience 192
consensus 50, 67–8, 71, 76, 121, 237, 241
consent 77
consequentialism 229, 239
considerateness 175
consilium 64, 70, 72–5, 80, 80–3, 87, 89, 92,
  148, 154–6, 169, 176
consistency 153, 159, 231
constantia, constancy 149–50, 152–8, 160,
  164, 169, 172, 176, 211
Constantinople 29
constitution 21, 41, 44, 47, 49, 79, 82,
  90, 233
  best 15, 19, 61, 63, 69, 79, 121, 124
  constitutional cycle 82–3, 86
  deficits in primary systems 69–75
  mixed theory 44, 62, 64, 69–70, 77,
    79–80, 84–6, 91–2
  Roman 122–5
consul 4, 30, 32, 34, 39–40, 77, 82, 119,
  197, 202
consultatio, deliberative enquiry 204
contio 34
contract 68, 76, 150, 196
convention 105
cosmic 62–3, 109, 111, 124
cosmopolitanism 105–12, 124, 136, 158, 162
cosmos, *kosmos* 105, 107, 109, 124, 148
counsel 18, 20, 169
  See also *consilium*, deliberation
country 30, 47, 107, 111, 164, 166, 187–9,
  192, 198, 204, 209–10, 212
courage, *fortitudo* 84, 114, 148, 159, 169,
  171, 192–3, 207
courts 42, 111
Crassus, L. 9, 17–18, 72, 204
Crassus, M. 5, 166, 175
Crawford, M. 11–12, 27
criminality 133, 189–90
crisis 62–4, 72, 83
Critognatus 130
cultural history 11–14

cupidity 166–7, 175
custom 12, 14, 39, 42–3, 62, 81, 84, 117, 123–4, 128, 148, 158, 238
Cynics 105, 109, 173
Cyrus 71

Darius 69
death 166, 230
debate 20, 63, 65, 209, 229–32, 236
debt 82, 163, 196, 218
decemvirs 31, 38–9, 43, 51
decision-making 20, 161, 185–214, 229, 236
decorum 149, 153, 159, 167, 175, 183n.83, 201, 211
  as scope of 'fourth virtue' 170, 172
  definition 64–6
  deliberation 41, 44, 70–2, 74–5, 77, 81, 122, 201
demagoguery 214
Demetrius 117
democracy 40–6, 64, 67, 69, 74, 123, 229
  See also popular rule
Desmoulins, C. 2
despotism 3, 218
dialogue 8–9, 15
dictator 6, 24n.28, 85, 88–9, 101n.72, 206–7, 209, 218
dignitas 18, 36, 43–4, 54n.26, 70–1, 74, 94, 157, 173, 198, 200, 214
  dignitas civilis 87–8
diligentia 156–7
Dio Cassius 28
Diodotus 8, 110
Diogenes of Babylon 162, 195
Diogenes the Cynic 105
Dionysius of Halicarnassus 33, 49
Dionysius II of Syracuse 203, 205
diplomacy 134
disagreement 230
discretion 170–1, 173, 175
disciplina 80, 152
dominatio 30, 34, 52n.3, 198
dominatus 52n.3, 206
Dugan, J. 17
durability 75–7, 79, 84–5, 122
duty 1, 14, 19, 44, 77, 107–8, 112, 119, 159, 164–5, 175, 185–6, 189, 196, 198, 201
  filial 187–9
Dyck, A. 117, 119, 195

economic individualism 163
education 159–60, 207
elections 10, 32, 34, 45–6, 77
Eleusinian mysteries 112, 125
embassy of philosophers 126
emotions 89, 133, 148
empire 14, 20–1, 32, 84, 107, 128, 129–35, 147, 190
enemy 112, 131, 134, 194, 214
English commonwealth 2, 28
Ennius 84, 123, 158, 166
Epicureanism 7–8, 109, 154, 234–6, 239–40
epistemology 125, 230
equality 37–46, 67–71, 74, 77–8, 85, 91, 121–2, 124–5
equity 68, 70–1, 74, 150
Erillus 240
ethics 7, 19–20, 112, 114–15, 117, 119–20, 131, 152, 185–6, 205, 229–31, 233, 236, 238–9
  ethical relativism 110
  ethical universalism 112
Euripides 218
exceptions 193
expertise 72

Fabricius, C. 190–1
facilitas, accessibility 155–7
faction 30, 34–5, 51
fairness, *aequitas* 148, 150, 196
family 111, 158, 188–9, 199–201, 205
Fantham, E. 45
father 187, 189, 192
fear 18, 168, 192, 194
felicitas 176
Ferdinand II 168
Ferrary, J.-L. 87, 129
fides 134, 148, 150, 152, 155, 156–8, 160, 163–5, 168–9, 173, 193–6, 209
Fimbria, C. 150
foreigners 155, 162
formula 195, 215–17
fortuna, fortune 80, 117, 147, 166, 202
Fott, D. 76
foundations 20, 32, 62, 94, 153, 157–8, 163–4, 229, 233, 235, 237, 238
Founding Fathers 2, 28
freedom 3, 10, 28–9, 31, 37–8, 41, 45, 71, 82, 170, 173–4, 232
  See also liberty, people
French Revolution 2

GENERAL INDEX 279

friend, friendship 20, 62, 111, 131, 154–8, 164, 186, 188, 189, 200, 202, 204, 205, 208–13, 218
frugalitas, moral control 171
funeral and burial practices 117

Garnsey, P 164
generals 133–4
generosity, *liberalitas* 150, 158, 162, 167
Gildenhard, I. 218
Glaucon 68, 125, 129, 239
gloria, glory 106–7, 161, 167–9, 175, 182n.69, 190, 201
god, gods 108–9, 113–14, 117–20, 125, 129, 132, 157, 166, 194–5, 218, 236
good 14, 52, 125, 231, 233–4, 236, 238–9, 241
good citizen 18, 37, 149, 175–6
good faith 88, 134, 148, 150, 165, 173, 193–4, 196, 211
good man 149–50, 191, 193, 211, 217
goodwill 168, 190
Görler, W. 232
government 20–1, 36, 47, 49, 61–93, 118–21, 133, 148, 169
Gracchus, C. 35, 42
Gracchus, T. 15, 63, 85, 88, 106, 134
gratia, kindness 155
gravitas 149, 152–8, 160, 166, 169, 176, 211
greatness of spirit 153, 159;
see *magnitudo animi*
Greece, Greeks 84, 115
See also Romanization
Griffin, M. 48, 51, 131, 188, 214–15
guardian 87–8, 134
gubernator 87
guidance 230
Gyges 191

happiness 90, 230–1
harm 159, 161–2, 194, 196, 215, 215–16
health 231
Hecato 188–9, 193, 217
Hellegouarc'h, J. 167
Herodotus 41, 69
hêsuchazein 206
Hirtius, A. 154–5, 176
history 10, 16, 62, 64, 78–83, 85–6, 123, 124–5
Hobbes, T. 1–2, 29, 219
honestas, nobility 153
honour 70, 166, 168–9, 173

honourable 1, 32, 66, 160, 167, 185–6, 188, 190, 192–5, 197–200, 204, 206, 208, 210–11, 214–15, 217–18
Horatius Barbatus, M. 39
Horatius Cocles 114
Hortensius 17–18
human impulses 76, 159, 161, 170, 172–3, 185–6, 200
humanitarian intervention 165
humanitas 155–6, 176, 206, 209

ideology 11–12, 17, 33, 36–7, 45, 168–9, 218
immortality of the soul 107
imperialism 21, 111, 119, 123, 125, 129–36, 156
imperium 31–2, 34, 37, 41, 70–2, 82, 93, 113–14, 118–21, 148, 166, 176
individual 29, 39, 51, 72, 76, 112, 128–9, 149
See also private
ingenium 156, 176
injury 161–2, 164–5, 171
injustice 126, 129–32, 134, 161–2, 164–6, 175, 192–3, 197, 216
innocentia 71, 156, 171, 176
institutions 62, 158
integritas, integrity 150, 156–7, 159, 166, 169
Irwin, T. 196
ius, iura 28, 31–2, 37, 39, 42–4, 49, 64–9, 71, 74, 77, 109, 118, 134, 214
aequo et pari iure 37, 42, 68, 149
consensus iuris 66–7, 121
ius civile 38
ius connubii 66–7
ius suffragii 80

Jekyll and Hyde 172
judge 41, 93–4, 196, 215
judgement 43, 86, 123, 171, 207, 232–4, 240
junta 65, 74
justice, *ius, iustum* 115, 118, 121–2, 136, 163, 198–200, 232–3, 235–6, 238–9
bond 50, 68, 71, 236
consensus 49, 64–9, 71, 76, 121, 125, 168
contractual theory 68, 76
deficit 70–1, 74
equal 42–4, 67–8
foundational 63, 90
legal 37, 43
natural 128

justice, *ius*, *iustum* (*cont.*)
  objective value 125
  theory 20, 109–10, 116, 125
  war 119, 131, 133–4, 197
  weakness 128
justice, *iustitia* 153, 206, 234, 239
  cardinal virtue 148, 171, 175
  civic virtue 148
  definition/specifications 74, 129, 196
  in argument of *On the commonwealth* 62, 76, 108, 122, 125, 198, 235, 239
  in argument of *On duties* 111, 151, 159–66
  in government of empire 112, 175
  in relation to *fides* 152, 158, 193
  of the good man 150
  relation to harm and advantage 193–4, 215–16
  virtue of rulers 71–3, 120

Kant 109, 113, 241
Kaster, R. 174
kathēkon 185
kings, kingship
  as system of government 1, 40–2, 44, 64–9, 133
  Caesar's dictatorship 192, 209, 213
  friendship with aspirants to kingship 211
  historical prevalence 120
  king as *rector* 88
  regal element in constitution 44
  regal element in mind 72
  Roman kingship 29–31, 39, 46–7, 68, 77, 79, 82, 91
knowledge 231, 233
Knoche, U. 166

Lactantius 61, 90, 126–9, 132
Laelius 15–16, 51, 62, 65–7, 72, 80, 85, 88, 105–6, 108–9, 112, 125–34, 159, 198, 235
Latin 7, 9
Latins 134
law 14, 50, 73, 88, 94, 112–22, 148, 173, 238–9
  ancestral 123
  autocracy 192
  categories 116
  civil 43, 148, 153
  contract 150–1
  designed for advantage 128
  equality before the law 37–9, 42–3, 68, 71
  governing philosophical procedure 232
  immutability 115–16
  legal code 90–1, 115–22
  legal conception of basis of popular rights 51–2
  legal justice 37, 42–3, 66–8
  legal positivism 236
  'measure of law' (*norma legis*) 117–18
  moral 66, 109, 113, 115, 119, 121, 125
  natural 108–9, 113–15, 119–20, 161, 208, 215, 236
  of Caesar 212
  overridden 33
  religion 116–18
  right reason 122, 236
  Roman 38–40, 112, 117–18, 122, 124, 152, 215
  theory of law 20, 108–10, 113
  war 194–5
  written 43, 114, 116
leadership 20–1, 33, 61, 64, 78, 83–90, 93
leading citizens, *principes* 14, 77, 81, 82–3, 89, 91, 93, 166, 213
legal code 90–1
legislation 10, 32, 34, 45–6, 77, 240
legislator 78, 148–9, 153, 234
legitimacy 49, 52, 65
lenitas, mildness 157
lepos, charm 155
letters 4, 7, 19–20, 29, 131, 154–5, 157, 186, 197–208
lex, law 42, 66–7, 109, 120
liberalitas, liberality 111, 155, 159, 161, 167
liberation 1, 4, 28, 82, 176, 207–8
libertas 10, 27, 29, 31, 36, 38–9, 81, 92
liberty
  'authors of' 210
  deficit under aristocracy and kingship 70–1, 73, 80, 82–3
  fraudulent catchword 10
  liberty and equality 40
  'liberty and safety of the Roman people' 208, 214
  liberty of country vs. life of friend 209
  lost under ambition/regimes of Caesar and Augustus 94, 167, 192, 206
  negative vs, positive 3
  popular liberty and its inalienability in the mixed constitution 81, 91–2, 122

GENERAL INDEX 281

rights implicit in popular liberty 31–2, 36, 39–40, 51, 81
Roman ideology of liberty and of its historical achievement 20, 27–36
taking risks for liberty 88, 201, 204, 207
See also freedom, non-domination
licence 28, 37
life 31, 66, 84, 89, 153, 209, 231, 238
See also way of life
Licinius Macer 40–2
Lintott, A. 90
litterae 155
Livy 2, 20, 28–31, 33, 37–41, 46–7, 79, 81, 87, 134–5, 147, 157
Loeb edition 67
Long, A.A. 168
Lucca 29
Lucretia 27, 114
Lycurgus 66, 78

Macer, P. 34
Machiavelli 28, 33, 81, 86–7, 147, 168
Mackie, N. 11, 32
Macrobius 61
magistrates 32–3, 42, 44, 71, 77, 81, 83, 88, 94, 112–13, 118–21, 133–4, 149, 173, 187, 215
magnitudo animi 151–3, 158–60, 166–70, 175–6, 192, 206
maiestas 58n.70
manager 87–8
Marcellus, M. 206
Marius, C. 191
Marius, M. Gratidianus 191
Mark Antony 6, 30, 33, 168, 176
Massilia 73
master 129, 133
Matius, C. 155, 157–8, 186, 208–13
McConnell, S. 205
Memmius, C. 29, 34
'men' 84, 87, 124, 158
methodology 72, 232–5, 237, 241
militarism 239
Milton 29
mind 43, 72, 89, 106, 109, 113, 119, 133, 236
Moatti, C. 12–13, 48
mob rule 65, 69, 74, 186
moderatio, control 18
moderation 170–2, 190, 209
moderator, calibrator 89

modestia, discretion 170, 172, 212
monarchy 29, 47, 68–9, 71–2, 74, 88, 239
money 166–7, 175, 212, 229, 239
monster 217–18
Montaigne 188
Montesquieu 77
moral error 231
moral realism 68, 110
moral theory 236
morality 185, 239
moralization 119
mos, mores 38, 152, 158, 174
  mos maiorum 12, 84
Mouritsen, H. 36, 83–4
multitudo 35, 44, 65, 168
munus 77

Napoleon 168
Nasica, P. Scipio 88, 134
nature
  human 108, 125, 172–3, 185–6, 200, 215
  individual natures 211
  natural order of things 1, 108, 132–3, 232, 235–6
  natural sociability of humans 161–2, 167, 191
  natural society of human race 215–16
  natural world 106, 236
  of commonwealths 116
  Roman predisposition for virtues 152, 153, 158
necessity 80, 91, 123
neoconservatives 123
neo-Roman 3, 29, 86
Nicgorski, W. 72
Nicolet, C. 45
nobility 10, 13, 33, 37, 55n.32, 82, 93
Noble Lie 234
non-domination 3, 29
Numa Pompilius 46, 80

oath 112, 117, 158, 193–5, 211
obligation 111–12, 131, 159, 161, 163, 165, 171, 175, 185–7, 189, 196, 198, 200, 231, 238
Octavian 6, 94, 176
  See also Augustus
officium 77, 159–62, 170–1, 173, 185, 193–4, 198, 201–2, 209, 211–13
oligarchy 10, 51, 69, 186
optimates 35, 42, 198, 202, 204

oratory 4, 7, 14, 16–19, 29, 154, 205, 234
order (in behaviour) 170–2
Oropus 126
otium 94, 206
Ovid 111

Panaetius 25n.51, 153, 159, 161–2, 166, 170, 172, 187, 201, 211, 240–1
Pansa, C. 154–5, 176, 206
parents 30, 111, 133, 164, 187–9
parricide 192
partnership 96n.14
passions 72, 114, 132–3, 167
paternalism 133–4
patricians 33, 38–9, 43, 82
patrocinium 134
patron 134, 157, 165
patronus 134
peace 18, 71, 94, 130, 149, 156, 197, 199, 201, 209–10
Peisistratus 218
peithananké, persuading compulsion 202–3
Peloponnesian War 165
people
  a people, peoples 71, 74, 133, 233, 235
  ambiguity (citizen body vs. *plebs*) 34–5, 73
  definition 49, 65
  'free peoples/nations' 41, 112, 120–5, 136, 217
  'good and stable peoples/nations' 112, 113, 122–5
  in definition of a commonwealth 42, 46–52, 71
  in theory of constitutional change 123
  liberation of the Roman people 176
  'liberty and safety of the Roman people' 208, 214
  Roman people 10, 29–30, 32–3, 37, 71, 74, 80, 82, 85, 91, 106, 157, 210, 215, 218
  sector represented in the mixed constitution 44, 77, 81, 92
  the people's safety as the 'ultimate law' 119, 208
Peripatetics 204, 230–1, 240–1
persona 88, 172–3, 201–2, 202, 211
Pettit, P. 3, 29, 75, 86, 148
Phaedrus 236
Phalaris 217–19
Pharsalus 206

Philo of Larissa 8, 204
Philodemus 109
philosophy 2–3, 5–9, 11–12, 14–17, 19, 86, 135, 152, 159, 169, 203–5, 207, 209, 212, 217–18, 229–42
  method 232–3
  philosopher kings 107
  philosophers 14, 148, 153
Philp, M. 86
Philus 37, 66, 68, 76, 105–6, 109, 125–34, 235, 238–9
piety 113, 116–17, 121, 148, 153, 156, 187, 194
Pindar 218
Piso, Cn. 188
Plancius, Cn. 38
Plato 1–2, 7, 14, 41, 63, 69, 75, 77, 106–7, 109–10, 114, 135, 148, 159, 161, 163, 218, 233, 236–7
  and *On the commonwealth* 16, 62
  as caged bird in Syracuse 203, 205
  as politically engaged intellectual 15
  attraction to monarchy 72
  dialogues
    Gorgias 171
    Laws 110, 116–17, 234, 239
    Phaedrus 107
    Republic 47, 62, 68, 72, 80, 85, 107, 125, 129, 164, 191, 239
    Seventh Letter 203
    Statesman 72
    Symposium 153
  Forms 72
  immortality of the soul 107
  Noble Lie 234
  Platonic dialogue 6, 8–9
  Platonic proem 116
  utopianism 62, 85
pleasure 234
plebs 10, 34–41, 43, 46, 53n.19, 73, 91–2, 157
Pliny the Elder 14
Plutarch 1–2, 127, 147, 170
Polemo 240
policy 75, 92, 241–2
political
  judgement *See prudentia*, wisdom
  leadership 86 *See also* leadership
  philosophy 86, 204, 240
  sphere 195, 229 *See also* public sphere
  theory 233, 235–41

Polybius 16, 49, 63, 69, 74, 110, 123, 130, 135, 168
Pompey 5–6, 19–20, 27, 33, 89–91, 93, 131, 147, 156–7, 174, 191, 197–203, 206, 210, 213
Popper, K. 75
popular rule 40–6, 64, 67, 69–71, 74
  See also democracy
popular sovereignty 31–2, 34, 46–52, 65, 73
populares 35, 37, 41, 163
populus 32–6, 46–52, 65, 68, 70–1, 75–6, 80, 82–3, 87, 92
  constitutio populi 76, 96n.11
  definition 49, 64–9, 122
  populus liber 28
  populus Romanus 33–4, 36–7
  res populi 47–9, 51, 65–6, 71, 75, 186
  voluntas populi 57n.68
Posidonius 190
potentia 32
potestas 31
Potidaea 165
Powell, J. 127
power 28, 32, 34, 37, 41, 70–1, 73, 81, 83, 92, 106, 122–3, 131, 166, 175, 190–1, 204, 213
powers 32–3, 72, 81, 83–4, 94, 121
  separation of powers 77, 84
practical 233, 235, 239–41
practice 62, 186, 233, 238, 242
praecepta 196, 231
praetor 27, 215
principles 195–6, 216, 233, 235, 236–7
private 18, 31, 37, 39, 43, 88, 149, 162–4, 169, 187, 198, 213
probabilis, persuasive 200, 233, 241
probitas, uprightness 152, 156, 158
procurator 87
promises 112, 193–6
property 31, 48, 51, 129, 162–4, 196, 214, 217
proportion 45
provinces 94, 111–12, 130–1, 134, 157
provocatio 32, 39
prudentia 159, 169
  civilis prudentia, 86–7, 121, 123
  See also wisdom
psychology 72, 106, 125, 133, 148, 159, 214, 218
public cause 198
public good 214

public policy 32, 89, 229, 236
public sphere 18–19, 31, 47, 49, 92, 148, 152, 154, 159, 169, 186–7, 195, 202, 204, 206–7, 209, 213, 229, 233–4
pudor, sense of propriety, shame 148, 156–7, 202
punishment 115, 117, 131, 134
purity 117
Pyrrho 240
Pyrrhus 190
Pythagoras 80
Pythagoreanism 106–7

quaestio infinita, question not relating to particular circumstances 204

Rawls, J. 135
Realpolitik 130
reason 12, 80, 82, 108–9, 112, 113–17, 119, 123, 132, 149, 159–60, 169, 236
rector 64, 72, 87–9, 207
regula 121, 186, 211
Regulus, M. 158, 192–5
relativism 128, 236
religio 156
religion 80, 84, 94, 112–13, 116, 121, 148, 153, 157, 195, 239
Renaissance 2
republicanism 2–3, 20, 28–9, 75, 84, 86, 147–8, 175–6
reputation, repute 190–1, 202
res publica 20, 61–93, 124–5, 159, 188, 206
  best constitution or form 15, 19, 61, 63, 69, 79, 120, 134, 238
  conception of *res publica* 23n.16, 28, 34, 42, 46–52, 121
  definition 64–9, 163
  duty to *res publica* 186, 188–9, 193, 207, 211
  health 216
  immortality 134
  its advantage 198–9, 202, 212, 214, 217
  its own values 190
  its political *modus operandi* 213
  justice in government 126, 128–30
  legislation 240
  liberty and rights of *populus* 29, 36–7
  relation to moral universalism 112–22
  safety 18, 208

res publica (cont.)
  valuation by Cicero 7, 20, 33, 186, 189, 194, 202
  virtues required 175–6
respect 175
restraint, *continentia* 148, 150, 153, 157, 159, 170–1, 190
rhetoric 8, 13, 16–17, 20, 66, 134, 201, 203–4, 207, 209, 212, 230
Rhodes 41–2, 123, 131
Richardson, J. 70
right, rights
  citizen rights and equality in Cicero's theory 37–8, 68, 71, 73–4, 88
  civil rights in neo–Roman republicanism 29
  extension to inhabitants of Italy 17
  in argument for democracy in *On the commonwealth* 42–4
  in formula of Cicero's mixed constitution 44, 77, 83
  in Twelve Tables 39
  in warfare 165
  ius as legal right 66–7
  popular political rights in Cicero's theory 36, 49, 51–2, 91–2, 186
  rights of allies, Italians, and provincials 131, 134
  rights of 'free peoples' 217
  Roman citizens and people 10, 31–3, 39–40, 80–2, 173, 218
  Roman right of liberty 31–2
  shared rights with the enemy 195
Romanization
  antiutopian political theory 16, 78, 80
  Latinizing philosophy 7, 9, 152–3
  of Greek democratic theory 43–4
  On the commonwealth as riposte to Plato's *Republic* 62
  theory of nature of a political system 52
Romulus 46, 78–80, 88, 111, 135
Rousseau 63, 78
Rudd, N. 68
rules 114, 117, 185–6, 195–6, 215–17
Rullus, P. 31, 34

safety 18, 29, 76, 85, 107, 208
Sallust 2, 20, 29–34, 37, 40–1, 92, 135, 147, 167
sapientia 106, 148, 152, 159–60, 176, 200, 212
  See also wisdom

Scaevola, P. 18, 196
scepticism 7, 20, 127, 229–36, 238, 241
Scipio 15–16, 24n.28, 40–2, 44–5, 50–1, 61–83, 106–7, 109, 121–6, 135, 159
secret ballot 91–2, 112
Segesta 123
self-control 166
self-interest 235
senate 5, 10, 17, 32–3, 36, 40, 42, 46, 80–1, 83–5, 92–4, 106, 127, 133, 154, 190, 193, 208, 218
  moral conduct 92–3, 119
senatus consultum 33
senatus populusque Romanus 54n.22
Seneca 1–2, 189
servire 133
servitus 28
Servius Tullius 46, 80
Sestius, P. 214
severitas 157, 167
sexual gratification 191
Shackleton Bailey, D. R. 7, 19, 202
Shakespeare 28
Skinner, Q. 2–3, 29, 48, 147
slave, slavery, servitude 28, 30–1, 41, 130, 132–4, 174
slavish 133, 174
Socrates 106, 197, 203, 205, 238–9
Solon 78, 82, 117, 239
sôphrosunê 148, 159, 170–1
soul 107, 109, 132, 148, 231
Speusippus 240
stabilitas 158
stability 75, 79, 81–2, 89, 122, 124, 136, 233, 235, 237
state 48
statesman, statesmanship 14–16, 18–19, 90, 94, 106–7, 149, 169, 198, 204, 207, 238
Steel, C. 14, 85
Stoicism
  Cato as Stoic 6, 153–4
  Diodotus 8, 110
  in Cicero's oeuvre and philosophizing 7, 110
  in *On the commonwealth* 63, 66, 106
  in *On duties* 240–1
  methodology 232
  on community 109, 112, 160, 163–4
  on the good 230–1, 236

on the honourable and the
    advantageous 199, 215
on justice 62, 162
on kingship 1
on law and reason 109–10, 113–15, 121,
    125, 136
on *magnitudo animi* 166
on virtues 161
Panaetius 201
psychology 159
Stoic sage 150, 200, 212
universalism 110, 112, 215, 217
stranger 112
Straumann, B. 120
Struggle of the Orders 38–40, 81
Suetonius 13
Sulla 134
Syme, R. 10–11

Tacitus 2, 30, 130, 188
Tarquins 27, 30, 46, 74, 87, 114, 207
taxation 190
temperamentum 46, 83
temperance 148, 150, 159, 193
temperantia 16, 156, 170, 172
Thebes 126
theft 187, 216–18
theology 19, 62, 107–9, 116, 194
Theophrastus 86
theory 78, 107, 186
thesis 204–5
Thirty Tyrants 51, 74, 197
Thrasymachus 125, 239
Thucydides 69, 130, 135, 165
treason 187–9
treaties 134
Trebonius, C. 176
tribunes 33–4, 38–40, 53n.19, 83, 85, 88, 91,
    106, 112, 119, 123
trust 94, 134, 148, 157, 168
truth 158, 160, 164, 233–4, 235, 240
Tullus Hostilius 46
tutela 134
tutor 87
Twelve Tables 39, 43, 117
tyrannicide 1–2, 20–1, 176, 186, 188, 210, 214
tyrant, tyranny 1, 5, 28–9, 35–6, 50–1, 69,
    74, 80, 86–7, 94, 153, 165, 176,
    186–7, 203–6, 214, 214–15, 217–19

universalism 66, 108, 112–22, 215, 217
universe 105–7, 109–10, 113, 118, 119

utilitarianism 229, 236, 241
utilitas 49, 65, 96n.12, 169

Valerius, L. 39
Valerius Antias 40
Varro 12, 174
verecundia, considerateness 151, 170–5
Verres 5, 131, 134
vice 74, 93, 132–3, 175, 230
vinculum 67–8
vindicatio, *vindiciae* 42, 51
Vindiciae, Contra Tyrannos 165
violence 161, 215–16
virtue, virtues 6, 20, 62, 66, 71, 76, 80, 83–4,
    90, 114, 129, 147–75, 185–6, 230–1
    cardinal 20, 148, 159, 166
    civic 20, 147
    imperial 156–7
    Roman 148, 152, 160
    social 152–3, 159
virtus 12, 152, 155–6, 166, 169
vis 81, 134, 227n.99

Wallace-Hadrill, A. 13
Walsh, P. 160
war 83, 119, 131, 133–4, 165, 169, 190,
    193–5, 197–8, 204
way of life 21, 84, 87, 94, 169
wealth 90, 106, 117, 129, 131, 161, 166,
    191, 231
Wirszubski, C. 37
wise, wisdom
    Christian conception 129
    in rule of the mind 133
    perfect rationality 106–7, 109–10, 112–13,
        119–20, 150, 160, 171, 200,
        217, 234
    political 18, 71, 80–1, 83, 120–1, 123,
        148–9, 152, 169, 176, 190, 206
    sapientia and *prudentia* 159
    shrewdness in calculating advantage
        126, 128–30, 235
Wiseman, P. 48
Wolff, J. 229, 236, 241
women 79, 125, 128
Wood, N. 163
Woolf, R. 191, 195, 236

Xenocrates 240

Zeno 231
Zetzel, J. 43, 49, 66, 238